I0824213

FROM LAPLAND TO SÁPMI

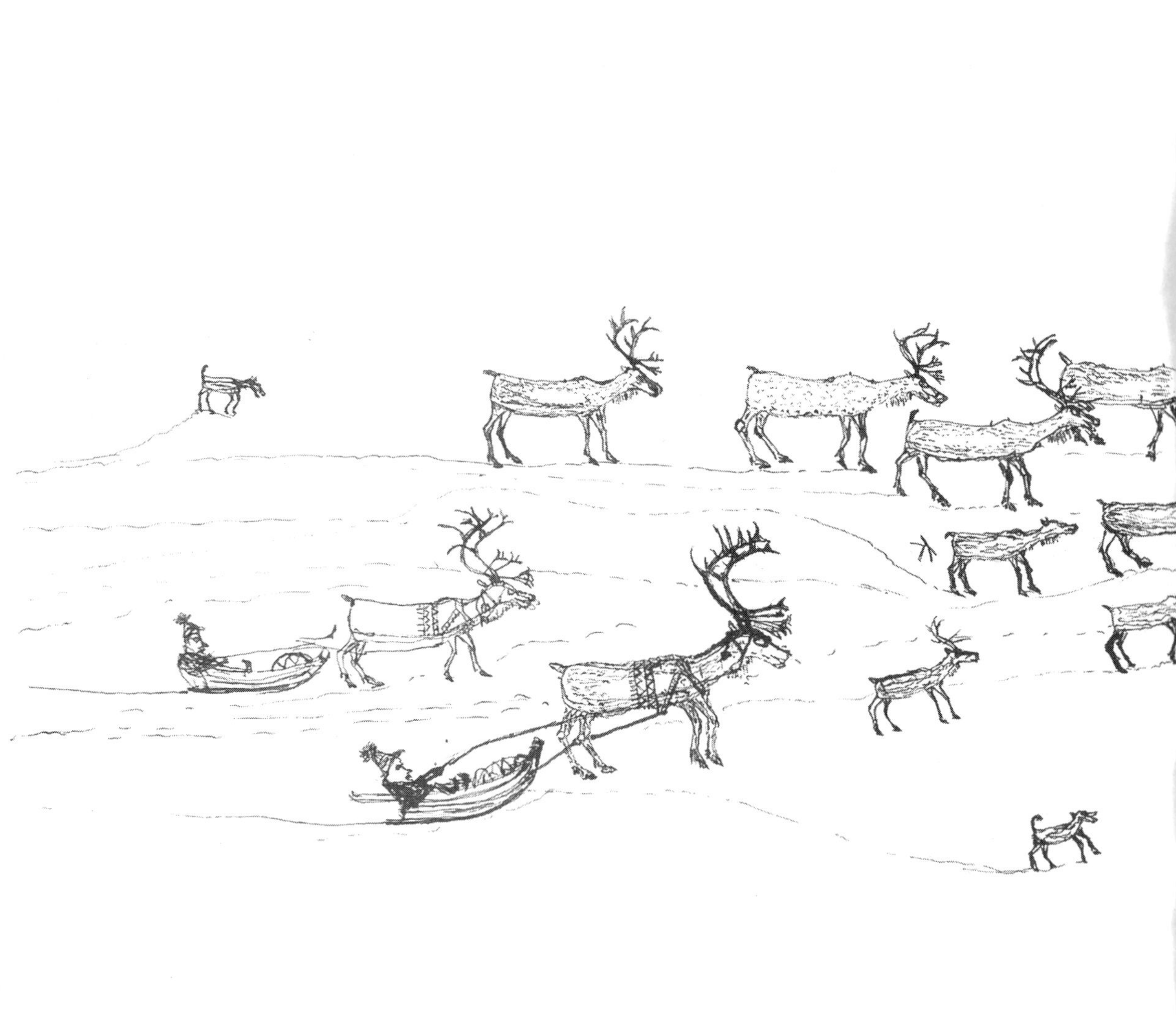

FROM LAPLAND TO SÁPMI

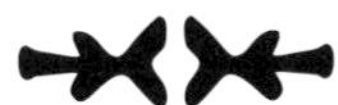

Collecting and Returning Sámi Craft and Culture

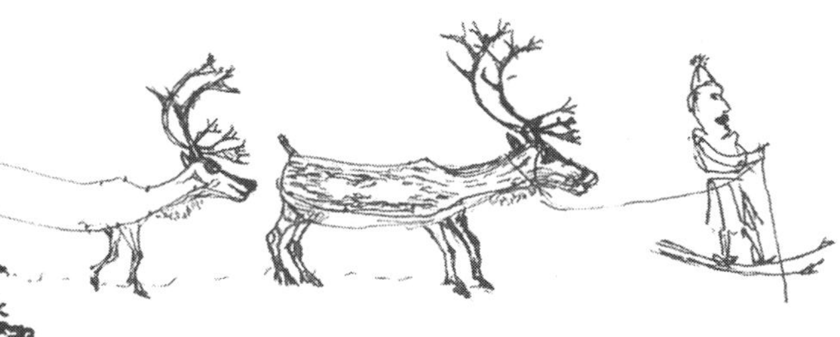

BARBARA SJOHOLM

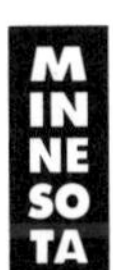

University of Minnesota Press
Minneapolis
London

The publication of this book was assisted by a bequest from Josiah H. Chase to honor his parents, Ellen Rankin Chase and Josiah Hook Chase.

Illustration on pages ii–iii by Johan Turi, Jukkasjärvi, Sweden. Ink on paper, circa 1910. Photograph courtesy of the Nordic Museum, Stockholm.

Map on pages vi–vii by Rhys Davies

Published by the University of Minnesota Press
111 Third Avenue South, Suite 290
Minneapolis, MN 55401-2520
http://www.upress.umn.edu

ISBN 978-1-5179-1197-3 (hc)

Library of Congress record available at https://lccn.loc.gov/2022040621

Printed in Canada on acid-free paper

The University of Minnesota is an equal-opportunity educator and employer.

30 29 28 27 26 25 24 23 10 9 8 7 6 5 4 3 2 1

Contents

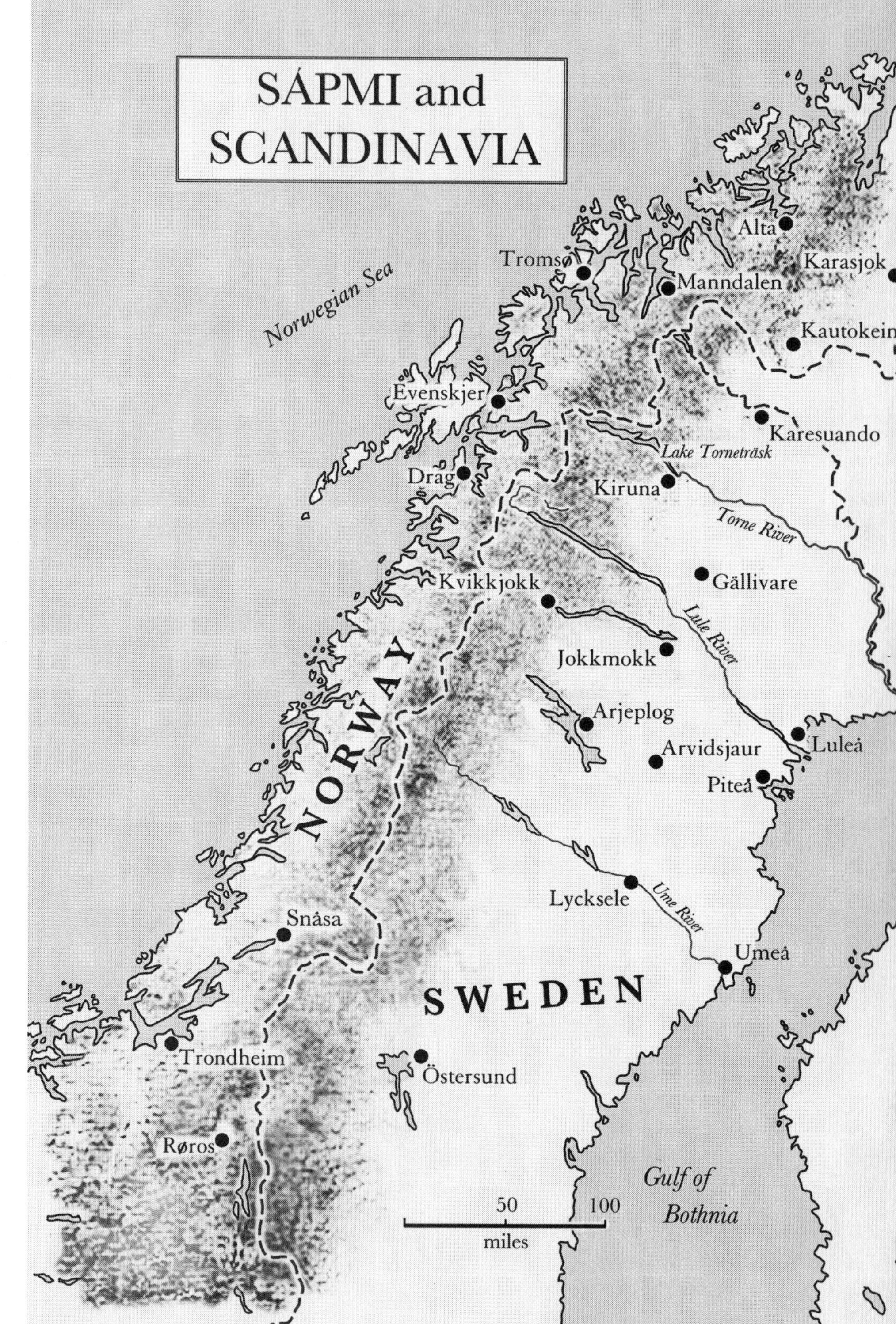

SÁPMI and SCANDINAVIA
Norwegian Sea
Alta
Tromsø
Karasjok
Manndalen
Kautokeino
Evenskjer
Karesuando
Lake Torneträsk
Drag
Kiruna
Torne River
Kvikkjokk
Gällivare
Lule River
Jokkmokk
Arjeplog
NORWAY
Luleå
Arvidsjaur
Piteå
Lycksele
Ume River
Snåsa
Umeå
SWEDEN
Trondheim
Östersund
Røros
Gulf of Bothnia
50
100
miles

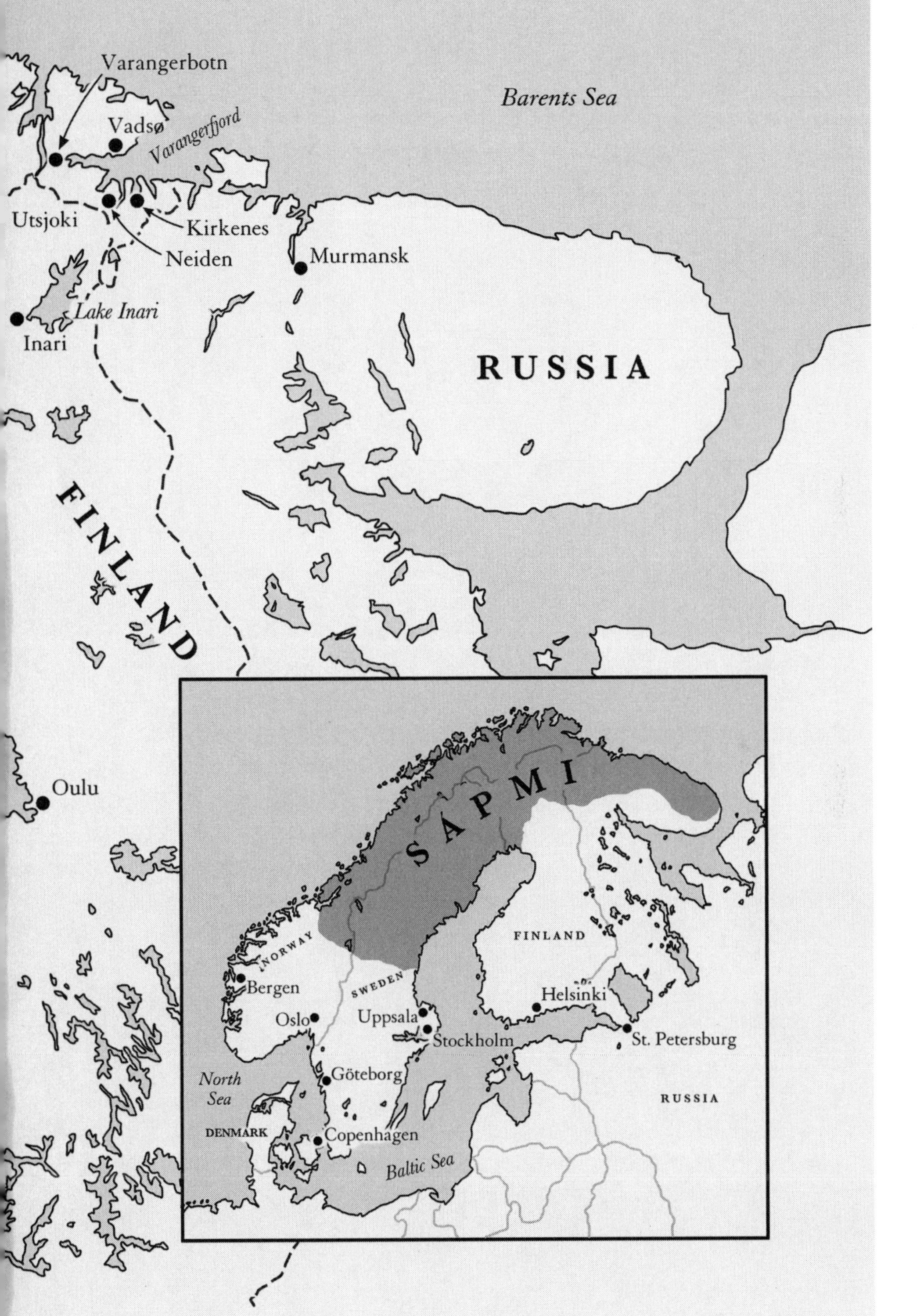
Varangerbotn
Barents Sea
Vadsø
Varangerfjord
Utsjoki
Kirkenes
Neiden
Murmansk
Lake Inari
Inari
RUSSIA
FINLAND
Oulu
SÁPMI
NORWAY
FINLAND
SWEDEN
Bergen
Helsinki
Oslo
Uppsala
Stockholm
St. Petersburg
North Sea
Göteborg
RUSSIA
DENMARK
Copenhagen
Baltic Sea

Sápmi's Geography and Languages

Over the four centuries covered in this book, national boundaries in Northern Europe and Russia were created and dissolved until they assumed the shape they have today. Throughout this time, Sápmi, the Sámi homeland, has endured as a geographic, historic, and imaginative space, spread across the borders of four countries. Sápmi encompasses thousands of square miles from Røros in Norway and Idre in Sweden to the northern provinces of Norway, Sweden, and Finland and east along the coast of the Kola Peninsula in Russia. My emphasis in this book is primarily the historical kingdoms of Denmark–Norway and Sweden–Finland and the present-day countries of Norway and Sweden. For that reason, I'll sometimes speak of "Scandinavia" to include Denmark and Finland and occasionally of "Fennoscandia and Russia" or the "Nordic countries."

Sámi and Sápmi are the English versions of *Sámit* and *Sápmelaš,* both meaning Sámi people. Sámi (also spelled "Sami" and "Saami" in English) is both noun and adjective, singular and plural. The words "Lapp" and "Laplander" are used in this book in the historic sense, when quoting from early texts. "Sápmi" often replaces "Lapland," with the understanding that Sápmi also has a larger meaning than a geographic territory and may also refer to people and material culture, as in this book's subtitle.

Today, the Sámi are the minority in most of Sápmi, except in certain regions of Finnmark in Norway. There is no exact census of Sámi people, but estimates range from eighty thousand to one hundred thousand, with the majority living in Norway. The Sámi are further divided into ten language groups, most of which correspond to geographic regions of Sápmi. North Sámi is spoken by twenty-two thousand people in northern Norway, Sweden, and Finland; Lule Sámi, by about twenty-three hundred people in central Norway and Sweden; and South Sámi, by six hundred speakers in south central Norway and Sweden. In the Inari region of Finland, between three hundred and four hundred speak Inari (Aanaar) Sámi, and the same number speak Skolt Sámi in Russia. Most of the other languages have relatively few speakers and are critically endangered. Sámi languages are Finno–Ugric languages, closely related to Finnish.

In Sweden and Norway, the two Scandinavian countries that are the main focus of this book, the official Sámi languages are North, Lule, and South Sámi (with Ume Sámi increasingly taught and spoken in central Sweden). That means there are always several spellings for most objects. For example, drum is *goavddis* in North Sámi; *goabdes* in Lule Sámi; and *gievrie* in South Sámi. In general, I've chosen to use the English name or the North Sámi word. In common with others writing in English, I've chosen to keep a few frequently used North Sámi words in their nominative form and to add an *s* when using the plural for words kept in the original, for example, *noaidi, joik, siida, sieidi,* and *duojár.* In other cases, when using a Sámi word for an object, I note its plural.

I've also chosen to use the most familiar Norwegian or Swedish spelling for villages and cities—for instance, Jokkmokk instead of Jåhkåmåhkke (Lule Sámi) or Karasjok instead of Kárášjohka (North Sámi). This choice was made primarily to ease the way for English readers. Many Fennoscandian maps now show both names in the Sámi homeland.

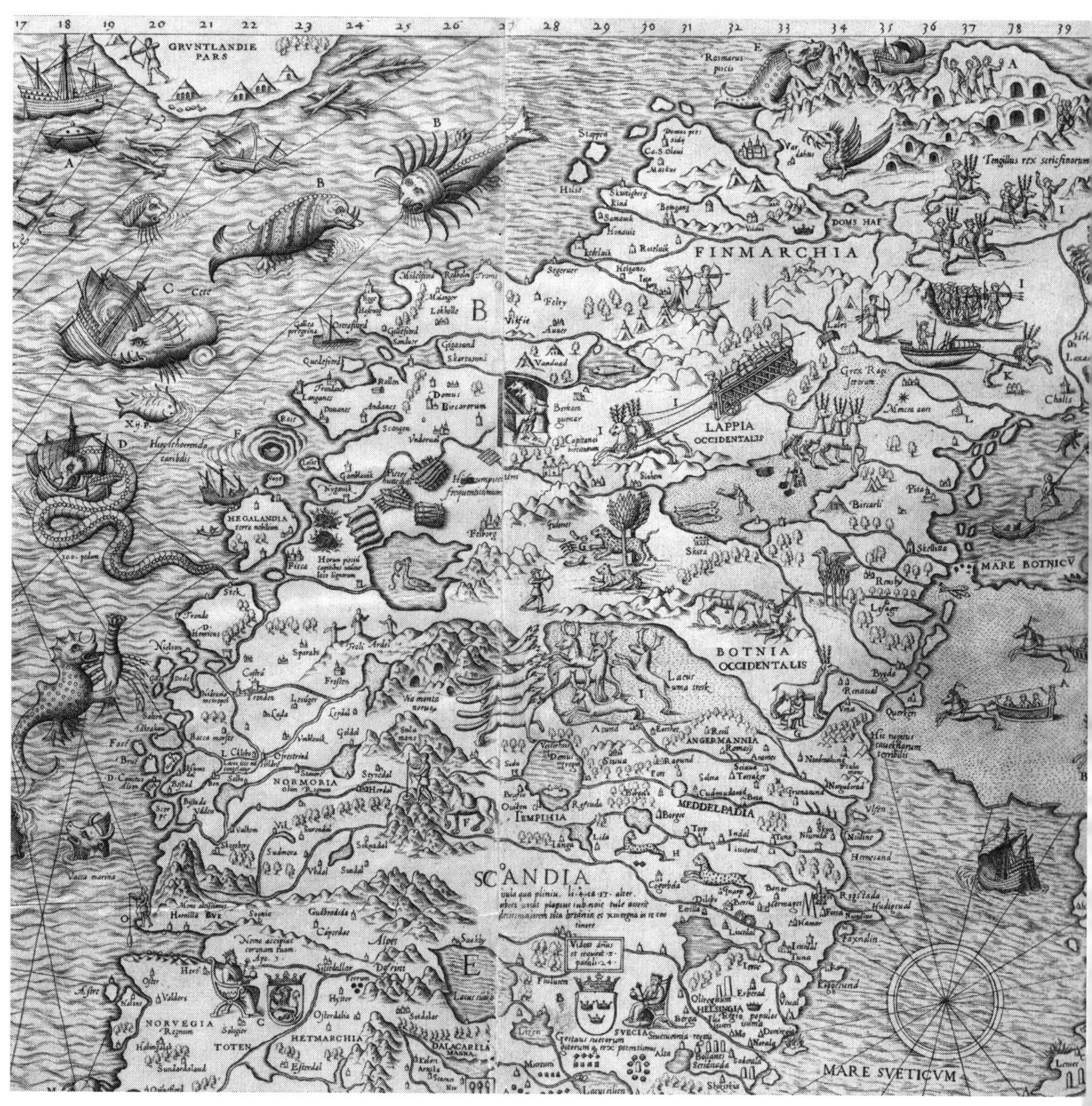

Olaus Magnus, *Carta Marina,* detail from second edition, 1572. This map was an early attempt to show the variety of people and ways of life in the Nordic countries. The exiled Swedish bishop Olaus Magnus was the author of *A Description of the Northern Peoples,* 1555. Courtesy of the James Ford Bell Library, University of Minnesota.

Introduction

Sea serpents and whales undulating in the coastal waters off Norvegia; elegant-antlered reindeer high-stepping around the fairy-tale realms of Finnmarchia, Biarmia, and Scrifinia; small warriors on skis armed with bows and arrows; even smaller houses and castles scattered like peppercorns around the frosty plateaus of the northern hinterlands of Europe. These are images from the famous Renaissance map the *Carta Marina* of 1539, created by the Swedish Catholic bishop Olaus Magnus after he went into exile in Rome following the Reformation. The bishop's map and his 1555 three-volume *A Description of the Northern Peoples* held many of the first published images and texts about the Indigenous people of Sápmi, a region stretching from the North Atlantic fjords to the Gulf of Bothnia, from the Barents Sea to below the Arctic Circle.

Olaus Magnus had never been farther north than his bishopric in Uppsala, and he wrote his books using material brought with him to Rome and sources he found in antiquarian volumes in the papal state there. His descriptions of the northern peoples are filled with "things to be marveled at, rather than explained," and cover everything from pirates at sea to warriors on horseback, from winter markets held on ice to the homely arts of beekeeping and baking bread.[1] Some of his chapters are about hunters, men and women on skis who wield bows and arrows and travel in sleds drawn by reindeer. These descriptions of the "Lapps," or the Sámi, include hearsay tales of shaman-like rituals and divination through drumming, as well as of sorcerers who stir up storms at sea and cast spells to harm enemies. Such tales of "Lappish magic" blend with the everyday wonders of the northern lands to create a picture of a world like no other, full of rare curiosities to be studied and treasured.

From Lapland to Sápmi is a cultural history of objects and collections originating in Sápmi, the home of the Indigenous Sámi people who live in Norway, Sweden, and Finland and on Russia's Kola Peninsula. The book begins in the seventeenth century with early modern collecting by clergymen, magistrates, botanists, and antiquarians. Such collecting efforts went hand in hand with the religious and political colonization of Sápmi by the post-Reformation Protestant Church, which reviled ceremonial objects as tools of the Devil, and by the crowns of Denmark–Norway and Sweden–Finland, which regarded objects of "Lappish sorcery" as status symbols for their treasuries.

These ceremonial and ethnographic objects also made their way to Europe as early as the 1600s, curiosities coveted by influential collectors from Paris to Florence and Madrid. "Magic drums" ended up in the Kunstkammers of kings and queens, as well as in more scientific collections, for instance, the famous Repository of the Royal Society in London. Missionaries accumulated objects in Scandinavia; so did European explorers and tourists. They often competed for the same objects, some of which were displayed in private museums. The belongings of the reindeer-herding Sámi, whether sleds, cradles, or fur clothing, were sold in curiosity shops in European capitals, and the "Laplander," along with family members, was a frequent performer in the living exhibitions in Scandinavia and Europe that began in the early nineteenth century and continued into the twentieth.

By the mid-nineteenth century, collecting in Sápmi had become linked with archeology, anthropology, and ethnography, often in order to categorize the Sámi people as separate from and lesser than other Nordic people. As industrialization and resource exploitation in the northern provinces of Sweden and Norway changed everyday existence for the Sámi, more of the objects they had created for trade and domestic use found their way into university and national museums in large cities to the south, where curators devised exhibits that, over time, have shaped public understanding of Sápmi. Beginning in the 1930s, Sámi artisans and activists began to play a larger role in how their belongings were displayed. This eventually resulted in conflicts and negotiations with institutions and the establishment of Sámi museums. New initiatives in the twenty-first century have included limited repatriation and truth and reconciliation commissions, as well as a renaissance of Sámi music, arts and crafts, theater, and literature and new ways of exhibiting Sápmi.

The title *From Lapland to Sápmi: Collecting and Returning Sámi Craft and Culture* reflects not only the linguistic and political shift that has taken place in recent decades but also a sense of movement, suggesting the historical origin and the contemporary repatriation of crafted objects collected *from* the mythologized and colonialized lands of the Far North and returned *to* the Sámi homeland: Sápmi as both place and Indigenous community. The North Sámi term for craft, *duodji,* encompasses traditional domestic articles and clothing as well as artisanal goods and artworks fashioned by *duojárs,* or craftspeople. But the concept of *duodji* is also spiritual and communal; it reflects the long heritage of makers in Sápmi who shaped sacred drums for their families, decorated reindeer harnesses for the migratory caravans, tanned and sewed leather shoes and fur tunics, embroidered elaborate hats and wove shoe bands, twisted and wound roots into baskets, and spent winter hours carving patterns onto spoons and knife handles. For the Sámi, *duodji* is both object and practice. Collectors of Sámi material culture who transported Sámi goods to private and public museums, while also recording joik music and writing down ethnographic information, were interested in both the object and the culture from which the object, tradition, or joik arose. In the contemporary process of returning many of these objects from Nordic institutions to museums in Sápmi, what is also being restored is the history of how, when, and why the objects were coveted and collected in the first place.

Sápmi is geographically defined at present as the traditional cultural region of the Sámi people within four countries or, more forcefully, as the territory of the Sámi people, divided by four countries. Sápmi, the homeland of Europe's only Indigenous people, is also the name for the Sámi people in the North Sámi language. The presence of their ancestors on the Fennoscandian Peninsula is recorded archeologically from the end of the Ice Age. The histories of Sápmi and Fennoscandia and Russia have been intertwined for over a thousand years, in chronicles unwritten and written, particularly since a more intensive form of colonization of Sápmi began in the 1600s. These days, Sápmi includes urban centers, large and small, where Sámi people have studied, raised families, found work, and built community.

My aim here is not to offer a comprehensive history of Sápmi over the past four hundred years. Instead, each chapter in Parts I and II takes on a time period and a series of events and personalities to create a narrative around one or more collections—of religious objects, of ethnographic artifacts, and of assemblages of art, music, and craft. Midway through Part II there is a shift, when stories from the early and mid-twentieth century often move into the present to discuss changing attitudes toward the Sámi and increasing agency among the Sámi themselves as they conserve and explore their past and develop aspects of traditional culture. By Part III, the focus is on the cultural currents of the past fifty years, with the Sámi as the main actors.

Although I'll often speak of "the Sámi" so as not to qualify every observation, it's important to recognize that to be Sámi in the past is not exactly the same as to be Sámi today, after generations of change, loss, assimilation, and society-wide modernization. Sámi life has varied widely throughout history, place, and occupation. Those Sámi who fished and hunted on the coasts of northern Norway had different experiences from those who herded reindeer in the Swedish–Norwegian mountains; they were different still from the Sámi who lived in the forests of Sweden and Finland, fishing and trapping, or who worked in mines or on railways; they were different, too, from urban Sámi who became teachers, artisans, and museum curators in the twentieth century. Because my emphasis is on specific objects and collections, this book can touch on only some of these differences, as well as the many social and cultural encounters that make up Sámi history within the shifting boundaries of the four countries.[2]

From Lapland to Sápmi is also the story of the Sámi people's relationships, collectively and individually, with their neighbors and colonizers, particularly the Scandinavians who collected objects from Sápmi, whether sacred drums, clothing, utensils, or souvenirs. Some of these Scandinavians were righteous Protestant missionaries intent on stamping out perceived paganism; some were early scientists eagerly adding rarities to their private collections; some were physical anthropologists and "Lappologists" who saw the Sámi as an inferior race to be studied; some were well-meaning ethnographers eager to preserve the remnants of a "disappearing" culture or to document languages and customs that remained; some were merchants or amateur collectors of art, music, or *duodji* that they sold to tourists or donated to museums. The narratives in this book are not solely about museums, but most do investigate the ways that collectors collected and how those collections became part of regional, national, and ethnographic museums, particularly those in Sweden and Norway. Objects move through museums and in and out of museums as well—through theft, trade, sale, and donation and through loans, negotiations, and repatriations. These shifting custodianships, within and without Sápmi, are mirrored in these movements, some of which reinforce old stereotypes and many of which now radically reimagine meanings and audiences.

Nicholas Thomas, director of the Museum of Archaeology and Anthropology in Cambridge, England, has written: "Material artefacts, for the most part, do not directly represent the events and developments foregrounded in conventional historical narrative, but often have oblique and incidental relationships to them; they bring particular and curious aspects of past life into view."[3] Most of the material objects I describe here have precisely that connection to history; while crucial to the meaning of Sámi history and Sámi identity, they have played a more incidental role in Nordic societies as curiosities to be coveted and forgotten. Yet Thomas's words also suggest that relationships between objects in collections, and between the makers and the collectors, are just as important as the objects themselves.

There has been a good deal of interest in recent decades in "the biography of the object" in books and articles about the meaning and history of singular artifacts. Here I hope to look not only at the significance of unique objects as they were transported from Sámi communities to private homes and museums but also at how Sámi collections were positioned and repositioned in museums. I want to focus attention on who collected and why, to examine stories of punishment, avarice, curiosity, and appropriation. I want to explore the rationales that led collectors to view the Sámi as Other, while at the same time interacting with individual Sámi people as colleagues, collaborators, and sometimes personal friends.

By delving into relationships between the collectors and the collected, I'm hoping to present a more complex and entangled picture of how objects were transported away from the Sámi people who created them and displayed and stored in local, ethnographic, and national museums. Some of these museums were in Denmark, Germany, Russia, and England; most were in Sweden, Norway, and Finland, including the Nordic Museum (Nordiska Museet) in Stockholm and the Norwegian Museum of Cultural History (Norsk Folkemuseum) in Oslo. These national museums later became sites of interrogation and reinterpretation, where familiar objects are presented in new contexts and where modern objects, sometimes based on older artifacts, become part of a changing narrative about the place of the Sámi in contemporary Nordic culture.

At the same time, new museums funded by the Sámi Parliaments and administered by a Sámi staff play an increasingly larger role in the Nordic countries as sites for exhibitions as well as for community building and research. In the current century, the emphasis has turned to repatriating objects from national museums to Sámi museums and to identifying the locations and fates of many of the Sámi objects in European and British institutions. But repatriation is only one aspect of return. An understanding of how Nordic national and regional museums conserve and exhibit their Sámi collections now takes place amid public discussions of Indigeneity and colonization. Such conversations and occasional confrontations have moved the question of who owns what into new directions, with consequences for the future. The discussions also complicate definitions of what it means to be Sámi and how the existence of Sápmi, a region divided by four countries, complicates notions of national identity.

I'm mindful, in my decision to highlight relationships between historical figures, especially those of unequal power (which for much of Sámi history was the case), that Sámi voices are hard to come by in most histories of collecting until the mid-twentieth century, and that is especially true of women's voices. For most of recorded history, Sápmi had an oral culture. The Sámi were largely described by outsiders from some of the first sightings and encounters a thousand years ago until the seventeenth century, when their own explanations for religious and cultural beliefs begin to appear, insistently argumentative, in government records, court cases, and letters and accounts by Protestant missionaries. These voices are few and far between yet stubbornly constant as the Sámi considered what these strangers felt entitled to know and what the Sámi decided to tell them—if anything. In nineteenth-century travelogues and early ethnographic studies, Sámi voices are often trapped in the narrator's perspective or appropriated and retold in poetry, tales, and myths published by Scandinavians and Europeans.

Such books about the Sámi became a flood of thick volumes by the end of the nineteenth century. In the words of many of these philologists, folklorists, and tourists, the Sámi had no history; they were romantic nomads destined to disappear. Such attitudes continued for decades. Yet by the early twentieth century, Indigenous texts—political, literary, and autobiographical—became more prevalent, and some of these writers were also artists and artisans and collectors. Their pamphlets, articles, and accounts create an alternate history of resistance and demands to be seen and heard. Although most collectors, ethnographers, and curators were men in the first half of the twentieth century, a variety of women, Sámi and non-Sámi, played an important role in creating and collecting objects. The Nordic countries' support of women's rights and parity in the late twentieth century had an effect on Sámi women as well, as they took the lead in many organizations, including museums and cultural centers. In addition to being museum directors and curators, Sámi women are artisans and artists, writers, filmmakers, and musicians. Their voices are strong and present, and their perspectives are reflected in new creative work and scholarship emanating from Sápmi.

The three parts of *From Lapland to Sápmi* break down Sápmi–Scandinavian cultural history into historical periods, with excursions into how the Sámi have also been seen in other countries in Europe. Part I, "Northern Curiosities," begins with the early scholars and scientists, often botanists and medical men, who put together some of the first collections of objects from Sápmi in the seventeenth and early eighteenth centuries for their own private curiosity cabinets and who traded and gifted the more valued objects, particularly sacred drums. In spite of active Sámi resistance, the drums and other ceremonial objects were, if not destroyed, removed to universities and royal collections, eventually to be labeled and displayed in state museums as examples of "Lappish sorcery."

Part I also explores the beginnings of images and performances of the Sámi as picturesque "wanderers" and "noble savages," living a pure and primitive life in the wilderness. In drawings, prints, books, and living exhibitions, Sámi people were usually represented wearing traditional clothing, posed in mountain settings, surrounded by domestic objects and items connected with herding, including tents, sleds, and reindeer (Plate 1). After the worst of Scandinavian religious persecution came to an end in Sápmi in the latter eighteenth century, settler colonization took hold, in the form of seizures of former reindeer-herding territories for agriculture and mining and eventually for hydropower, railways, and industrial logging. At the same time, tourism came to the fore; travelers began to explore and write about Scandinavia, cementing images of nomadic reindeer herders as the only authentic Sámi. The production of images from Sápmi, as well as the first instances of Sámi participation in constructed habitat displays in the early nineteenth century, showed the Sámi together with the objects they had created and used. These exhibits, which would continue until the 1930s, turned the Sámi people into ethnographic "things to be marveled at."

Part II, "Collecting," moves into the mid-nineteenth century and looks at appropriation and collaboration, at the interest in ethnography and ethnographic objects, at the founding of national and regional museums, and at the rise and fall of racial biological research in Sweden and Norway in the first half of the twentieth century. The years before and after World War II continued policies of assimilation and social and educational discrimination against most Sámi. Yet Sámi political organizing also took place, and by the last decades of the twentieth century a significant political movement had emerged that included the establishment of three Sámi Parliaments in Norway, Sweden, and Finland. Museums took note but were often slow to change their exhibits. At the same time, Sámi museums were established and artisanship found its way into collections and the public eye. While "things" (i.e., material objects) were sometimes less to be "marveled at" and more to be "explained," a new and renewed appreciation arose for other forms of Sámi cultural and aesthetic expression. Swedish musicologist

Karl Tirén's collection of wax cylinders of Sámi songs, or joiks, for instance, is significant in both its materiality and its preservation of past voices that have provided inspiration for Sámi musicians in the twenty-first century.

I end Part II by telling the more personal story of how the Danish ethnographer and artist Emilie Demant Hatt collected ethnographic objects from Sápmi for the National Museum of Denmark as part of her travels and fieldwork in the early twentieth century. A number of those objects were gifts from Sámi friends, including several that were courtship gifts from the artist and writer Johan Turi, and are now part of collections in Copenhagen and Stockholm. My questions and reflections about where these objects belong lead readers into the third and final part of the book.

Part III, "Two Directions," takes a deeper look at collecting, displaying, and returning Sápmi since the 1980s, in both Nordic national and regional museums and Sámi museums, such as Ájtte in Jokkmokk, Sweden; Siida in Inari, Finland; and the Sámi Museum in Karasjok, Norway. In 2012 the Sámi Parliament in Norway and the Norwegian Museum of Cultural History in Oslo began the legal process of repatriating half of the national museum's Sámi collection to Sámi museums around the country, a project called Bååstede, a word from the South Sámi language meaning "the Return." The National Museum of Finland in Helsinki also recently transferred the majority of its collection of Sámi objects to the museum Siida in the north of Finland. In Sweden, while direct repatriation is not yet on the table, the Nordic Museum in Stockholm has loaned objects, particularly the ceremonial drums, to regional and Sámi museums in the country. Denmark, which once ruled Norway, also has a significant collection of Sámi material culture. In early 2022, the National Museum of Denmark agreed to turn over ownership of a seventeenth-century ceremonial drum to the Sámi Museum in Karasjok. Repatriation has taken on new momentum in the past few years, as Sámi researchers identify and inventory objects originally from Sápmi in the Nordic countries and elsewhere in Europe. In Part III, I also look at exhibits in several national and regional museums in Norway and Sweden that reimagine displays of Sámi culture and act as cultural meeting places for both Sámi and non-Sámi visitors. "The Return" is a process that goes two ways, as Sámi culture becomes more visible and valued in Nordic societies.

For some readers, the history of Sápmi's existence within the known geography of Northern Europe may be novel and unsettling. Even more disturbing may be learning about the centuries of active persecution of this Indigenous people and an equally long period of resistance, often ignored in history books, on the side of the Sámi. Many of the stories I tell here will be new to those of us more familiar with the Nordic countries only as some of the wealthiest and most progressive nations on earth. This book tells alternate and parallel histories and makes clear that these countries are as complicated and complicit in social and cultural injustice as other Western powers, though in ways that have gone unrecognized for centuries.

The narratives in this book explore questions I've asked myself. How have Sámi-made objects been categorized, successively and simultaneously, as ceremonial, utilitarian, ethnographic, and aesthetic? Who collected these objects from Sápmi and why? Where did the objects go, how were they displayed, and, in some cases, why were they sometimes returned to Sápmi? Are these objects still being made, and who makes them? What do these "things to be marveled at" expose about relationships between the makers and the collectors? What can these objects and collections tell us about the history of Sápmi, a geography and a diverse array of people, within the borders of the High North but at the same time often outside the past historical narratives of Northern Europe?

I'm not a collector, aside from my ever growing library of books about Sápmi, but I've long been interested in the intertwined histories of Sápmi and Scandinavia, and I have visited many of the museums, archives, cities, and landscapes I describe here. Over the years I've learned from Sámi curators, historians, and artists and from others in the Nordic countries active in the fields of museology and cultural history. *From Lapland to Sápmi* reflects and builds on the new scholarship in those countries and elsewhere, especially that which looks at colonialism and Indigeneity past and present in Sweden, Norway, and Finland. My previous work on the Danish artist and ethnographer Emilie Demant Hatt, who collected experiences, objects, and friends in Sápmi in the early twentieth century, gradually sparked a desire to tell some of the many fascinating, troubling, and inspiring stories of how Sámi-made objects were created, stolen, lost, displayed, remade, and remembered. While *From Lapland to Sápmi* can't answer all my questions, these narratives of makers and collectors in Sápmi are worth sharing and exploring, particularly in a time of historical transition, when many of the objects are again on the move, sometimes physically back again to Sápmi but also, importantly, back again into the hearts and hands of the Sámi people.

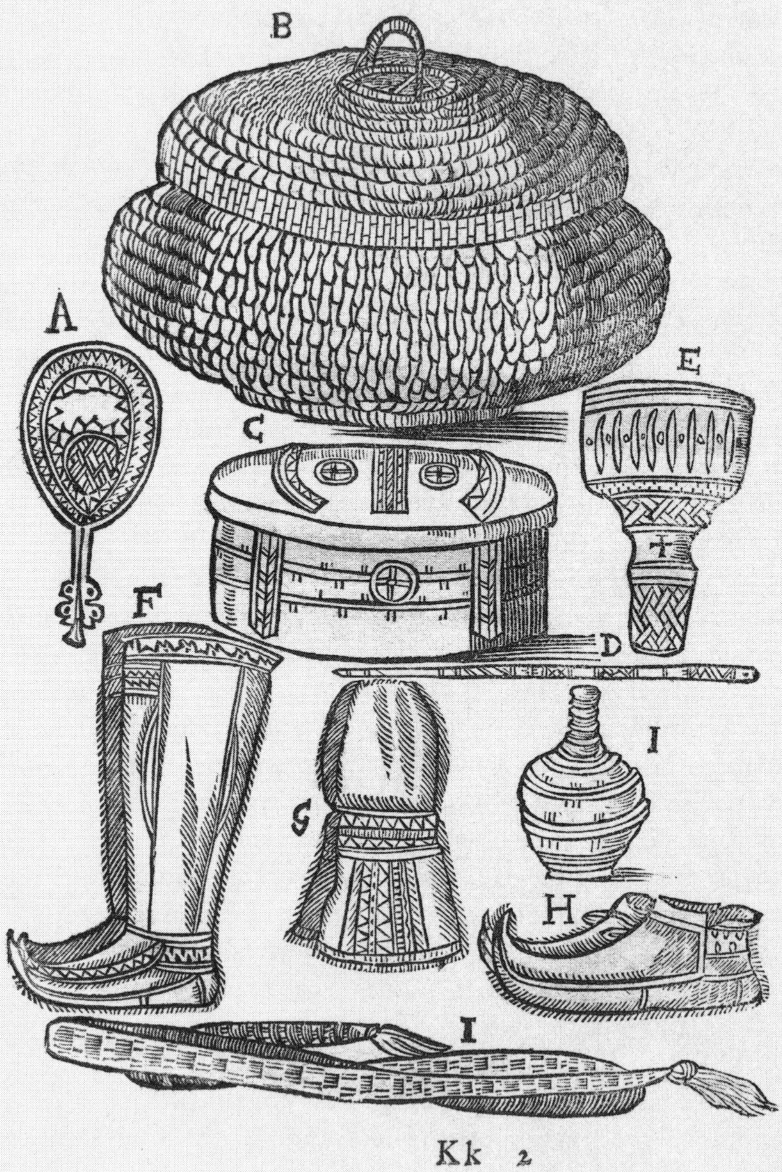

Many of these traditional Sámi objects, illustrated in *Lapponia,* first published in Latin in 1673 by scholar Johannes Schefferus, were to be found in his private museum in Uppsala, Sweden. Courtesy of Uppsala University Library.

PART I
Northern Curiosities

Lapponia

They came on the north wind, lead arrows sent at faster-than-light speeds and over huge distances, usually southward, malicious projectiles that struck their victims suddenly out of nowhere. An explosion, followed by instant death. These shots, or *skudd,* called *Gandskudd, Finnskudd,* and *Trollskudd,* were part of the maleficent arsenal of *gand* sorcery that so-called Lappish wizards routinely employed to inflict pain and disease on others. Olaus Magnus wrote, "For this purpose they craft small spell-spears, about the length of a finger, and shoot them as far as they want against those who are the object of their revenge."[1]

Although *gand* came to be almost exclusively associated with the Sámi and the Far North, the word's origin is not Sámi. *Gand* is from Proto-German and appears in Old Norse as *gandr;* one of its meanings is "magic staff." The word still survives in Norway in contemporary slang as a half joke: You've been *ganda* if life is giving you one misfortune too many. More people in pre-Christian Viking times believed in and performed some form of magic than just Sámi *noaidis*—community religious leaders with powers to heal the sick and forecast the future. Yet by the Reformation in the mid-sixteenth century, when Olaus Magnus wrote *A Description of the Northern Peoples,* spell casting was largely written about as a Sámi phenomenon. After Olaus Magnus came state-sponsored Lutheran clergymen to warn of the dangers of *gand.* Norwegian pastor Peder Claussøn Friis, born in 1545 and best known for his translations of Icelandic sagas, included a chapter on the Sámi in his book, *Description of Norway and Outlying Islands.* Like many people who wrote about the Sámi, he based his stories of "Lappish sorcery" on hearsay and imagination and exaggerated freely. Friis believed that *gands* were magic spells, created for the purpose of self-defense. You had to be able to send off a curse in order to repel one coming at you, as in a modern video game. Like

Olaus Magnus, Friis visualized the curses as embodied objects, "spell-arrows," which could be directed not just at people but also at animals and other natural phenomena that annoyed them, like the wind itself. If a wizard were in the mood, for instance, he could fire off a *gand* in the direction of a mountain boulder and explode it just to show off.

But Friis expanded the wicked vehicles of *gand* sorcery to include not just lead arrows but also insects, blue-black flies that the Sámi kept in special pouches. If a sorcerer were irritable or bored, he might open this pouch and unloose the *gand* flies into the North Wind, to carry them south and to wreak random havoc on humans and beasts alike. North Norwegian poet and pastor Petter Dass called the dark blue insects "Beelzebub's flies," while the Norwegian missionary priest Johan Randulf described the *gand* flies in a manuscript from 1723 as emanating from certain flying fowls of the air: "The bird spews out these *gand* flies from its beak, and some shake out of the bird's feathers and wings. They are no doubt natural flies, but poisoned, that this Satan in his guise as a bird has brought down from some other place in the world, to the wicked service of the Sámi. The Sámi collects the flies and puts them in a box, so he has them to send out as *gand*."[2]

Since accusations of *gand* figured prominently in the rash of sorcery trials of Sámi people in the late seventeenth century in Norway, the historical records offer other means of describing and visualizing objects that cast a spell. In 1680 in Vadsø in Finnmark, a Sámi man on trial for witchcraft described the *gand* as a small animal the size of a mouse with two heads, front and rear. Arrows and insects were the most common depictions of *gand* objects, occasionally illustrated in a manuscript or in the record of a witchcraft trial; yet at least one author, the German-born Swedish scholar Johannes Schefferus, believed that a *gand* could also be a round ball, about the size of a walnut or a small apple. He called it a *gand-tyre,* from the Swedish-Finnish word *tyrä,* which means "sorcery ball."

This object was made of fur, hair, or moss, he wrote in his 1673 book, *Lapponia*: "very smooth, and so light it seems hollow, its color is a mixture of yellow, green, and ash."[3] If the object of your revenge or wrath were human, it was best to make the *gand-tyre* of human hair and nails; if the object were an animal, fur and wool were your best bet. Sometimes these materials were stuck together with tree pitch. Wizards created these balls, enlivened them, and sold them. They might employ the *gand-tyres* against their own enemies or sell them to anyone who had a grudge. The balls were, in Schefferus's opinion, lacking a fine sense of direction. Instead, barreling through the air "like a whirlewind," they sometimes

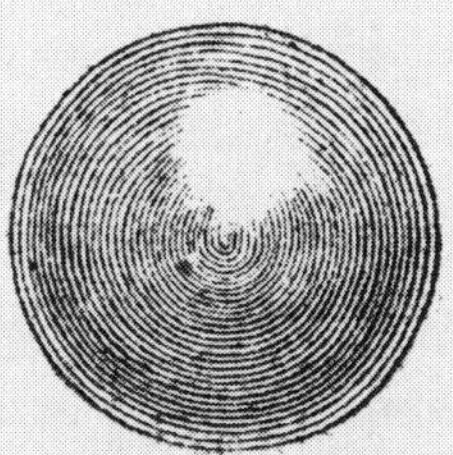

This *Tyre* they ſay is quickened and moved by a particular art? it is ſold by the *Laplanders*, ſo that he that buies it may hurt whom he pleaſes with it. They do perſwade themſelves, and others, that by the *Tyre* they can ſend, either Serpents, Toads, Mice, or what they pleaſe into any man, to make his torment the greater. It goes like a whirlewind, and as ſwift as an arrow, and deſtroies the firſt man, or beaſt, that it lights on, ſo that it often miſtakes. Of theſe we have too many inſtances in this time, which are too long to inſert here: having therefore done with all, or at leaſt the chiefeſt matters concerning their ſacred, and ſuperſtitious rites, or worſhip; we proceed to other affairs.

A rare illustration of a *gand-tyre* from the English translation of Schefferus's Lapponia, *The History of Lapland,* 1674. These objects were said to be imbued with magic and came in many forms, but few were conserved. Courtesy of the National Library of Norway.

missed their targets and destroyed whatever was in the way. It also appears from his account that the *gand-tyre* might itself not fly but instead cause to fly through the air a variety of serpents, toads, and mice, "or what they please into any man, to make his torment the greater."[4]

Unlike other authors who described various forms of *gand* in books and historical records, and very occasionally offered a simple sketch of an arrow tip or an insect-like thing, Schefferus included an illustration of one of the round balls in a chapter dedicated to the "Magicall Ceremonies of the Laplanders" in *The History of Lapland,* the English translation of *Lapponia.* Schefferus wrote that the ball was given to him by Mr. John Otto Silverstroem, a master of metals. Thus, Schefferus seems to have been one of the few writers on the subject of the Sámi to have held any sort of *gand* in his hand and to have displayed it, along with other Sámi objects mentioned in *Lapponia,* in a small museum near the cathedral in Uppsala.[5] It was the first private museum in the world to exhibit a Sámi collection.

Magic objects like the *gand-tyre* were not limited to these "Lappish sorcerers." European royals had their own form of sorcery ball, the bezoar, a word that comes from the Persian and means "antidote." A natural bezoar is a stony concretion that forms in the stomachs of some ruminants. Other bezoars were made by humans. The animal bezoars came from the stomachs of goats, sheep, oxen, and llamas; the lumps were created when layers of calcium and magnesium built up around a pebble, a scrap of undigested vegetable matter, or hair. Over time, the contractions of the gastrointestinal tract squeezed the lump into a smooth round shape. Other bezoars were created by hand, often by artisans in Goa, India, using a paste of minerals and spirits. Both forms of bezoar, often housed in elaborate metal cases, were a kind of currency among royals and were known to physicians in the Renaissance as being effective against poisons. Elizabeth I of England and Erik XIV of Sweden were known to wear rings set with small bezoars—possibly as a ready antidote if regicide was contemplated.[6]

Twenty-two of these rare bezoars had belonged to the emperor of the Holy Roman Empire, Rudolf II, whose Kunstkammer in Prague was legendary, not just for his Titans and Tintorettos but also for archeological antiquities; curios from India, Africa, and the Far East; and objects of natural history collections. In his palace were ancient jawbones and ivory miniatures, silk wallpapers and beetles. He had collected everything possible, the better to replicate in his palace museum an "encyclopedia of the visible world."[7] In 1648, a good part of Rudolf's treasures and his impressive library was removed from his palace in Prague, loaded onto barges on the Moldau River, and towed north to Stockholm, part of the compensation paid to Sweden as the victor of the Thirty Years' War, in which Sweden's king, Gustav, had died on the battlefield. The royal who received them in Stockholm was the young Queen Christina, who had a love of learning, pomp, and accumulation.

Queen since she was six but crowned only in 1650 at age twenty-three, Christina was an unusual royal: a superb horsewoman, well versed in classical literature, and able to converse on all subjects in several languages. She had the deep voice of man, a hunched shoulder from being dropped as a baby, and a disinclination to marry. She thought nothing of depleting the treasury to pay for masques and balls or feasts and jousts in one of her several castles. Her notion of governing mainly extended to racking up debt and then ordering her parliament to find new ways to raise money. Christina conflated herself with Sweden; what came into the treasury through taxation and plunder was hers to spend. With one hand, she showered attention on her favorites; with the other, she withheld and punished.

As the "Pallas of the North," she invited European scholars to Stockholm to curate her collections of treasures, art, and curios; to act as archivists and librarians; and to become professors at Uppsala University. Philology was a particular passion of hers. As a means of deciphering the world, philology harkened back to the Renaissance, when searching for the occult correspondences between words was seen as scientific and when learning as many ancient languages as possible was a scholar's joy. Along with philology came collecting and assigning objects to a diversity of categories. The making of "encyclopedias of the visual world" continued into the mid-seventeenth century. One of Christina's pet projects was the formation of a Swedish Academy to rival the Académie Française. No sooner had she learned of Descartes than she decided he must attend her at her court and instruct her on the new empiricism he had so elegantly put forth in *Discourse on Method.* Although the famous French philosopher politely refused her invitation, she managed to kidnap him and bring him back to Stockholm at the beginning of one of the coldest winters in Swedish history. Within two years he was lonely and frustrated in his attempts to instruct the young queen in the fine points of the scientific method. He died of a chill in 1650.[8]

Christina's reign was short. She converted to Catholicism and abdicated in 1654 to move to Rome. But one of the scholars Christina invited to Sweden would leave a lasting legacy. This was the young philologist Johannes Schefferus, from Strasburg, who arrived in 1648 to take up a professorship in law and rhetoric at Uppsala University. Although many foreigners left Sweden after Christina's abdication, Schefferus stayed on in Uppsala, amid a quarrelsome and impecunious group of professors who scrabbled to be paid by the Crown for their scholarly pursuits. He is remembered mainly for the short black cape he always wore and for his volume *Lapponia,* a compilation of information about the Sámi in the north of Sweden considered the first book about the Sámi ever written—and one of the most influential.

In 1671 the chancellor of the realm, Magnus de la Gardie, now regent to the son of Christina's successor, Charles X Gustav, charged Schefferus with the task of writing a description of the inhabitants of Lapland. De la Gardie was concerned about the rumors that had plagued Sweden for decades, spread mainly by Germany, which had often lost to Sweden on the battlefields during the Thirty Years' War. Pamphlets full of spleen and insinuation held that it was only witchcraft performed by the notorious "Lappish wizards" in the North that had allowed Swedish victories.

De la Gardie wanted a more realistic portrait of the Sámi, specifically of their conversion to and practice of Christianity, which would refute claims that "Lappish magic" was responsible for Sweden's prowess at warfare. The chancellor didn't expect Schefferus to travel north to observe the Indigenous people in situ, nor did the professor have any inclination to leave his comfortable home in Uppsala for the wilds of Sápmi. Instead, the two of them rummaged through the private collections of several nobles, including that of the chancellor, for objects from Lapland: cups carved from birch boles, spoons shaped from reindeer horn, embroidered tunics and bonnets, boat-shaped sleds, and long, wooden skis. These objects, an encyclopedia of the visible Sámi world, were the basis for Schefferus's descriptions and drawings and soon, with other objects sent by informants up in Sápmi, sat on the shelves of the museum he built to contain them.

Uppsala is one of Sweden's oldest cities and its oldest seat of learning. Since 1477 students from all over the country have flocked to study there, including students from Sápmi. The medieval cathedral on a hill still dominates the old city center near the university, surrounded by winding streets and squares. Off one of these old market squares, St. Eriks Torg, where a Swedish king was beheaded by Danes and near where Ingmar Bergman shot scenes for his film *Fanny and Alexander,* is a chunky, one-story, square structure. Measuring about seven hundred square feet, with one heavy wooden door and three large windows, it's painted the warm orange ochre of many of Uppsala's old buildings; the pitched roof is covered with rounded, terracotta clay tiles. Inside are thick walls plastered white, a stone floor, and a vaulted ceiling. The three rooms are divided unequally; one is long and rectangular and probably where objects were once displayed from Schefferus's collection of natural history, antiquities, and Sámi artifacts. Another small room probably held his library of several hundred volumes, and another was a workroom.

Many of the treasures of Sweden at the time were stored safely away from the people in various castles around the country, including the vast sixteenth-century Three Crowns castle in Uppsala and the formidable palace in Stockholm. The modest square building on St. Eriks Torg seems to have been the first building in Sweden purposely constructed as a museum. From around 1671 to

Schefferus's death in 1679, its collections drew scholars, students, and wealthy European travelers through its doors. They came to see the rocks veined with iron ore, copper, and silver from the Swedish mountains; fish and plant fossils; Viking runestones; stuffed foxes and wolverines; and natural history oddities. Many also came to view the collection of Sámi clothing, reindeer gear, skis, and sacred drums. The Museum Schefferianum had six drums; three came from de la Guardie's home.

As a physical object, the Sámi drum falls into one of two types, both of them oval shaped: a bowl drum and a frame drum. In the bowl drum, reindeer skin is tightly attached to a hollowed-out birch burl. Two slits at the back form a handle. Most bowl drums, or *goavdát* (pl.), are from central and northern Sápmi. The frame drum, or *gievrie,* is created from bentwood, usually spruce but occasionally pine. These frame drums are generally from southern Sápmi; many of them had attached metal rings and dangling strands of leather wrapped with pewter thread and bone or metal charms. Almost all the drumskins were decorated with reddish alder-bark ink: the pictographs of animals, people, tents, mountains, and the sun and moon were usually simple figures, much like the petroglyphs found in parts of Sápmi, which were carved and painted on stones dating back thousands of years. By the 1600s some drumskins also featured Christian imagery, including churches and crosses. Because so many drums were destroyed and because so few accounts were given of the meaning of the figures—and those accounts were usually given under duress—researchers have been left to guess at the symbols or to attach more fanciful meanings.

The drums were used for several purposes. *Noaidis,* often men but women as well, acted as intermediaries between the physical and spirit worlds. The sound of the drum enabled them to fall into a trance of one or more hours in which they lay apparently unconscious. During the trance they were able to leave their bodies and to move freely as a spirit or a breath of wind. They might shelter in the form of a reindeer or fish; they had the ability to fly long distances. They traveled in the realms of the dead and the almost dead. Sometimes they could bring an ill person back to health or even a dead person back to life. The greatest skill of this representative was to restore harmony to the community, or *siida.* By outsiders *noaidis* were called sorcerers and magicians, wizards and witches; in later literature they were identified as "Lappish shamans."[9]

But it was not only the *noaidis* who possessed and used a drum; almost every household had one as well, for purposes of divination and general consultation.

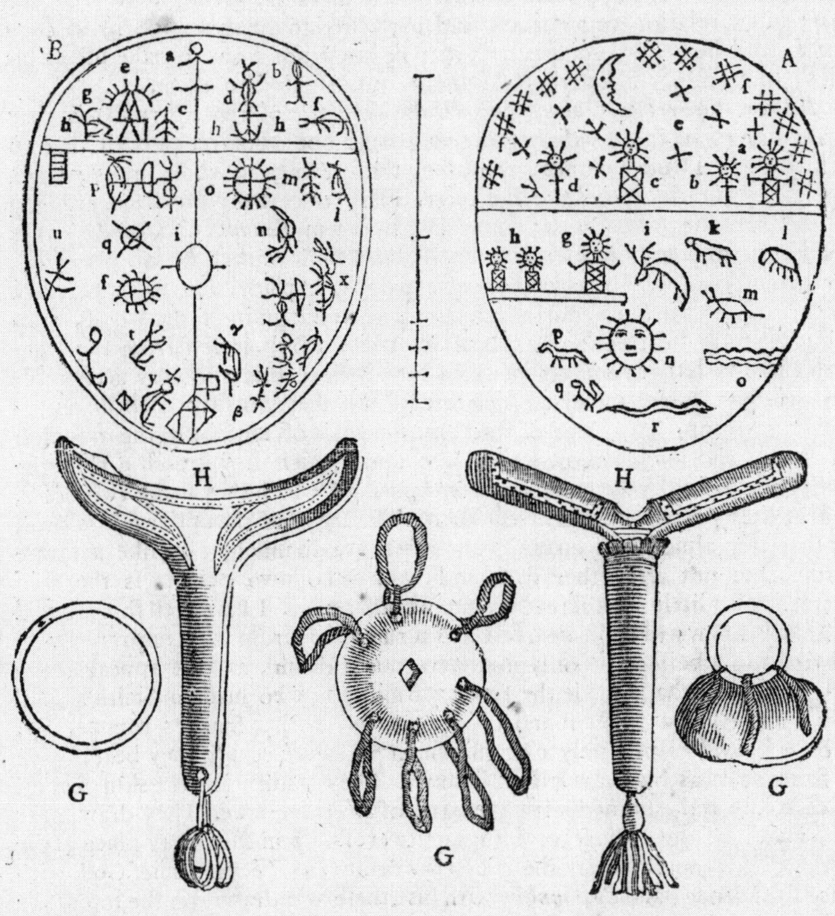

50 *Of the magicall Ceremonies*

The Explication of the Figures.

In the Drum A. a markes *Thor.* b *Thors Servant.* c *Storjnnkare.* d *his Servant.* e *Birds.* f *Stars.* g *Christ.* h *his Apostles.* i *a Bear.* k *a Wolf.* l *a Rain-deer.* m *an Ox.* n *the Sun.* o *a Lake.* p *a Fox.* q *a Squeril.* r *a Serpent.*

In the Drum B. *a* denotes *God the Father.* b *Jesus Christ.* c *the Holy Ghost.* d *S. John.* e *Death.* f *a Goat.* g *a Squeril.* h *Heaven.* i *the Sun.* l *a Wolf.* m *the fish Siik.* n *a Cock.* o *Friendship with the wild Rain-deer.* p *Anundus Eerici* (whose Drum this was) *killing a Wolf.* q *Gifts.* r *an Otter.* ſ *the friendship of other Lapps.* t *a Swan.* u *a sign to try the condition of others, and whether a disease be incurable.* x *a Bear.* y *a Hog.* β *a Fish.* γ *one carrying a Soul to Hell.*

Sámi ceremonial drums illustrated in Schefferus's *The History of Lapland,* shown with hammers made of reindeer antler and pointers in the form of rings. Courtesy of the National Library of Norway.

The method used here was not to play the drum as an instrument but to hold it parallel to the ground and beat the drumskin with a hammer made of reindeer antler. This caused a small object—a *vuorbi,* or pointer (which had other names, including "frog")—placed on the membrane to vibrate and bounce. When the hammer stopped, the pointer lay on one symbol or another and could be interpreted. Thus, the drum acted like the hexagrams of the *I Ching* or a pack of tarot cards—a method of prediction and a means of understanding.

As an Indigenous people who lived off the land and the rivers and seas and who cared for and tried to protect small and large herds of reindeer, the Sámi used the drum to seek advice on herding or fishing conditions and to predict weather patterns. The *siidas* collectively had millennia of traditional knowledge to draw on; some of it was shared in the form of stories and music, while some of it was embodied in the family drums. The drum offered a way of teaching and a way of understanding; it was a solace and a compass. Many drums were passed down through the generations and were treated as the precious and powerful heirlooms they were, wrapped carefully in fur or cloth when not in use and placed in secure parts of the tent or in the last sled in a reindeer caravan.

But to travelers, traders, and the pastors sent to Christianize the northern hinterlands, the drums were connected only with sorcery and evil. To the missionaries, the drum was "the Devil's bible," not just in the way it was used but in itself, as an object. The Devil lived inside the drum. Beating on the membrane called the Devil forth. That was a large part of the reason why, beginning in the 1600s, the drums themselves had to be destroyed and why the Sámi *siidas* began to hide the drums and deny that they knew anything about them, claim they had never used them, or else explain that possibly their ancestors had used them but they themselves had no idea what the missionary was talking about. Few confessed to being *noaidis,* and most claimed they were Christian. Some said that their drum was more like a compass: it was necessary when migrating through the mountains with reindeer to have a directional tool.

Ripped, smashed, and burned in bonfires, hundreds—perhaps thousands—of drums vanished over a period of about a hundred years, from the early seventeenth to the first decades of the eighteenth century. Those that survived were confiscated by magistrates and missionaries and eventually sent to kings and collectors in the larger cities. One of the drums found its way to Copenhagen around 1630–40, to the collection of the famed Danish physician and scientist Ole Worm.

If you had visited the Copenhagen home of Ole Worm, polymath and physician to King Christian IV, here are some of the astonishing natural history objects you

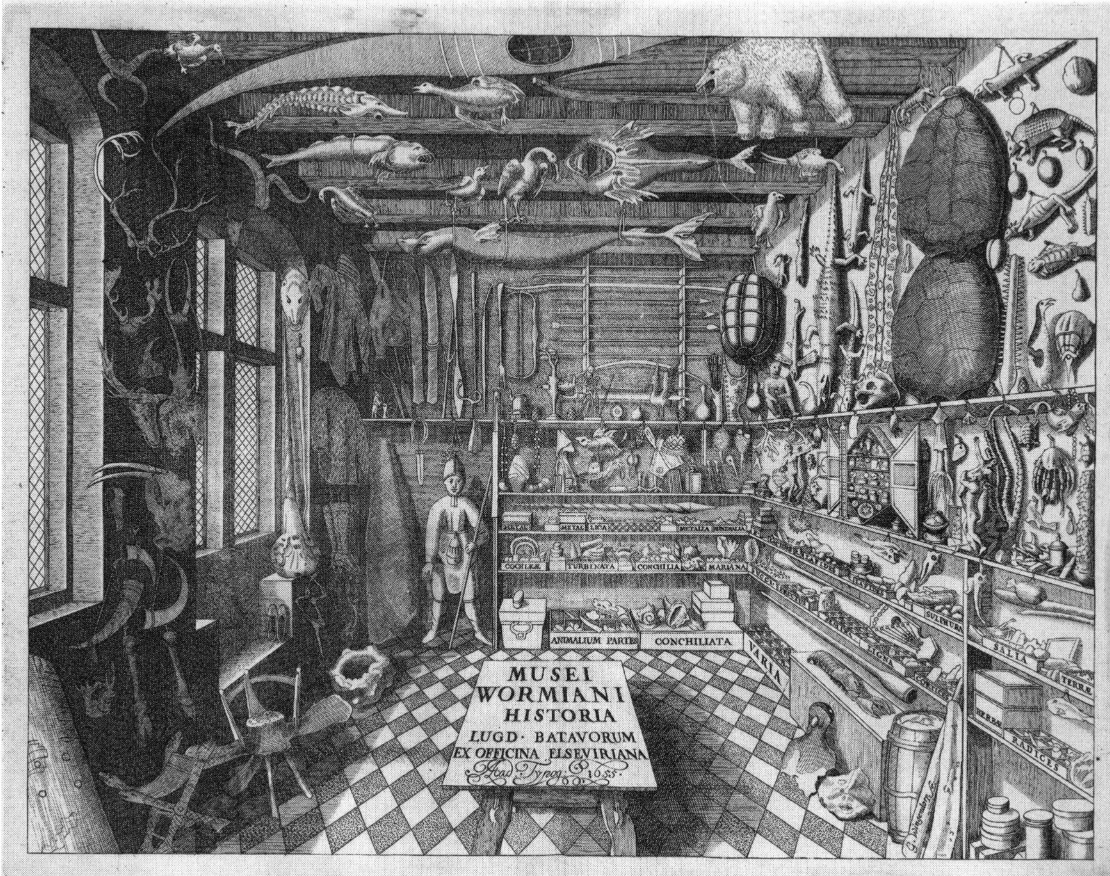

Frontispiece in the catalog for Museum Wormianum, 1655. Danish scholar Ole Worm displayed hundreds of natural and humanmade objects in his private museum in Copenhagen, including a few objects from Sápmi. Courtesy of the Science History Institute, Philadelphia.

might have encountered, arranged in cabinets and cupboards and on shelves up to the ceiling: the tusk of a narwhal from the North Atlantic and a giant tortoise shell from the South Seas; mysterious marine and avian fossils from long-vanished eras; monkey paws and tiger jawbones; fleshy embryos preserved in spirits; and several hundred botanical specimens, including a wooly fern that, it was suggested, might be related to a sheep. The Museum Wormianum also contained human-made objects. By ship and horse, baskets intricately woven of reeds arrived from Africa, decorated spears from Indonesia, a navigation compass from China, runic stones and metal armbands from Viking Age sites, as well as sleds, skis, kayaks, and paddles from the North: Iceland, Greenland, and Scandinavia. Ole Worm followed in the footsteps of other learned men around Europe, whose cabinets of natural history and anatomy served as laboratories to study the variety of God's creations in a scientific way, with an eye toward taxonomy and the material properties of each marvelous object. What the Museum Wormianum contained is known today from the catalogs he and his assistants produced; each edition included more items, until by the time of his death in 1654, the count was around 1,600, some 220 of which can be seen in the famous frontispiece to the catalog. Among the items collected by Ole Worm were various things from Sápmi, including a ceremonial drum and its hammer and pointer (Plate 2). There's no indication in the catalog where the drum was taken from or who made it, though a description explains how the instrument is meant to be operated.[10]

It's possible that Ole Worm didn't think of the Sámi drum in his collection as any more of a magic item than a Chinese navigation compass or the runic calendar that came from the Swedish island of Gotland. As one of the leading runic scholars of his time, he was curious about all manner of symbols, letters, and inscriptions, and he may have found the ceremonial drum from Sápmi intriguing because of the pictographs. He was a learned man and had read the sagas that spoke of the Sámi as soothsayers and sorcerers. An anonymous medieval text in Latin, *Historia Norwegie,* written in the late 1100s, gave an account of a ritual in which the wizard "lifted up a small vessel like a sieve, which was covered with images of whales and reindeer with harness, and little skis, and even a little boat with oars."[11] After dancing to give the instrument magic power, the sorcerer fell to the ground, foaming at the mouth. In his trance he traveled through time and space and fought with another wizard, throwing *gand* shots.

Schefferus's book *Lapponia* became an influential bestseller of the Enlightenment, even more read abroad than in Sweden. Originally published in Frankfurt am Main in 1673, it was soon translated to German and French and appeared in England as early as 1674 in the translation *The History of Lapland.*[12] For almost two centuries *Lapponia* remained the most comprehensive and most quoted ethnography of the Sámi. For historical background, Schefferus relied on Pliny and Tacitus, the medieval Danish scholar Saxo Grammaticus, the Icelandic scholar Snorre Sturleson, and Bishop Olaus Magnus's *A Description of the Northern Peoples.* These past historical accounts of the Sámi were updated with details from Sámi students in Uppsala. One of them was Olaus Simma, from Finnish Sápmi, who had converted to Christianity and would return north as a pastor. Along with the information he provided, Simma contributed transcriptions of the words to two joiks, a form of musical vocalization, which Schefferus placed in the book's section on Sámi courtship and marriage.

Other sources for Schefferus (and by far the largest) were pastors in Sweden's central and northern parishes who were familiar with Sámi communities. Magnus de la Gardie had written to the Lutheran clergymen requesting that they send back descriptions of the parish Sámi, their language and family life, their housing arrangements in winter and summer, their habit of skiing, their hunting and herding of reindeer, their weddings and funerals, and their churchgoing practices. Along with a great deal of ethnography and natural history came descriptions of sacrificial rites and trances undertaken by *noaidis* with the help of sacred drums. These were the sections that were translated into other languages and disseminated most thoroughly abroad. Nicolaus Lundius was one of these informants. He was a Swedish-educated sexton, son of the first recorded Sámi pastor in Arvidsjaur, and author of a text in Latin about the Sámi, *Descriptio Lapponiae,* that interjects the perspective of a Sámi observer into the historical record, noting, for instance, that attempts by Swedish authorities to find out Indigenous knowledge, especially about religion, from the Sámi were often unsuccessful. "They do not reveal their art; except it happens when they are drunk and one can then with care find out something from them, as well as from their children, but they sternly admonish their children not to tell anything to Swedish people."[13]

Part of the Enlightenment project in Europe consisted of efforts to civilize "primitive" people. For many countries, this mission took place in colonies often very distant from the mother country, but in Sweden it took place within the nation's own borders. Christianization went hand in hand with the Crown's growing interest in exploring and exploiting the country's natural resources, particularly in the mountains and the northern half of its land mass. For that reason, Schefferus was directed to collect and discuss not only ethnographic objects but also the natural history of Sápmi. The mineral collection in the Museum Schefferianum was not for show but for science. Silver began to be mined in the mountains of Sápmi in the early 1600s, with many Sámi forced to provide reindeer-sled transport from the mines to the village of Kvikkjokk on the Lule River; Sámi and Finnish mine workers would also be employed in the seventeenth century in the Torne River Valley.

The internal colonization of Sápmi and its Indigenous population began with

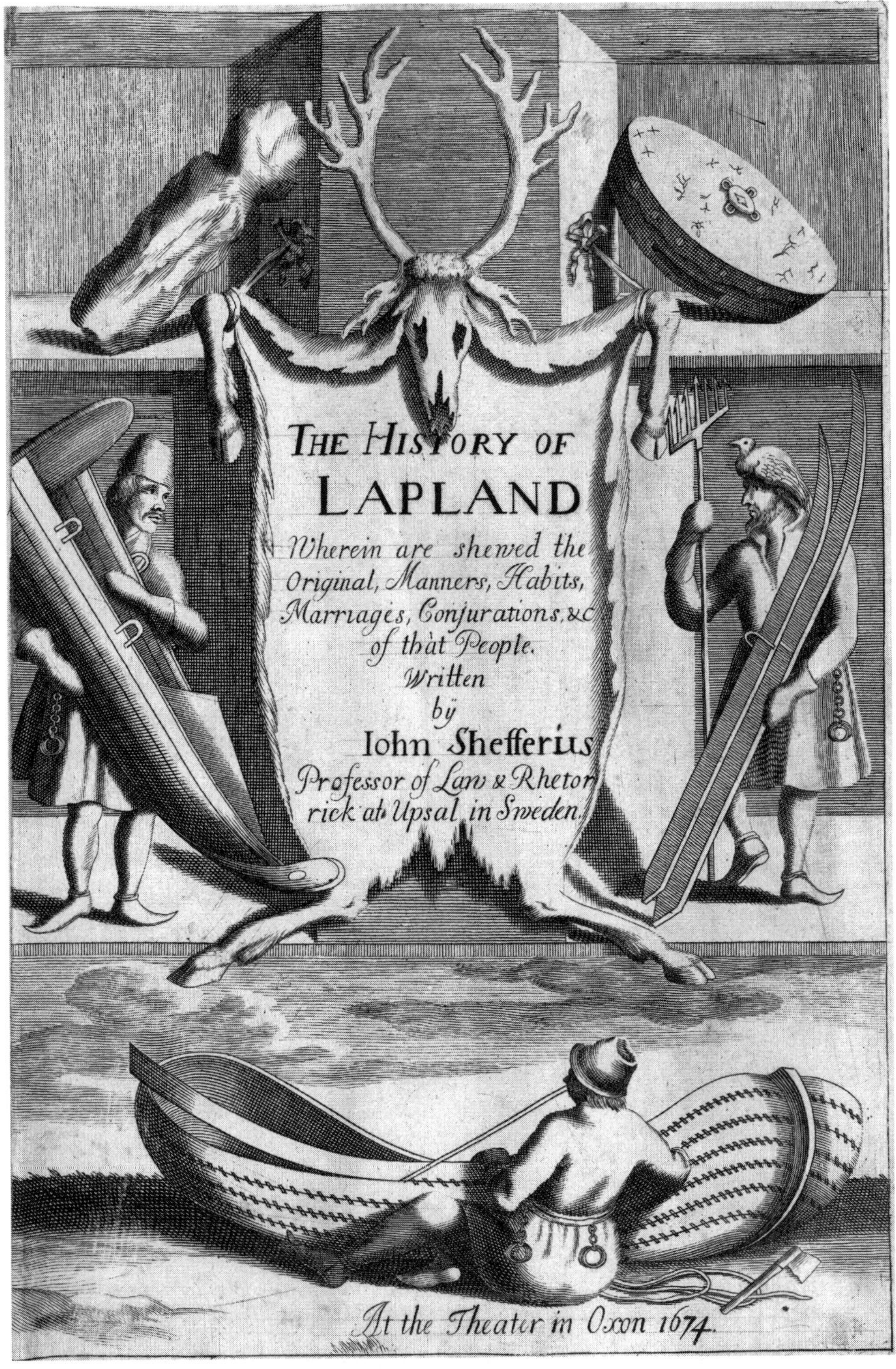

The frontispiece to *The History of Lapland* illustrates a sacred drum and a *sieidi* of stone, often used as an altar at sacrifice sites. Along with a driving sled and a pair of skis is a riverboat, sewn together with reindeer sinews. Courtesy of the National Library of Norway.

natural resource extraction but was abetted by the establishment of Lutheran churches throughout the northern provinces of Sweden. Christina's grandfather, Charles IX, given to war abroad and an aggressively Protestant stance at home, undertook to impose Lutheran teachings and Swedish state control on his subjects, particularly the Sámi. This began with building churches and sending seminary-trained missionaries northward to educate the Sámi and convert them to Christianity; but as the century progressed and many Sámi refused to attend church or continued to practice their heathen traditions alongside Christian traditions, punishment began to increase. The line between clergymen and authorities with legal powers, like the bailiffs who could make arrests and bring charges and the district governors who presided over yearly court sessions in the countryside, was a fine one by the end of the seventeenth century.

The Sámi drum became a potent symbol of conflict between those who resisted giving up their traditional worldview and their sustaining religious practices and those who were determined to force the Sámi population to accept and embrace the Christian faith fully.

About ten years after Schefferus's death in 1679, the district governor and the bishop began a tour of the "Lappmarks" in Sweden (a term used particularly in Sweden to designate the different language districts, such as Lule Lappmark and Pite Lappmark). In each place they visited in 1688 they demanded that the Sámi turn over their drums and other sacred objects, that is, their "idols." Those Sámi who bowed to their authority and gave up their drums were not punished, but anyone who denied owning a drum yet had been denounced by family or neighbors was hauled before the court. Some went to prison; others were flogged. The only man who was sentenced to death in Sweden was Lars Nilsson, in Pite Sápmi.

Nilsson initially handed over his drum, perhaps explaining to the authorities that his use of the instrument was only something he had learned from his ancestors and that he had no idea drums were prohibited. Perhaps, like others before him, he claimed that the drum was just a household item, something to forecast the weather or to check on the status of the herds in the mountains. Yet later, in 1691, when his young grandson died by drowning in a well, Lars Nilsson became distraught. He found another drum and tried to resurrect the boy, as a *noaidi* might do. A couple of Christian Sámi men were sent to investigate this case of sorcery and found Lars Nilsson singing and drumming on his knees outside his tent. The Christians argued with him that this was the Devil's doing and he must stop; when Nilsson refused, they forcibly took the drum, after which he attacked them with a knife for interrupting his efforts to save his grandson.

At the district court trial in 1692 in Arjeplog he showed no remorse but said he felt that the Sámi gods had helped him more than the Christian god ever had. He asserted that he now planned to continue to "observe and use the custom of his forefathers, in spite of what higher or lower authority in this case would now or in the future prohibit him from doing." As an example to the local Sámi, Lars Nilsson was sentenced to death. In April 1693, he was first decapitated and then burned at the stake, together with his drum and other idols. His family was summoned to watch his execution. Afterward the local pastor wrote that he hoped Nilsson's trial and death would be a "warning for other idolators and such sinners."[14]

The objects in Schefferus's museum were never cataloged during its eight-year existence. Most of what is known of the museum's contents comes from the correspondence or notes of a few visitors describing what they encountered in Uppsala. One of his visitors, during the summer of 1670, was a prince of Germany, who was doing a grand tour and visiting private museums. Prince Albrecht and his entourage had passed through Copenhagen and viewed the Museum Wormianum. Here in Uppsala, according to a journal written by an anonymous friend or secretary traveling with the prince, the entourage was able to look at even more objects from Sápmi and to watch Professor Schefferus demonstrate how the drum was used. Prince Albrecht's companion added a note that "the king allows his government officials in the Lappmark to confiscate these drums, and those who use the drum are punished for that reason."[15]

Aside from some of the drums, which went from being objects of witchcraft to objects much valued and desired by aristocrats and scholars, it's difficult to trace the fate of most of the Sámi objects in the Museum Schefferianum after its founder's death. The art of museum preservation was hardly known in the Enlightenment. Clothing made of skin and fur is prone to bugs; leather crumbles; wooden skis and sleds may rot. Many of the items disappeared over time, forgotten or destroyed. Other items made of more durable materials like antler and bone or metal—spoons, belt ornaments, and jewelry—were dispersed and lost their provenance.

Two large *sieidis,* or sacrifice stones, were once housed inside the ochre-painted building at St. Eriks Torg, and one is there still. Other objects went to the royal collections of Sweden's kings and queens, overseen by the College of Antiquities, a research organization formed to promote and study what was unique in Swedish culture. This college became the Antiquities Archive, an institution eventually disbanded in the nineteenth century as interest in ancient runes and mythic Swedish kingdoms diminished. Its duties were taken over by the Royal Academy of Sciences in Stockholm. The objects from Sápmi remained together, and the collections increased; the number of drums grew to twenty-nine, many of them confiscated in the 1720s in court sessions in areas around Åsele and Lycksele in central Sápmi, where Sámi families were compelled to hand them over on pain of flogging or imprisonment to clergymen and other authorities.

Some Sámi drums were given by Swedish royals as exotic presents to Swedish noblemen; in other instances, foreign aristocrats approached Swedish diplomatic contacts and agents who dealt in art and artifacts, which is how some drums made their way to palaces in Europe. It's recorded that the British king Charles I had a Sámi drum in his royal collection.[16] Schefferus's *Lapponia* had made an impact in England and on the Continent among dukes and princes looking to build their own collections of northern curiosities. Already in 1674, Lorenzo Magalotti, a poet, traveler, and envoy of the grand duke of Tuscany, had written to Professor Schefferus, asking for help with completing a collection of *Lapponica* to be sent to his employer in Florence. "What I already have of such items is: their dress, boots, shoes, gloves, feather cap—all embroidered with lead [pewter]. You need not therefore trouble yourself with anything of this kind. I also have a drum and a hammer. What I would like is one of the rings which they make jump on the drum when they hit it, a bow, some arrows of their own manufacture and above all a pair of skis."[17]

It's not known where this particular Tuscan collection is now, but other drums over the next hundred or so years were sent to Italy, as well as Germany, France, Spain, and England, and they now are in the possession of national and ethnographic museums. Some drums ended up in the hands of agents and antiquarians who sold them. Others were given by clergymen or their families to interested parties. Still others were passed on by scholars to scientific institutions. One drum said to be from the Museum Schefferianum accompanied Schefferus's former secretary, Johan Heysig (later Heysig-Ridderstjerna), on a trip to England in 1681. It was presented to members of the Royal Society for Improving Natural Knowledge, along with an explanation, duly written down during the society's meeting in London in November 1681, of how the drum functioned as a source of divination.[18] In later years the drum was displayed in the Royal Society's museum, the Repository, to scientists and the public, catalogued under "Mechanical Engins, Modells, etc."[19]

Of Schefferus's *gand-tyre* no further mention has ever been made. There's no reference to a "Lappish sorcery ball" (or to *gand* flies or to spell-spears) in any museum inventory in Sweden, though Queen Christina must have left behind a few bezoars when she decamped to Rome with chests full of the royal treasures. One, in Göteborg's Ethnographic Museum, is a hardened sphere from the stomach of a Japanese horse; another small bezoar from the seventeenth century, cloudy gray and set into a gold ring, was worn by Queen Hedvig Elenora, wife to Charles X Gustav and regent to their son; it's now in the collection of the Royal Armory in Stockholm. Aside from the fact that a bezoar was a rarity belonging to emperors and queens, a magic object prized for its ability to counteract poisons, and that a *gand-tyre* was an object of the greatest disgust and fear, a magic object that could fly through the air and wreak havoc on intended and unintended victims, there's not much to distinguish two balls that may have come from the stomach of a ruminant.

Unlike other material objects from Sápmi, the *gand* was more described—as arrows or projectiles, as blue flies, as two-headed beasts the size of a mouse—than ever seen or held. The one thing that the various forms of *gand* had in common is that they flew through the air and their trajectory often soared north to south, somewhat like the traffic route of many objects from Sápmi that for several centuries were transported from the northern forests, headlands, and mountains to private and public collections in the South.

Curiosity Cabinets

As the *gand* arrow flies, it's about fifteen hundred miles from East Finnmark to Copenhagen. Overland. To sail to or from Copenhagen along the islanded, fjord-indented Norwegian coast would have taken several weeks before the age of steam, and that's in good weather—of which there's precious little most times of the year in those latitudes. Nevertheless, many sea voyages were made from Denmark to the Barents Sea and back again. Long before Queen Margaret of Denmark united Norway, Denmark, and Sweden in 1397 with the Kalmar Union, vessels were plying these northern waters. In the Icelandic–Norwegian sagas and other medieval writings, the Arctic reaches of the Nordic–Russian landmass are described as a place of strange beasts at sea and on land, a dark, frozen wilderness where great sorcerers cast spells and foretell the future. As we've seen, later writers like Olaus Magnus and the Protestant clergy in Norway and Sweden reinforced many of those beliefs: the High North was the home of black magic, and the wizards who practiced it were servants of the Devil himself.

Yet Finnmark was also known for its abundant natural resources: the fishing was fantastic. The coastal Sámi had long been recognized as boatbuilders and fishers, both along the inner fjords of the northern coastlines of the Norwegian and Barents Seas and along some of the rivers of Finnmark. Dried cod was stacked in Viking longships and traded in England as well as the Mediterranean Catholic countries. By the 1500s Norwegian and Russian fishing boats were regularly seen in those northern seas, often converging on the Varanger Fjord. They transported dried and salted fish down the Norwegian coast to Bergen, the hub of the trade since the time of the Hanseatic merchants. The Danish state coveted that trade and by the seventeenth century fully controlled it. The Danes set up trading posts along the coastline, from Bodø to Vadsø, each with a mercantile, a church, and a thin layer of Crown appointees to administer the fishing village: a merchant with the license to buy fish and sell goods; a bailiff to keep the peace; and a pastor to teach children and to tend to souls. Some districts also had a governor in residence; court sessions were held once a year, by traveling prosecutors and magistrates from Denmark.

Finnmark, the size of Denmark, was sparsely inhabited, with a population of only around three thousand in the mid- to late seventeenth century. The Indigenous Sámi lived both on the coasts and in the interior, on the tundra of the Finnmark plateau, in villages like Utsjoki, Karasjok, and Karasuando. They crossed the snowy plateau most of the year on skis and with sleds, herded reindeer, and often had very little contact with the authorities. They sold furs as well as dried reindeer, dried fish, and berries to traders in Norway, Sweden, and Russia and were largely economically independent. But during the seventeenth century greater efforts were made to tax their income and to convert them to Christianity, forcibly if necessary.

Beginning in the late 1500s and gathering strength in the 1600s, the combination of ancient fears of evil sorcerers in the North and the authority imposed by a royal court far to the south resulted in a series of witch hunts and trials in Norway. They were especially prevalent in the northernmost regions of Finnmark. Here, over 175 people were put on trial from 1593 to 1695, and many were burned at the stake for conspiring with the Devil and causing harm to others. The majority of cases involved Norwegian women who lived along the northern coast, but about a quarter of those tried and sentenced were Sámi men and, to a lesser extent, Sámi women.

The allegations and prosecutions for witchcraft in Finnmark at the end of the seventeenth century took place around the same time as those in Salem, Massachusetts, and in Scotland. It's notable that the Norwegian female witches were condemned in waves of denunciations. Implicating other women during torture, they confessed to all the things women witches are accused of doing: flying through the air, meeting in covens, and consorting sexually with the Devil. The Sámi, the majority of whom were men, were largely accused of other sorts of mischief connected with dark magic: casting spells, causing storms at sea, and aiming destructive *gands* at physical objects and people. Of the thirty-seven Sámi tried for such crimes, few went free, and about twenty-three were burned at the stake. Few witchcraft cases involved the sacred drum or ritual sacrifices, even though the ecstatic trances and healing work of the *noaidis* in the North were also cause for consternation.[1]

The first death sentence pronounced in a case of Sámi sorcery in Finnmark was against Morten Olsen in 1601. Anders Poulsen was the last Sámi to be convicted, in 1692. Poulsen (Poala-Ánde) was said to be in his nineties, a herder who brought his reindeer to the Varanger Fjord seasonally. He was reported to the authorities by Sámi converts to the Christian faith, who stood by as he was arrested in December 1691 in Nesseby. He was brought to Vadsø, a fishing town on the coast and the administrative center of East Finnmark. There he was interviewed, charged with "diabolic sorcery," and kept in prison until a trial could be held after the new year. The main evidence against him was that he owned and used a sacred drum, which was by this time forbidden by law, both by the Church and by the state. He had no lawyer, only a translator who was also on the side of the prosecution. His answers to his interrogation formed most of his written "confession," which was then used as a basis for the trial. The drum itself, as Exhibit A, was on trial as well, an object of fascination and revulsion to the magistrate and prosecutor.

Anders Poulsen's "confession," along with the record kept of the court proceedings, is biased and contradictory: his words come through only indirectly through scribes who also insert such language as "He claimed," "He denied," and "supposedly." Yet, this Sámi elder's explanation of what the symbols meant and how the drum functioned as part of the Indigenous religion, though tainted by the prosecutor's surviving record, is one of the few sources extant from someone who practiced this religion all his life. Even indirectly it's possible to hear Poulsen's faith and anguish, to see his attempts to clarify, deflect, and dispute his guilt in a setting where he had no rights and few sympathizers. Although several of his children came to the trial and stood up to say that their father had never done any harm or been involved with the darker arts of sorcery, opinion was against Poulsen from the beginning. He had contradicted himself numerous times between the first interrogation in December and the trial in February, telling his questioners initially that he had made his drum himself and that the figures on the drumskin were painted with his own blood. He later claimed that he had gotten the drum from another Sámi and that the inked symbols were scratched on with alder-bark paste.

He also said that he had learned everything about the drum from his mother and that he had gone "wild and reckless" during his years of instruction. She herself had been "insane for nine years" during her own spiritual instruction. He tried to take these details back during the trial, but the prosecutor would have none of it, referring to the text of the forced confession: "His immensely godless and devilish art, which he has learnt in the family, from his godless mother, a woman he says was not of the right faith in God in Heaven, like other people."[2] His mother was not a Christian, opined the prosecutor, nor was Anders Poulsen, even though, as the trial progressed, he hoped to convince the authorities that many of the symbols on the drum—an angel, Mother Mary, a church building—had to do with the Protestant faith. But vague on Church doctrine, he fumbled his answers repeatedly, which added to the sense that he was lying to save his skin. He did not understand that what was so upsetting and criminal to the authorities was the mixing of Christianity and Indigenous religion—believing in both God and gods and thinking that was acceptable.

Most of the two-day trial involved the meaning of the symbols on the drum. None of them involved black magic, it was clear. The drum was largely employed to benefit and protect people, to aid in divination and in healing. With a drum, Poulsen explained, you could remove a spell or a *gand* placed on someone; the drum could locate reindeer thieves and increase reindeer luck. Playing on the drum could help women in labor. You could also use the drum to find out how your relatives were, even if they were far away.

Poulsen's drum was oval and divided into five sections by horizontal lines. Stick figures stood on the lines, along with other images. On the second row were five images: a circle, two figures, a building with crosses, and another figure. Poulsen said they represented the sun, Jesus, God the Father, a cathedral, and the Holy Spirit. But they also had names that corresponded to Sámi gods. The court, which had confiscated his drum on his arrest, now asked him to demonstrate how the drum worked, to use the hammer on the surface and chant spells. He picked up the well-worn drum that he had owned almost all his life, that he had perhaps made himself, and made the sign of the cross on his chest and over the drum.

It is recorded that tears ran down his wrinkled cheeks as he complied, forced to reenact what had been private and sacred in front of men wearing black robes, pleated white collars, and wigs. He told the court that the gods would not answer him, that they "were skeptical that any appeal to them would come from a 'Norwegian building.' He called loudly to his gods not to be afraid of the Norwegians. Even though he played in a Norwegian building, the Norwegians didn't wish them any ill."[3]

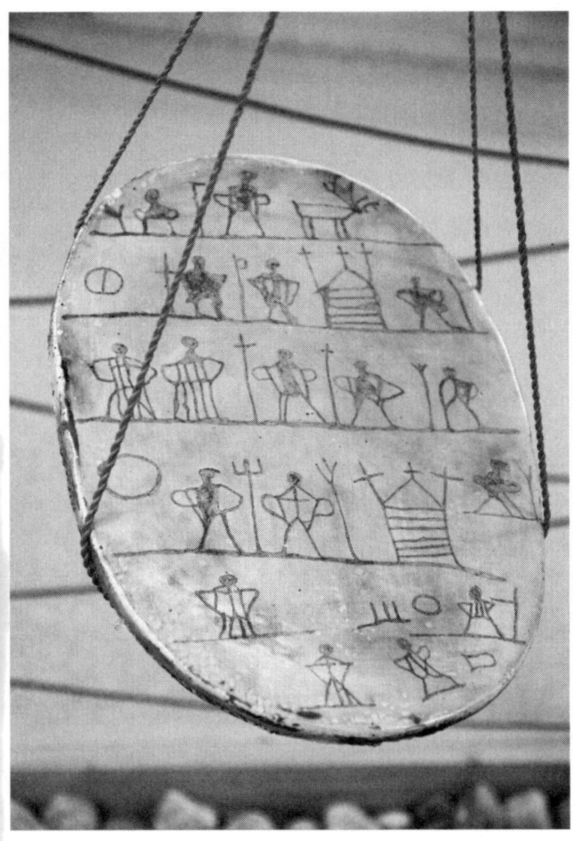

A reproduction of Anders Poulsen's drum, Varanger Sámi Museum, Varangerbotn, Norway. The original was permanently transferred in 2022 by the National Museum of Denmark to the Sámi Museum in Karasjok, Norway. Photograph copyright Bente Haarstad.

This was untrue, of course. The prosecutor conducting the case, Olle Andersen, was convinced by the appearance of the drum in court that punishment should be severe. According to Andersen, every time the sorcerer beat the drum, he set evil demons in motion. Satan worked through the drum, and the verdict and sentence should reflect this terrible sin against the Christian god. Poulsen was clearly a sorcerer and in league with the Devil, yet the magistrate, Niels Knag, was in doubt as to what the exact sentence should be for possessing and using a drum. He consulted with the governor of Finnmark, Hans Lilienskiold, who was also at the trial, and together they made the decision to defer sentencing until they heard from higher authorities in Copenhagen. In the meantime, Poulsen was to remain in Vadsø and all his possessions were to be inventoried and seized.

Only a day later, as Poulsen lay sleeping, a young male servant in Lilienskiold's household, already known for his unstable and bizarre behavior, murdered the

Sámi elder with three blows of an axe, explaining that the man was a sorcerer and deserved to die. There was little justice in this case, given that Poulsen had already been found guilty and would have been executed anyway—a decision confirmed by the high court in Denmark the following year. The children of Poulsen petitioned for half of the money raised from selling Poulsen's reindeer for their mother's welfare.

Once Anders Poulsen was dead, his drum belonged to the Danish Crown. It was not destroyed but sent down to Copenhagen, where it became part of the Royal Kunstkammer and eventually the Ethnographic Collection in the National Museum of Denmark. It is one of only a few drums remaining whose figures were explained in some way by its original owner.[4]

After the worst of the persecutions passed in the late 1600s in Finnmark, the drums and other Indigenous religious practices went underground in most of Sápmi. Part of what drove the clergy and authorities to undertake such witch hunts was not that the Sámi did not externally embrace Christianity—many had been baptized and appeared to have accepted the rituals surrounding the Lutheran Church—but that some Sámi continued to use their drums and to worship their gods at the same time. The drums came to function as a symbol of resistance. While the Sámi wanted to preserve their traditions, including the drum, as a way of connecting to their ancestors and culture, the Church labeled the drums as heathen, evil, and symbolic of defiance toward ecclesiastical authority. Not all drums were burned, and not all drums were taken away by the Church. Sometimes newly converted Sámi or their descendants, repulsed by their former beliefs, destroyed or sold the drums themselves. It was said, and it seems likely, that occasionally Sámi people made a new drum, rubbed some dirt on the skin to make it look older, left it out in the rain, knocked its frame a bit, and offered it to the missionaries in lieu of the true drum. Some drums were buried or hidden in mountain clefts, to be retrieved in some safer future. Some drums were doubtless demanded as payment for taxes or debt and spirited away from Sápmi by those who hoped to sell them to collectors. And like the drum of Anders Poulsen, more than a few drums ended up in the curiosity cabinets of scholars and kings and queens.[5]

Across the square from the cathedral of Uppsala, not far from Schefferus's former museum, is another, but much grander, ochre-painted building. This is the Gustavianum, constructed in the early seventeenth century, with a printing press, student halls, and, most remarkably, an anatomical theater on the third floor, commissioned by the professor of medicine Olaf Rudbeck. If you visit the Gustavianum, you can see the steeply raked seats of the anatomy theater where dissections were performed and wander halls with displays of old medical and scientific instruments, including Anders Celsius's first thermometers. But one of the great draws of the Museum Gustavianum is an extraordinary cabinet of curiosities created in Augsburg, Germany, in 1632 for Gustavus Adolphus, Christina's father, who died on the battlefield. The Augsburg Cabinet, about four feet tall and just as wide, was crafted of polished dark woods with inlaid stones and enamels; its four doors open to smaller doors and drawers, each with a treasure. The cabinet still contains its original collection: over a thousand items, most of them small or miniaturized replicas. It houses everything from tiny paintings of religious landscapes and portraits to parlor games and drawers for toiletries. There are hundreds of items from the natural world, shells, precious stones, and fossils. Like almost all such cabinets, this intricate collection had the dual aim of presenting both art and nature. It was an aesthetic blend of precious rarities and science.

Most curiosity cabinets have disappeared, in part because many were actually rooms in palaces, not self-contained, movable cabinets. The term came to include pieces of furniture, like the Augsburg Cabinet, and the Kunstkammers of royalty, whose treasures could not fit into a single room. The term often seems to encompass any private collection created from the 1500s through the mid-1700s that combines artistic treasures with natural history oddities and ethnographic marvels. Yet not all private museums were in palaces; more modest collections were also assembled by learned men of the time for the purposes of study and teaching. Olaf Rudbeck, who apparently had a Sámi drum or two, used his collections as a laboratory, as did, on a more modest scale, Johannes Schefferus.[6]

Ole Worm, an inspiration for both men, had the larger collection, almost sixteen hundred objects by his death; the catalogs and inventories from his museum are all that remain, and most of them are intact because his scientific museum was absorbed into the Kunstkammer of the Danish king. In the summer of 1654, as the plague tore through Copenhagen, Ole Worm didn't leave the city like most of his well-off friends. A conscientious medical doctor, he stayed on to help. He wrote to his eldest son, Willum, warning him to stay away, however: "The majority who die make the mistake right at the beginning of weakening their powers either by blood-letting or by purging. If they don't in the first six hours take precautions against the disease, it's all over with them."[7] Worm had already made his will in early June. He left the collection to Willum, in hopes that it might be kept together, but he also suggested that, if the family was not able or interested in maintaining the museum, the new king, Frederick III, be offered a chance to purchase it. Two months after making the will, as the plague continued to carry away some six hundred people a week, Ole Worm succumbed and died.

Willum soon approached Frederick III, who bought the contents of the Museum Wormianum the following year to increase the size and scope of his Royal Kunstkammer, which was relatively sparse by comparison to the collections of two of his notable contemporaries, Queen Christina of Sweden and the duke of Schleswig-Holstein. Denmark's king was well educated and well traveled; during his reign he continued to make purchases and expand his collections, initially in the royal palace and later in a new building in the center of Copenhagen, constructed specifically for the Kunstkammer and library. The royal collection was housed in a narrow, thick-walled, two-story building that still stands. Today the ground floor contains the reading rooms of the Danish State Archives.

There were nine rooms of treasures in this Kunstkammer. The staff published catalogs regularly, and the number of objects grew, added to by merchants and explorers as well as missionaries. By the end of the 1600s two further drums from Sápmi had become part of the ethnographic collection begun by Ole Worm. The illustrated catalog from 1696, *Museum Regium,* shows a drum in the hands of a kneeling figure, a *noaidi,* who is moving the hammer on its surface, an image popularized by Schefferus's *Lapponia.*

For the next 150 years the Kunstkammer would be maintained by a long series of alternating Christians and Fredericks. By the mid-nineteenth century the collection was encyclopedic and rarely visited by any members of the royal family. Visitors were limited, and curators handled the purchases and cared for the objects. It's very likely that during this period a quantity of objects from the Museum Wormianum showed signs of age or disintegration and were discarded or were judged not important enough for the Kunstkammer. Of the multitude of objects that Worm had painstakingly collected, only about forty were in the inventory by the mid-nineteenth century, including Worm's original drum.

What made the Sámi drums worth keeping, when the narwhal horn and the kayak disappeared over the decades? One reason was their association with magic, even with evil spirits, and another was their extreme rarity. The drums had not been initially created by Sámi artisans to become an exotic object representing their entire religious culture; they likely expected only to make a good drum that would last two or three generations if cared for properly. What made the drums that survived so valuable was the fact that these instruments of wood and skin, painted with alder bark, once owned by almost every household in Sápmi, were so increasingly few in number.

They became rarities because so many were destroyed.

Depending on which history you read, the Danish–Norwegian theologian Thomas von Westen was either a tireless missionary and teacher on behalf of the Lutheran Church who succored and educated the Sámi in the Trondheim region or a ruthless Christian proselytizer who tried to stamp out Sámi culture and language and made off with around a hundred drums that he coerced from Sámi across a wide region from Trondheim northward, using threats of damnation and hellfire if they did not comply. In line with the majority of colonialist religious figures, he believed he was doing God's work by saving souls, even as he carried out an implicit political mission of bringing the often resistant Sámi population of Finnmark and North Trøndelag under the control of Denmark–Norway.[8]

Europe in the seventeenth century had large populations of Catholics and smaller groups of Jews, Orthodox Christians, and Muslims. Scandinavia had also once been Catholic. Trondheim was already a pilgrimage site before the pope decided to build Nidaros Cathedral there in honor of Olaf Haraldsson, later Saint Olaf. Even after the Reformation the cathedral retained something of its former dominance over the surrounding region. In 1714 Frederick IV of Denmark established a government department for missionary work. Sápmi had its own subdepartment, the Seminarium Scolasticum, placed within the school of the Diocese of Trondheim in Norway.

Spearheading the missionary efforts among the Sámi was Thomas von Westen, born in 1682 in Trondheim and sent to Copenhagen in adolescence to study. He completed his theology degree at the university and hoped to become a professor, but having fallen into deep debt as a student, he married Anna Pedersdatter, who ran a boarding house for Norwegians in Copenhagen. She was twice his age. In 1710 he took up a post in western Norway as a district priest. Like many at the time, he was influenced by Pietism and Church reform; with a group of like-minded churchmen he discussed how to organize the Sámi mission in Norway. In 1716 the Danish king sent von Westen to Trondheim to oversee thirteen missionary districts. Traveling extensively in northern Norway, von Westen shifted the harsh tone of previous attempts to convert the Sámi and brought about an end to the death penalty given to *noaidis* and others who held on to their religious beliefs and rites. He met with the male heads of Sámi *siidas* and discussed building assembly houses and schools in their far-flung communities. Education was a priority for von Westen, a necessity to Christianize the Sámi population, beginning at an early age. Like many missionaries, he was horrified to realize that although many of the Sámi nominally accepted Christianity and its rituals—baptisms, weddings, and funerals—they continued to trust in the gods, spirits, and worldview of the Indigenous religion. Abhorrent to him was the idea that individuals thought they could combine the two belief systems. He reprimanded one Sámi man who had sacrificed to the goddess of fertility, Saaraahka, so that his wife would be protected during childbirth, implying that his wife could not be both "Jesus's bride and the devil's whore."[9] Floggings and fines for not attending church had brought up attendance rates, but much more remained to be done to destroy "the tool and instrument of Satan": the drum.

By some accounts von Westen was mild mannered, but he had a core of righteousness that brooked no opposition. His was a sensual but suspicious face: full lips, lifted eyebrow, accusing eyes. He's been described as "gifted and energetic but unbalanced."[10] While he made it a point to speak Sámi and to ask the Sámi (*noaidis* in particular) about their beliefs and write down some of what they told him, he didn't learn the language in order to listen deeply or to have his mind changed on any point. The more the Sámi resisted him, the more determined he became to force them to recant their evil ways and turn over their drums. Some Sámi people found the clergyman simply annoying. They apparently had other things to do, according to an early biographer, than listen to the pastor's lectures and answer his questions. Even getting to church on a regular basis was inconvenient for reindeer herders; added to that were von Westen's peremptory demands that they appear whenever he wanted to speak to them about their pagan rituals. Some Sámi threatened him verbally; others took to the mountains west of Trondheim and even crossed the border to Sweden.

In 1722 and 1723 von Westen traveled to an area north of Trondheim known for its widespread and intransigent resistance to Christianity. When the Sámi in the village of Grong heard he was on his way, they organized to keep him out, and at least two Sámi elders, Bendix Andersen and Jon Torchelsen, disappeared into the mountains and then into Sweden with a drum that had been in Andersen's family for four generations. Von Westen wrote to fellow pastors in Sweden, asking for their help. He said he only wanted to help the poor Sámi and bring them into God's fold but instead they were disappearing over to Sweden. They were telling lies about him, von Westen complained, "that he locked them in dark rooms, tied them up, and tortured them in countless ways." This was not true, he wrote the Swedish pastors. He "loved them," and all he wanted to do, "in all gentleness,

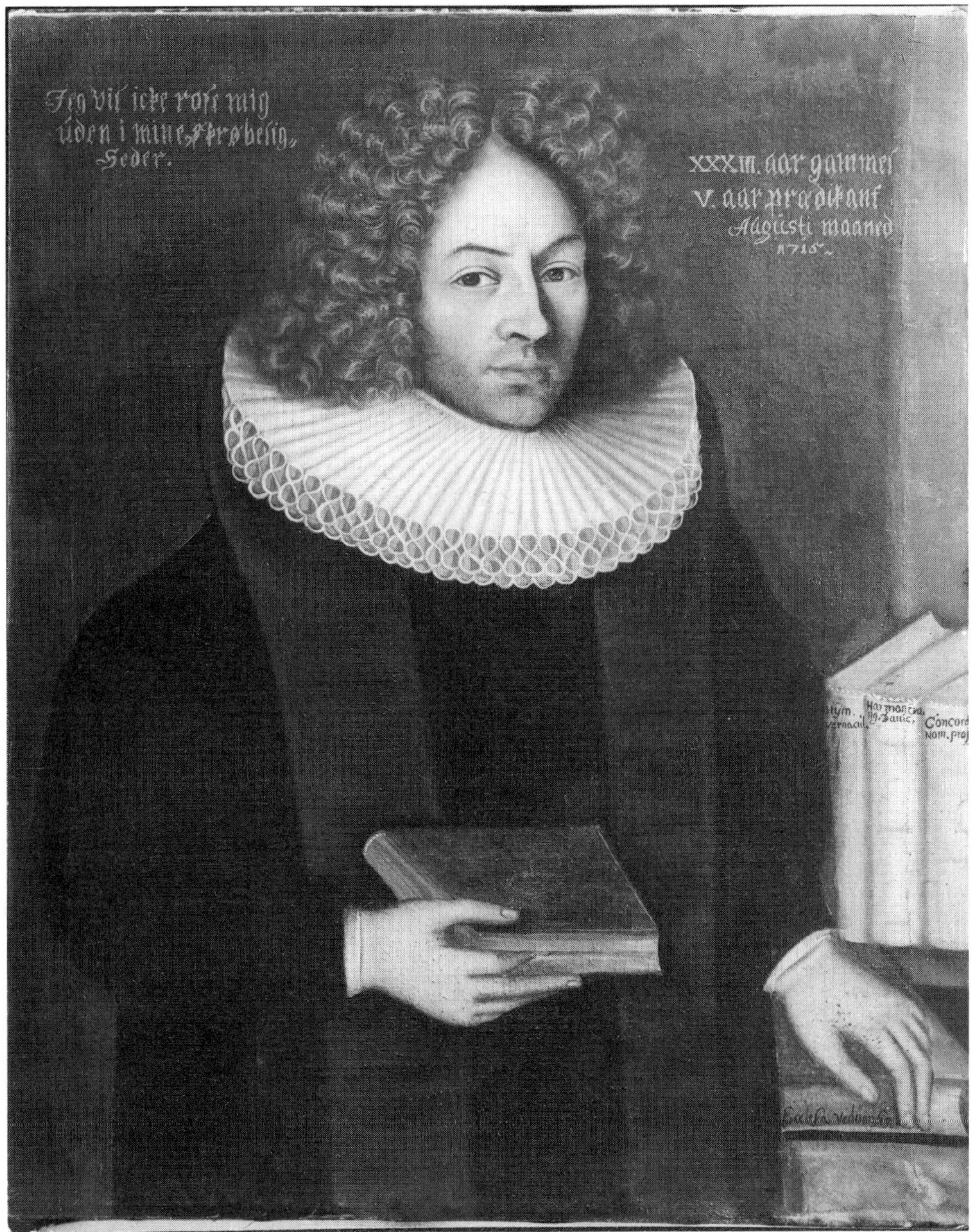

Thomas von Westen, engraving, circa 1720s. Clergyman von Westen sought to minister to the Sámi people in northern Norway, while gathering information about their beliefs and pursuing individuals to obtain their ceremonial family drums. Courtesy of Helgeland Museum, Norway.

was keep them from hell and the devil." He concluded by asking the pastors to return these runaway Sámi, and he would promise to do the same for the Swedish pastors should any of their Sámi folk run to Norway, away from them.[11]

It took many months for von Westen to get his hands on Andersen's drum, called the *Freavnantjahke gievrie* in South Sámi or the "drum from Frøyning Mountain." It is a remarkable object, oval, with a spruce frame. From one end of the frame hang 134 strands of leather wrapped in pewter thread, gathered in fifty bundles; each strand has a small metal token attached or hanging from its end. These were gifts to the drum, explained Bendix Andersen to von Westen. The drum frame also had a small cross made of eleven tin nails, and these nails were also gifts, each one given in thanks when a bear was killed. Aside from these identifying marks, the Frøyning drum is inscribed with the name "Bendix Andrei" on the inner side of the drumskin.

Von Westen's account of the meaning of the symbols on the drum comes from Andersen and Torchelsen; wolves, churches, reindeer, birds, a *gand* fly, herders, hunters, gods, and much more decorated the drumskin. Considering how little the voices of Sámi drum owners were recorded and the fact that not a single Sámi person wrote down their own stories about the drums, this makes the *Freavnantjahke gievrie* all the more remarkable. However, von Westen was leery of their explanations of some of the symbols; he feared that in order to evade punishment they gave some of the pagan pictograms a more Christian spin. He also was of the opinion that only when a Sámi person was drunk did anyone have the chance to hear the truth. Regrettably, he said, his moral beliefs prevented him from giving them strong spirits. All the same, he wrote down what the two told him about the drum, just as he tried to record the words of other Sámi men when he coerced their drums away from them. It seems not to have occurred to von Westen to try to learn about the religious practices of Sámi women, who worshipped their own set of goddesses. For the most part, women rarely spoke to the missionaries, and few of their voices appear in any of the church records of the time. An exception was Karen Arnesdatter, a Sámi woman married to a colleague of von Westen, Jens Kildal, who assisted in translating and gathering information for her husband.

Altogether, von Westen managed to collect, on his own and from other missionaries whom he supervised up and down the northern coast, about a hundred drums. Even though he considered them the Devil's instruments, he did not destroy them. They were in his mind proof that the Sámi could give up their

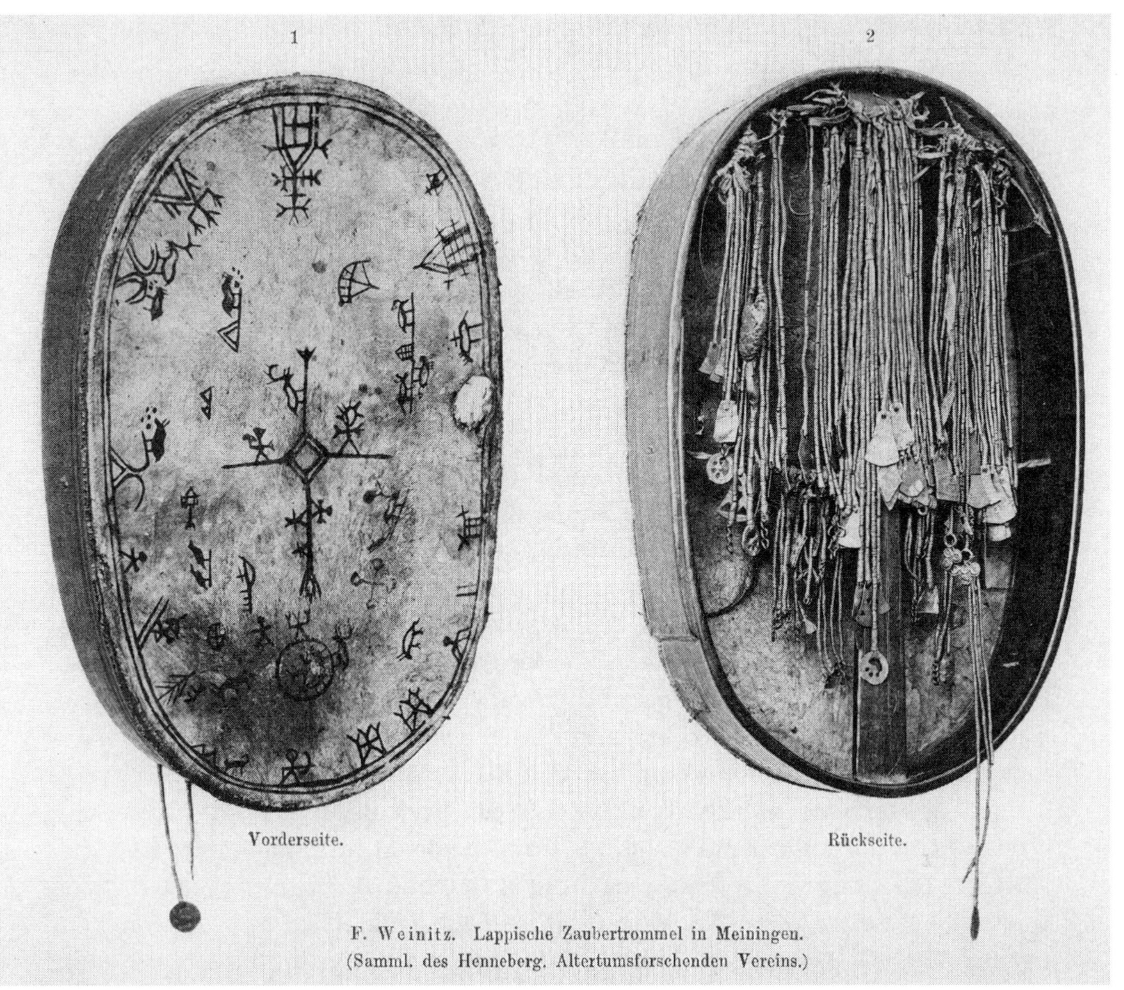

***Freavnantjahke gievrie*, or the "drum from Frøyning Mountain," owned by Sámi elder Bendix Andersen. The drum, now at the Meininger Museum in Germany, was taken from Andersen by Thomas von Westen around 1722–23 and sent to Copenhagen. Photograph from *Zeitschrift für Ethnologie*, 1910.**

pagan ways, once and for all. Did he place them in a cupboard somewhere in the home he shared with his wife in Trondheim? After a falling-out with the bishop of Trondheim, von Westen convened a school for Sámi boys, the Seminarium Domesticum, and he opened his home to the students and other Sámi who visited. Did any of them ever see this grand collection?

A hundred drums would have taken up a good deal of room. It was, both temporarily and for all time, the largest collection of Sámi drums ever assembled.

Thomas von Westen died in Trondheim in 1727, at only forty-five years old. He had run through his wife's money and gone into debt again; he was poverty stricken and broken in health. In 1725 he'd shipped his collection of drums to the College of Missions in Copenhagen, which occupied part of the Vasjenhus, a building in the square of Nytorv that also housed an orphanage, printing press, and pharmacy. Nytorv was the location of Copenhagen's pillories and stocks, where most public executions took place. It's possible that some scholars and collectors, including Frederick IV, visited the missionary association to view the drums.

The *Freavnantjahke gievrie* ended up in the Kunstkammer, along with a drum that had once belonged to a man named Joen Andersen, from the same area of Trøndelag. Frederick IV was the royal patron of the College of Missions and had personally taken an interest in the arduous task of converting the Indigenous people of his northern colonies to Christianity. Perhaps the drum's dangling metal strands caught the king's eye, marking it as something special for his collection. It was as well for the fate of the drum that it joined the other thousands of curiosities in the royal library and Kunstkammer, for only by this stroke of luck did the drum escape the conflagration that would shortly engulf the city.

Copenhagen was in the early eighteenth century a warren of narrow, winding streets with many timbered buildings from medieval times, contained by still-standing outer city walls. On the evening of October 20, 1728, a neglected candle started a fire near present-day Vesterport. The blaze roared for over two days, and in the end about a third of the city had been destroyed, including almost half of the inner medieval streets, which included the university. Twenty percent of the population was left homeless, and rebuilding would go on for ten years. In addition to private book collections, the University of Copenhagen library lost thirty-five thousand texts, many irreplaceable. By strenuous efforts, the Icelander Arni Magnusson managed to save most of the handwritten manuscripts he'd painstakingly collected from homes all over Iceland, including originals of many of the sagas. Other unique Icelandic manuscripts were destroyed when the university library burned down. Professors were driven from their flaming homes near the university, house by house, street by street. The work of past scholars and scientists went up in smoke, including manuscripts and notes by Ole Worm, whose house burned, too.[12]

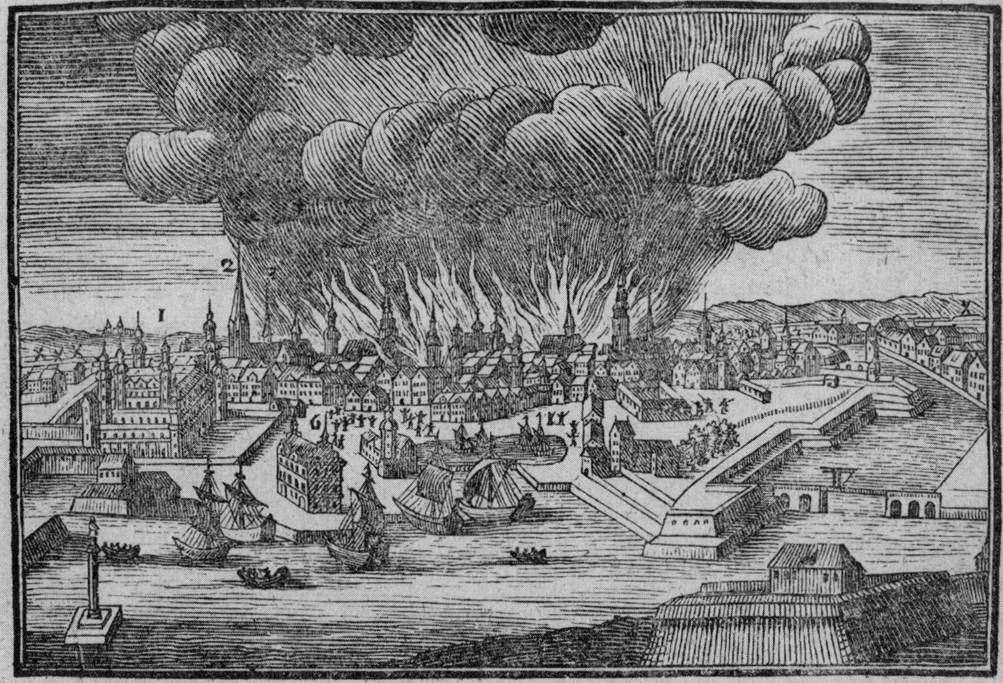

The great fire of Copenhagen, newspaper woodcut, 1728. The fire destroyed many priceless manuscripts, books, and objects, including most of the drums collected by Thomas von Westen in Sápmi. Courtesy of the Museum of Copenhagen.

Nytorv burned, and so did the Vasjenhus and all the records of the College of Missions. It's said that most of the drums from Sápmi, painstakingly crafted and reluctantly surrendered by individuals and families who treasured them, were reduced to ashes.

About a hundred years later, after the death of Frederick VI in 1839 and as a result of talks that had been going on for some time between the court and the Danish government, the treasures of the Royal Kunstkammer began to be redistributed to new museums in Copenhagen. In 1845 the ethnographic material was separated out to become the first stand-alone ethnographic museum in the world, under the direction of Christian Jürgensen Thomsen, an archeologist who developed the concepts of Stone Age, Bronze Age, and Iron Age. Other ethnographic museums began to appear in Europe around the same time, many formed in just the same way as Denmark's, from the private collections of royals and scientific societies, supplemented by objects sent back home by merchants, colonizers, and missionaries. This ethnographic collection, which includes half a dozen ceremonial drums from Sápmi, would be transferred in 1892 to the National Museum of Denmark, which now takes up a full block in Copenhagen on Prinsenstræde.[13]

Today, four of the Sámi drums are displayed in a glass case in the section of the National Museum called "Peoples of the Earth," along with other beautiful examples of Sámi handiwork. In this area of the permanent exhibit, the Sámi of the Nordic countries are classed together with the Siberian peoples of Russia and Asia, with mention of their shared shamanic cultures, which gives a flawed impression of Sámi history past and present. The text on the website about the collection is brief and respectful with a distancing nod to "increasing colonization" that took place in the early 1900s over the issue of resources, that is, when Sweden and the newly independent country of Norway were in charge.[14] Inexplicably, Denmark–Norway and its two hundred years of colonizing Sápmi, beginning in the 1600s, is missing from this historical summary, along with information about the witchcraft trials and the College of Missions. There's no mention of Ole Worm's museum here either, though his original drum is on display, its reddish pictographs now faded to near invisibility.

The *Freavnantjahke gievrie* did not burn in the great fire of 1728, but in 1757 Frederick V removed the drum with the dangling leather strands, inscribed with the name of Bendix Andrei, from his Kunstkammer and presented it to the Duke of Hildburghausen, who had been married to his sister Louise before her death. The duke put it in his own curiosity cabinet in his castle in Saxe-Hildburghausen, a small duchy in central Germany. During the next 180 years a number of things from the duke's collection were sold or given away. The next recorded mention of the *Freavnantjahke gievrie* came in 1837, when it was listed as a gift by Ludwig Bechstein to a historical society in Meiningen, Germany. Bechstein was a folklore collector of note whose book of German fairytales was more popular than that of the Grimm Brothers when first published. Eventually the objects belonging to the Meiningen historical society were moved to a castle, Elisabethenburg. In the early 1930s the drum was tracked down by the Swedish writer and ethnographer Ernst Manker, who was in the process of compiling his long scholarly monograph on many of the remaining Sámi drums.[15]

For a long while, that was the last known sighting of the drum. During World War II, Meiningen was heavily bombed, but the castle escaped damage. Later, the Iron Curtain descended, and the drum was inaccessible in East Germany until 1991, when the staff of the National Museum of Denmark, in the course of investigating the location of the objects that had once been part of the Danish Royal Kunstkammer, made contact with the Meininger Museum and discovered the drum there, exhibited as a musical instrument.

Anders Poulsen's original drum was on long-term deposit from the National Museum of Denmark to the Sámi Museum in Karasjok, Norway, from 1979 to 2022, when, after yearslong negotiations, the drum passed into the Sámi Museum's ownership. A facsimile copy is on display at the Varanger Sámi Museum near Vadsø, where Poulsen's trial took place more than three hundred years ago. The replica is painted with red pigment made from alder bark, symbolizing blood. In his confession, Anders Poulsen said he'd painted his drum with his own blood, something he later contradicted. But whether or not it was his own blood, it might just as well have been.

The Magic Drum

> *In Norway I heard of a curious method that someone had used in order to take away drums and various pictures from the Lapps. Having got wind of such objects, he would ask the Lapp to hand over the drum and the Lapp would refuse. Having asked the Lapp for a long time without any success, he takes his arm, pulls up his tunic, and before he notices, opens the vein, at which the Lapp swoons, begs for his life and agrees to hand them over. He is then immediately bandaged up and the same procedure is applied to many others.*
>
> —Carl Linnæus, *The Lapland Journey,* 1732[1]

In the spring of 1735, en route to Holland, a young Swedish scholar by the name of Carl Linnæus gave a performance in Hamburg to a select group of learned men. Dressed in clothes from Sápmi—a heavy fur tunic, with a belt from which hung a knife, a horn of tobacco, and two small leather bags embroidered with pewter thread; leggings and boots of reindeer skin; and a rakishly tilted, pancake-flat hat—the young man chanted in imitation of a Sámi joik, banged on a skin drum, and even pretended to fall into a deep trance. He wasn't Sámi, he did not speak or understand the language, and it's almost impossible to imagine that he had ever seen such a drum used, much less observed a *noaidi* going into a trance state. Yet his performance made enough of an impression to be recorded by someone who attended and who wrote it up for the *Hamburg Journal of the Newest Learned Things,* taking particular care to describe the *Zaubertrommel,* a "magic drum" with painted figures on its drumskin, a brass ring on top, and two sticks. "The Lapps use it, for instance, when they want to go hunting and want to know in advance where the game is best and where they are likely to encounter it."[2] The German author of this account was already familiar with the writings of Johannes Schefferus, but here was an extraordinary opportunity to see the alleged sorcery of the drum in action.

The young Swede would go on to wear the same costume when he defended his doctoral thesis in Harderwijk a few weeks later at a Dutch equivalent of a diploma mill. He gave other performances that included pretend joiking in Amsterdam and Leiden. He was not in Europe as an entertainer, however, but as a botanist who was already famous before he arrived in the Netherlands for what turned out to be a stay of over three years. In 1736 he would publish the acclaimed first edition of *Systema Naturae,* which introduced the revolutionary system of binomial nomenclature: everything living, beginning with plants, would now have two names in Latin, genus and species.

The public demonstrations of Sámi drumming and singing given by Linnæus, who was known in Sweden as Carl von Linné, were self-promoting sideshows to the serious work as a botanist and zoologist that would make him among the most famous of European scientists by the time of his death in Uppsala in 1778. Yet his public accounts of the Sámi people and their culture, later published in 1811 in English as *Lachesis Lapponica, or, A Tour in Lapland,* weren't all wrong.[3] Some details were certainly based on hearsay and reading; others were founded on first-person observations made during his travels in Swedish and Norwegian Sápmi in the summer of 1732, when he was given a stipend by the Royal Society of Sciences in Uppsala.[4] The society wanted more information about the vast tracts of northern Sweden for purposes of future mining, hydropower, and industrialization. They also requested data on the Sámi people. Linnæus obliged their interest, picking up mineral specimens, shooting birds to stuff, making notes on the local Sámi and their culture, and describing landscapes and river systems. His own plan was to collect botanical specimens in an area of Sweden that was little known from a scientific standpoint, and he collected so much that he was able to publish a flora of Lapland in 1737. Oddly, the frontispiece of *Flora Lapponica* shows very little in the way of flora. Instead, against a background of looming clouds and a bright-rayed sun low on the horizon behind two tall craggy rocks that wouldn't be out of place in a medieval religious painting is an illustration of a man in a sled pulled by a reindeer. In the foreground another reindeer rests peacefully near a man in Sámi costume who sits with a drum in his lap next to a tent. In the extreme foreground is another drum, placed to show the pictographs on its surface.

Linnæus's published journal of his five-month expedition is naturally enough packed with descriptions of animals and plants; he often jumps off his horse to

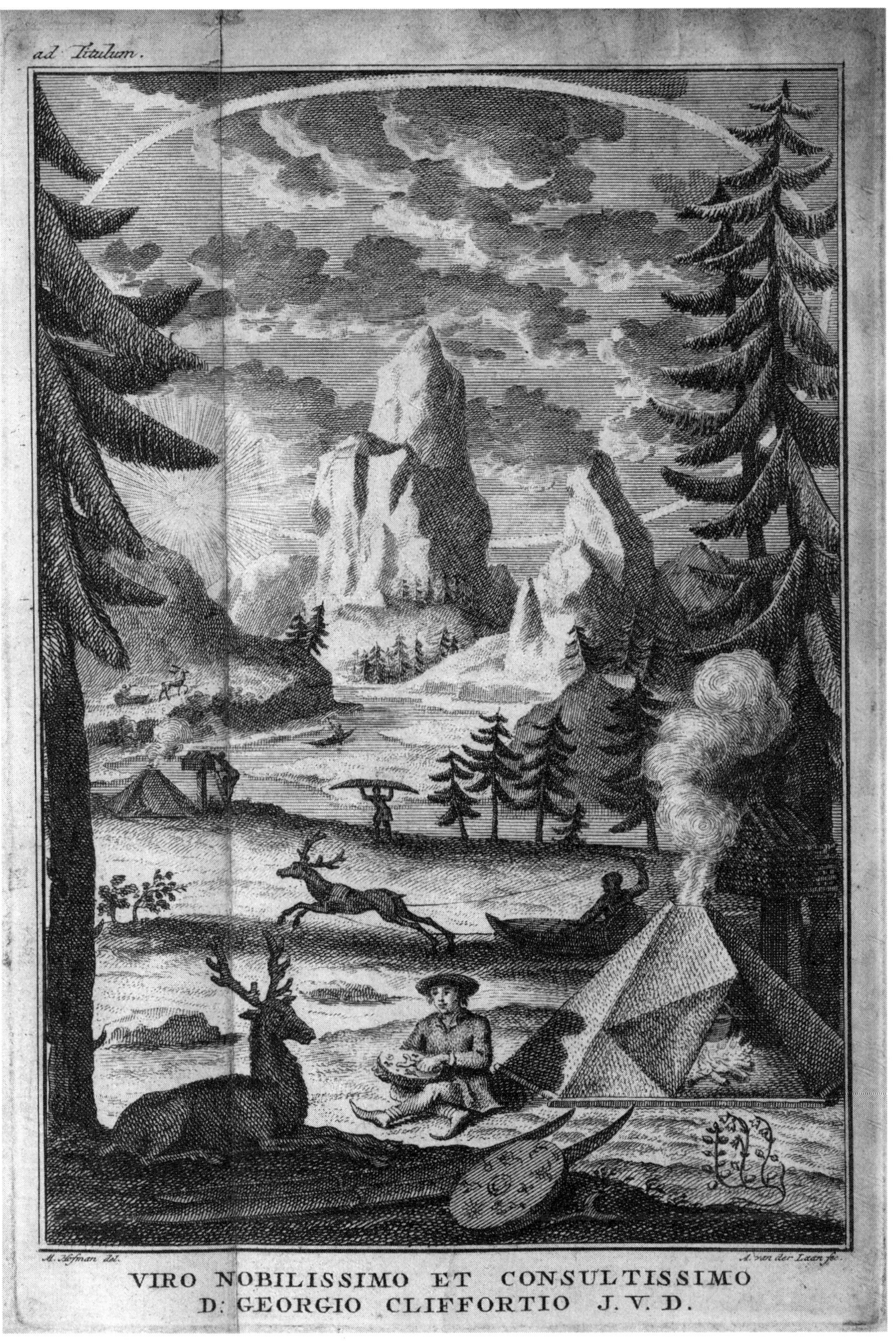

Frontispiece, *Flora Lapponica*, 1737. Carl Linnæus's compendium of botanical observations was based on his early travels in Sápmi. Courtesy of Wellcome Collection, London.

survey a tiny flower or takes a potshot at an owl, sometimes defeating the purpose of taxidermy by blowing it to pieces. His itinerary, by horse, riverboat, and foot, took him from Uppsala, where he had lived and studied, up into the interior, north and then northwest, over the mountains to Norway and then back again and into Finland. Often uncomfortable with the outdoor life, he later exaggerated to the Royal Society about some of the dangers he'd faced—"No sooner had I moved 2 feet than a rock broke away below the first man and, with an eruption of sparks and smoke, struck right where I would have been following. Had I not altered course exactly where I did under the guidance of the Eternal Creator, that would have been the last of me"—and about exactly how far he'd traveled, adding on a few hundred miles.[5]

He exaggerated his contact with the Sámi people as well, later boasting that he'd met a thousand Sámi on his journey. In reality he visited perhaps eight to ten different *siidas* and sometimes had a local Sámi guide with him. Along the route, especially in Norway, Linnæus jotted down ethnographic observations on all manner of things concerning the Sámi: from diet to diseases and infirmities (boils, blindness, prolapsed uteruses); from herding reindeer to sewing with sinew thread; from courtship to children's games. Many of his notes on the Sámi show admiration for their general agility and ease in nature. He asked himself, "Why are the Lapps so fleet of foot?" and came up with a list of answers: boots without heels, practice in running from the time of childhood, freedom from heavy farm labor, and suppleness of muscles from always flexing and moving.[6]

He thought their diet heathy—"The Lapps are completely carnivorous creatures"—and suggested emulating their habit of drinking "fine, sparkling, and delicious water" from snow-melted mountain streams.[7] Later in life he lectured his students at Uppsala on the importance of diet and exercise, sometimes bringing up the Sámi as examples. Even when he observed that the Sámi seemed to be invariably short, he found good reason to think that the Sámi were paragons of health compared to the heavy-treading, hard-drinking, pot-bellied Swedish farmers.

But very deeply into the religious and cultural life of the Sámi he did not venture. He wrote down the story of opening a vein of a man's arm to force him to turn over a drum as if it were a mere anecdote. He witnessed no rituals nor saw any drums himself. As if he were describing the call of a bird, he wrote down the notes of a "Lapp song": *"Jejee vu vu aa vujaa, ai: Teelee, e eee, uau Tali, Tuu, T, etc."*[8] He learned only a few words of Sámi (just as he was never to learn Dutch, French, or English) and seems to have had little interest in questioning the Sámi about their intellectual lives or spiritual beliefs. He spent only a few nights during his five-month journey in a Sámi tent or turf hut. For the most part he traveled in the company of Swedes and Finns; he stayed in farmhouses, occasional inns, and sometimes the homes of various Swedish clergy. These pastors, like the Reverend Carl Solander of Piteå, acted as interpreters of Sámi culture for Linnæus—from the point of view of the Lutheran Church, which worked to Christianize and convert them. Some of these men are named, and later he kept in touch with them.

For someone whose fame rests on binomial classification of flora and fauna, the botanist seems to have fallen short in writing down the names of the Sámi people that he encountered along the route. The journal is replete with the names of trees, mosses, minerals, birds, and plants, plants, plants. But Sámi names there are none.

During his travels in Lapland, Linnæus was given traditional Sámi clothing and other ethnographic objects—a snuffbox, a boat model, Sámi shoes, and small items that later hung from his belt. He didn't pick up a drum and perhaps didn't even see one. The drum that would later go with him to Holland, Germany, Belgium, and England to be hammered on in public was given to him after his return to Uppsala by a clergyman. This could well have been Reverend Carl Solander, whom Linnæus had stayed with in Piteå. Solander took an interest in Sámi artifacts and seems to have sent at least one drum south to Uppsala before Linnæus came up to Sápmi. In the late seventeenth and early eighteenth centuries, the religious authorities employed by the state often became the means by which learned men and aristocrats came into possession of drums confiscated from Sámi individuals. Later, academics would play a role in helping ethnographic collectors and museums secure the increasingly rare and sought-after magic drums, whose provenance only grew more vague as the drums changed hands.

However the drum came to Linnæus, its original owner was Anders Nilsson Pont; his name was written on the inside drumskin. Together with four other Sámi men, Pont went on trial at an ecclesiastical assembly held in the parish village of Lycksele in January 1723.[9] Nils Grubb was the judge presiding in the case. He was not a magistrate but the dean of the district of Umeå, which stretched from the town of Umeå on the Gulf of Bothnia to the Norwegian border and included the parish of Lycksele, which was sparsely inhabited by Forest Sámi speaking the Ume Sámi language. Umeå, about four hundred miles north of Stockholm, was Nils Grubb's birthplace; he came from a family of local governors and clergymen.

He studied theology in Germany and Stockholm and, like Thomas von Westen, was a Pietist, interested in reforming the Lutheran Church. In 1713, in Stockholm, he had married the fifteen-year-old stepdaughter of Göran Törnqvist, an architect who had recently been ennobled and given the new last name Adelcrantz.[10]

Anna Charlotta Adelcrantz accompanied her new husband to Umeå. It could not have been an easy time to live in the town. For one thing, hardly any of the town was left. The Great Northern War raged from 1700 to 1721 around the Baltic, as an alliance among Denmark–Norway, Saxony, Poland, and Imperial Russia under Peter the Great took on the Swedish Empire. Although Sweden had some successes early on, the Swedes lost the war, and their control of the Baltic territories staggered to an end, along with the absolute monarchy that had prevailed. While the peace treaties stalled, Russian forces pillaged and set fire to much of Sweden's eastern coast. Umeå was burned to the ground in 1721.

Perhaps because of the ongoing wars, there had been a lull in persecuting the Sámi in Sweden. But in March 1723, Thomas von Westen, many years into his mission in Trondheim and shocked at the degree of paganism he found on his travels, sent out a letter to all Swedish and Norwegian clergymen ministering to the Sámi, including to Nils Grubb in Umeå. Von Westen firmly suggested that they investigate the parishes for continued use of the forbidden drum. This is likely the reason for the court sessions and seizures that took place in the Ume, Lule, and Pite areas in Sweden in 1723–25.

These were somewhat different kinds of trials than the one in 1693, where Lars Nilsson was convicted of sorcery and burned at the stake in Arjeplog. Von Westen had successfully lobbied for the death penalty to be removed in the case of drums, and it's possible that many of the more enlightened clergy of the eighteenth century had no taste for witch burnings. That doesn't mean that the Sámi were let off easily. In Sweden, a clergyman or two turned up at least once a year, usually at the winter market, where Sámi and non-Sámi traditionally met up for trade and where taxes were generally collected. The Sámi came also at the demand of the Church to show their outward acceptance of Christianity by holding weddings and baptisms. Frequently, a baptism was followed back at home by a Sámi naming ceremony, where the Christian name was ritually removed and a Sámi name bestowed on the child.

During the early 1720s the Sámi were called to church more often: they had to listen to a sermon by the traveling pastor or bishop and then come up to the altar to be questioned about their knowledge of the catechism, after which, while still in the church, they were interrogated about their heathen practices and whether they continued to own and use a drum. They were bullied into giving up their drums on pain of eternal damnation. They were pressured into informing on each other for the same reasons. Those who confessed were required to appear before the full assembly, which included interpreters, a judge, and a clerk to record the proceedings.

Some of those historical records still exist; they list the names of those who surrendered their drums and were then saved from damnation but sentenced to floggings and fines. The records show that at the assembly in Lycksele in 1722, eleven drums were handed over. The largest cache of drums collected at one time in Sweden—twenty-six altogether—took place in 1725 in Åsele, a village to the northwest of Lycksele. Like many churches in the province of Västerbotten, the Åsele parish did not see its Sámi congregation often; the likeliest time to find them was during markets that took place at church feast times. Bishop Peter Asp gathered forty-five Sámi families together in Åsele at one of these markets and forced them to turn over the drums on pain of punishment.

In 1722, Nils Grubb, the dean in Umeå, sat in judgment on four men, including Anders Nilsson Pont, who were suspected of possessing a drum. Grubb found the men guilty. Pont and the others were required to relinquish their drums by the next assembly. The sentence consisted of eight days in prison and the order to attend church on Sunday one time. As it turned out, neither was Pont imprisoned, nor did he voluntarily turn over his drum; instead, after his natural death in 1723, his drum was seized by the local pastor in Lycksele and eventually made its way into the hands of Carl Linnæus. What happened to the drums that were confiscated from the others in Lycksele is not known; perhaps Grubb simply took them back to his home in Umeå.

According to Norwegian–Swedish scholar Håkan Rydving, whose book *The End of Drum-Time* explores the confrontations and coercions around Sámi Indigenous religion in the seventeenth and eighteenth centuries, the outward resistance of the Sámi to Christianity ended in the years around 1740, the same time Linnæus acquired his Sámi costume and dress. Few written sources from the eighteenth century give the Sámi perspective on how their religious practices were denigrated and erased or how the practices went underground, kept alive in families, often by Sámi women, whose voices clergymen rarely listened to. One of the few Sámi narrators of this cultural loss, recorded in 1745 by the Swedish clergyman Pehr Högström, was Anders Erson Snadda. He explained how Sámi spiritual and economic life had waned since the Church had dispossessed his people of their drums, burned their sacrificial sites, and publicly punished many Sámi for continuing to embrace the old ways:

> Since they began to deviate from the customs of their ancestors, they have become scattered, and nowadays there are in the whole of the community, not more than a few, and most of them are beggars. He told about his father, that he used the drum *[goabdes]* and was well; he himself had now put it aside, but found himself not understanding anything else, but soon having to walk before others' doors [i.e., beg]. . . . To all this, the other Lapps added their words, from which I could notice that they were of the same opinion as he.[11]

The ceremonial drums of the Sámi moved from being an integral, valued part of family and community life to becoming curiosities to be exhibited, displayed, and traded beyond the borders of Sápmi, beyond the borders even of Scandinavia.

In a painting of Linnæus done in 1737 by the Dutch painter Martin Hoffman, the young botanist wears his Sámi clothes—the fur tunic; the flat hat; the belt with a bag or two, a needle case, and a knife attached—and in his hand is a drum. Hoffman ended up making two copies of this painting for Linnæus's admirers in the Netherlands, such was the Swede's popularity. Many in the Netherlands hoped—and expected—that Linnæus would become a professor at a Dutch or Belgian university. Instead, for a time he went to work for George Clifford III, a member of a wealthy Dutch–Anglo banking family and a director of the Dutch East India Company. Clifford owned a great estate west of Amsterdam called Hartekamp, which had a famous botanical garden that contained specimens from around the world, including many from Indonesia. He invited Linnæus to explore and inventory Hartekamp's garden; this became another book, *Hortus Cliffortianus.*[12]

With financial backing and letters of recommendation from Clifford, Linnæus made a monthlong trip to England in the late summer of 1736 to meet with other scientists and share his work. He promised Clifford he would also bring back plant specimens from such well-known nurseries in London as the Chelsea Physic Garden. Thanks to the efforts of merchants, amateur botanists, and nurserymen in Britain and America, London was fast becoming an epicenter of botanical interest. One of the great collectors of plant specimens was Hans Sloane, a doctor who in his younger years had spent a year or two in Jamaica as the physician to

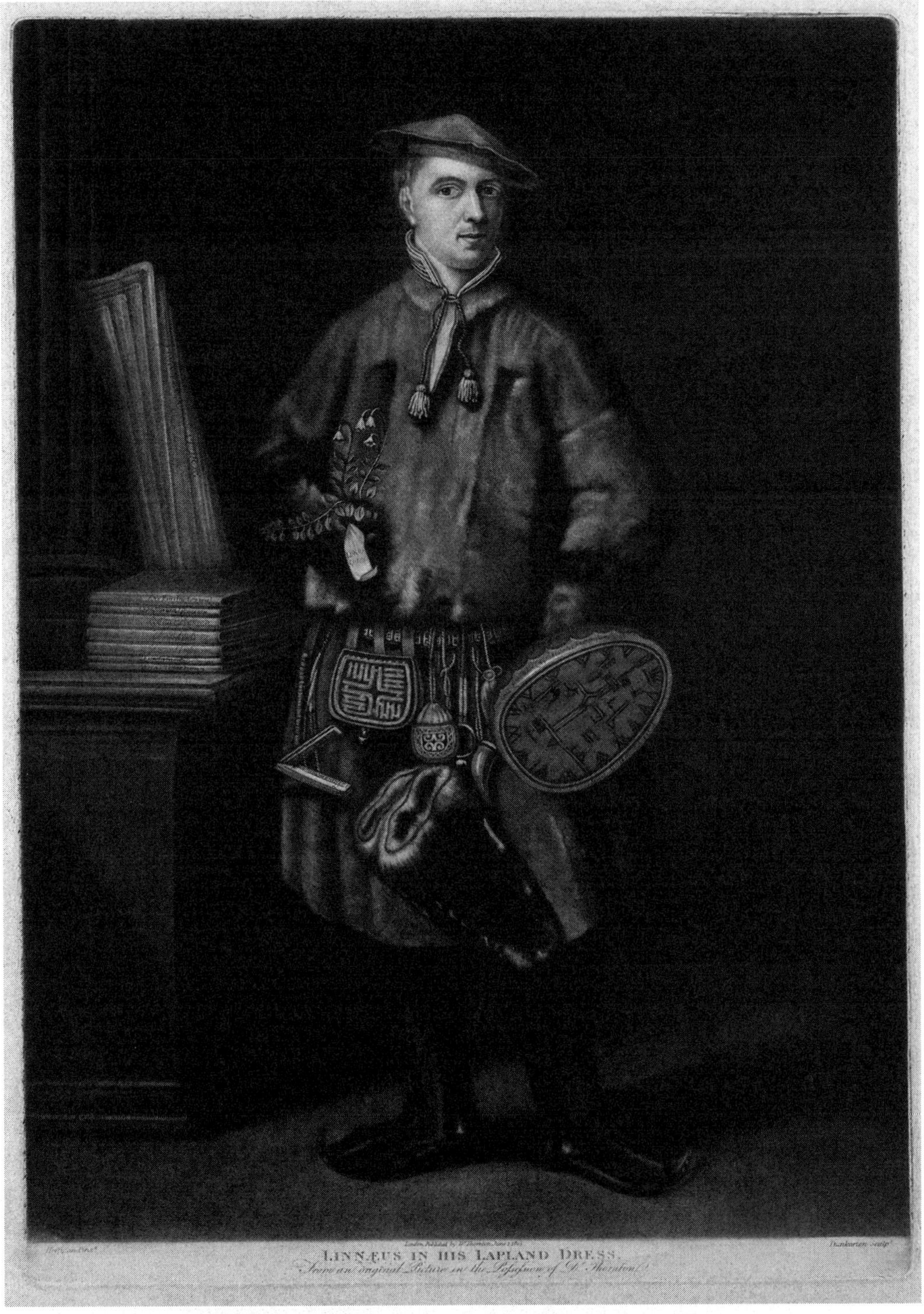

Carl Linnæus in Sámi dress, with the drum that originally belonged to Swedish Sámi Anders Nilsson Pont. Mezzotint engraved by H. Kingsbury after a painting by Martin Hoffmann, 1807. Courtesy of Wellcome Collection, London.

the island's new governor. After the governor's death, Sloane returned to London with notes and an herbarium of hundreds of dried plants from the West Indies. He became a society and royal physician; however, it was his marriage to a wealthy widow, Elizabeth Langley Rose, heiress to lucrative slave-worked sugar plantations in Jamaica, that gave Sloane the means to collect on a vast scale. In 1702, he acquired the curiosity cabinet of William Courten, a formerly wealthy merchant who had financed the colonization of Barbados, and from then on Sloane purchased other people's collections when they or their descendants needed to sell their libraries and curios for economic reasons. He developed extensive contacts around the world. After his trip to Jamaica, Sloane never traveled again. He didn't have to. The world came to him.[13]

By the time of Linnæus's visit to London, Sloane was at the height of his fame. He was the president of the Royal Society, which met once a week in rooms in Crane Court near Fleet Street, after having moved there from Gresham College. The Royal Society of London for Improving Natural Knowledge, as it was first named, is the world's oldest independent scientific academy; it was first established in 1660 by a dozen men, including Robert Hooke and Christopher Wren, as a society for the exchange of knowledge based on reason and observation. The highlights of the meetings were scientific presentations, often experiments either reported on by members or actually performed on-site. Membership was by invitation only, but it was open to men of all classes and had an international reach from the beginning. In addition to its journal, *Philosophical Transactions*, the Royal Society also maintained a museum of objects for scientific study that included everything from anatomical specimens to mechanical models. In 1711 the Royal Society constructed a galleried building for the Repository in the back garden of Crane Court, where anyone might view the collections. Over the years many of the objects in the Repository decayed, particularly the animal specimens. Foreign visitors were more than a little shocked at the disorder. Periodically, there would be a reorganization and some dusting, but the collection diminished over the years through pilfering and crumbling. Some members of the Royal Society, like Hans Sloane, may have felt that certain important objects belonged in safer surroundings—such as his own home.[14]

Sloane's collection comprised thousands of objects, from the tiniest of insects and bird's eggs to the skeleton of an elephant, housed in eleven overstuffed rooms in Montague House in Bloomsbury. His private museum held thousands of geological specimens, including fossils and precious stones. His medal and coin collection was staggering. Added to that, he collected fine art—some three

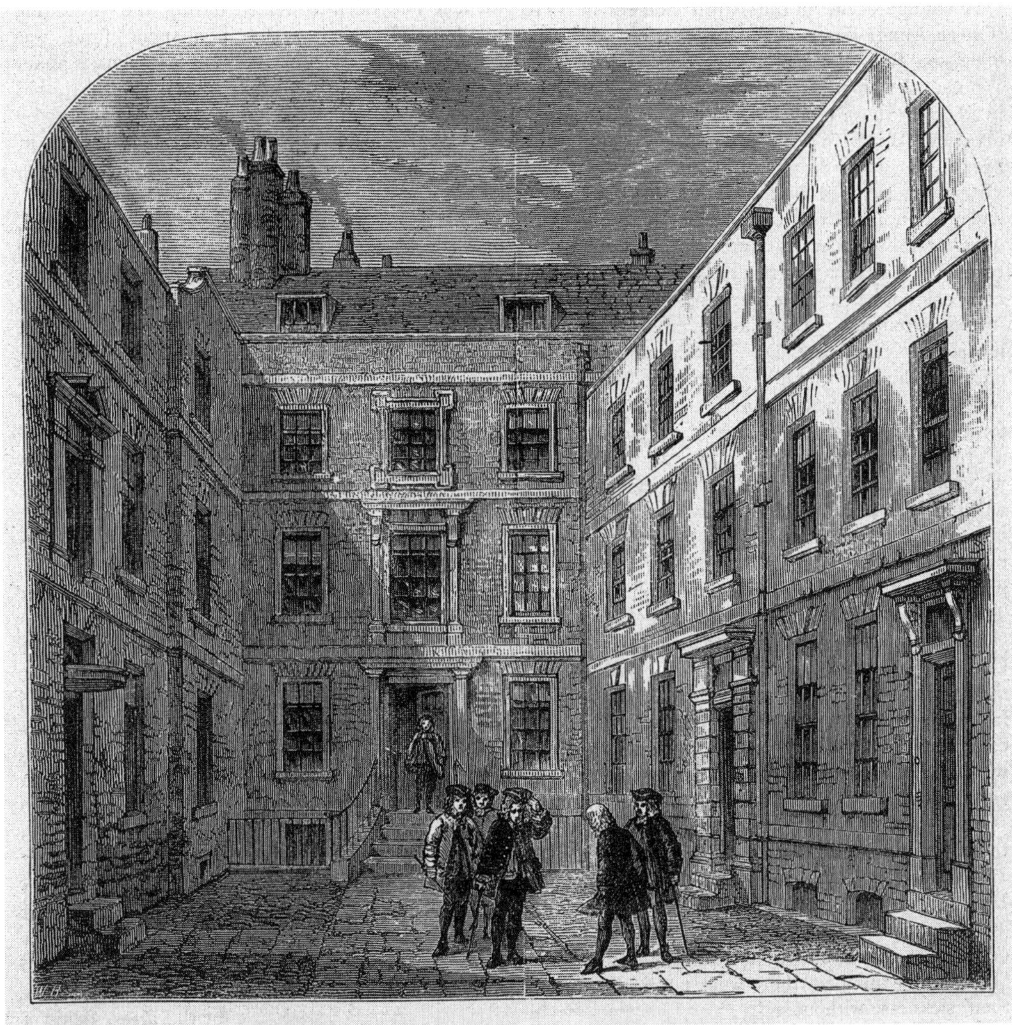

In 1681, a drum from Sápmi was presented to the Royal Society in Britain and became part of the Repository, a museum of humanmade and natural history objects built in the back garden of its building at Crane Court in London. Courtesy of Wellcome Collection, London.

hundred paintings—and possessed a library that included manuscripts and drawings as well as 50,000 bound volumes. The collection included ethnographic items from all over the world, some acquired as part of other people's curiosity cabinets, many from merchants and agents. Of greatest interest to Linnæus, of course, were Sloane's 230 volumes of herbaria, ordered in various systems that other botanists besides Linnæus would find confusing.

Much as Linnæus longed to be invited to one of the Royal Society's meetings and to become a member, he was thwarted that summer of 1736 and for many years to come. He seems to have made a poor impression on Sloane, and it was not until Sloane's death that the invitation to become a fellow of the Royal Society was finally extended. Nevertheless, Sloane did ask the young Swede to come to his home in Bloomsbury and to view his botanical collections.

Linnæus spoke only Swedish and Latin, so he and Sloane must have conversed either in Latin or very little. Sloane walked him through the collections and gave an overview of the specimen volumes. Later Linnæus would write to a friend in Sweden, "Sloane's collection is in complete disorder."[15] Since one of the aims of the generally self-confidant Linnæus was to ingratiate himself with Sloane and his botanical circle so that his own "sexual" systems of plant classification (identifying flowers by numbers of pistils and stamens) would become the norm, Linnæus held his tongue regarding the lack of labeling in the volumes of plant specimens, fearing that the famous man, now seventy-six, would not be particularly open to new methods of taxonomy. He was correct. Sloane's avid accumulation over many decades followed his own methods of typology, which struck many visitors as random, unscientific, and old-fashioned. Yet Sloane's collection, which he showed gladly and often, was one of the wonders of London. In 1742 he moved the entire collection to his new home in Chelsea, and in 1753 the government purchased everything. Most of it became the nucleus of the British Museum.

Among Sloane's collections, according to an inventory done in 1742 during his move from Bloomsbury to Chelsea, were three Sámi drums. They were classed with all the other musical instruments owned by Sloane, including Jamaican banjos, Chinese organs, Norwegian trumpets, and drums from Africa and Bengal.[16] One of the drums, according to Sloane's records, was acquired from the estate of Engelbert Kaempfer.[17] German-born Kaempfer is best remembered as an explorer, physician, and early scholar of all things Japanese. But the route that led him to the closed courts in Edo and Kyoto had earlier passed through Sweden. As a younger man, he studied in 1681 in Uppsala, where he likely acquired a Sámi drum. He made friends in high places and was soon attached to a diplomatic mission to Russia and the Near East by the Swedish king Charles XI. In Iran he changed employers and accompanied the Dutch East India Company as their chief medical officer to Batavia, Ceylon, and Japan. Kaempfer died in 1716 in Germany, and his nephew inherited his collection. The nephew approached Hans

Sloane, who eagerly purchased Kaempfer's collection in 1723–25, giving him, and later the British Museum, an unparalleled collection of Japonica.

A second drum recorded in Sloane's inventory was linked with "Mr. Grubb, a Swede," certainly the deceased rector of Umeå who had presided over assemblies in Lycksele, Lappmark, in 1722 and 1723.[18] It was likely procured in 1736 from Sweden, perhaps indirectly through the clergy pipeline that funneled drums into the larger world. One possible facilitator of the sale might have been Hans Sloane's co-fellow at the Royal Society, Jacob Serenius, pastor of the Swedish church in East London. Serenius was sent to England in 1723 as a young man and became a devoted Anglophile. In 1735 Serenius returned to Sweden and was appointed bishop of Strängnäs, a diocese near Stockholm. A year later, a shipment arrived for Sloane from Sweden, together with two lists, one in Swedish and one in English, of items from Lapland. Both lists, dated July 7, 1736, are signed "A. Charlotta Adelkrantz," and both include mention of a "Lapland-drum with its hammer."[19] Anna Charlotta Adelcrantz, the wife of Nils Grubb, had returned to Stockholm after her husband's death in 1724. There she lived with her mother and her mother's second husband, the architect Göran Adelcrantz. The items she inventoried for Hans Sloane are the same items that turned up in Sloane's handwritten *Catalogue of Miscellanea* from the 1740s, the language only a little altered: fur clothing, a cap, snowshoes and a staff, a bag with steel and flint, tobacco and a spoon, and "a Lapland sledge with the bridle & trappings for the Rene deer."[20]

Is it possible that Jacob Serenius put the word out that he was looking for material objects from Lapland for his Royal Society colleague Hans Sloane? Is it conceivable that Serenius knew Anna Charlotta's stepfather, Göran Adelcrantz, who was one of the listed subscribers endorsing the publication of Serenius's Swedish–Latin–English dictionary?[21] Adelcrantz was no stranger to the business of agenting drums, as it turns out. In his younger years, before he was ennobled and was still Göran Törnqvist, he was recruited by his mentor, the well-known architect and courtier Nicodemus Tessin, to help with an exchange of goods. The young king, Charles X Gustav, coveted some Florentine engravings by Callot belonging to the duke of Tuscany; in exchange, the duke asked for a magic drum from Sápmi to add to his collection of rarities.

The drum, complete with instructions on how it worked, was to be sent to Paris and forwarded on to Monsieur le Grand Duc at his palace in Florence, while Göran Törnqvist traveled by another route to Italy to pick up the engravings. Törnqvist's part in the scheme went well; at least the engravings came to Stockholm in good condition and now belong to the National Museum of Sweden. But the business of the Sámi drum was much more fraught. First there were difficulties obtaining a suitable instrument from Sápmi. Then, when a drum finally arrived at the halfway point in Paris, it had been damaged in transport. Next, according to the envoy in Paris, Monsieur le Grand Duc asked if, in addition to the drum, he might also have *un petit garçon lappon,* "a little Sámi boy," to accompany the drum and play it for him. Eventually a Sámi youth was persuaded to go to Paris, but it's unclear what happened to him after that, except that the envoy complained of him drinking and carousing.[22]

The British Museum is currently in possession of two seventeenth-century drums from Swedish Sápmi. Neither of these two drums came from Sloane's collection, raising the question of what happened to the drums purchased by Sloane in the 1730s from Anna Charlotta Adelcranz and the estate of Engelbert Kaempfer.[23] One drum in the museum's present collection is said to have been bequeathed by Hans Sloane in 1753, but as befits the general uncertainty surrounding so many of the drums, the extended catalog text is more cautious: "Possibly acquired by Sloane from the Royal Society, and thus likely to be the drum given to the Royal Society in 1681 by Johan Heysig-Ridderstjerna of Sweden."[24] It is described at length, both in appearance and use, as a "magic drum." Its shape, carved from a single tree bole, and its images mark it as possibly being from Pite Sápmi in central Sweden.

The second seventeenth-century drum at the British Museum has a different provenance and history than those associated with Kaempfer and Adelcranz. This frame drum, its drumskin so worn that the pictographs are barely visible, is said to have belonged to Bengt Sjulsson from the village of Vapsten in Lycksele parish.[25] The museum acquired it in 1868 when it purchased a large collection of European prehistoric antiquities from the private estate of Gustav Klemm, a German anthropologist who worked most of his life as the director of the royal library at Dresden. In a ten-volume series of books on culture and mankind, Klemm developed the idea of cultural evolution as a three-stage development from savagery to domestication and then to freedom. He divided humanity into active and inactive races. Germans were at the apex of the races. Where Klemm placed the Sámi whose drum he collected is probably clear. Bengt Sjulsson, who lived from 1672 to 1748, was likely forced to give up his drum at the Lycksele assembly around 1722, when Nils Grubb presided over the court and Anders Nilsson Pont was tried and sentenced. But how did the drum come into the hands of Gustav Klemm?

As is so often the case, the full story of this drum's history is lost to time. Once confiscated and robbed of their context, the drums from Sápmi became something other than what they had been, particularly when they left their homes in the North and were transported to curiosity cabinets and private museums on the Continent. No longer companions of the household or guides on the path of healing and understanding, they became objects connected in the public and scholarly mind with magic and witchcraft, coveted treasures or ethnographic artifacts, whose original makers and owners were simply referred to as necromancers and witches. In rare cases, a drum's maker is known, as are the circumstances in which it was taken, sold, or given and to whom. It's possible to follow the trajectory of certain drums, like the one belonging to Anders Poulsen, which was filched from him after his trial in Vadsø in 1691 and eventually came to the Royal Kunstkammer in Denmark, or the drum that belonged to Bendix Andersen, confiscated by Thomas von Westen in 1722 and shipped to Copenhagen to end up in a museum in East Germany. The drum belonging to Anders Nilsson Pont, which for centuries has been known as "Linnæus's drum," also has a traceable path, thanks to its famous custodian.

Linnæus did not settle in Holland but returned to Sweden in 1738. He married a young woman to whom he had been engaged before he went to the Continent and fathered four daughters and a son. He took up a professorship at Uppsala University. He never left Sweden again and rarely left Uppsala. He created a garden that mirrored his classifications and that he used in his very popular botany classes. Always self-confident, he grew vain and touchy; allowed to name many of the world's plants in Latin, he honored allies with the names of beautiful plants, while slighting some of his enemies by attaching their names to tiny mosses and stinkweeds. Bitter and crabby as he could be at times, he invested energy in his students and had high hopes for several disciples, particularly Daniel Solander, son of the Reverend Carl Solander in Piteå. During his studies, Daniel Solander lived in the home of Linnæus and his family in Uppsala, but he returned to northern Sweden in the summer, where he botanized in Sápmi. He was gifted, energetic, and sociable, and Linnæus had big plans for him that extended to offering him the hand of his daughter Lisa Stina in marriage.

In 1760 Daniel Solander arrived in London with his professor's encouragement to study and make connections in England; he made so many connections that he never returned to Sweden. He never married Lisa Stina and almost never wrote to his mentor again, refusing to answer Linnæus's repeated pleas for plants or to offer a word about his own health or whereabouts. Instead, Solander improved his English and threw in his lot with the wealthy amateur scientist and avid plant collector Joseph Banks. Along with Banks, Solander sailed as a botanist in the *Endeavor* to the South Pacific on the first of Captain James Cook's voyages. Solander later worked for the British Museum, cataloging Hans Sloane's herbarium. The seventeenth-century Sámi drum now displayed at the Museum of Archaeology and Anthropology in Cambridge was a gift from either Solander or Banks to Trinity College.[26] The acquisition date listed, 1760, suggests that Solander could have brought it with him when he first arrived in England. Some evidence suggests that Daniel Solander, like his father, Carl, may well have acted as an agent for others who wanted drums from Sápmi.

In time, Linnæus gifted Anders Nilsson Pont's drum to Carl Peter Thunberg, another disciple and botanist. After Thunberg's death, the drum went to Uppsala University and then to Sweden's Royal Academy of Science, which traded it to the Musée d'Ethnographie du Trocadéro in Paris for some other objects in 1883. In France, as in Denmark and Sweden, national museums began to appear in the early to mid-1800s. In 1878, following the Universal Exhibition in Paris, a new museum of ethnography was created out of private and royal collections and from scientific societies. As in other countries, paintings, sculptures, and archaeology were separated out; the Louvre and other museums became the home of artistic treasures and loot collected from around the world wherever France had a colonial toehold. Ethnographic collections came from some of the same sources and were spurred on by a growing obsession with Native peoples and cultures, as evidenced by the frequency of universal expositions and traveling exhibits that often included mannequins, dioramas, and live human beings as specimens and actors.

Newly established ethnographic museums all over the globe took part in exchanges of objects in the late nineteenth and early twentieth centuries. The Musée d'Ethnographie du Trocadéro fell on hard times in the first decades of the twentieth century, however, perhaps superseded by the Colonial Museum, which competed for collections from French possessions in Africa and the South Pacific. The Colonial Museum was transformed in 1935 into the Musée de la France d'Outre-mer, and in 1937 the ethnographic museum became the Musée de l'Homme, which was reestablished on different principles than exuberant, disorganized collecting. Anthropological expeditions sent back material culture, and the collections became more scientific in their labeling and presentation. It was around this time, in 1933, that the drum used and revered by Anders Nilsson Pont was returned to Sweden, not to Lycksele but to the Linnæus Society in Uppsala, where it still is exhibited in the museum dedicated to Linnæus, along with a copy of the famous portrait of him in Sámi dress.

Mr. Bullock's Exhibition of Laplanders

The formal name was the London Museum of Natural History and Pantherion, but it was usually called the Egyptian Hall for the facade that suggested a temple from the land of the pyramids. Its cornices were supported by sphinxes and two statues that represented Isis and Osirus; every surface of the street entrance was covered with hieroglyphs. Until 1820, the owner of the museum on Piccadilly Street, William Bullock, had drawn crowds by displaying stuffed giraffes and tigers in a tropical setting, along with attention-grabbing purchases like Napoleon's carriage and other mementos of the late war that ended with the Battle of Waterloo.

In 1819 Bullock held a great auction that emptied out his museum of its fifteen thousand natural and manufactured objects, and he turned his attention to exhibitions that would satisfy a growing public interest in educational entertainment. The visitors who eagerly filled the Egyptian Hall from January through March 1822 had come to see four live reindeer and three live "Laplanders" from Norway. The Sámi and reindeer were positioned against a vast painted backdrop of snowy mountains said to be of the North Cape, together with a summer tent and a winter turf hut and some of their domestic objects, including a sledge and a cradle. On the walls of the great hall hung more than a dozen examples of fur coats, tunics, boots, shoes, and hats, along with skis, reindeer harnesses, and even a "drum of the Lapland Necromancers."

The "Laplanders" on view that winter consisted of reindeer herders Jens Thomassen Holm, his wife, Karen Christiansdatter, and their four-year-old son, Thomas, originally from the Røros district in southern Sápmi. Over the first six weeks, the living exhibition of this modest family, a few animals, and several dozen objects welcomed fifty-eight thousand visitors, attracted largely by the unusual presence of reindeer in London. Yet beyond the excitement of stroking the tame beasts and talking through an interpreter with Jens and Karen—the fur-bundled couple was always described as "diminutive" but also as mild in character and quick in intelligence—was the instructional value of being able to observe the dwellings, means of transport, and beautifully made clothing from Arctic lands. Remarkably, the *Exhibition of Laplanders* offered the most extensive assemblage of Sámi objects in one place since Schefferus had put together his museum in Uppsala, this time in a distinctly urban setting and with the intention of drawing a mass audience.[1]

"A natural inclination to possess every thing that is extraordinary either in nature or art has impelled me, from my earliest years, to collect and preserve whatever objects of that description it was in my power to draw into one collection," wrote William Bullock, in his introduction to a booklet that accompanied the *Exhibition of Laplanders*.[2] Bullock was only one of many in a long line of Englishmen and -women who indulged a love of collecting not only to enhance their private curiosity cabinets but also to buy and sell items and display them to the public.

Until the second half of the eighteenth century, the paltry number of Sámi objects in England, like most natural history specimens, antiquities, and curios, had been restricted to viewing by members of the upper classes, scholars and university students, and foreigners with a scientific bent. The Royal Society's Repository, in a new building in the garden of Crane Court, was open to the public, but relatively few ventured there, and some of those who came expressed disappointment with the state of the exhibit. Hans Sloane's magnificent library, herbarium, and collection of thousands of objects were off-limits to most, and even after the British Parliament acquired the collections for the nation and moved everything into the mansion on Montague Street, viewing was strictly monitored. Although the British Museum was ostensibly the first museum in the world to open its doors to the public, its educational purpose was thwarted by limited access: prospective visitors had to appear at the museum, sign their names in a book, and wait to receive a ticket and timed appointment, sometimes months in the future.

Several other examples of collections are known besides those of Hans Sloane and the Royal Society, which offered limited viewing. Beginning in the late seventeenth century, the Tradescant family, John the Elder and John the Younger, horticulturists and nurserymen, had displayed antiquities and exotica from abroad in their home in Lambeth and had published a printed catalog that included treasures from early Virginia—wampum, bearskins, and a garment embroidered by shells that had belonged to Powhattan—along with hundreds of botanical cuttings and dried specimens. The collection was snapped up in 1664 by Elias Ashmole, who donated it to the city of Oxford, which built the Ashmolean Museum to contain it. Another important collection in Britain was the library and herbarium of explorer and botanist Joseph Banks, housed in Soho Square and opened to the public in 1777. After Banks's death, his library was acquired by the British Museum, and the botanical specimens ended up at the Museum of Natural History in London. Banks specialized in plants, but he had rarities from the South Seas and other geographies in his possession, including at one time a Sámi drum that he or his first librarian Daniel Solander gave to Trinity College.

In these early scientific collections, the few items from Lapland were treated as curiosities, as examples of magic from the near and distant past. There was no great attempt to categorize them other than by type (musical instrument or magic talisman). But alongside the private and public collections was an increasing interest in accumulating and displaying exotica for pleasure and profit in London, which was increasingly the center of massive imperial trade with the world. Shipments from the Americas, Africa, and Asia—cotton, silk, spices, teas, coffees, and useful and decorative items—were hourly unloaded from sailing ships in the great docks that lined the river. Auctions abounded, and private collectors, often titled aristocrats of both sexes but also newly wealthy families in trade, spent fortunes acquiring rare objects from around the globe.

London's inhabitants, primed by illustrations, travelogues, and other published accounts of the foreign, found in many of these curios and the stories behind them a way to satisfy their curiosity about how the rest of the world lived. The coffeehouses that sprang up in the eighteenth century, where a man could meet friends, argue, drink coffee, and read the latest issue of *The Rambler* or *The Spectator,* also in some cases provided displays of exotica on the walls. Don Saltero's, in Chelsea, was one of the best known of these informal museum–coffeehouses. Its owner, John Salter, previously a barber, set up his museum with castoffs from his neighbor Hans Sloane and added to them over the years, printing a catalog that included some 293 motley objects.

With Don Saltero's coffeehouse, the word *museum* became a synonym for any sort of attraction that displayed rare and bizarre objects, while curiosity shops high and low proliferated in lanes abutting the docks of London and in glittering arcades in more affluent neighborhoods. As curio shops and coffeehouses arranged their exotic wares on shelves and walls and in glass cases like the Kunstkammers of old, entrepreneurial curio collectors became museum owners and impresarios who increasingly offered a combination of amusement and education in the form of public museums. One such establishment, often compared favorably with the less accessible British Museum, was the Holophusikon in Leicester Square, more generally known as Sir Ashton Lever's Museum, established in 1774. Lever, originally from Manchester, collected on a grand scale, and his museum proved it. Sadly, it proved unprofitable and closed in 1788, its collections dispersed. Lever's Museum demonstrated that the public could be tempted to pay to see novelties, but perhaps not the same novelties over and over. To an increasingly urbane public interested in knowledge acquisition, it was not quite enough to look at exotica. They wanted more spectacle and interaction, something that William Bullock understood and could provide.

William Bullock was born in 1773 in Sheffield, where he began his career as a jeweler and silversmith. Along with practicing his craft, he bought and displayed collections of natural history specimens and global exotica, including items from Cook's South Sea voyages. Eventually he created a Museum of Natural Curiosities, which he moved to Liverpool in 1801 to draw larger crowds. But even Liverpool wasn't big enough for him, and ten years later he built his London Museum of Natural History and Pantherion on Piccadilly, which remained a fixture of public entertainment for the next hundred years. While Bullock expanded his talents as a showman, he remained a serious natural historian. He belonged to the Linnean Society of London, for instance, the world's oldest active biological society, established in 1788. Its founder and president, James Edward Smith, was the English translator of Carl Linnæus's *Lapland Journey,* which he'd arranged to have published in London in 1811. It was through Smith's efforts that Linnæus's botanical, zoological, and library collections were purchased from his widow and brought to London in 1829.

William Bullock's personal interest in biology was the quadrupeds, and his London Museum had featured a variety of taxidermied four-footed beasts, often arranged in habitats, using both painted murals and real trees and plants to suggest a largely imaginary "Tropical Forest." Bullock was one of the first museum curators in England to display his animal and vegetable specimens in a habitat group, a concept still very much with us today. For all his love of quadrupeds, there was one "that I was never to obtain, either in a preserved or living state. . . .

I allude to the Reindeer: a creature of the most extraordinary and beautiful form; an animal whose domestication is of more importance to its master, than that of any other, or probably the whole of the quadruped species. The Laplander and his reindeer appear to have been created for each other."[3]

It was this fascination, Bullock suggests, that led him to make three attempts to obtain reindeer from Norway, initially because he believed that herds of this animal could be established in the hills of northern England and Scotland or even "in the neighborhood of London," on one of the remaining heaths. Having read Linnæus, he believed he knew something about the Indigenous people of Scandinavia who lived in such close harmony with this animal. Bullock was also influenced in his desire to obtain reindeer by Sir Arthur de Capell Brooke, a member of the Royal Society and an early traveler to northern Scandinavia. In his lengthy and leisurely travelogue, *Travels through Sweden, Norway, and Finmark, to the North Cape, in the Summer of 1820,* published in 1823, Brooke writes chiefly about the Sámi in the North. But he also encountered a few Sámi people in the area of Røros in the Dovre Mountains north of Oslo (formerly called Christiania). On his return to London, he described his adventures to William Bullock, who, "fired with a description of this singular race of people, set off into Norway, for the purpose of bringing to England a family of them with their rein-deer, &c. This, after numerous difficulties, he at length accomplished; and it is almost unnecessary to add, that they have been exhibited to the public, who have strongly marked the interest they have felt on the occasion."[4]

Whatever the exact reason, William Bullock did manage to locate a dozen reindeer to import and a Sámi couple willing to come to London to care for the animals. Initially Bullock did not plan to exhibit the reindeer in the Egyptian Hall but rather intended to allow their appearance onstage in a theatrical piece written and directed by actor and playwright Thomas Dibdin, to be performed with Jens Thomassen Holm and Karen Christiansdatter in the Haymarket Theater. This plan was given up when eight of the reindeer died while detained at an English port by a customs official who couldn't find "reindeer" on his list of tariffs and had to write to London for instructions. Nor did the Sámi couple seem to conform to Dibdin's expectations of how "Laplanders" should sing and dance. In the end, Bullock, with Brooke's help, organized the *Exhibition of Laplanders* at his museum, where a wildly popular exhibit of Egyptian archeological items, including sections of a temple, was just ending its run.[5]

Lapland proved just as popular as Egypt in satisfying the public's appetite for exotic novelty. It also marked the first time Sámi people and their belongings had

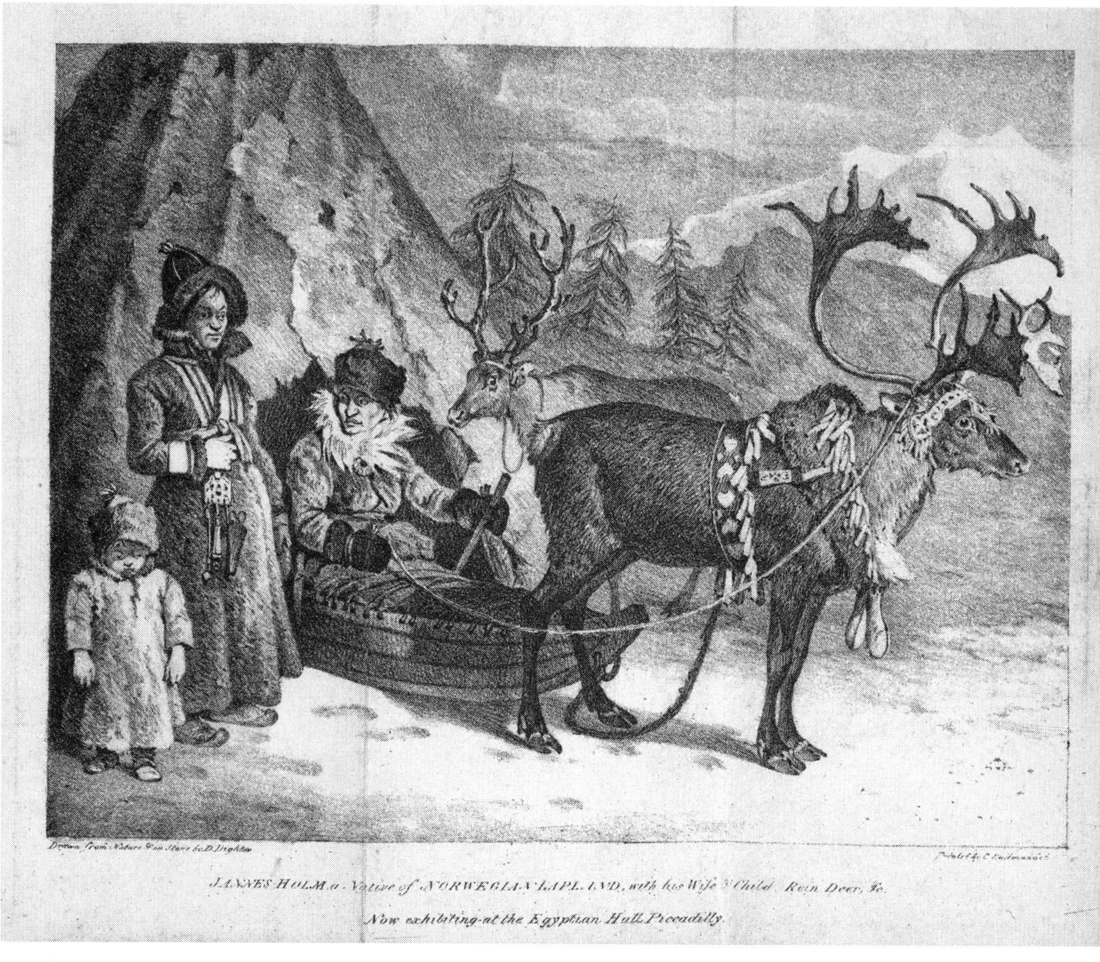

Illustration depicting Jens Thomassen Holm, Karen Christiansdatter, and their son, Thomas, from the catalog of William Bullock's *Exhibition of Laplanders* at the Egyptian Hall, Piccadilly, 1822. Courtesy of Wellcome Collection, London.

been exhibited together to a foreign audience. Such displays from Sápmi would become a feature in Northern Europe and even in North America over the next century. These living exhibitions took place, often outdoors, in zoos, parks, and the grounds of national exhibitions and world expositions in Hamburg, Paris, Copenhagen, and Chicago, as well as in many smaller European cities. Over the years the exhibitions grew ever more elaborate, with recreations of Sámi tent encampments, reindeer sled rides for children and adults, and performances of caravan migrations and even wedding processions.

The most well known of these were arranged by Carl Hagenbeck, a German supplier of animals to zoos and owner of a zoological park in Hamburg. In 1875 he engaged a group of six Sámi from Karesuando and Tromsø to come to Hamburg and live for a while on the grounds behind his house, outdoors and on exhibit. As Hagenbeck relates in his memoir, *Beasts and Men,* his expectations that the Sámi would be a huge success in Germany were immediately realized. "All Hamburg came to see this genuine 'Lapland in miniature.'"[6] Several years later, from 1878 until 1879, a group of about a dozen Sámi, this time from Karasjok and Kautokeino, was installed at Hagenbeck's zoo, and for the next decades Sámi families and individuals came regularly to Hamburg, along with reindeer, tents, sleds, cradles, and all the domestic items that Sámi herders used in daily life.

Hagenbeck made a large profit with these exhibits and soon expanded his definition of a zoo even further, including different displays of Indigenous people from Greenland and Africa. Unlike Bullock, Hagenbeck emphasized the anthropological interest for viewers in simply observing the Sámi go about their ordinary lives. It was domesticity as spectacle. Yet, that didn't prove to hold enough value for zoo goers. Soon, exhibits of lassoing and harnessing reindeer and of setting up and pulling down the tent on "migrations" were performed several times a day, along with faux wedding processions and ceremonies.

Like displays of other so-called primitive people, these living exhibitions would take on an ethnographic character, where public curiosity merged into racialized studies of people from elsewhere around the globe. Such exhibitions were not neutral; by exhibiting Sámi families in zoological gardens, by making it a condition of employment that the Sámi perform "migrations" and "wedding processions," the impresarios who organized such shows limited the means by which the Sámi could communicate their traditional culture. Some Sámi participants returned home to Sápmi from Germany with unhappy memories of being exploited and fenced in with their suffering reindeer. Sámi and non-Sámi journalists alike protested in print in the early twentieth century over the poor conditions of these "capitalistic business schemes."[7] Yet, as the Norwegian scholar Cathrine Baglo has explored in detail, such living exhibitions could also be sites of agency for Indigenous Sámi people, particularly by the end of the nineteenth and early twentieth centuries, when families chose to accept employment in order to share their cultures, travel, make money, and return home with stories of Paris and Berlin.

Jens Thomassen Holm and Karen Christiansdatter were two of the pioneers of this mode of travel and contact. Bullock and the London journalists might have seen the pair through the lens of romance as noble savages, as "wanderers" typical of their race, but in fact they were, like many in South Sápmi at the time, gradually being dispossessed of territories that had traditionally been part of the reindeer grazing lands and were now, through theft, intimidation, and government legislation, becoming the property of small farmers and larger landowners. Their "native habitat," not mentioned in articles published about the exposition, was Røros, which had become a mining town in the seventeenth century. Holm and Christiansdatter owned few reindeer and had worked for others. Eventually they ended up in the Stavanger area on the coast of Norway, which is where Bullock seems to have encountered them. The stories that appeared in the press had very little to do with the reality of their lives, which was less romantic and more hardscrabble.

Along with the press coverage it received in British newspapers, the *Exhibition of Laplanders* was documented and publicized by several publications and pictorial reproductions, all of which make reference to the material culture of the Sámi that formed part of the show. Although there seems to have been no detailed catalog, it's possible to get a sense of the objects Bullock, assisted by Arthur de Capell Brooke, thought worthy of display as part of the "habitat group" but also as museum pieces arrayed on the walls. For urban Londoners, these objects helped define and emphasize the exotic nature of Sámi culture, even though it's unlikely that most of the things displayed were the actual belongings of the Holm–Christiansdatter family. They traveled light, Bullock wrote, when they accompanied the herd down to Flekkefjord in the south of Norway to embark for England. Instead, it seems probable that the large and small objects that made up the scene in the Egyptian Hall and that were hung on the walls were gathered by agents in Norway or in some cases belonged to Brooke. The cloth-covered tent and its poles as well as the turf hut would have been either purchased in Norway and shipped down to London or constructed under supervision in the Egyptian Hall from materials obtained more locally. It's very possible that some of the objects, especially the clothing, were created especially for display.

Bullock's booklet, *An Account of the Family of Laplanders, Which, with Their Summer and Winter Residences, Domestic Implements, Sledges, Herd of Living Reindeer, and a Panoramic View of the North Cape . . . Are Now Exhibiting at the Egyptian Hall, Piccadilly,* is intriguing for many reasons, not least because of his fascination with reindeer as a species and his generous excerpts from Linnæus's *Lapland Journey* about the habits and manners of the Sámi. But it also includes a one-page list of some of the objects displayed on the walls and in the staging area of the museum. Among them were the following items:

- A superb Lapland lady's dress, made of the skins of the beautiful White Deer, fringed and ornamented with the fur of the Black Bear, with gloves and shoes to correspond.
- The curious Cradle, or case, in which the Lapland women carry their children, so contrived as to enable them to suckle the infant without disturbing it.
- A Lapland sledge, the same used by Captain Brooke in travelling from the North Cape to Norway.
- Drum of the Lapland Necromancers, now becoming extremely rare.[8]

Although Brooke, in his descriptions of his northern travels in 1820, makes frequent mention of the "Sea" or the "Shore Laplanders" and seems to have recognized that, especially along the Norwegian coast above the Arctic Circle, fishing, often combined with other occupations, was the primary means for sustenance for the Sámi, this was not the picture presented at the Egyptian Hall. There was no fishing gear and not a single boat, a choice that would reoccur in the foreign exhibitions to come, where the material culture and clothing would reinforce the impression that the Sámi were mountain nomads from a distant land, with a history that was simultaneously continuing and disappearing. In *Lapland Sketches,* a thirty-six-page educational manual for young people published at the time of the Piccadilly exhibition, we can read that "the proper Laplanders . . . are constantly wanderers. It is only those whose herds have perished by disease, or fallen a prey to wolves, who have become colonists; and from want of the means to follow their usual mode of living, have recourse to fishing or tillage for their subsistence."[9]

Lapland Sketches offers some descriptions of the material culture of the Sámi, particularly the dresses and cradle. The anonymous writer also weighed in on the ceremonial drum, noting that "great pains have been taken by the Swedes and Danes to instruct the Laplanders on the subject of religion: yet most of them retain a variety of superstitions and idolatries, and have among them considerable remains of Druidical institutions. Their magicians have a sort of tambourine, which

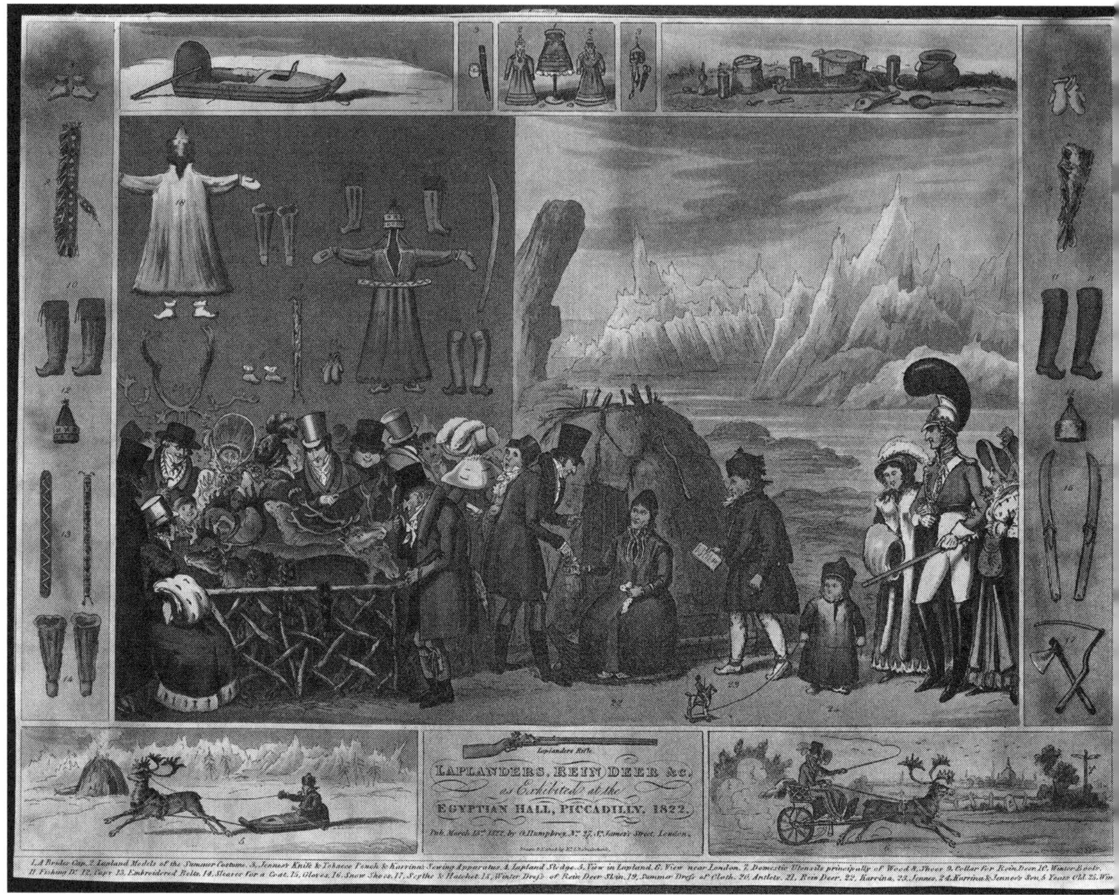

***Laplanders, Reindeer, etc., As Exhibited at the Egyptian Hall, Piccadilly, 1822.* Illustration by Isaac Robert Cruikshank. The detail on the next page shows objects with numbers corresponding to the key at the bottom of the illustration. Courtesy of the National Library of Norway.**

they call a drum, and which is ornamented with figures of the sun, moon, stars, birds, rivers &c."[10] Was this drum an original from the seventeenth or eighteenth century, or was it recreated for the exhibit? Although mentioned in both Bullock's list of items and *Lapland Sketches,* the "Drum of the Lapland Necromancers" doesn't appear in drawings of the exhibition, nor did Holm or Christiansdatter apparently perform on it, as Linnæus had done on his, to demonstrate that sorcery was still alive and well in Sápmi.

The drawings produced by the popular artists Thomas Rowlandson and Isaac

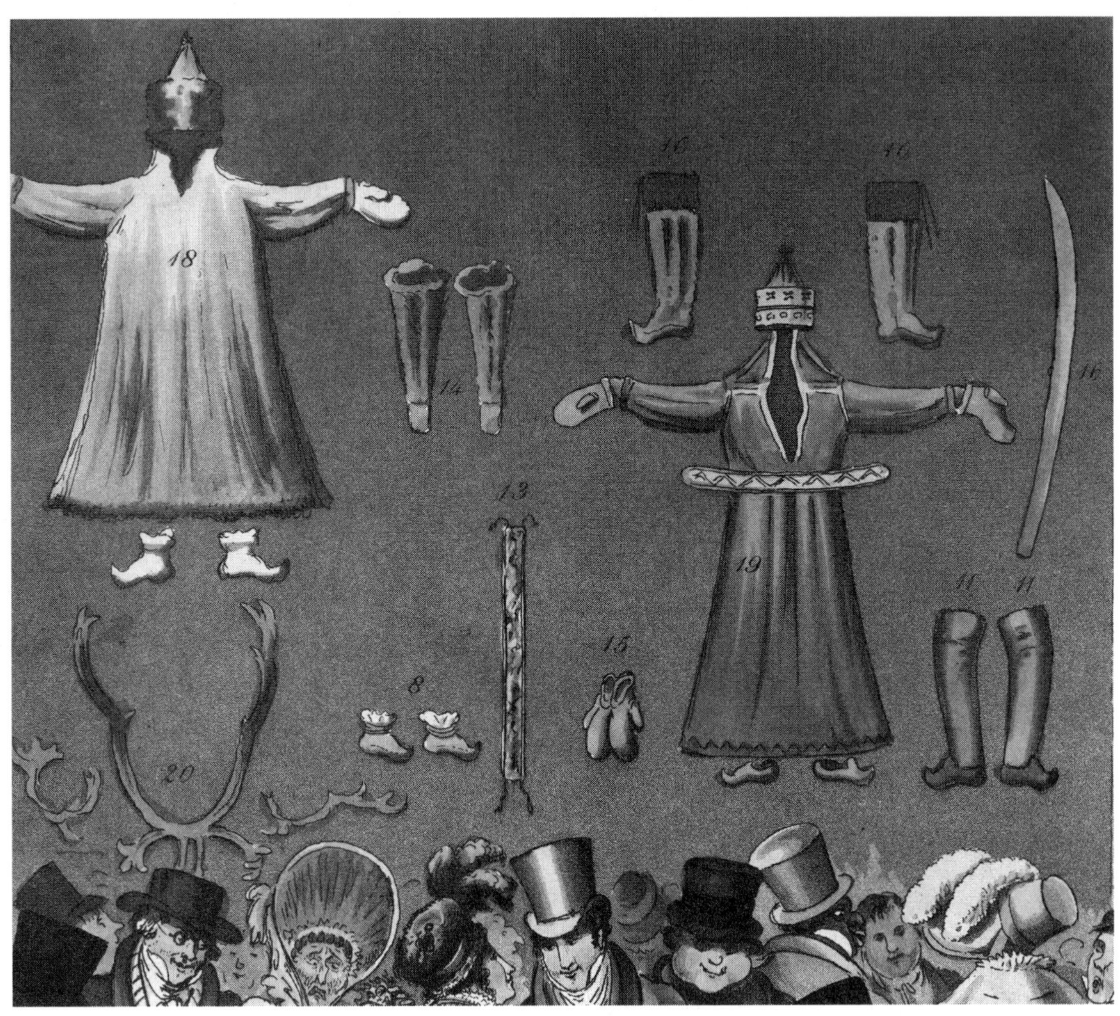

Robert Cruikshank and later turned into hand-tinted etchings for sale provide the best visual guide to the show and act as a catalog of sorts. Rowlandson places a prancing reindeer in the center foreground of his picture, with the fur-coated Sámi family to the side (Plate 3), while in Cruikshank's illustration, Karen Christiansdatter is seated in front of a turf-covered hut, with her husband on one side and Thomas Bullock in a top hat on the other. As befitted their interest in caricature, both artists juxtapose ladies and gentlemen in Regency dress jostling to get a better view of the reindeer in a corral, but they also add a number of accurately drawn objects to their pictures. Rowlandson's drawing captures the evocative mural of the icebergs and crags of the "North Cape" at one end of the hall and the side walls where fur coats, tunics, hats, fur gloves, and reindeer antlers hang. In Cruikshank's illustration, the border includes small scenes of people driving reindeer in a sled and riding in a modern open carriage, as well as various items of Sámi make: tall boots, long fur gloves, skis, and a rifle. The objects are numbered, and a key can be found at the bottom of some of the etchings that gives the names of the objects.

An illustration produced by Cruikshank a few months later in 1822 forms an intriguing parallel with his picture of the exhibition in Piccadilly. This one is titled *The Laplanders Return to Their Native Country Under the Care of Mr. Bullock and His Son*. The image in the center shows William Bullock, four times as large as Jens Thomassen Holm and Karen Christiansdatter, both wearing English dress. Oddly, the rest of the Sámi people in the picture are normal size, on par with Bullock's son and his wife. While a very few Sámi-made objects are shown in the possession of the Indigenous crowd, the majority of items, many of them toys spilling out of a basket or being borne by a procession of laborers in the background, are of English make, including a grandfather clock and furniture. The border of this picture matches the style of Cruikshank's exhibition picture and includes tiny but grand scenes of British life: a boxing match, a horse race, imperial guards, a steamship at sea, and along the sides various objects that seem to suggest military dress and weaponry.

The Holm–Christiansdatter family did return to Norway in April 1822, but they were back in London for a resumption of the exhibit in November. This time there were no reindeer but a breed of deer from North America. After London, the family and the exhibit went on tour through the provinces before a final return to Norway in 1823. Somewhere along the way their son, Thomas, seems to have died. For decades afterward, Jens was remembered as "English-Jens."

What of the objects that were displayed in the *Exhibition of Laplanders*? It seems unlikely that they were returned to Norway with the Holm–Christiansdatter family and very likely that they were not kept long by Bullock, who spent most of 1823 in Mexico collecting everything from casts of Montezuma's calendar stone to specimens of minerals, fish, and birds for his next astonishing Piccadilly exhibition, *Ancient and Modern Mexico*. Perhaps Arthur de Capell Brooke took all or some of the Sámi objects, given that he maintained an interest in Scandinavia and traveled up to the North Cape and Finnmark again in 1823, publishing two more illustrated books, *Winter Sketches in Lapland* (1826) and *A Winter in the North Cape* (1827). Perhaps the fur dresses, skis, and even the drum were sold to an antiquarian or curio dealers in London. Perhaps the hats or gloves decorated a London coffeehouse for a time, or perhaps a private collector acquired a few objects that passed to descendants and then were discarded or donated to local museums. There are relatively few documented Sámi objects in British museums, and many of them came from later ethnographic expeditions at the turn of the nineteenth century, but it's always possible that a few are unlabeled remnants of the 1822 exhibition. For the most part, English museums rarely collected Sámi artifacts in a systematic way. The largest collections are in the British Museum and the Pitt Rivers Museum in Oxford. The Museum of Anthropology and Archaeology in Cambridge is the only British institution with a permanent installation; this exhibit was arranged in 1947, some 125 years after the *Exhibition of Laplanders* in the Egyptian Hall.

In Germany, as a result of the living exhibitions organized by Carl Hagenbeck, many of the items of clothing and utilitarian objects illustrating Sámi nomadic and domestic material culture eventually found their way to ethnographic collections in German museums in Berlin, Leipzig, and Dresden. These ethnographic objects brought to Germany were not often or always the belongings of the Sámi from Finnmark and northern Sweden who were hired by Hagenbeck's company. They were purchased separately and shipped to Hamburg and other cities by agents such as the Norwegian Johan Adrian Jacobsen, who traveled the world collecting for Hagenbeck and others. The same would have held true for the expositions in Paris, Berlin, and Chicago at the World Exposition of 1893. The material culture of the Sámi performers was crucial to how they were to be represented, as fur-clad nomads living in tents and traveling in sleds drawn by teams of reindeer, yet the objects used in the attractions seem to have been treated differently than the objects obtained by antiquarians and eventually agents for museums, which were increasingly identified by district and often by their maker, especially if their maker was considered a quality craftsperson, or *duojár.*

Increased travel and commerce, beginning in the eighteenth century and reaching every part of the globe by the nineteenth, was responsible for the transfer of hundreds of thousands of exotic curiosities into the hands of collectors, shopkeepers, exhibitors, and museum curators, some to be displayed, some to be stored, many to be discarded or misplaced in the burgeoning storerooms of local and national museums. From the Royal Kunstkammer to the scientific curiosity cabinet to the curio shop on a London street, from living expositions to

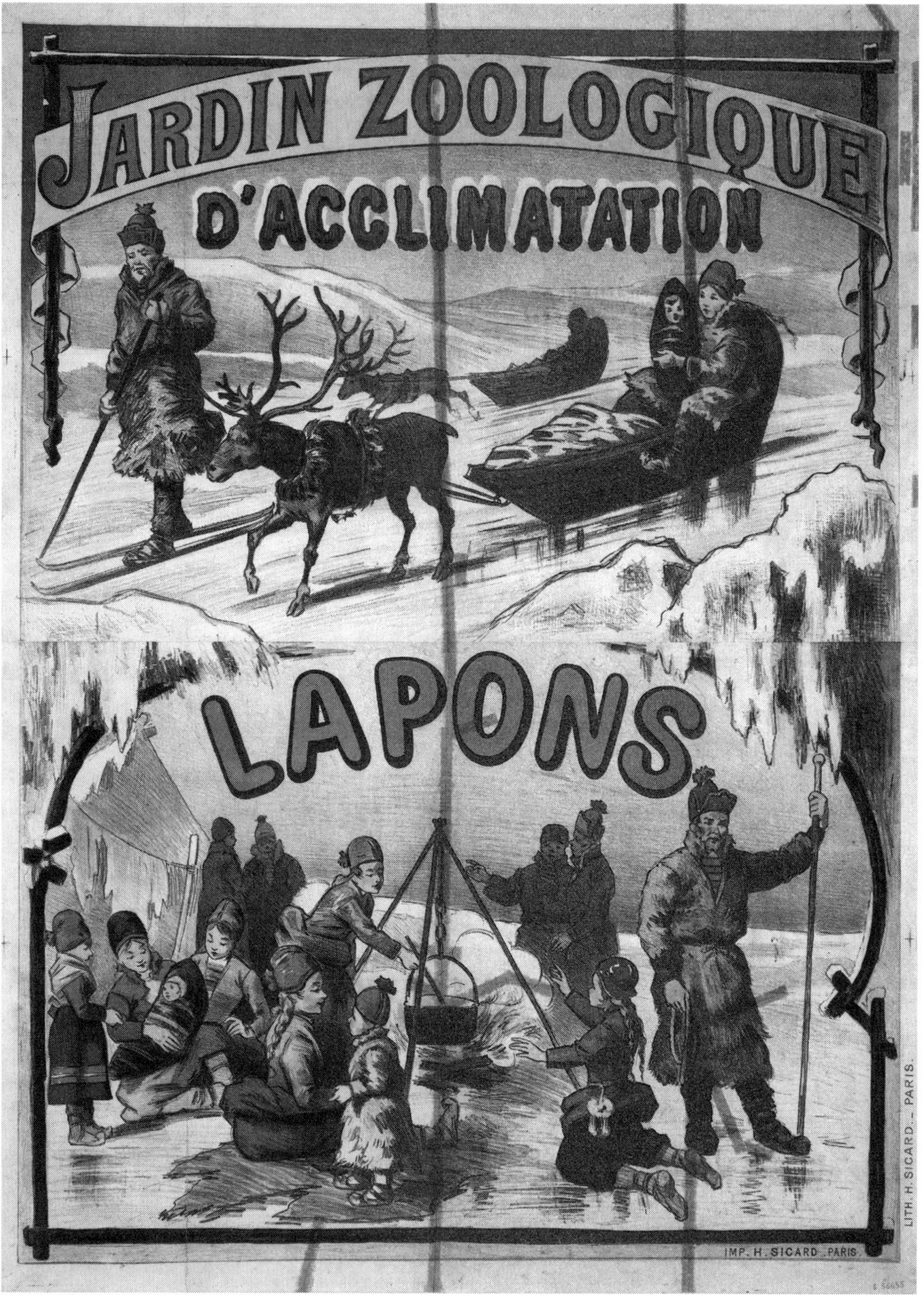

In 1878–79, an exhibition of Sámi people, reindeer, domestic tools, tents, and sleds toured multiple cities in Europe under the auspices of Carl Hagenbeck and his Hamburg Zoo. This poster from 1878 shows typical images of the Sámi at the Jardin Zoologique d'Acclimatation in Paris. Almost a million people are estimated to have visited the exhibition in 1878, many in Paris for the concurrent World's Fair that year. Courtesy of the Historical Library, City of Paris.

ethnographic museums, Sámi objects, even the choicest rarities, like the ceremonial drums, would gradually filter out of Sápmi into England and Europe and largely be forgotten.

But in Fennoscandia and Russia, in all regions where the Sámi people continued to live, the mid-nineteenth century was the beginning of serious collecting not only of antiquarian objects when they could be found but also of all forms of *duodji* made of bone, wood, silver, skin, and pewter thread. The collecting of objects, along with the collecting of folklore and myths, would take place against a backdrop of continued colonization of Sámi lands and resources, intensified state persecution, coerced education, language loss, and cultural appropriation and erasure.

Outside Sápmi, the Sámi would remain exotic "wanderers" portrayed through the prism of Lapland and the Arctic, almost always pictured with reindeer and sleds. The living exhibitions in England and on the Continent painted a romantic picture of an ancient people given to chanting and drumming under the northern lights. In modernizing Scandinavia, the "problem" of the Sámi, often called "the Lapp question," would grow increasingly intertwined with notions of racial and cultural hierarchies. Where did the Sámi come from? Where did they fit into Scandinavian history and culture? Were they a race apart, a primitive society at an earlier stage of civilization, destined to fade away? Or were they an active, political threat to Nordic nationalism, to settlement, to the new industries and transportation systems, a people to be controlled, segregated, or forcibly assimilated? How Sámi objects were collected, described, stored, and displayed, beginning in the second half of the nineteenth century, the so-called golden age of museums, is part of the history of the Sámi within and apart from Scandinavia. Yet, as the nineteenth century came to a close and the twentieth century began, another story emerges of agency, resistance, and creative renewal. It's the story of how the Sámi began to contest discrimination and to work together, individually, and at times with collectors and allies, to preserve and reinvent their material and intellectual culture.

By the closing years of the twentieth century, Lapland would have become Sápmi.

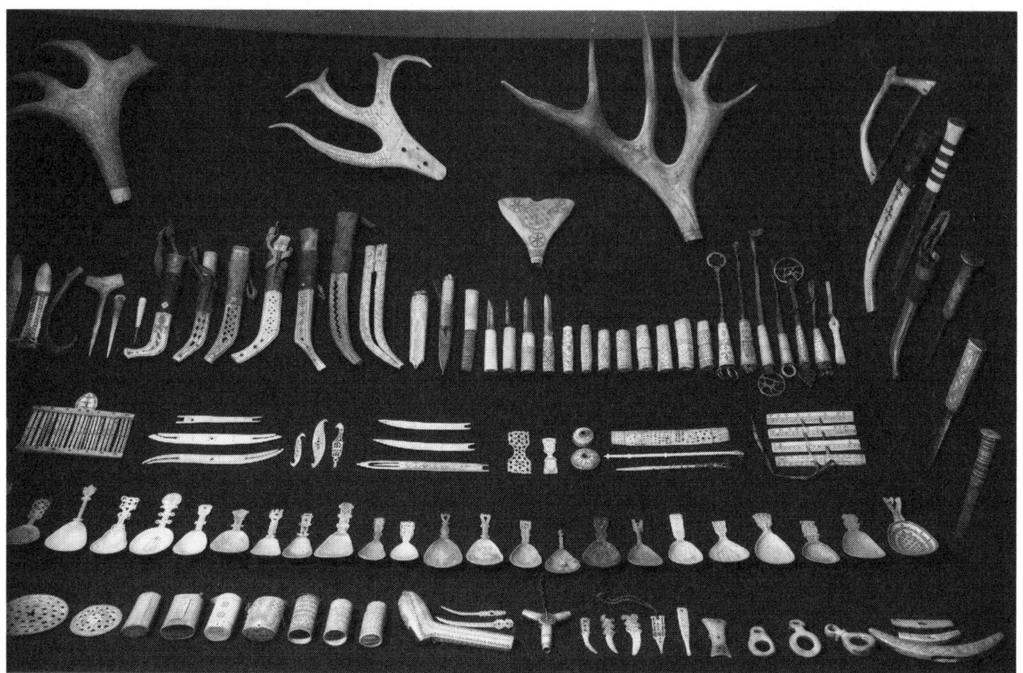

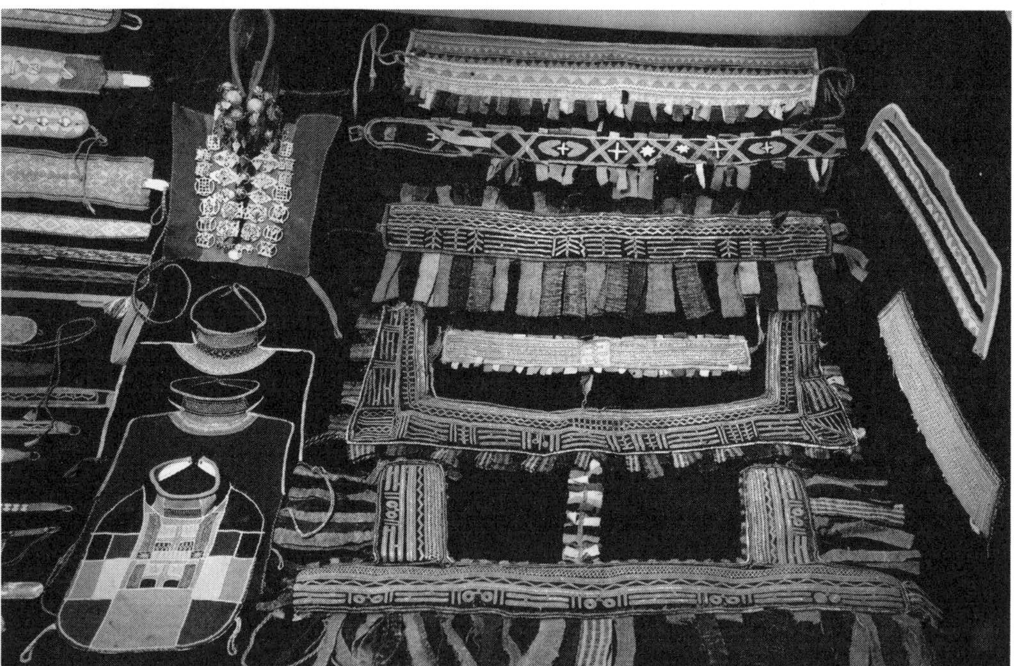

Sámi *duodji* displayed in the 1947 exhibition *Lapparna* at the Nordic Museum in Stockholm. The upper case displays male or "hard handicrafts," and the lower case shows female or "soft handicrafts." Photographs by Lennart Nenkler. Courtesy of the Nordic Museum, Stockholm.

PART II
Collecting

A Model Prisoner

On a promontory high above the entrance of Oslo's harbor, a stone fortress has stood for over seven hundred years. The original Akershus Festning was finished in 1300 by Haakon V, son of Magnus the Lawmender and Ingeborg of Denmark. The growing city that Akershus protected was partially destroyed by a fire in 1624. When reconstruction commenced, the city was renamed Christiania, in honor of the Danish king Christian IV, who rebuilt the fortress in the style of a Renaissance castle, with turrets and towers. In years to come the fortress complex took on other purposes than protecting the city's harbor; it was variously a royal residence and a prison called the "Slavery," as well as the headquarters of the Ministry of Defense. It was surrendered to the occupying German forces in 1940. The Norwegian traitor Vidkun Quisling was executed on its grounds after the war. The buildings now house the Armed Forces Museum, the Resistance Museum, and the Royal Mausoleum. It has been a symbol of the Norwegian capital for centuries.

To Lars Jakobsen Hætta, a young Sámi man from Kautokeino who arrived in Christiania as a convicted criminal in 1856, Akershus was a prison: stone cold in winter, damp the rest of the year. A place of beatings and poor food, where prisoners died of malnourishment and ill health and hopelessness. The seven Sámi men sent to Akershus from a prison in Trondheim came at the request of an unmarried scholar devoted to his studies of Finno–Ugric languages, especially Sámi languages. His name was J. A. Friis, and he built a good part of his career on intellectual relationships with Sámi prisoners, particularly young Lars Hætta, who had been tried and found guilty, along with his older brother, Aslak Hætta, of taking part in a bloody uprising in Kautokeino over the course of two days in November 1852.

The story of the rebellion in Kautokeino, a Sámi village with a church, a trading post, and a few scattered wooden houses on the Finnmark Plateau, had its beginnings a decade before, when a Swedish–Sámi pastor initiated a religious revival within the state Swedish Church. Lars Levi Læstadius, born into poverty outside Arjeplog in Pite Sápmi in 1800, managed to get an education and obtain a degree in theology from Uppsala University. Most of his career as a Lutheran clergyman took place in northern Sweden. He was unusual for the time in that he knew and could preach in Finnish and two Sámi languages, Pite Sámi and North Sámi. In 1844 on an inspection tour to Åsele, he encountered a woman who told him of her spiritual awakening. This sparked a change in Læstadius's own life, and his sermons took on a different tone. He spoke directly to the Sámi using examples from the scriptures that echoed their own experiences with dishonest merchants, sheriffs, and priests. He told them about a more caring God, a God who wanted them to rouse themselves, to save themselves, to live better, purer lives with God-given energy and far less drinking. The revivalist movement that resulted would come to be called Læstadianism.

Many Sámi in Finnmark were initially wary of the first wave of "the Awakened," who showed their faith by jumping, shouting, and preaching hellfire and damnation—in rousing group meetings that would later come to define the sect as it took firm hold in northern Norway and Sweden. But others in the scattered and colonized villages of Finnmark welcomed the revival for social and political reasons as well as spiritual ones. The local sheriff in Kautokeino, Lars Lohan Bucht, along with a trader named Carl John Ruth, had no use for the herders except as customers for liquor sales. As alcoholism grew widespread, with the subsequent loss of reindeer that were sold or seized in payment for food and drink, many Sámi began to suspect that these men, along with the government and the Church, were conspiring to destroy traditional Sámi life and steal their means of subsistence. Protests to the Church officials were ineffective. By 1851, Sámi activists, inspired by Læstadian beliefs, took matters into their own hands.[1]

Lars Jakobsen Hætta, or Jáhkoš-Lasse (the son of Jacob), was born in 1834, one of six siblings whose parents died when he was in his early teens. He inherited a few reindeer, but his future was made uncertain by poverty. He had a little schooling and lived with members of his family. Two of his three brothers, Mathis and Aslak, were jailed for months beginning in 1851 after protesting in churches in Kautokeino and Skjervøy. Mathis was still in prison in Trondheim when Aslak was released and returned to Kautokeino to find that Sheriff Bucht was threatening to confiscate his reindeer for nonpayment of fines. By now a confirmed Læstadian given to shouting that he was chosen by God, Aslak organized a group of thirty-five men and women from Kautokeino, including his eighteen-year-old brother Lars, and they began a series of protests that culminated in a march on the church at Kautokeino on November 8, 1852. They punished the new pastor, Fredrik Hvoslef, by beating him and then moved on to Sheriff Bucht, attacking him and stabbing him to death. When the merchant Ruth arrived to stop them, they killed him as well and burned his shop.

Not all Sámi people were happy about the violence and looting that followed, and many, along with the inhabitants of a nearby village, were moved to counterattack the Læstadian rebels. Eventually Aslak Hætta and his followers were arrested by the authorities and sent to Alta for a trial. Two of them, Mons Somby and Aslak Hætta, were sentenced to death and beheaded two years later. Along with several others, Aslak's younger brother Lars was also sentenced to death for his part in the murder of Bucht. Because of his young age, his sentence was commuted to life imprisonment with hard labor. He was packed off, along with other male and female rebels, to prison in Trondheim.

Several years after the bloody event, Lars Hætta, Anders Bær, and five other men were transferred from Trondheim to Akershus Fortress in Christiania on the request of Professor Friis. Friis was at the time working on a grammar of Sámi, "as spoken in Finnmark," and other projects. His plan was to teach two of the more promising prisoners, Hætta and Bær, to read and write in Norwegian and North Sámi in exchange for their assistance. When Hætta proved capable of translation, Friis set him to work on the New Testament for an edition in North Sámi. Eventually the professor would encourage Bær and Hætta to write memoirs of their lives. These two accounts—*muitalusat,* from the singular *muitalus,* meaning "account" or "history"—were some of the first preserved texts written in the North Sámi language.

The men were not the first Sámi prisoners that Professor Friis had worked with. In 1851 he had requested the presence of two Sámi men convicted of theft, Peder Rik and Nils Karasjok, and they were transferred from Trondheim to the capital. The following year, in 1852, Friis had petitioned for two other Sámi convicts to be transferred from Trondheim to Christiania Prison. One of them was Lars's brother Mathis Hætta, and the other was Rasmus Rasmussen Spein, another young man in his twenties and a fierce Læstadian. Christiania Prison, unlike the "Slavery" at Akershus, was a penitentiary in the center of the city where both men and women were imprisoned for lesser crimes: begging, homelessness, theft of bread to feed themselves and their children. Both Rasmus Spein and

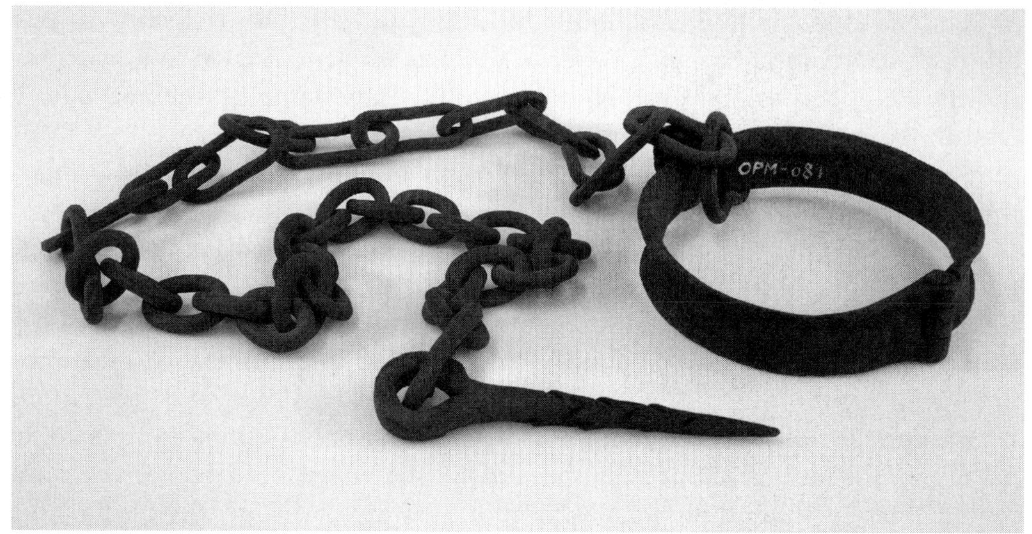

Shackles used in the arrest of the Kautokeino rebels, 1852. Courtesy of the Norwegian National Museum of Justice.

Mathis Hætta refused to work with Friis. Spein died in Christiania six months after arriving there, while the uncooperative Mathis was eventually returned to Trondheim.

His younger brother Lars would prove more tractable and would, in fact, become Friis's most trusted collaborator, a relationship forged in prison with religious overtones. Although Friis's letters to Lars Hætta no longer exist, Friis kept those sent by the younger man, beginning in the late 1850s. The early letters brim with humble thanks for Friis's goodness to all the prisoners. "For we will never manage to return the gift," Hætta wrote. "For me it is often very hard to have to beg so many things from you for free. Because I was never used to that and when I had my freedom I didn't need to ask or beg anything from other people."[2] Hætta would never stop thanking Friis for his help. Even though in the future Hætta would begin to recognize his own value, he could not fully acknowledge how much Professor Friis benefited from his Indigenous knowledge and language skills.[3]

Jens Andreas Friis was born in the fjord country of Sogn in 1821, but his scholarly interests lay farther north. During his university studies in Christiania in the 1840s he discovered Finnish and Sámi, and although he graduated with a degree in theology, his real passion was for Finno–Ugric languages and folklore. With a stipend he traveled in 1849 to Finland to study with Elias Lönnrot, a medical doctor and the founder of folklore studies in Finland. Friis made his first trip to Finnmark in 1850. He was a fisherman, hunter, and hiker, with a balding pate and a neatly trimmed beard and glasses. He was said to have loved and lost a sweetheart in his youth and to have had a child with his housekeeper in Oslo, but a bachelor he remained.

Before Friis became a full professor of the Sámi and Finnish languages in 1866 at the university, those languages were only taught occasionally, mainly to clergymen destined for parishes in northern Norway. The initial dictionaries were created for these pastors, so that they could communicate with their congregations. Friis based his grammar book and his first dictionary, both published in 1856, on earlier efforts by Nils Stockfleth, his older mentor at the university.[4] Posted to Vadsø in the far north of Norway, Stockfleth took an interest in the Sámi's souls, which led to an interest in linguistics. He didn't believe that Sámi children should be forced to learn Norwegian; it was better they read Bible studies in North Sámi to get the full benefit of Christian teaching. During a teaching stint in Kautokeino in the 1840s, he used his own pamphlets to try to teach Sámi children the word of God in their own language.

Stockfleth was an irascible man who showed his anger at students who couldn't spell or read by knocking them about the head with a copy of the New Testament, as Anders Bær recorded in the memoir of his childhood. One of the boys about to be thumped left his place in line and hid in a corner of the schoolroom, hoping to avoid punishment. "But the pastor came over to where the impossible boy had been standing, and went through the line to him and hit him and said, 'The same goes for you!'" Stockfleth also raised his stick and chased out of the classroom an older woman who wanted to listen to his lessons.[5]

When Stockfleth retired from the university, Friis took his place teaching clergymen the rudiments of Sámi in preparation for their mission work in Finnmark. Although Norway had three main Sámi languages—South Sámi, in the areas around Røros and Trondheim; Lule Sámi, in the fjord and mountain areas around Bodø and the Saltfjord; and North Sámi, the most widely spoken, in Troms and Finnmark—Friis concentrated largely on the North Sámi–speaking population. He created an orthography for the language that is still in use, though modified by three spelling reforms.

For Friis it was essential to have Sámi people to listen to and talk with. It was a welcome opportunity for his studies that he was able to help bring prisoners from the core language region of Finnmark to Akershus Fortress. After creating his initial dictionary and grammar book in 1856, Friis would go on in 1887 to publish an 868-page "Lappish dictionary" with definitions in Norwegian and Latin and a grammatical overview.[6] But Friis never limited himself to linguistics. As the foremost interpreter of Sámi life and culture, he eventually had an influence on most aspects of how the Sámi were seen by the majority of Norwegians, in scholarly publications and literary representations and not least in how Sápmi was collected and displayed.

Friis was working on his "Lappish grammar and dictionary" in 1854, the same year that the Crystal Palace exhibition hall opened in Sydenham, an affluent suburb in South London. The original structure of cast iron and plate glass was constructed in Hyde Park for the Great Exhibition of 1851. The exhibits displayed everything from British and European industrial goods to domestic belongings; raw materials, fabrics, and clothing; and artifacts and art from all around the globe, many from countries within the British Empire. Six million visitors came from May to October 1851, and the event was considered such a success that the Crystal Palace buildings were disassembled and reconstructed as a permanent exhibition space in South London and ethnographic exhibits were planned. Included among the representations of Indigenous people from elsewhere was to be a small exhibit from Lapland.[7]

The curator of the ethnology department of the new Crystal Palace exhibit hall in Sydenham was Robert Gordon Latham. A Cambridge man, Latham in his younger years traveled to Germany and Denmark to study philology before heading to Norway. Afterward, in 1840, he published *Norway and the Norwegians*. He had a favorable opinion of the country—except for the Sámi inhabitants. He seems to have met only a few, including one who was learning to become a carpenter in Christiania. But, in general, Latham had the fixed opinion that Laplanders were savages. "Few of them sow and reap," he wrote, and many were "lazy, suspicious, and drunks. All this I write from report. The Norwegian government deserves all credit for trying to raise the degraded national character of these stunted Hyperboreans."[8]

Robert Latham may not have met J. A. Friis, but he did get to know Friis's older cousin Ludwig Daa during his visit to Christiania. He wrote to Daa in 1853 to ask for his help in gathering and sending Sámi artifacts for the Crystal Palace. Ludwig Daa was a man of many parts: a politician, a newspaper editor, and a professor of history. To satisfy Latham's request, he turned to Friis, who put together two sets of Sámi objects from his travels and from purchases from agents

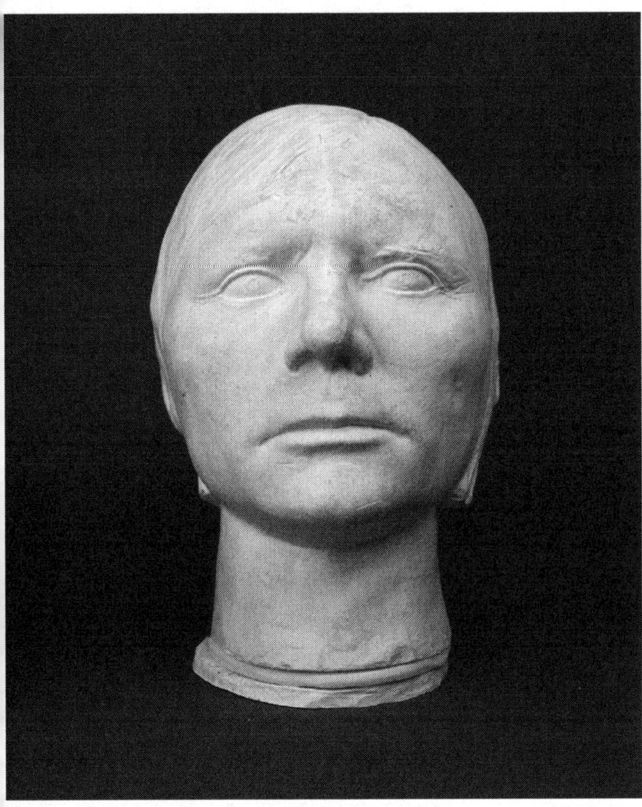

Mathis Hætta, portrait head in plaster, cast in the 1850s at the Christiania (Oslo) Prison, where he was imprisoned with others from Sápmi. Photograph by Mette Bing Espedal. Courtesy of the University Museum of Bergen.

and traders. One set was to be for the Crystal Palace. The other set was to be for an ethnographic museum, to be located in rooms at the new university building under construction in central Christiania. The items collected by Friis were largely clothing (fur coats and trousers, tunics, belts, and boots), along with a sled, harnesses, and smaller domestic belongings. But the collection also contained three plaster casts of the heads of the Sámi convicts in Christiania Prison—Peder Rik, Nils Karasjok, and Mathis Hætta—from which multiples had been made, apparently on the request of Latham.

By the middle of the nineteenth century, Christiania had a population of around thirty-two thousand, a university that was established in 1811, a theater in 1827, and a national art collection in 1836—all created on Danish models. There were newspapers, a commercial sector, a stock exchange, and banks. A railway from Christiania to Eidsvoll was constructed in 1854, and other lines would follow. New Norwegian institutions had also begun to spring up, including the

Christiania Norwegian Theater, whose first director was Henrik Ibsen. Norway's first ethnographic museum opened in 1857 and consisted of three small rooms on the top floor of the main university building. Its initial collection was meager: when the first museum catalog was published, there were only 197 items listed, about a quarter of them sent in trade from Robert Latham. It rankled some Norwegians that, like so many things Norway was trying to establish in the mid-1800s, the new museum with its cramped attic rooms, hot in the summer and freezing in the winter, was but a weak copy of Denmark's Ethnographic Museum. Established in 1849, replete with choice items from the Royal Kunstkammer, the museum in Copenhagen was said to hold the finest ethnographic collection in the world.

In 1862 Ludwig Daa took over as director of Norway's Ethnographic Museum. The first thing he had to do was throw out a number of moth-eaten furs from Sápmi. He then attempted to organize the collections by geographic area and to add to them through purchases from different regions of Norway, including Sápmi. One of his acquisitions was around twenty objects collected by District Sheriff Abraham Brun from Nesseby on the Varanger Fjord. In the summer of 1870, Brun had participated in a large exposition held in Tromsø, where Norwegian and Sámi objects were displayed, including clothing, sleds, skis, toys, and various models of boats and houses, made by both Sea Sámi and Mountain Sámi (Plates 4 and 5). A few years later Brun brought his collection with its Sea Sámi objects south to another exposition in Drammen, near Oslo, and Daa bought it for the museum. According to Yngvar Nielsen, a later director who published a history of the museum in 1907, most of Brun's objects had little ethnographic value, given that they were created expressly for the Tromsø Exposition. In the 1870s, public and professional interest in the Sea Sámi, who lived a settled life fishing and farming along the many fjords of northern Norway, was greater than it would be later, when items connected with reindeer herding were far more likely to be prized and displayed in Norwegian museums. In 1874, in a corner of the university's garden, Daa even had constructed a small replica of a farm with turf dwellings of the type associated with the Sea Sámi.[9]

Yngvar Nielsen's history of the Ethnographic Museum portrayed Ludwig Daa working hard to expand the collection by traveling to London and Amsterdam to arrange exchanges of objects and make purchases. Daa wanted the museum to contain all human races, including the Scandinavian race. Nielsen disapproved of this; he later blamed Daa for not separating the European (i.e., Norwegian) objects from the primitive ones. When Nielsen took charge in 1877, he also traveled but concentrated largely on the Norwegian countryside, gathering painted wooden chests and carved chairs. Many of these would become part of the Norwegian Museum of Cultural History (Norsk Folkemuseum), founded at the end of the nineteenth century.[10] Most of the Sámi objects would remain part of the university's ethnographic collection until the 1950s, but some were traded away for other exotic treasures, which is partly how Sámi artifacts from Norway made their way to museums abroad. One of the more unusual collections of Sámi objects consisted of around 160 miniature models of Sámi domestic items created by one of the prisoners at Akershus Fortress, Lars Jakobsen Hætta.

Lars Hætta described himself as "a thirteen-year-old, miserable, orphan boy" when he encountered followers of the teachings of Lars Levi Læstadius, those known as "the Awakened," for the first time in Kautokeino in the fall of 1847. "And I saw that they were neat, pale people, and that they looked serious. I also noticed that people were afraid to ask them about anything and barely chose to speak with them." All that winter Læstadianism moved through Finnmark, attracting more attention and more adherents, many of whom were angry about the "bad habits," especially drunkenness and fighting, that had become frequent among the Sámi. "The Awakened" tried to intervene and often said to the drunks and quarrelers, "Think, think about the eternal suffering in hell, which is where you'll be going if you don't turn over a new leaf."[11]

After Lars's parents died, the younger children were farmed out to relatives and elder siblings, some of whom had started families of their own. He had an interest in learning and managed to attend school in Kautokeino when it was in session. He did not learn how to read or write much, but he was instructed in the basics of the Gospel. Like most adolescents, he was searching for identity. He was under the sway of older family members, including his older brothers Mathis and Aslak, both of whom had become radicalized, personally and politically, by the Læstadian movement. Lars Hætta never wrote about the terrible day and night in November 1852, but the events in which he played a role were described vividly by Sophus Tromholt, a Norwegian scientist and photographer. Tromholt, who spent a winter in Kautokeino in 1884, wrote a long book in two volumes, *Under the Rays of the Aurora Borealis.* One chapter, "The Reign of Terror in Lapland," is devoted to the episodes leading up to and including the Kautokeino Uprising, which though "mere dry facts . . . reads more like the ravings of a diseased mind."[12] Tromholt's main informant was Pastor Stockfleth, who naturally disapproved of the "confused ideas of Law and Government" held

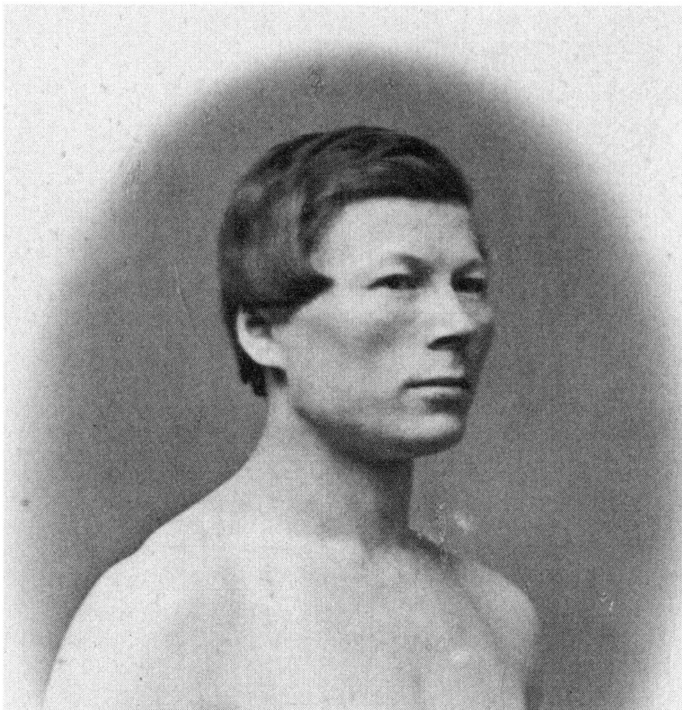

Lars Hætta, photographed at Akershus Fortress, Oslo, circa 1860. Photograph by Adolf Christian Moestue. Courtesy of the Cultural History Museum, University of Oslo.

by the rebels, "which prevented them seeing that those who acted against them in such a severe manner were solely stimulated by the purest motives."[13]

Tromholt also had access to the court records, however, so at least part of his lurid tale is based on "dry facts." Perhaps the scene of Aslak commanding his younger brother Lars to "commit the deed," since his own knife was too blunt, and of Lars taking his knife to Sheriff Bucht's already much battered and stabbed body and hammering the knife "into the hilt with his staff" is too dramatic, given that Tromholt certainly wasn't there, but no one denied that Bucht was violently murdered and that Lars gave the final blow that killed him.[14]

Lars came to Akershus at age twenty-two. The one photograph of him taken in prison shows him in three-quarter profile, clean-shaven, with a bare chest. He seems to glance warily at the photographer from the corner of his eye. While photographs of undressed Sámi people became more common, especially in Sweden in the 1920s and 1930s during the "scientific" investigations performed by certain eugenicists at the State Institute for Racial Biology in Uppsala, this camera view was unusual for its time. In the second half of the nineteenth century,

Sámi men, women, and children were usually photographed fully clothed, very often in heavy fur clothing, the better to show off their exotic ethnicity. Perhaps this photograph was the preliminary step to a plaster cast, like those made of Mathis Hætta and the two other prisoners.

By the time Lars Hætta arrived at Akershus, he had been jailed in one way or another for several years in harsh conditions in Alta and Trondheim. He knew that his brother Aslak and Mons Somby had been executed. By this time, as is clear from later writings, he experienced deep and abiding remorse for his part in the murders of Bucht and Ruth. Most likely Hætta attempted to control his fate as best he could. If that meant assisting Professor Friis with language issues, definitions, and cultural history—and eventually being excused from hard labor in favor of revising and continuing on with Niels Stockfleth's partial translation of the New Testament—he accepted it. In the process, he turned himself into one of the first Sámi writers and translators, as well as an Indigenous cultural broker.

Most of the intellectual work that Lars Hætta performed for Friis during his prison years was in exchange for learning Norwegian and Sámi, as well as in expiation for his sins, but Friis set Hætta on another task that gave him more latitude for creating something of his own. The Sámi models that Hætta produced in the late 1850s were miniatures of objects in daily use among reindeer-herding families in Finnmark: bowls, barrels, spoons, cups, cheese molds, cradles, skis, ski poles, reindeer saddles, and oval chests. Most of them had no moving parts, such as lids that opened. No sharp knives were included, though there was a small axe and a shovel. The objects were usually only a few inches long, but not uniformly scaled. A sled was the same size as a *lokke giisá,* or lidded chest, for example. There seem to have been no drums, hammers, or *sieidis,* natural objects of stone or wood used in ritual worship and sacrifice ceremonies. The objects were rarely decorated, and they displayed no obvious personal touches like initials or symbols.

Along with the miniatures were several larger objects: tents made of cloth and sticks, with a door that opened, and an array of tiny belongings that went with it. Sometimes the tent was placed on a board, with a figure of a man and perhaps a dog and a reindeer (Plate 16). Lars Hætta also carved and painted wooden reindeer, including their antlers, and fitted them with colorful braided harnesses. Many of the small-scale models appear to have been used for teaching the clergymen going north what to expect in Finnmark among their new parishioners. The miniatures had labels in Sámi and sometimes in Norwegian pasted on or attached by wire. Some fitted into carrying cases, perhaps for easy transportation to a classroom. But the painted reindeer and the tent scenes may have been created or used

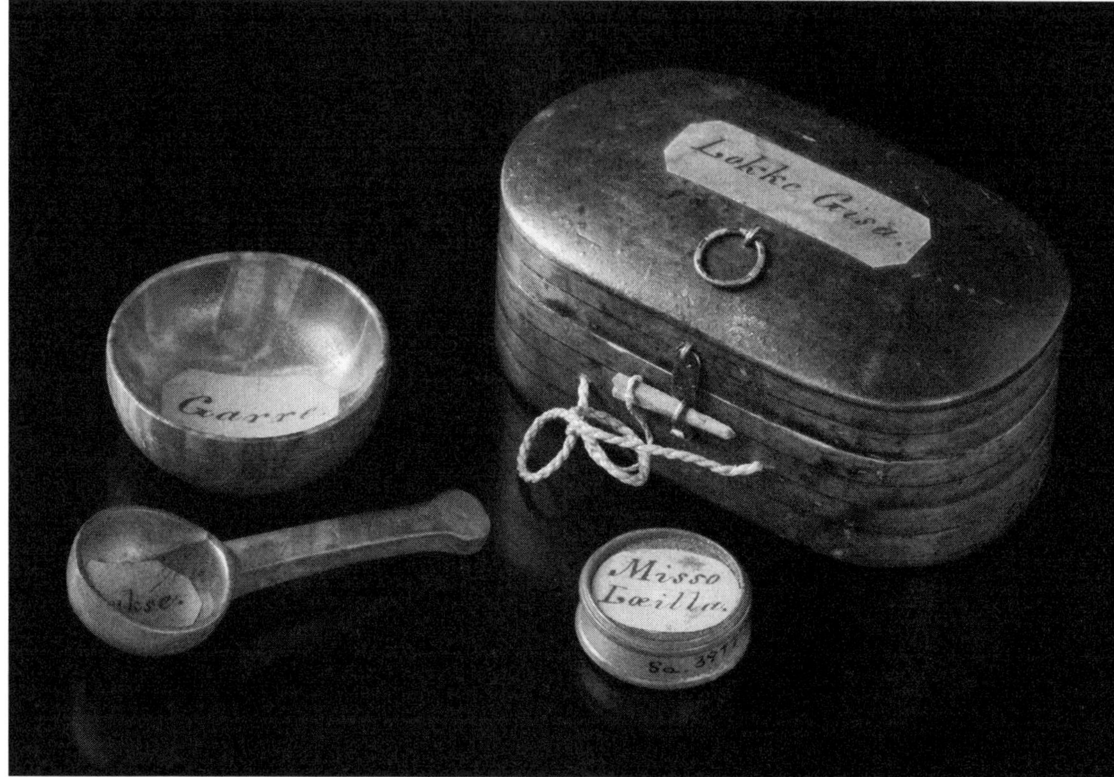

Miniatures created by Lars Hætta while he was in prison, circa 1860. The miniatures were later sold and traded in Europe for ethnographic objects for the Ethnographic Museum in Oslo. Photograph by Anne-Lise Reinsfelt. Courtesy of the Norwegian Museum of Cultural History.

for another purpose—as a means of exchange or sale. The whole collection was purchased in 1860 by the University of Oslo, but it was never cataloged for the Ethnographic Museum, and ultimately a number of the miniatures went elsewhere. The collection would not presumably have been purchased from Hætta himself, nor were the objects tagged with his name when they were further sold or exchanged outside Norway. The only descriptor of their maker was "convict" or "Lappish prisoner."

To carve many of the objects from wood and to cut string and cloth, Lars Hætta would have needed a knife; it's unlikely he was left alone with a sharp object, so he must have been watched as he whittled and trimmed cloth for the tent. He would have also needed to cut minute pieces of leather, reindeer pelt, and sinew thread or rope. In the Akershus "Slavery" the prisoners did not have their own cells but rather lived and slept in large common rooms. It's possible that Hætta worked on his translations and on his model objects in such a common room, but since the prison also had workshops, he may well have used the tools available there. The question remains: Where did he and Friis meet to discuss the finer points of North Sámi syntax and grammar? It's not likely that a professor would have enjoyed visiting the cold jail cell shared by the Sámi prisoners.

During the time of their imprisonment at Akershus Fortress, three of the seven Sámi men died. One perished by drowning in the sea, where the prisoners went to bathe. Two others died from "weakness of the chest"—pneumonia perhaps or tuberculosis. While Hætta, as Friis's informant and collaborator, was allowed to avoid hard labor, the others were sent out into the city in their prison uniforms, always in shackles that clanked with every step they took, which sometimes caused foreigners to the Norwegian capital to write that the treatment of the Akershus prisoners was barbaric. Hard labor was usually stonework or construction; in the 1820s and 1830s, for example, the "slaves" worked to even out the hill on which the royal palace was to be built.[15]

Beginning around 1861, Friis and Daa began petitioning for the remaining Sámi prisoners to be pardoned and released early. Finally, the state agreed to allow three of the prisoners to return home. One of them was Anders Bær, who was released in 1863. Although Bær, like Lars Hætta, had learned to read and write and had obliged Friis by composing an autobiographic narrative in North Sámi, he, unlike Hætta, had continued to perform hard labor during the day. Sometimes, he later told his son, he couldn't write in the cell at night because his hands were too cold. Bær's account gives a picture of Sámi life in the mid-nineteenth century in Finnmark, a valuable source for historians. It was valuable at the time as well, and Friis browsed freely through Bær's work when creating his own descriptions in later books. After Bær returned to Finnmark in 1863, he reunited with his family and apparently had nothing further to do with Friis.

But Lars Hætta, because of his life sentence for murder, lived, worked, and slept in Akershus Fortress until 1867, the only Sámi prisoner left by the end. That year, in May, he was pardoned and released with the stipulation that he accompany J. A. Friis and his cousin Ludwig Daa on their journey north that summer. This stipulation may have been the way Friis managed to free Hætta, but certainly Friis also benefited from making Hætta their guide. The journey began in Vadsø, where they took on a second guide, who was fluent in Russian. After exploring the Sámi and Kven communities on the Varanger Fjord, the group set off east along the coast and then south along the Kola River to document the lives and language of the Finns, Sámi, and Karelians who lived in these regions. At the end of the journey, they went their separate ways. Friis traveled south to Helsinki for six months to further research the languages and history of North Karelia and Russian Finland; Daa returned to Christiania; and Lars Hætta was finally allowed to make his way back to his home in Kautokeino after fifteen years in some form of captivity.

By 1867, the Kautokeino Uprising was only a memory, though a still vivid one, of a time when "the Awakened" rebelled against what seemed to be the collusion of Church and state. The Norwegian–Swedish union had attempted to strengthen its control and assert the state religion by building a new church and school in Kautokeino. Although the Læstadian sect would remain the dominant form of worship among the Sámi in northern Norway, Finland, and Sweden, among outsiders the moniker "Læstadian" was generally preceded by the adjective "fanatical." The rebels of 1852, those who had not been executed or had not died in prison, had trickled back to Kautokeino, including Berit Hansdatter Gaup, who had spent twelve years as a convict in Trondheim.

Gaup and Lars Hætta married and began their life as a couple in their thirties with few possessions and no reindeer. They eventually had six children, including twins, whom they struggled to support. Lars tried fishing at sea and building up a small herd but struggled with reindeer thieves and wolves. He had hoped to teach, but wasn't allowed to do so because of his criminal record. Instead, Lars Hætta's skill as a translator, for Professor Friis and the Norwegian Bible Society, became one of the family's main sources of income, and it meant that Hætta and Friis would continue to correspond and cooperate for many years.

Hætta had started at Akershus by translating psalms and sermons into North Sámi, but as his Norwegian improved, he moved on to the Bible. His translation of the New Testament came out in 1874. He completed a North Sámi translation of the Old Testament in 1876, under contract to the Norwegian Bible Society, an organization that seems to have had financial problems and was often late in paying him. It may not have made things easier that payment from the Norwegian Bible Society was administered by Bishop Hvoslef of Tromsø—the same clergyman who had been publicly beaten during the uprising. While Lars Hætta had some income from his translation work, he was sometimes ill and tired, and reindeer thieves stole his animals when he couldn't watch them properly. He wrote to his "Dear Teacher" or "My Dear Teacher and Friend" from Finnmark, always grateful but often trying to explain the ways in which life was difficult. The letters, which at the beginning had been full of humility and gratitude, were more businesslike as the years passed. Though Hætta still asked about his friend's health and offered sympathy when needed, he also inquired about further translation work and mentioned his challenges of obtaining payment for the work he had done.

Norwegian was the colonizer's language, learned in prison, but for Hætta it was also a meal ticket, the only one he had. It's possible that he didn't particularly like the Norwegian language. At one point in his memoir he compared *davvisámegiella,* or North Sámi, "a soft, flexible" language with many long words, to Norwegian, which was "stiff and hard, an impoverished, curt, and jumpy language."[16] The word that Hætta uses for "jumpy"—*byksende*—comes from an older Norse expression meaning "to jump like a goat." Anyone familiar with both languages can see some truth in this. Norwegian can be poetic, but there's a sharp briskness in the one- and two-syllable words that begin with hard consonants: *knut* (knot), *gate* (street), and *trekke* (to pull). Longer compound Norwegian words also use plenty of hard *g*'s, *k*'s, and *t*'s, such as *knekkebrød* (crackers) and *knausgård* (rocky farm). The vowels in North Sámi are soft and drawn out, and the consonants are sibilant or slightly plosive, for example, *s, šš, ž,* and *đ.* Even the *k* sound is softer in Sámi, for example, *joik* and *johka* (river), with the emphasis on the drawn-out vowels.

The syntax of Norwegian is similar to that of English: subject, verb, and object, with similar adverbs and prepositions. But Sámi, with case endings for all nouns and pronouns that affect prepositions and verbs, has a different rhythm and variable syntax, along with more prepositions and postpositions, many having to do with ways of moving from place to place. The locative case so frequent in Sámi sentences is surprisingly adaptive. Aside from its use locating a noun (a person, animal, or thing) "at" or "in" a place, it is often used in possessive sentences. In Norwegian and English, one says, *Jeg har en hund,* or "I have a dog." In North Sámi one says, *Mus lea beana,* or "A dog is in my vicinity."

Although both Anders Bær and Lars Hætta created written records, it appears that only Bær's account was fully composed at Akershus. Hætta's account was written later in Kautokeino. His work has less direct autobiography compared to Bær's and much more reflection about the state of religion and morality in Sámi culture after Christianity was first introduced and before the Læstadian movement came along. In this telling, there was little positive about life in Sápmi over the last two centuries. Instead it was all sin.

> To put it briefly: alcoholism, thieving, fornication, coarse speech, shameless talk, quarreling, disputatiousness, cursing, worldliness, lust for money and goods, and miserliness that makes one complain about too much food and meat being consumed. These were the most usual and general major sins that beset the Sámi and caused the greatest damage, unhappiness, conflict, and lack of harmony among them, in soul and body.[17]

According to Hætta, the reason for this way of life was lack of Christian teaching for Sámi children and the fact that many pastors sent up to Sápmi were unable to preach in Sámi. The languages generally used were Norwegian for the Sámi living on the coasts and Finnish for the reindeer herders residing inland. He believed that only when Niels Stockfleth published Bible stories in Sámi in 1840 did the situation improve, though idolatry, drunkenness, cursing, and fornication unfortunately continued. Hætta's short account in North Sámi, which only goes up to the year 1848, was likely written either only for Friis or for Friis to demonstrate to the authorities how the prisoner had reformed and become a productive Christian member of society. Whether the text reflects the extent of Hætta's beliefs and preoccupations isn't known, but there's no reason to believe that Hætta had not become a true believer in the Gospel. The account wasn't published until 1927, in a translation by another Norwegian clergyman and philologist, Just Knud Qvigstad. The writing (in a new translation published in 2019) shows power and style, with novelistic turns of phrase and description.

Some of Anders Bær's and Lars Hætta's descriptions and stories were repeated by Friis in the books he began to write for scholars and the general public, stories and travel tales that became popular in his lifetime, at least one of which, the novel *Laila,* had an afterlife long into the twentieth century. In 1871, Friis published *A Summer in Finnmark, Russian Lapland, and North Karelia.*[18] The title was misleading; as he admits in his foreword, he spent little time in Finnmark that year. Having been there twice before, he was eager to press eastward while the days were long and light. As a result, the Finnmark section was more of a mishmash of statistics and texts from "published and unpublished sources" (the unpublished sources were often noted as "a mountain-Lapp") about language, religion, and reindeer herding. Friis's information on herding seems cribbed from Anders Bær's detailed descriptions of nomadic life in his memoir, and at least one story told by Lars Hætta in his memoir appears in Friis's text. This is the tale of Garra-Rásttoš ("Tough Rasmus"), or Rasmus Andersen Spein, who kept on with some pagan practices of sacrificing to a *sieidi* to ensure his reindeer herd flourished. In his travel narrative, Friis tells in similar language this same story, now about a Sámi man named "Rastus."[19]

A Summer in Finnmark, Russian Lapland, and North Karelia was not the only book Friis published in 1871. Substantial as it was, it was nothing compared to the doorstopper in two volumes, *Lappish Mythology, Folktales, and Sayings.*[20] The first volume was a scholarly overview of aspects of Sámi religion and mythology, with chapters on *noaidis* and a variety of gods and other supernatural figures. Of note were illustrations of eleven drums and explications of their meanings. It was the fullest published description of drum imagery to date, and Friis relied on multiple sources for his information. In the second volume covering folktales, Friis showed a surprising change of style. Here the scholarly tone turns to storytelling. He had collected the tales from different parts of Norwegian Sápmi, it seems, over a period of years, perhaps inspired by the folklore journeys of Peder Asbjørnsen and Jørgen Moe, whose own efforts were based on the work of the Grimm Brothers, with an eye to defining the true Norwegian character, and whose stories began to be published in the 1840s. Friis's book was the first collection of Sámi folktales to come out in Scandinavia.

Ten years later, in 1881, Friis published a novel originally titled *From Finnmark.* It recounted a story of a young Norwegian couple, the Linds, who were traders in Karasjok. While taking their baby daughter in winter to Kautokeino to be baptized in the church there, the reindeer-sled caravan with two servants and the infant went astray, and they were set upon by a pack of wolves. The baby and her cradle fell out of the sled, and after a desperate search that revealed only an empty cradle, the parents returned home, convinced their daughter had been eaten by wolves. The little girl, however, was found by a Sámi servant of Aslag Laagje, a "rich Lapp" in Kautokeino who adopted her and named her Lajla. A year later Laagje, having realized the identity of the girl, traveled to Karasjok to return Lajla to the Linds, only to find out that the couple had succumbed to a plague and Lajla was now an orphan. Laagje and his wife took the girl home again and raised her to believe she was Sámi; they betrothed her to her "cousin" Mellet. But by chance Lajla met her real cousins, Ingrid and Anders Lind, handsome young Norwegians who lived on the coast. Love sprang up between Lajla and Anders, and complications ensued, until all was revealed and Lajla and Anders married.

This novel was so popular that it was translated into seven languages, including English in 1888. When a second edition of *From Finnmark* came out in 1890 in Norwegian, the title was changed to *Laila.*[21] It has an enduring place in Nordic literature and has remained in print since its first publication. Three movies have been made of *Laila*. The first and most famous is an epic silent film made by Danish–German director George Schnéevoigt in 1929 (Plate 6), which shows an athletic girl at a reindeer race, lashing her steed to first place.

On the surface, *Laila* is a simple pastoral work of fiction within the National Romantic tradition of *bondefortelling,* or "peasant tale," transposed from Norway's mountains and valleys to Finnmark. Given its spirited heroine, *Laila* is also reminiscent of a George Sand novel set in the French countryside. Beautiful, clever, emotional, and skilled at lassoing and steering a reindeer sled, Laila is a noble orphan. The novel clearly profits from its author's immersion in Sámi language and culture and from his long conversations with Lars Hætta over the years, as well as from Anders Bær's detailed explanations of herding. The novel includes set pieces about reindeer management and migration, festive yearly markets, schooling, and the importance of Sámi children being able to read Bible stories in their own language. But the twists and turns of the story involving Laila's identity and what happens when she meets the Lind siblings and grows conflicted about her life as an "ignorant Lapp girl from the mountains . . . who can do nothing, understand nothing, know nothing" are the twists and turns of Friis's own mind as he grapples with how he really feels about Sámi people, not just in the aggregate, as objects of study, but as individuals.[22]

Laila is an unusual novel for a sixty-year-old professor of Finno–Ugric languages to have written. Although a few different characters have points of view, nineteen-year-old Laila, with her light eyes and blond hair—who speaks and reads Sámi and identifies with all that is nomadic but who also picks up Norwegian easily in school and can converse in that language as well—is the core protagonist, who eventually struggles with a double consciousness. Who did Friis have in mind in describing an adolescent girl grappling with her identity and what that means for her love life and her future? Is there a tinge of homoeroticism in the scholar's fevered prose and scenes of Laila waiting in vain for Anders Lind to come to her one midnight? Or in Lind's rescue of Laila, who dangles over a frothing waterfall? Or in his declaration that he would have married Laila even though she was a Lapp! (But how wonderful it turns out she's actually Norwegian and his long-lost cousin). Is Laila really Lars, as reimagined by Friis? Certainly, Lars Hætta struggled with his own version of double consciousness, one that would follow him back to Kautokeino and mark his days.

Friis and Hætta continued corresponding off and on for many years. In the winter of 1876–77 Hætta traveled down to Christiania for five months at Friis's request to work with him on the "Lappish dictionary." Where did Hætta stay in the city—with a member of the clergy, at a boarding house for Christian men, or with Friis himself? What was it like for Hætta to see the city where he had lived for eleven years but where he hadn't been able to visit a restaurant, browse a shop, or simply walk the streets like any other person? Did he wear his Sámi clothes? Did he visit the Ethnographic Museum with Friis and Daa and perhaps look again at the miniatures he'd created so carefully years before? The historical record doesn't answer these questions. We can only wonder if he and Friis sat together in the professor's office at the university or in a café or if Friis asked him for more stories and details of life in Finnmark that he would soon incorporate into his sketches for the newspaper, which would result in the story of Laila and other tales. Did Friis ever send his collaborator the newspaper sketches or the finished book to read? Did he mention his popular writing to Hætta? There's no indication in the letters that Hætta thought of Friis as anything but a language scholar devoted to grammar and the Bible.

After this visit and Hætta's arduous journey back to Kautokeino, the two likely never saw each other again. Over the years, others in Finnmark reported on Lars Hætta, including Sophus Tromholt, the scientist who had written about the Kautokeino Uprising in his book. It seems that Tromholt was angry with what he saw as Hætta's exploitation by Friis. In 1882, he wrote an article about Hætta for a Christiania newspaper, calling Friis out, and suggested starting a public fund for the Sámi translator. Friis disputed this in his published reply in the paper: "Lars Hætta has been well paid and well recognized for the work he carried out."[23] But he agreed that there could be fundraising on the translator's behalf and in the end helped secure a government stipend for Hætta, which acknowledged his work on the New and Old Testaments. In his last ten years, Hætta worked as a church sexton.

The two men died within one day of each other but thousands of miles apart, Friis on February 16, 1896, at age seventy-five, and Hætta on February 17, 1896, at age sixty-two. In early recountings of their work together, Hætta was either ignored or described as "contributing" to Friis's work. Certainly, there was a mutual decision to collaborate and to share knowledge within an unbalanced power relationship. There was also, both consciously and unconsciously, appropriation. Friis taught Hætta to read and write both Norwegian and Sámi, and, in trade, Hætta offered Friis valuable language information for Friis's grammars and dictionaries and cultural and historical stories for his popular works. Hætta's reward was the release from a life sentence at Akershus. By most measures, Friis,

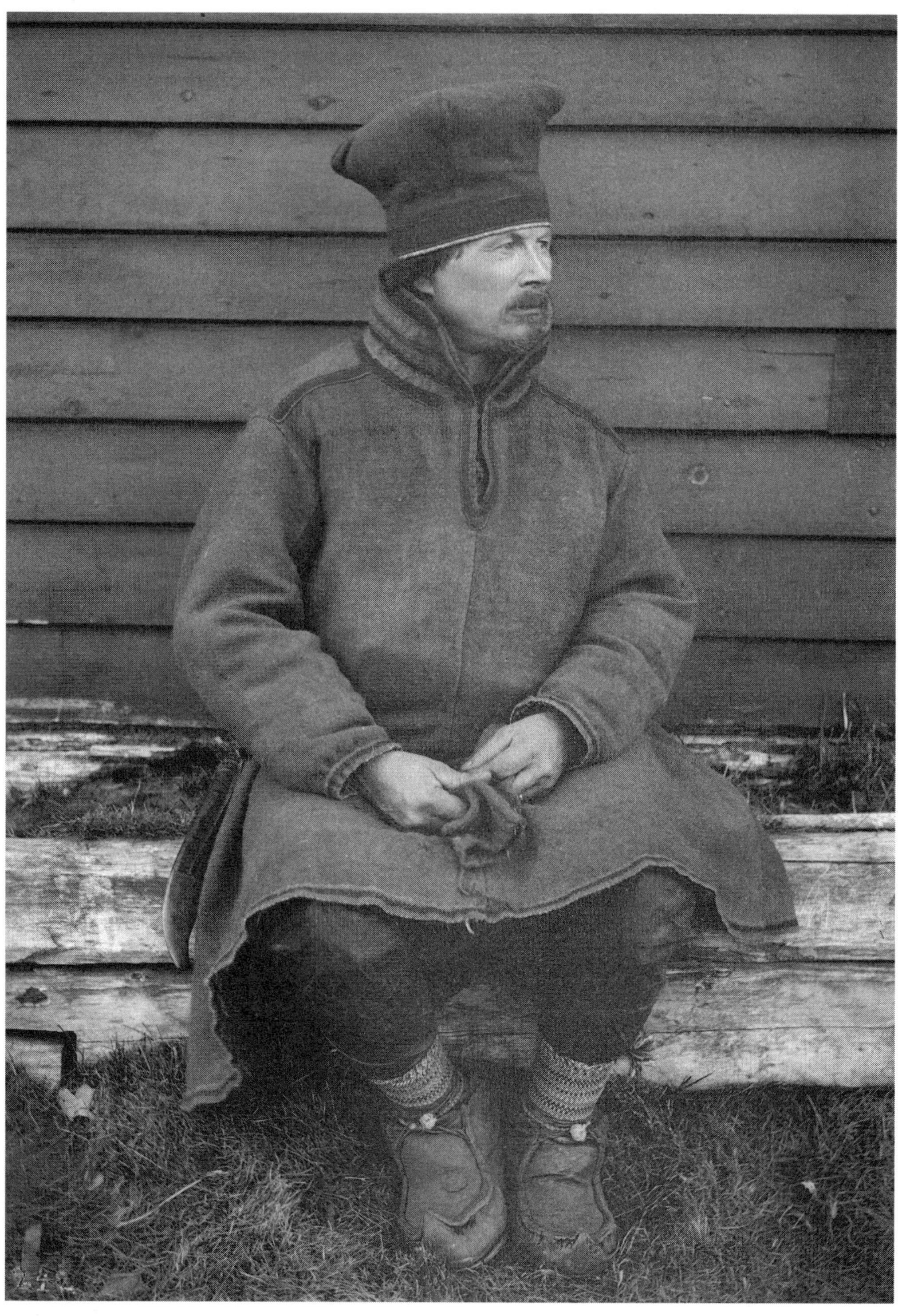

Lars Hætta, Kautokeino, Norway, 1883. Photograph by Sophus Tromholt. Courtesy of the University of Bergen Library.

a respected professor with a salary from the university and the author of many popular books, some of which earned him a handsome income, received far more from Hætta than Hætta received from him. On the other hand, Hætta didn't die in prison or starve when he returned home to Kautokeino. He had a skill, one that made life possible.

In a quiet corner of South East London lies the Horniman Museum, first established in 1890 by Frederick Horniman, scion of his father's tea business. Horniman's Tea Company, founded in 1826, was the first to fill and seal tea bags and was at one time the largest tea trading company in the world. Frederick Horniman, a Liberal MP, was a traveler who built the Victorian museum to house and display his collections from Africa, Asia, and North America; he bought objects that "either appealed to his own fancy or that seemed to him likely to interest and inform those who had not had the opportunity to visit distant lands."[24] Expanded and rebuilt, the Horniman Museum and adjacent gardens are a popular draw and now contain some 350,000 objects, including eleven small objects that originally came from Sápmi, but with no accession notes about how they arrived at the museum. For a long time, these eleven things were uncataloged, but they included a little milking bowl, a pair of skis, a sled, and a box with a false lid. Some had tiny labels in delicate copperplate script in Sámi or Norwegian.

One of the labels, *Jorbba Gisa,* pasted on to a miniature chest with two miniscule rope handles, led a member of the museum staff to contact Leif Pareli, then the curator of the Sámi department at the Norwegian Museum of Cultural History in Oslo. Pareli said the object was a model of a *giisá,* or chest that was usually attached to a pack saddle, one of several models made by Lars Hætta in the late 1850s. The Oslo museum held thirty-six of them and a record of provenance. They'd been transferred from the Ethnographic Museum in the 1950s, along with other Sámi ethnographic objects.[25]

Of the 160 models said to have been made by Hætta, some later turned up in unlikely places, including the Smithsonian Museum in Washington, D.C., which holds a small, painted, wooden reindeer with a sled.[26] Ludwig Daa, who became the director of the Ethnographic Museum in Christiania in 1862, was given a budget by the state to purchase more ethnographic objects, but the budget didn't cover all he wanted for the museum, and it turned out that Haetta's models were useful trading currency. He began at home in Norway by sending a box of twenty of the models to Bergen's University Museum in 1863, along with three of the plaster casts of Sámi prisoners.[27] Daa also made acquisition forays in 1863–64 to Amsterdam, Copenhagen, Paris, and London, with the announced intention of bartering some Sámi objects for global ethnographic artifacts. As a result, the National Museum of Denmark received seven Sámi objects in trade; five of them were miniatures made by Hætta.

Ludwig Daa had connections in London, including his old acquaintance Robert Latham and a clergyman, Reverend Graham Smyth, who brought Daa to William Wareham, a curiosity dealer with a shop on Charing Cross Road. Wareham was known to sell to the British Museum and to the collector Augustus Pitt Rivers, who later founded the eponymous archeology and anthropology museum in Oxford. Wareham apparently purchased the Sámi objects, and in exchange Daa received, among other things, a canoe and three oars from New Zealand and two busts of Indigenous people from Tasmania.[28] The Pitt Rivers Museum still has a few examples of Hætta's models, including miniature skis, a tent, and a painted wooden reindeer that are the near cousins of those in Norway. Until recently Lars Hætta's name was unknown at the Pitt Rivers Museum. A few of the models are displayed by type, as is the custom at the museum, under the label "transport."[29]

The 1860s began almost a full century of ethnographic collecting on a grand scale in Fennoscandia, as well as in Europe and elsewhere around the world. Eventually thousands of Sámi objects would end up in ethnographic museums in Nordic cities. Many would also make their way to collections in Germany, France, Russia, and England. Lars Hætta's miniatures were not exactly ethnographic objects, nor were they toys, charms, or souvenirs. They remain, in their scattered collections, small, sturdy testaments from a prisoner's life and one man's longing for home.

Autumn Migration in Lule Lappmark

Summer, 1868. Two Swedes from Stockholm, Baron Gustaf von Düben and his younger wife, Lotten, both well fed and dressed for a long journey (in Lotten's case, in a wool skirt and bloomers), began to wander off into the roadless territory of Sápmi, known then as Lule Lappmark. Not alone, of course; they advanced in a pack train of reindeer, with their cook and a research assistant from Stockholm. They had also employed a Sámi guide and porters, a dozen of them, for the von Dübens had a great deal to carry and much of it was heavy. Gustaf von Düben was a doctor and professor of pathological anatomy at the prestigious medical university in Stockholm, the Karolinska Institute, with a mission to study the Sámi people in situ. Lotten von Düben was the photographer on the journey. Her camera alone weighed over a hundred pounds, and then there were all the glass plates, packed carefully in birchbark hampers, as well as a portable darkroom tent where she planned to prepare the plates with iodized collodion and to develop them after photographing Sámi people, face front and profile.

Professor von Düben had chosen Lule Lappmark for this ambitious reconnaissance because it was more accessible than many areas of Swedish Sápmi before the age of rail. The couple, their cook and assistant, and their little dog, Tove, had taken a steamer up the Baltic coast to Luleå and then boats up the Lule River to Jokkmokk, at which point they hired the porters and set off with the reindeer for the mountains and lakes around the village of Kvikkjokk and surrounding areas. What the baron knew so far of Sápmi mainly came from reading: Schefferus, Læstadius, and Linnæus, with a few other travelogues thrown in. Although the two-month-long trip would be arduous, von Düben felt it necessary. He planned

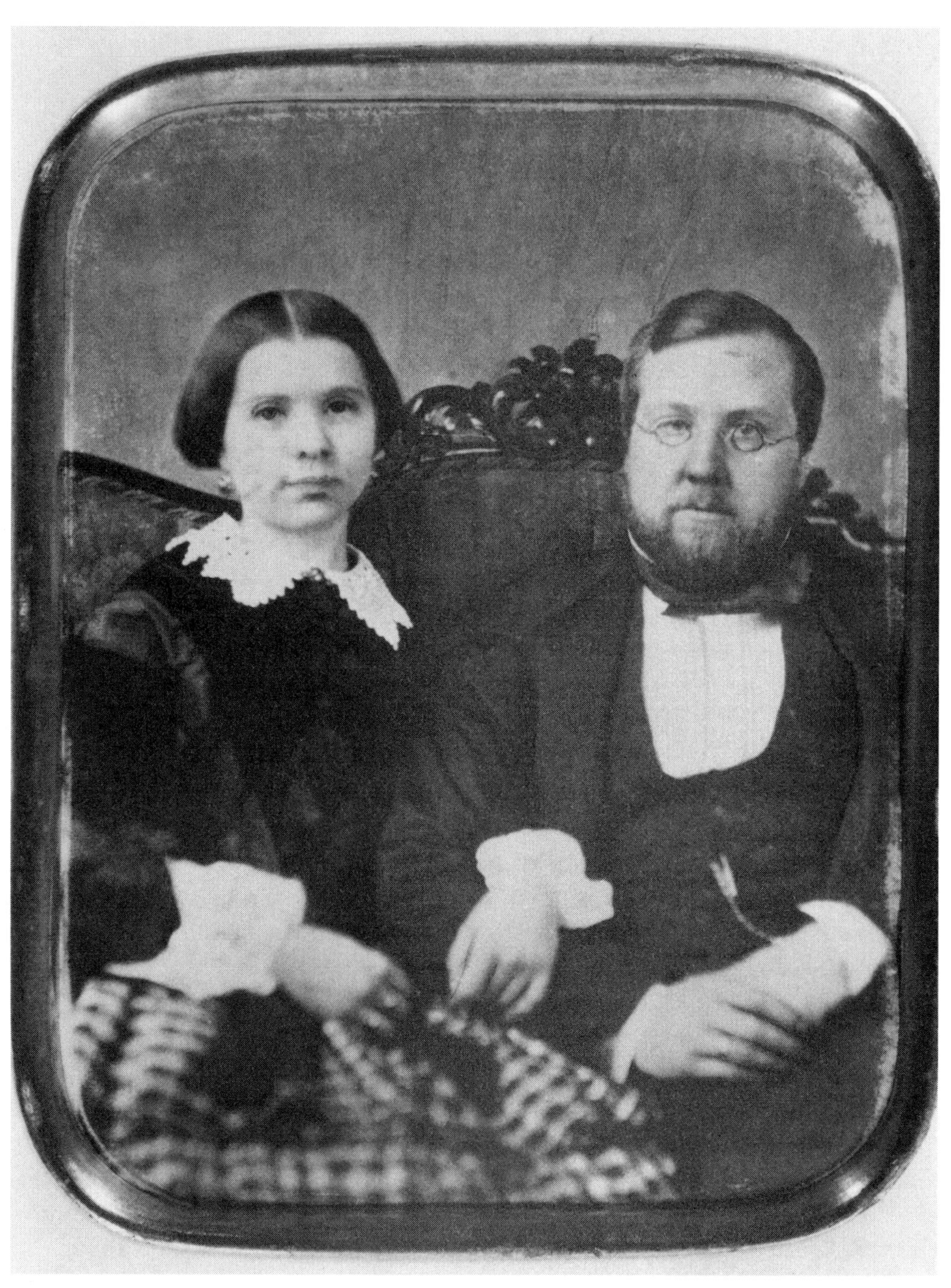

Lotten and Gustaf von Düben, 1860. Courtesy of the Nordic Museum, Stockholm.

to write a brief introduction about the ethnographic and physiological characteristics of the Sámi to accompany a scientific catalog of Sámi crania, a collection of twenty-two skulls that were part of a larger assemblage of skeletons and skulls of humans and animals displayed at the Museum of Anatomy at the Karolinska Institute.[1]

Gustaf von Düben was a medical man from an aristocratic family, a man industrious and widely traveled (Africa, the East Indies, and China), whose social rank and abilities allowed him to move steadily up the career ladder. In 1860 he was offered the post of the previous professor of anatomy at the Karolinska Institute, Anders Retzius, who had died. Soon after assuming the job, von Düben was made aware of the cache of Sámi skulls in the institute's anatomical museum, which formed an important part of Retzius's studies on the physical anthropology of the Nordic people, research he had been conducting since at least 1842 when he lectured on "The Shape of the Crania in Northern Lands" at the Congress of Scandinavian Naturalists.

Anders Retzius, whose interests extended from studying primitive vertebrates to investigating teeth grinding, was the inventor of the cephalic index (the ratio of the width to the length—front to back—of the skull, multiplied by 100). He had measured and recorded the indexes of many of the skulls in the collection and organized them into different races: long skulled (dolichocephales) and round skulled (brachycephales) being the most convenient description at the time. The Sámi were said to be round skulled; the "Nordic races," long skulled.

Craniometry as a tool for classifying living people into different races had grown in respectability among physical anthropologists and medical men in the late nineteenth century. Comparative measurements based on fragments of skulls and bones were widely employed in archeological research as the fossil remains of Neanderthals and Hominoids were uncovered; such calculations helped construct a key to human physical development from ape to *hominus erectus*. But skull measurement also had less scientific aspects—the amateur practice of phrenology was one—as well as more sinister sides. The mid-nineteenth-century interest in physiognomic types and racial difference had solidified into a growing body of work that separated "savages" from people of "higher culture" and then was used as a self-justifying tool of social bigotry and political discrimination.

Anders Retzius used calipers to measure skulls of both the living and their remains. Such calipers would become a tool for several generations of physical anthropologists, some of whom used their measurements to promulgate theories

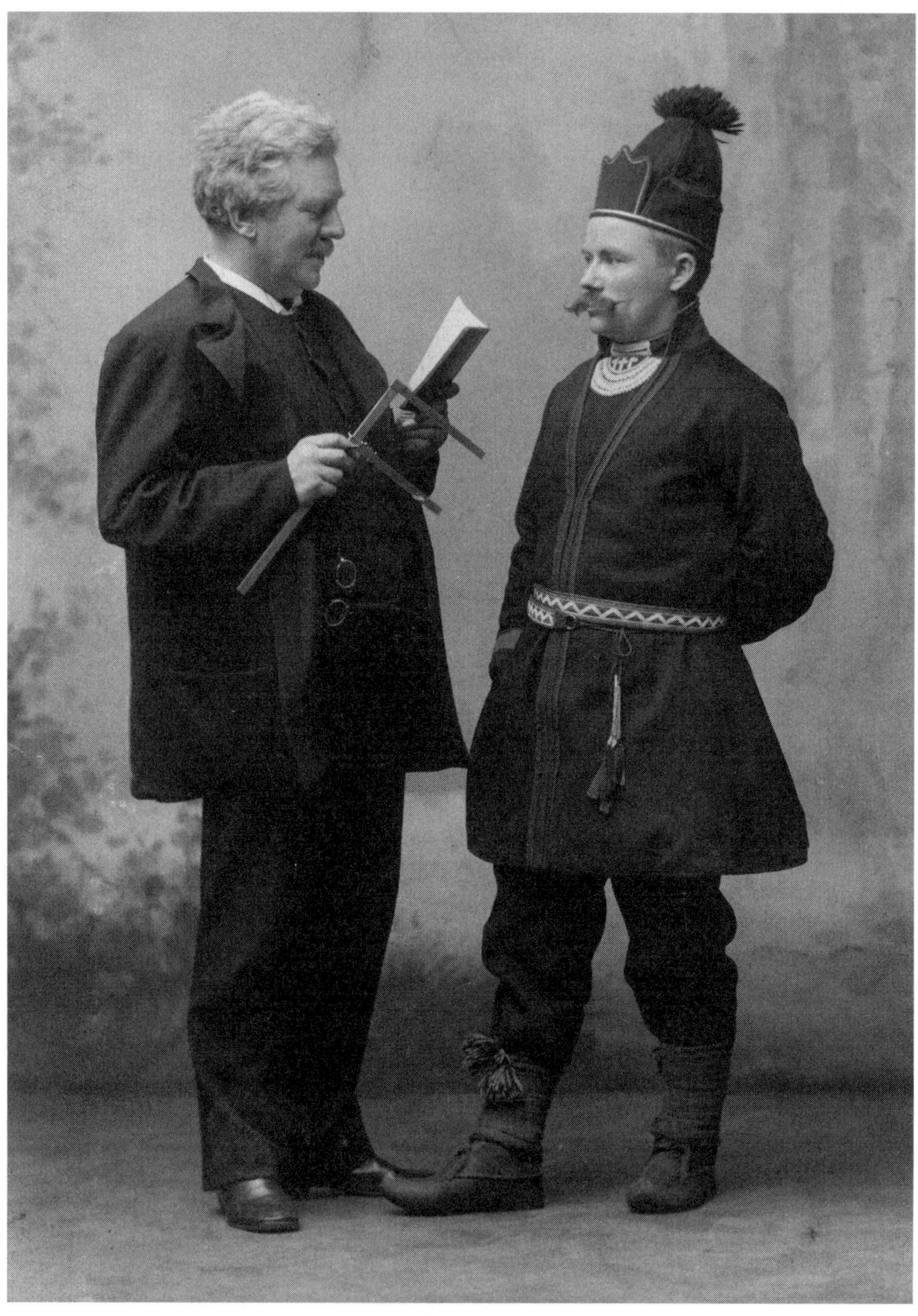

Anders Retzius and the Sámi Fjallstedt, 1905. Retzius, the father of "craniometry," is holding calipers to measure his subject's skull. Photograph by Alfred Dahllöf. Courtesy of Uppsala University Library.

of racial biology. Aspects of Retzius's work in Sweden were particularly taken up in Norway, Germany, Britain, and the United States. In Scandinavia the targets of such research were the Sámi and to a lesser extent Jews, Roma, and people of Finnish origin.[2]

Von Düben would likely have carried calipers in his toolbox on the scientific journey to Sápmi in 1868 and again in 1871, when he and his wife made a second overland trip that began on the coast of the Gulf of Bothnia and moved inland along the Lule River before circling back to the gulf. It was the camera, not the calipers, however, that proved the most important tool for research, among the Sámi who posed for them and back in Stockholm, where the objects they had collected were photographed. Pictures of both people and things would soon be disseminated as representations of Sámi life in various contexts, including illustrations that accompanied texts, starting with von Düben's own. His initial idea of writing a brief introduction to a catalog of skulls instead turned into a five-hundred-page book, *On Lapland and the Lapps, Especially Those in Sweden,* which came out in 1873. This substantial volume represented the Sámi people less as tourist attractions and more as primitive specimens of humanity for physiological study and classification, a perspective that would become more and more prevalent in the coming decades.

By the time the von Dübens set off on their first trip to Sápmi, the image of the Sámi people had already undergone several revisions in the Nordic countries: from masters of the ski and sled, to fearsome wizards who cast spells and caused storms at sea, to pagan worshippers who must be converted to Christianity, to fur-swathed noble savages under the Aurora Borealis, to colorfully dressed folk similar to Swedish peasants but with reindeer. The days of the clergy putting individuals on trial and punishing them for witchcraft were long over. Instead, by the early 1800s the Sámi had been recast by travelers and artists from southern Scandinavia, Britain, and the Continent as part of the picturesque landscape of the High North, a region of sublime beauty and mystery. As the nineteenth century wore on, foreign travelers complained that the Sámi were not as interesting as they had been. In his 1858 book, *Northern Travels,* Bayard Taylor bemoaned the loss of the "barbaric poetry," that is, joiking, of the Sámi; confronted by a Læstadian prayer meeting in Kautokeino, he noted with disapproval that it would be more picturesque to see a "sabaoth [sabbath] of Lapland witches."[3]

Some tourists, however, welcomed and publicly promoted changes that took the mystique out of the North. In 1869, for instance, a year after the von Dübens' first visit to Lule Sápmi, a British couple, Alexander Hutchinson and his unnamed wife, also took a trip to Kvikkjokk, which resulted in a popular travelogue, *Try Lapland: A Fresh Field for Summer Tourists,* that refashioned northern Sweden as a gentle and welcoming landscape, full of short, friendly people: the Sámi. These early tourists were more interested in acquiring furs and other items of clothing, along with artisanal objects, for private collections than in making scientific studies. Eventually some of their souvenirs would end up in museums, while the romantic views of the Sámi would give way to the amateur and scholarly ethnographic investigations of the latter decades of the nineteenth and the early twentieth century, which offered observations and explanations of Sámi religion, folklore, domestic habits, and reindeer herding, as well as a slew of opinions about what should be done with this nomadic people in an age of industrialism.

Gustaf von Düben was among the first generation of Nordic men practicing Lappology, a semi-scientific, vaguely well-intentioned, colonialist-inspired, and largely racist bundle of ethnographic and linguistic studies, theories, and prejudices given a veneer of respectability by politicians and educators, who turned to the Lappologists as experts on the Sámi populations, especially the reindeer herders. The emerging field of Lappology went hand in hand with creating new museums that held Sámi objects. The ways that Sápmi was collected, understood, and displayed would reinforce and amplify the pernicious notion that Sámi individuals belonged to a primitive society, several steps lower on the evolutionary scale, and a group sadly destined to disappear in the near future. Interest in full-scale "salvage ethnography" had not yet begun when the von Dübens were first collecting in 1868.[4] Yet within ten years a Stockholm entrepreneur named Artur Hazelius would be gearing up with a grand plan to save traditional Swedish culture from extinction. In the course of creating Skansen, the world's first open-air museum, and laying the foundations for the huge Nordic Museum in Stockholm, Hazelius shaped expectations of how a national culture should be preserved, exhibited, and sold to the public. The objects gathered for ethnographic study by the von Dübens in Lule Lappmark, as well as Lotten von Düben's many photographs of people and landscapes in Sápmi, would be an early part of the Hazelius collections, repurposed and presented for decades to come in public exhibitions and museum settings.

The Lule River extends far into Sápmi from its mouth in the northern reaches of the Gulf of Bothnia. As well as an important salmon river, the Lule had been for centuries a major thoroughfare, allowing the Sámi to travel upriver and downriver to trade with others on the coast who had brought goods from Russia and the rest of Europe. On their journey northwest in 1868 the von Dübens traveled in boats on the river and trekked through meadows, bogs, and scrub forests. They passed through Jokkmokk, one of the larger Sámi villages, and on to Kvikkjokk, a hamlet built on the delta of two rivers. In the 1600s, silver was discovered in the mountains fifty kilometers away, and Kvikkjokk briefly became a mining center. But after the mines closed in 1702, only the Sámi inhabitants and the parish priest and sexton remained. Swedish settlers arrived in the nineteenth century, living from hunting and fishing.

After Kvikkjokk, the von Dübens and their entourage continued onward, into the mountains, the traditional reindeer grazing grounds of the Tuorpon Sámi. The von Dübens plunked themselves down for three weeks on the shores of Lake Virihaure, with its gray-blue glacier waters and idyllic setting. The Tuorpon *siida* generally spent the summer fishing, trapping, protecting their reindeer from predators, repairing tools, sewing, and preserving food. This summer, unexpectedly, they found themselves under scrutiny, measured by the baron and photographed by his wife.

Like her husband, Lotten von Düben, born in Uppsala, came from an aristocratic family. There's little known about her personally; the couple had no children, and her husband only mentions her in passing in his book—as the photographer. She left no words about herself behind. If it hadn't been for her husband's interests in the Sámi and the two excursions they made, she likely would have been as invisible as most bourgeois women of the mid-Victorian era. Instead, her photography lives after her in a collection of photographic albums and original glass plates and in reproductions of her photographs. She is considered one of Sweden's pioneer photographers, the more so because she was a woman taking pictures not inside a studio but in the open air.

Her improbable career as a photographer began around 1860 when she and her husband moved into a seven-room apartment on Hantverkargatan in Stockholm. The large apartment was one of the perks of Gustaf's new position as a professor at the Karolinska Institute. In the same building lived others who worked at the institute or were associated with it, including Carl Curman, an amateur photographer and balneologist who believed in the efficacy of spa treatments and set up several indoor medical baths in Stockholm (von Düben was, among other professional appointments, the director for several years of Sweden's oldest spa). Curman was asked by the institute to become the go-to man for medical photography. Accordingly, he set up a studio in the building and learned the technique of colloidal, or wet-plate, photography. Lotten, in turn, learned to photograph from him—not to amuse herself or to support herself, like many women of the time from different classes, but rather to assist her husband's research. Her camera work is different from that of most of the first generation of photographers in Sweden: her subject matter is largely documentary shots of people arranged for the purposes of anthropological study and comparison. But Lotten von Düben was also inspired to photograph scenes of natural beauty, one of the earliest Swedish photographers, male or female, to do so.

On her two trips with her husband to Lule Sápmi, she took several hundred photographs—mountains, waterfalls, and lakes among them—that document the beauty of the undammed Lule River and its shores. She also took photographs of the inhabitants along the river and in the nearby mountains. Although the Tuorpan Sámi were working all that summer, rarely did she photograph them engaged in any activity but pipe smoking in these poses. Sometimes Lotten took a family portrait or photographed a mother and child together, but in general she placed her subjects alone, seated on a camp stool or standing against a background of storehouses or reindeer corrals. Often she took two shots of each person, full face and in profile, in a three-quarter view so their clothes and hats are visible: face front and then head turned to the side, hands crossed in front or lying loosely on their laps. The intent of the poses is clear: to document the physiognomy of the skull shape and confirm that living Sámi people had the same "round-headed" crania as their dead forebears, whose skulls sat on shelves in the Karolinska Institute's anatomical museum.

Lotten von Düben's close-ups of the serious faces of her subjects, many of whom are women, are compelling. Their expressions are thoughtful, skeptical, even irritable. Many of them had not wanted to pose, it's said, especially with their silver jewelry, the sight of which might encourage the tax collectors to increase their annual demands. Were the Tuorpon Sámi paid to be photographed? Did they pose just to avoid conflict or encourage the Swedes to leave more quickly? There's something intrusive about these stiff mug shots, and yet it can't be denied that they're often riveting as well, for Lotten was a serious photographer. Her photographic record of the Sámi was the first sustained documentation of *siidas* in the Lule and Pite Lappmarks; Lotten took the time to record the names of those she photographed, enabling later researchers and family members to know them as individuals and ancestors.

Was Lotten interested in anatomy and racial biology or just adventure? Was she pulled into this project by the force of her husband's interests, or was she an

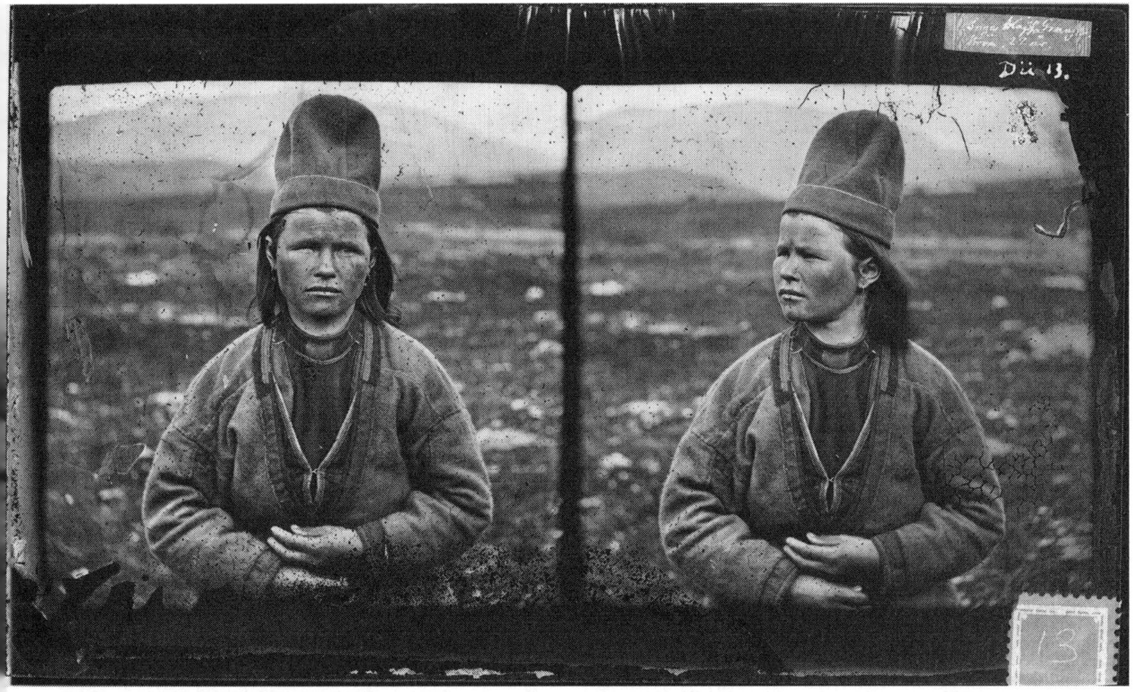

Inga Kajsa Granström, age twenty-two, Tuorpon Sápmi. Stereoscope image taken by Lotten von Düben on her first trip to Sápmi, 1868. Courtesy of Uppsala University Library.

eager and willing participant? It's tempting to see her as taking the opportunity to escape the confines of bourgeois Stockholm life for a while, to don bloomers along with the cook, Johanna Björkland, who accompanied the entourage in 1868 and was photographed, looking rather dauntless, by Lotten. It may have been a marvelous chance that Lotten seized to explore a wilder side of Sweden and meet people different than herself; to master a complex technique that had to be carried out quickly and competently; and to develop and refine a photographer's eye in the absence of having seen much imagery produced by the camera. We don't know: her female silence is as profound as that of the women she photographed.

Besides capturing the weathered faces and watchful stares of the Tuorpan Sámi in 1868, Lotten also took pictures three years later, during the von Dübens' second summer trip to Pite Sápmi. By that time, the professor had decided that a short ethnographic essay to supplement the catalog of skulls was not enough; a much larger study was called for. The couple, again with their little dog, Tove, but with a different cook and assistant, boarded a steamer in June in Stockholm and arrived in the small town of Piteå, south of Luleå on the coast. From there they made their way overland to Arvidsjaur, where since the seventeenth century Sámi had congregated in the summer around the church. For some weeks every summer and at other church festivals, the herders and their families stayed in around eighty wooden huts with grass roofs in small streets near the church, a *lappstan* or parish village. There Lotten photographed women and men in their Sunday best, as well as the collection of huts and the church. The research party, again accompanied by twelve porters, moved on to the village of Sorsele, crossing lakes and tramping through forests and marshes. The von Dübens were welcomed to Sorsele by a Sámi pastor, Anders Fjellner, and stayed with him for three weeks. Fjellner, a collector of Sámi folklore and early oral literature, including epic poetry and joiks, was a valuable resource for Gustaf von Düben. From there the party went overland to Ammarnäs, where again groups of nomadic and settled Sámi had gathered near the church for a time of christenings and weddings.

The journey homeward took in Arjeplog, Arvidsjaur, Jokkmokk, and Luleå, where they embarked for Stockholm. With them on the steamer, in addition to the photographic material, were objects they had collected, just as they had done on the first trip: leather bags, knives with etched handles of reindeer antler, and needle cases, also etched with figures and designs. Gustaf had also purchased sleds, reindeer harnesses, skis and poles, and many articles of clothing: reindeer-skin coats and tunics; skirts and aprons; weatherproof reindeer-skin trousers; breast cloths with high collars, tied around the neck; short jackets embroidered in pewter thread; silver jewelry and belts with silver medallions; and boots and snowshoes. A few of the items were valuable: they purchased no drums (all of them had long since been stolen, destroyed, or well hidden), but two examples of sacrifice stones, or *sieidis,* were packed in crates and sent south, along with a large bridal crown decorated with silver ornaments.

Back in Stockholm in the studio in the building on Hantverksgatan, Lotten confined herself largely to photographing these artifacts for her husband's research and the book he was working on. But another of her projects around 1871–72 was to take large-format photographs of the twenty-two skulls in the collection of the Museum of Anatomy. Even though they would not appear in *On Lapland and the Lapps* in 1873, crania were a core aspect of von Düben's work on racial types and categories of people, The story goes that Gustaf Retzius, the son of the original collector of the skulls, also employed by the Karolinska, was another student of Carl Curman. Enthusiastic about the idea of photographing and writing a monograph about the Sámi skulls, he was pulled off the project by

Professor von Düben, who declared that the Sámi were his property. Retzius had to content himself with publishing a book on Finnish skulls instead.

Anatomical museums were not rare in the nineteenth century, nor were collections of skulls and skeletons. Once illegal and otherwise forbidden to study for many Christian centuries, corpses and skeletons were now available to medical men for research and to professors for teaching purposes. Thanks to the assiduous work of Anders Retzius, the Karolinska's collections of animal and human remains were among the largest in Scandinavia, and they continued to grow after his death.[5]

Bird and mammal skulls were easy to obtain, and so were the skulls of indigent patients and executed criminals. Sámi crania were a different matter, as Anders Retzius and others complained. They pointed out that the Sámi did not tend to die in hospitals or prisons, the source of many human remains. Unsurprisingly, the Sámi often objected to the desecration of their churchyards; some gravediggers were bribable, but not all. All the same, this macabre practice was not only tolerated but encouraged. As Retzius popularized craniometrics, other institutions wanted skulls too, and he found himself competing with other researchers or trying to enlist them in collecting for the Museum of Anatomy. Johan Wilhelm Zetterstedt, a professor of botany, an entomologist at the University of Lund, and the author of a book about his travels in Umeå, would seem, as a specialist in mosquitos and flies, to have no reason to own Sámi skulls, but he was nevertheless excited after much effort to obtain "*two complete and genuine* Lapp crania" for Retzius.[6] Retzius also found help from the well-known revivalist pastor Lars Levi Læstadius, who enthusiastically made himself a party to the plundering of Sámi graveyards while he was acting as a guide and botanist for the French La Recherche Expedition of 1838–40. Læstadius wrote anonymously about these activities in the Karesuando area for *Norrlands Posten,* mentioning in passing that the local Sámi would be upset if they found out about it.

It wasn't only medical men like Retzius who wanted Nordic skulls, including those of the Sámi, to measure and categorize as long headed or round headed; explorers and amateur and professional scholars of archaeology and Nordic history also wanted them. One of these amateur scholars who later became well known as a trader in skulls was Andreas Georg Nordvi, a Norwegian from the inner Varanger Fjord in Eastern Finnmark. He had been born there into a family who owned a trading post in Mortensnes. These trading posts dotted the coastlines of northern Norway. Initially they had been set up as monopolies by the Danish state; later they were purchased and run as fishing fiefdoms by families who often saw their fortunes rise and fall depending on the catches, trade, and competition. As a young man, Nordvi sailed south to Copenhagen to study archaeology and zoology but had to break off his education to return to Finnmark and take over the trading post when his father died. Nordvi developed a fascination with Nordic prehistory, including burial sites of the Sámi, which were constructed in mountain and river scree. Eventually he began to excavate the burial sites of the pre-Christian Sámi and to study the skeletons and placement of the bodies. He was not primarily interested in the skulls at first. However, in the 1870s and 1880s, with his business in economic difficulties, he began selling Sámi skulls to researchers and scientific institutions in Scandinavia and abroad.

Most of the skulls that Anders Retzius obtained for the collection at the Karolinska were obtained in less dramatic ways, of course; a doctor friend in northern Sweden supplied a few, as did his students from the provinces who could curry extra favor with their professors by presenting him with a Sámi skull. The core collection of twenty-two skulls fluctuated at times, for Sámi skulls were in demand by other institutions in Sweden and abroad, and a certain amount of trading went on. That there was no shame in studying and writing about human skulls in von Düben's scientific circles, and in Scandinavian society in general, is obvious from *On Lapland and the Lapps,* where the professor explains that he began studying Anders Retzius's collection of Sámi crania eight years before. The intention was to publish a catalog accompanied by a description of the skulls. But since there had been no "systematic" description of the Sámi people for a hundred years, it also seemed of interest to include a short ethnographic study of this race, even though "they are small in number and are of limited political significance."[7]

On Lapland and the Lapps turned out to be a massive compendium, distilled from earlier writers and his own observations, both ethnographic and anatomic. Its fifteen chapters began with an overview of Lapland's landscapes and Sámi people and then progressed through descriptions of reindeer and herding, domestic work, clothing, language and poetry, prehistory and origins, and the use of the drum for divination and healing, ending with two chapters on the treatment of the Sámi and their future. Of note, since the professor specialized in anatomy, was a chapter on their appearance and physiology. He wrote about their hair, height, and body shape, adding his own negative opinions about their "wide" mouths, their skin color, and the way their ears "stuck out."

Reproductions of some of the individuals and their belongings from the two trips in 1868 and 1871 appeared in *On Lapland and the Lapps,* not as photographs but as woodcuts. Compared to the documentary strength of the original photographs,

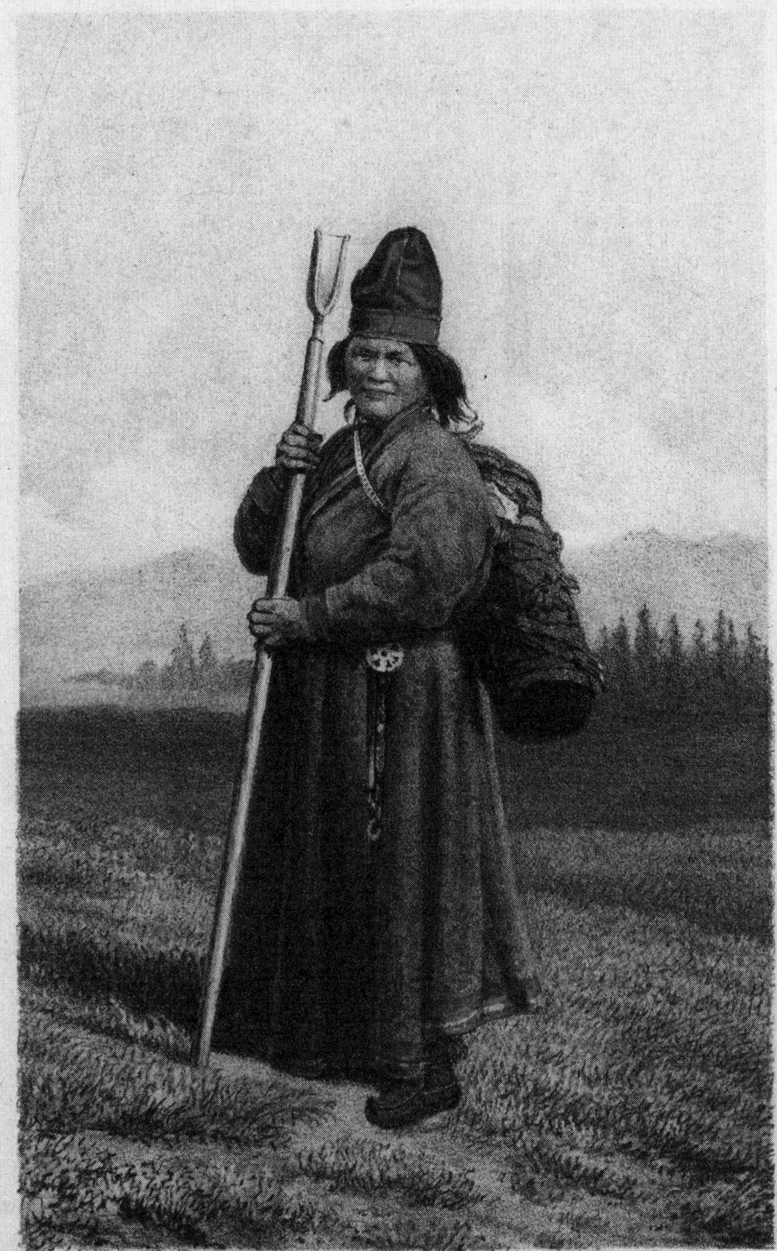

Eva Brita Mulka. Color plate from *On Lapland and the Lapps* by Gustaf von Düben, 1873. Based on a photograph by Lotten von Düben. Courtesy of Sainte-Geneviève Library, Paris.

in these illustrations the faces of the Sámi have a softer look. They have become types rather than individuals in whose living eyes we can see doubt and resistance. A few illustrations are in color, including the frontispiece of *On Lapland and the Lapps,* which shows a woman in a long Sámi dress, possibly tanned reindeer skin, possibly brown woolen cloth, with some touches of colored fabric at the neck and wrists. She is full figured, holding a long pole with a prod at the tip; around her waist is a traditional belt with a scissors, needle case, and knife hanging down from a decorative metal ring. On her strong back is strung a cradle of birch and cloth, with a sleeping baby's face peeking out. She wears the tall, conical, red hat that marks her as a Lule Sámi, and on her feet are boots of reindeer skin. The caption tells us she is Eva Brita Mulka, born Granström, twenty-eight years old, from Tuorpon village in Lule Lappmark. The background is only semi-distinct, with green grass underfoot and a line of trees and misty mountains. A second color plate on the opposite page shows Per Olof Amundsson Länta, twenty-seven years old, from Sirkas village in Lule Lappmark. He too is wearing *gákti,* or traditional dress, in this case a tunic belted at the waist, with a decorative collar or *slieppá,* embroidered with pewter thread. Other Tuorpon Sámi are rendered in woodcuts printed in sepia, in plates at the end of the volume.

The real Sámi people were not as conventionally attractive, perhaps, as Lotten and Gustaf von Düben might have liked, and their everyday working clothes were serviceable but not exotic enough. The von Dübens had collected, among around ninety objects altogether, many examples of *gákti,* from fur tunics to dresses to footwear and hats. Back in Stockholm, the authentic shoes and hats were combined with new tunics and dresses made up in fresh fabrics with trimmings and worn by members of the baron's family, his pretty niece and her teenage girls, who were then photographed by Lotten von Düben. These figures would serve as models for five life-size, plaster-cast mannequins created for a diorama soon to be exhibited in various world expositions, along with tableaus of Swedish peasants dressed in regional costumes (Plate 7).

This diorama, titled *Autumn Migration in Lule Lappmark,* would become a fixture at Artur Hazelius's Scandinavian-Ethnographic Collection, which he opened in 1873 as a private museum on Drottningsgatan in central Stockholm. By then Hazelius had purchased from Gustaf von Düben all the objects and clothing the expeditions had gathered in Sápmi. The air-brushed mannequins in their fresh new clothes were to be placed among the real objects of Sámi daily life, with a stuffed reindeer to pull their sled over suggested snow, against a backdrop of painted mountains with white peaks. The scene was wintery, though the von Dübens had visited at the height of summer. A few years later, as part of Sweden's contribution to the Paris International Exposition of 1878, Hazelius recreated *Autumn Migration in Lule Lappmark*. The diorama returned to Stockholm as a popular feature of his private museum, which in 1880 became an independent foundation renamed the Nordic Museum (Nordiska Museet).[8]

Artur Hazelius, born in 1833 in Stockholm, held an advanced degree from Uppsala University in Scandinavian languages. In his youth he was influenced by romantic notions of Swedish history and culture and the need to save traditional songs and folklore. His interests were broad and encompassed not only dialects and languages, his original field of study, but also architecture, agriculture, and archaeology. He enthusiastically joined the pan-Scandinavian movement of the mid-nineteenth century that supported the dream of Swedish–Norwegian–Danish unity, in parallel with similar unification movements in Italy and Germany. Pan-Scandinavianism faded after 1864, when Denmark and Prussia went to war, and Sweden–Norway did not support Denmark. Yet for Hazelius, the dream lived on with the union of Norway and Sweden, which was not dissolved until 1905. The problems faced in particular by Norway and Sweden were in many ways similar: land reforms, crop failures, and industrialization led many from the largely rural countryside to flock to cities and take passage for North America. On a walking tour of Sweden in 1872, thirty-nine-year-old Hazelius panicked upon seeing abandoned farms, wagons, and tools.

Watching the disappearance of Sweden's folk culture was the catalyst for both the open-air museum Skansen, founded in 1891 on a Stockholm hillside on the peninsula of Djurgården, and plans for the grand Nordic Museum to be built nearby in the style of a Dutch–Danish Renaissance palace. From the beginning Hazelius regarded the Sámi people and their culture as part of Sweden—an exotic part, to be sure, but still important to claim as Swedish. He was just as interested in saving and displaying Sámi artifacts as he was in rescuing painted furniture and farmhouses from the countryside. The first Sámi object collected and registered for the Scandinavian-Ethnographic Collection was a woman's belt embroidered with pewter thread. In time the Nordic Museum would come to house around sixty-two hundred objects from Sápmi. The items from von Düben's collection are among the earliest objects.

Gustaf von Düben never published his catalog of Sámi crania. He died in early 1892, after many years of teaching anatomy. In October of that year, an accidental fire roared through the Museum of Anatomy at the Karolinska Institute and destroyed many of the skulls and skeletons, including all twenty-two of the skulls from Sápmi, collected with such effort by Anders Retzius. His son Gustaf Retzius wrote to a friend at the time, "The greatest loss is the excellent Lapp series, probably irreplaceable, which was procured by my father during a long period of years, and to which were added seventeen skeletons from Lapp graves, bought by Düben from Nordvi."[9]

Years after the fire, Lotten's photographs of the skulls were used as the basis for a complete series of lightly tinted lithographs, published posthumously in a cloth portfolio under Gustaf von Düben's name in 1910 as *Cranius lapponica.* It was a two-volume work, edited by his past assistant C. G. Santesson, featuring twenty-two printed plates. Each large plate, measuring around 20 x 24 inches, had five scientifically drawn views of the same skull, with a printed caption at the bottom: "Laplander I," "Laplander II," and so forth. A text booklet in English accompanying the artistic–scientific portfolio included two tables of measurements taken of the crania, the chapter on Sámi physiology reprinted from *On Lapland and the Lapps,* and a preface by Gustaf Retzius.[10]

Although the collection of skulls at the Karolinska Institute disappeared in flames, that didn't mean Sweden no longer had Sámi crania in several institutions, including at the universities of Lund and Uppsala, where they were conserved and studied. The racial classification theories developed by Anders Retzius and Gustaf von Düben didn't die out but rather strengthened during the first decades of the twentieth century. In 1922 the Swedish State Institute for Racial Biology, the first institution of its kind, would be established in Uppsala for the purpose of studying human genetics. Norway also had its crania collections. Some had been collected in the nineteenth century. For instance, the skulls of Mons Somby and Aslak Hætta, who had been executed and decapitated in 1854 for their part in the Kautokeino Uprising, were part of the collection until 1996. That year, a determined descendent, Niillas Somby, after years of effort, managed to obtain the skulls and to have them buried in Sápmi. The largest number of Sámi skulls was collected in the twentieth century. There are some one thousand Sámi remains in the Schreiner Collection in Oslo, though permission is now required from the Sámi Parliament in Norway to study them.

There are today no skulls, Sámi or otherwise, in the Nordic Museum's vast holdings, and Lotten's photographs of Sámi crania are not to be found among her albums, prints, and negatives, which came to the museum in 1939 from family members. Yet the spirit of the von Dübens lived for decades in the "Lapp Camp" at Skansen and in the two rooms called "the Lappish Department," on the ground floor of the new building, which opened its doors to the public in 1907. Although Hazelius was not there to oversee the arrangement, the curators decided to include examples of both objects typologically organized and mannequins in *gákti*. A diorama of the original scene of five figures with a sled was pared down to one man and his reindeer sled. This figure of a man in furs and a stuffed animal was placed on a platform and titled *The Traveling Lule Lapp.* For decades the traveling Lule Lapp would keep his fixed pose, as if the reins were tethering him not only to his reindeer but also to the image of a static primitive culture.[11]

Razzias

Arctic Lapland Expedition completed! In 53 days covered 2070 km mostly by reindeer sled! 1039 items of ethnographica collected. Total cost 2252 kronor.

—Telegram from Hugo Samzelius to Artur Hazelius, April 27, 1891[1]

Of the several men Artur Hazelius engaged to build the collection of Sámi objects for the new open-air museum Skansen and for the Nordic Museum, Hugo Samzelius, a professional forestry consultant based in the north of Sweden, was one of the most eager and avaricious. On March 8, 1891, with detailed instructions from Hazelius, Samzelius departed by train from Luleå on the coast to the mining town of Gällivare. From there he took a horse sleigh on packed snowy roads north to the Torne River Valley, where Sámi, Finns, and Tornedalians (Swedes whose ancestors had come from Finland) had long coexisted. He continued to travel northeast, now by reindeer sled, over the frozen rivers and flat snowy terrain of the Finnmark Plateau to the Norwegian Sámi villages of Kautokeino and Karasjok, then to Utsjoki in Finland, and up along the Varanger Fjord to the Norwegian fishing village of Vadsø. He returned to Luleå through Finland.

Although Samzelius called his journey the "Arctic Lapp-ethnographic Expedition to the Lappmarks of Sweden, Norway, Finland, and Russia," he was largely traveling through northern Scandinavia. At the time Sweden and Norway were still in a political union. Finland, ceded to Russia by Sweden in 1809, was governed from Moscow.

March and April are traditionally some of the best months for a sled journey above the Arctic Circle. The days grew longer week by week, and the snowpack was thick and firm. Having studied at *Jägermeister* ("hunting master") school,

Hugo Samzelius was a thorough-going outdoorsman, yet he wouldn't have traveled such distances by reindeer sled on his own. He hired local Sámi men to guide his path, to make introductions, and to work as interpreters of the Finnish and North Sámi languages. He gathered information from his Sámi guides about the areas he passed through and collected "superstitions" and tales of past pagan practices from them. Samzelius stayed in parsonages, farms, and mountain huts; he ate only once a day. He bargained and bought, labeled and wrapped, and managed to send cases of what he called "ethnographica" back to Artur Hazelius in Stockholm. He also was in charge of seeing that some representative Sámi structures near Gällivare were dismantled and packed up to be freighted south for the Lapp Camp to be built at Skansen.

His enthusiastic intention was to visit every Sámi settlement he could and to "save Lappish ethnography from oblivion."[2] Already in the first three days, as he wrote in his travel journal, he had collected 239 objects, and not only that, he'd boxed them and sent them to Gällivare to be shipped by train to Luleå and then by steamer to Stockholm. Jovially he wrote that "now began the razzia for everything that could demonstrate a trace of ethnographic value and interest!"[3]

"Razzia," from the Arabic, had entered the vocabularies of many European languages by the mid-1800s, at a time when the Barbary pirates from Algiers attacked ships on the Mediterranean and Atlantic, plundered their contents, and kidnaped their passengers to enslave and/or ransom them. In Scandinavia, "razzia" described a "quick and thorough investigation," though in Swedish it also kept its earlier meaning as a pillaging raid that destroys and carries away.

Before Hugo Samzelius set off, Artur Hazelius wrote to him with comprehensive guidelines for collecting ethnographic material, specifically objects that illustrated the nomadic lifestyle of the Sámi: "The most important thing that should be inquired into is everything that touches on the Lappish ceremonies or worship of gods, their superstitions, anything of that sort."[4] Samzelius was instructed to gather objects having to do with reindeer herding and to inform himself by reading *On Lapland and the Lapps* by Gustaf von Düben, with its pictures of objects and explanations of how the Sámi used them. Hazelius also emphasized the need to record information about the object: "All names of the places where the object was found and the people should be written down very clearly, as well as the Lappish name of the object."[5] He particularly directed Samzelius to look for the naturally shaped stones and wooden objects known as *sieidis,* which in times past had been worshipped with offerings of antlers, meat, and fat.

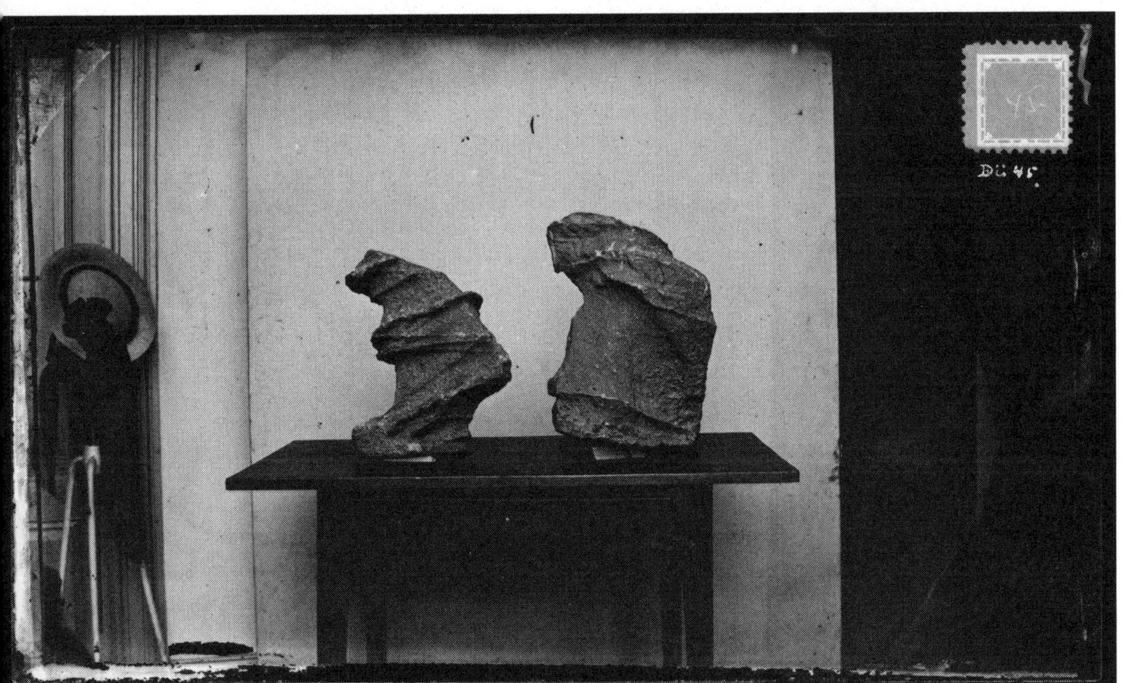

Two stone *sieidis* collected by the von Dübens on their expeditions to Sápmi in 1868 and 1871 and sold in 1873 to Artur Hazelius. They were photographed by Lotten von Düben in a studio and reproduced in Gustaf von Düben's *On Lapland and the Lapps*. The *sieidi* on the left came from near Jokkmokk, and the one on the right is from Arjeplog. Both *sieidis* are now in the collection of the Nordic Museum, Stockholm. Photograph courtesy of Uppsala University Library.

Parts of the travel diary that Samzelius kept on his Arctic Lapland Expedition on behalf of the Nordic Museum were excerpted in the newspaper *Stockholms Dagblad*. Samzelius was also written about by others, in breathless journalism: "The journey was not without adventure, since the wide-open plateaus had to be crossed, where among other things you could expect to encounter packs of wolves, often numerous in these regions. But Mr. S. had prepared himself with a pair of very good revolvers and set off with fresh courage and great expectations."[6] The lists in the diary of the many objects he collected and the people he met along the way give a flavor of his rapid progress over hundreds of miles in less than two months and his systematic gathering of whatever he could find. His ethnographic observations are brief and superficial, but his passing comments on the unexpected competition from other collectors and tourists and the bargaining he did with the artisans themselves shine a light on the trade in ethnographic artifacts and handicrafts in Sápmi at the turn of the nineteenth century.

Hugo Samzelius was not the only Swede who made an expedition in the early 1890s for Skansen and the Nordic Museum. Henning Nordlund, another forester, collected extensively in Lule and Pite Sápmi, buying some five hundred Sámi objects in Jokkmokk, Kvikkjokk, and Arjeplog. In some cases he had to bargain hard to get the objects. He was not always certain about what constituted authenticity, writing to Hazelius that he had purchased a "troll drum" recently made by Anders Pirkit in Kvikkjokk that was supposedly modeled on the drums of old. The price asked for it was one hundred kronor. Nordlund offered fifteen kronor and got it, along with a hammer. He explained to Hazelius, "There does not seem to be any genuine Lapp drum now except in the museums."[7] But Nordlund's razzias weren't given the newspaper coverage of Samzelius's more dramatic Arctic Lapland Expedition, nor did he keep a record of his travels. Most of the attention went to Hugo Samzelius, who wrote popular articles for the press as well as acted as a consultant on the Lapp Camp at Skansen.

What Artur Hazelius and Hugo Samzelius called ethnographica in need of saving from oblivion was to a large extent made up of ordinary domestic objects, often decorated in traditional patterns. These handcrafted objects, *duodji* in North Sámi, were used by Sámi reindeer herders and Sámi settlers who fished and farmed. Every family of reindeer herders in the 1890s would have owned several lasso rings, or *gielat* (sing., *giella*), which were made from reindeer antler and had two holes to run the rope through and secure it when it was thrown. Often these two-holed lasso rings were decorated with designs. The designs tended to be geometric in South Sápmi and often floral or with flowing lines in North Sápmi. In 1891 Samzelius collected around twenty-five of these lasso rings. He also collected a great number of needle cases, or *nállogoađit* (sing., *nállogoahti*), small tube-shaped containers for sewing needles; these were made of horn, etched like the lasso rings, and topped by a tiny lid of bone or a leather plug, with a braided leather string that would attach the case to a decorated ring that hung from a woman's belt. Samzelius purchased fifty-three needle cases from Sámi families in 1891. He also bought 154 spoons, or *basttet* (sing., *baste*); forty-four of them alone came from tent camps and farms in Finnish Enontekiö and were made largely from tree boles or from horn; those in horn usually had decorative, etched handles. For centuries the Sámi had taken their designs to silversmiths, who created spoons, cups, and jewelry for gifts and dowries (Plate 8). Samzelius preferred the "ethnographic" versions made by hand.

What did the planned Lapp Camp at Skansen and the Nordic Museum need with 154 Sámi spoons and fifty-three needle cases? Scrolling through the Nordic Museum's digital register of items connected with Hugo Samzelius, we can see pages and pages of images with brief notes on where the objects were collected and sometimes the name of the owner or maker. The registry entries from 1891 are extensive: knife sheaths and knives, buttons, hand-sized looms, salt flasks, silver belt decorations and belt buckles, shoe bands, a large number of caps and hats, and pipe cleaners. There are certainly some larger items, such as *giisás,* or bentwood boxes; coffee mortar bowls; and lidded baskets tightly woven from birch roots. But one of the main things that unites the majority of items from the 1891 razzia is size. They are on the small side, some very small indeed. Of course, nomadic people traveled light; hence the portability of the sewing tools, spoons, knives, and lasso rings. But we must also consider the possibility that in his desire to collect as much as possible within a short amount of time, to travel to as many places as could be reached before the snow began to thaw and melt in April, and to make it easy to transport objects on his sled and to pack and send them southward, Hugo Samzelius may have opted for spoons and needle cases over carved bread bowls and painted travel boxes and chests or knives and malleable hats over heavier woven reindeer harnesses and fur pelts.

In those days as today, Sámi handicraft was divided into "hard" and "soft" objects. Hard objects are created from wood, bone, antler, and metal; soft ones are from fabric, yarn, tanned leather, pewter thread, roots softened for basketry, and sometimes fish skin. Until recently, the first sort was created by men and the second by women. Samzelius showed a preference for the hard objects and for purchasing from men. Of the many artisans or donors named in the Nordic's register of objects collected by Samzelius, only a relative handful are likely women; their contributions are root baskets, clothing, and soft leather pouches. One exception is a traditional woman's hat fitted over a horn-shaped wooden mold, called a *ládjogahpir,* which Samzelius collected from its two makers, Beret Persdatter and Beret Isaksdatter, in Karasjok (Plate 9).

Although he was instructed to collect material from the nomads, Samzelius did not always buy directly from the Sámi herders; he also bought objects from doctors, clergymen, and settlers; from Swedes and Finns; and from Sámi farmers. He preferred often to buy from farmers because they sold their ethnographica for more reasonable prices. The members of the Sámi *siidas* around the area of

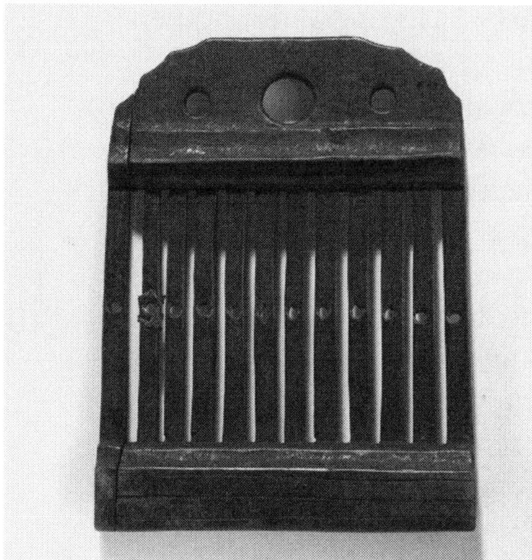

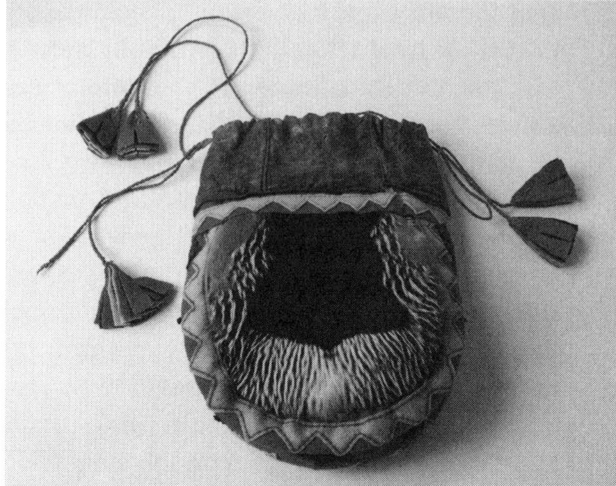

Examples of traditional "hard" *duodji,* a wooden heddle, or *njuikun,* for weaving shoe bands and belts, from Piilijärvi, northern Sweden, and "soft" *duodji,* a tobacco pouch, or *duhpátlávka,* made of reindeer skin, wool, and loon skin by Elin Andersdotter Spein, Kautokeino, Norway. Both collected by Hugo Samzelius, 1891. Courtesy of the Nordic Museum, Stockholm.

Karesuando and the Torne River, those who made the annual reindeer migration over the mountains to the Norwegian coastline to graze their reindeer for the summer, were apt to drive a hard bargain. "Their prices are high, as they steadily allege that they are well paid by the 'Englishmen,'" he complained in his published diary.[8] The "Englishmen" were the foreign tourists, male and female, cruising up and down the Norwegian fjords. Samzelius would eventually have the same experience in Kautokeino and especially Karasjok in Norway, where the Sámi seemed particularly entrepreneurial. "If he [a Sámi artisan] wasn't offered a high enough price he was just as likely to sell his ethnographica to the fishing English tourists, who would gladly pay what was asked."[9] For these tourists, Sámi artifacts were not precious ethnographica that belonged in a museum in Stockholm. Instead, a knife, hat, doll, or spoon ornamented with designs was a souvenir to take back to London, Hamburg, or Rome.

Duodji is often defined most simply in English as "handicraft," though the word itself means an act, activity, or product. The verb is *duddjot,* meaning "to work with one's hands," and those who do this work are *duojárs.* The making of useful and beautiful things for daily and festive wear, for cooking and weaving and sewing, for herding and hunting and fishing, and for gift giving and trade goes back far into Sámi history. Historical witnesses of the Sámi sometimes disparagingly described them in their winter furs as looking like primitive animals. But other travelers left detailed portrayals of Sámi wearing colorful hats and tunics reminiscent of Renaissance clothing or of wealthy herders loaded with silver belts, necklaces, and earrings. Many admired the Sámi skills of weaving and carving, basketry, and knife making. Most of these objects were created of natural materials, such as horn, birchwood, and tanned skin, sometimes in combination with silver, copper, and pewter. In centuries past, the symbols used on ceremonial items (e.g., drums, hammers, and pointers) had meanings connected with Sámi religious practices, something that still faintly resonated in images etched into spoons and knives. Most Sámi individuals at the turn of the nineteenth century still made everything needed for daily life, but others also made objects to sell to tourists and dealers to supplement their income.

It's worth asking whether Hugo Samzelius had an eye for the aesthetic value of what he was buying up on this expedition and on other, less ambitious purchasing trips or whether he, like Henning Nordlund, went shopping in Sápmi only for ethnographica. The instructions from Stockholm had been clear. For Hazelius, the basic configuration of knowledge about the Sámi—as written down by scholars and Lappologists—was already in place. What was needed were more objects, many more objects, to fill in gaps and to create a typological repository for comparisons. But the other reason Hazelius was trying to save and preserve Sámi ethnographica was related to the reasons he was also sending out assistants to every part of Sweden—and to Norway and Finland—to gather painted farm chests, violins, rocking horses, striped aprons, baroque altarpieces, and the contents of mercantile stores, cobbler shops, and bookbinderies: he wished to establish a comprehensive catalog of what it was to be Scandinavian and to put new value on Nordic folkloric and artistic heritage.

The Sámi, who were both artisans and the objects of ethnographic study, were to be part of this great project to protect and defend the folk arts and vernacular architecture of the many provinces of Sweden. That Sweden included the geography of Sápmi was still somewhat hazy in the minds of many in the South. When they thought about the Sámi, it was as nomads with reindeer, left over from some earlier time. According to the Lappologists, the Sámi were thought to be dying out; it was imperative to collect evidence of their lives before they completely disappeared. Yet Samzelius's experience in Sápmi seemed often to contradict the premise of cultural disappearance. Not only were the Sámi alive and well everywhere he traveled, but they showed an entrepreneurship out of character with a primitive people whose culture was vanishing. Not only did they insist on continuing to make traditional craftwork, but many of them seemed to have a sharp sense of its value and to be just as interested in selling a knife to a British tourist who was taking a salmon-fishing holiday in Finnmark as to the Swedish forester who arrived by sled from the South looking for ethnographica for a museum in Stockholm.

Foreign tourists had been visiting Sápmi in greater and greater numbers since the middle of the nineteenth century, when steamships brought mass tourism to the North Cape. By 1900 railway lines had been constructed through several regions formerly used for herding reindeer, and a post system of horse buggies and winter sleighs could transport sightseers through the mountains and valleys. The Swedish Tourist Association created a system of cabins and hostels used by Scandinavians as well as tourists from Europe and North America, and detailed travel guides began to be produced, with mentions of the Sámi nomad camps that visitors could encounter in Sweden and Norway, often not far from where the steamers put into port or where the train stopped at a mountain station.

One Victorian visitor was the Englishwoman Susannah Henriette Kent, who described her experiences in Sápmi in *Within the Arctic Circle,* published in 1877. She and others took an outing to see the Sámi herders and their reindeer near the small city of Tromsø in northern Norway. The encampment in Tromsdalen had long been established as a summer destination for *siidas* coming over the mountains from the Könkömä region of Sweden to graze their reindeer in the lush pastures of the valley, as well as to buy supplies in Tromsø. Like other foreign travelers en route to the North Cape, she described the camp in terms of a circus, in which the Sámi displayed themselves and their reindeer. Kent and the many tourists who followed her route up the coast and into the interior were some of the purchasers of Sámi-made clothing and other items; many of the objects were for sale at ports or train stations during stops.[10]

A firsthand account of the summer camp outside Tromsø by someone who was not Sámi but was living in the valley with a Sámi family in 1908 is given by the Danish artist and ethnographer Emilie Demant Hatt:

> In Norway you hear sharp comments about the Lapps' laziness and their living off tourists. Regrettably a form of tourism has developed: that is, the less well-off and the completely poverty-stricken make and sell small things. The

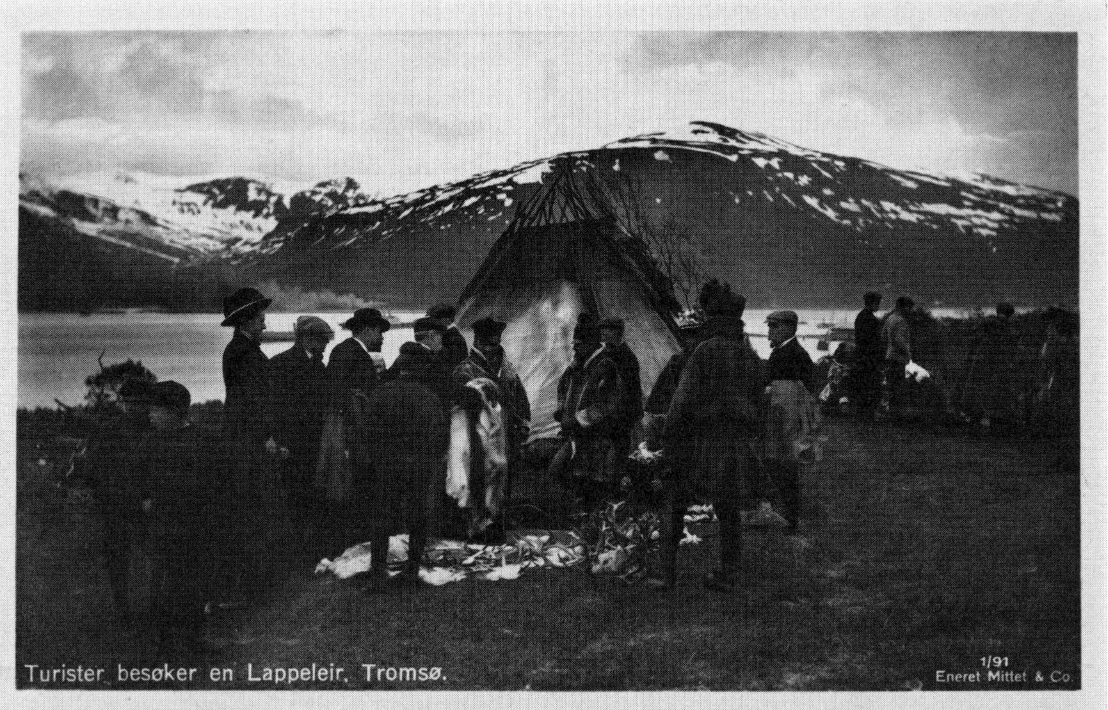

A postcard reading "Tourists Visiting a Lapp Camp, Tromsø," circa 1905, shows the trade in reindeer skins and antlers. Tourists traveling by steamer up and down the Norwegian coast often came to visit Sámi settlements or marketplaces to buy *duodji* and skins. Courtesy of the National Library of Norway.

women sell little pouches, dolls, and other toys, while the men offer objects made of antler. Most often these are meager and badly crafted items; in many instances they're completely warped versions of Lappish handiwork. But tourists want to have things cheap and they have no understanding of what they buy or any ability to judge the value of the work. When the bad craftsmanship is often the same price as the good, you can quickly understand how that soon demoralizes the craftsperson.

Some of the well-off Lapps, who don't admire this industry, can still find it necessary to find objects to sell, for example, duplicates of silver spoons and the little silver-plated pipe. They can't enjoy such things in peace because of the tourists and since the latter prefer to have used objects, the Lapps tend to smoke "tourist pipes" when they come to Norway. The tourist-buying mania knows no decency; they buy the strings of pearls from a girl's neck; they buy

> silver buttons from a woman's belt and everything precious they clap their eyes on. If the Lapps' everyday clothes were more tempting, the tourists would buy them off their backs. If you reproach the Lapps for selling things, they answer that it's difficult to avoid the foreigners' insistence. Often the tourists pay so well that the temptation is too great.[11]

Demant Hatt had been a tourist once herself. In 1904 she'd arrived in Lapland with her sister from Denmark. One of the earliest travelers to take the recently finished rail line from Kiruna through the mountains to the Norwegian coast, Demant Hatt described in a letter to her parents buying a pair of *komagers,* or soft Sámi boots, at the Narvik train station. But as she went on in the future to collect seriously as part of her ethnographic research, she obviously made a distinction between items sold as cheap souvenirs to greedy and ignorant foreigners and the material she bought on behalf of the National Museum of Denmark. Hers was a collection of representative domestic objects from Swedish Sápmi and personal memorabilia, including the gifts she received from Sámi friends. In spite of her attachment to the Sámi, we can easily see that she didn't give the herders who made objects for tourists much credit for their business sense. Yet the Sámi had long been traders, and one of the currencies of trade was their handicraft.

There are many parallels with the tourists who collected "authentic Lappish curios" to remember their travels by and the tourists who steamed up the Inside Passage to Alaska and scooped up baskets and replicas of totem poles, as well as with the tourists who bought thousands of baskets, pots, and figurines from Pueblo Indians in the Southwest, sometimes directly but more often from dealers.[12] Museum curators in both Scandinavia and North America also bought from artisans and dealers, though they often concealed the origins of some of the artifacts so that they could be displayed as ethnographic specimens. In the United States, at the end of the nineteenth century and the beginning of the twentieth, there were dozens of Indian trading posts in the Upper Midwest, Great Plains, Northwest, and Southwest that marketed beaded purses and turquoise jewelry, Navaho blankets, Tlingit baskets, and Pueblo pots, as well as portable curios for the modern American Craftsman bungalow, many of which featured an "Indian corner" in the living or dining room. On a more limited scale, dealers in Scandinavia also catered to tourists and locals with an interest in "old Lappish culture."

In 1907, a grocer named Franz Gustaf Wennberg set up shop in Kiruna, the mining town founded ten years before in the "wild west" of northern Sweden. Over

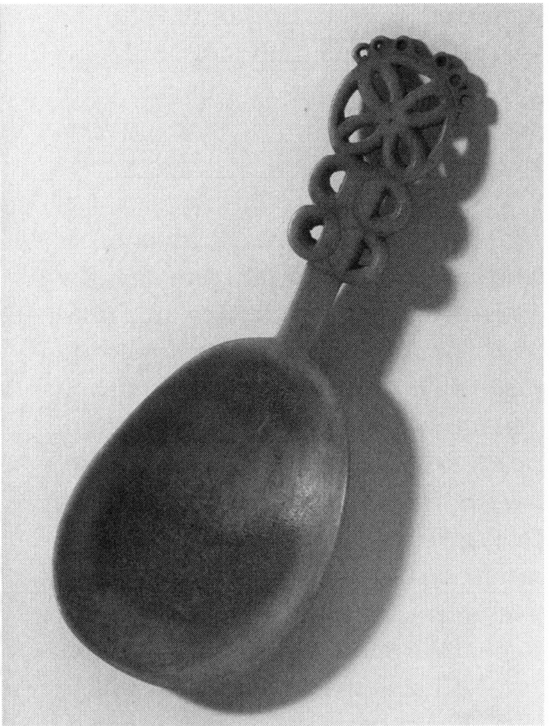
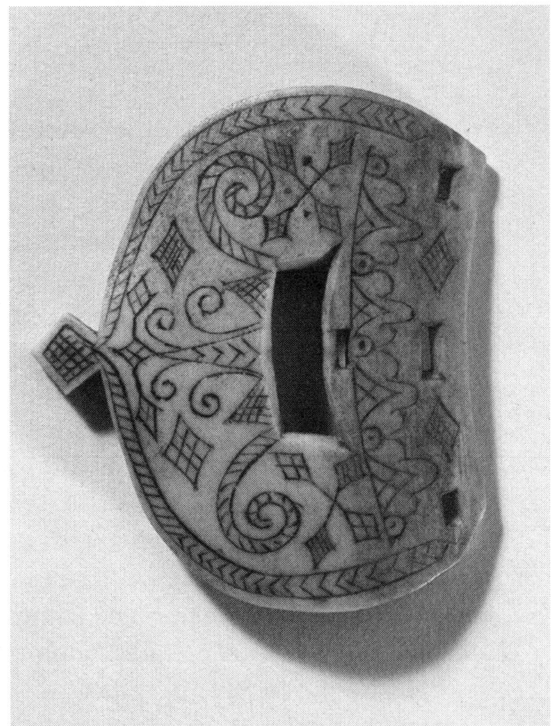

Spoon, or *baste,* of reindeer horn carved by Lars Jonsen Gaidno and a buckle carved and etched by Mikkel Josephsen Nekkala, both of Kautokeino, Norway. Purchased by Hugo Samzelius for the Nordic Museum in 1891. Courtesy of the Nordic Museum, Stockholm.

the next years, Emilie Demant Hatt passed through Kiruna to mail letters and packages, to visit acquaintances, and to buy provisions, some of which she purchased from Wennberg. Many of his customers were miners and their families; others were tourists who flocked up to the Land of the Midnight Sun in summer to hike in the mountains. Wennberg also served Sámi people from the surrounding areas, who bought flour, coffee, and other provisions. The Sámi had previously traded for many of these goods at the winter markets and from merchants along the coast of Norway or the Gulf of Bothnia. Wennberg may have accepted furs or reindeer meat in trade; he also took Sámi handicrafts as payment.[13]

Franz Wennberg was far from the only shopkeeper to buy and sell Sámi-made objects as souvenirs in Sápmi. When Samzelius arrived in Karasjok on his razzia after traveling up the frozen rivers from Kautokeino, he had two guides, Mikkel Josephsen Nekkala and Lars Jonsen Gaidno. The latter spoke Sámi, Finnish, and

Norwegian.[14] Gaidno had worked as an interpreter for Professor J. A. Friis in the past. He was missing his right arm but managed easily with his left. Samzelius noted that he was very good at engraving reindeer horn, and he commissioned two pieces from Gaidno for the Nordic Museum.

Nekkala and Gaidno brought Samzelius to stay with the merchant Carl Fandrem, and it was possibly here that the Swedish forester began to realize the extent of the competition he and Hazelius faced to save ethnographica from oblivion. The Fandrem family had a thirty years' start doing business with the Sámi in Karasjok and then sending Sámi-made objects down the Norwegian coast by ship. Carl Fandrem's now deceased father, Christian Fandrem, had owned the concession to the trading post at Komagfjord in northern Norway. The Fandrems collected and sold Sámi objects both as souvenirs and as ethnographica. Christian Fandrem displayed objects from Sápmi in the Tromsø Exposition of 1870, held at the Hotel du Nord. He later gifted some objects to the Tromsø Museum, and they became a core part of the Sámi collections there.[15] The university ethnographic museums in Bergen and Oslo also benefited from Fandrem's collecting interests. In 1894 there was another exposition in Tromsø, this time in a newly built museum that included "Touristic objects and antiquities" that blurred ethnographica and souvenir collecting in Sápmi. A local merchant, Cedorph Ebeltoft, who ran a shop catering to summertime steamer tourists in the center of Tromsø, was one of the exhibitors. He advertised his wares as the "greatest stock of Arctic and Lapp Curiosities." Along with furs and reindeer skins he sold Sámi dresses, caps, and shoes, "utensils of any kind and toys and knives, and a great variety of Arctic objects."[16] Samzelius noted Ebeltoft's name uneasily in his published journal excerpts as a competitor, one who, said a Sámi artisan, "pays much better than You!"[17]

The distinction among ethnographic objects for research and display in museums, souvenirs for tourists, and authentic artisanal works was blurred at the turn of the century, and this blurriness affected perceptions of Sámi handicraft. A strong argument can be made that tourism in Lapland and the fascination of foreigners in Sámi-made objects acted as an encouraging economic spur to artisans to keep making objects in the traditional ways they'd learned from their parents and elders in the community and to teach the traditions to their own children. Was the interest in Sámi-made objects also connected to the revival of the folk arts in Scandinavia in the late nineteenth century?

This zeal for craftwork was part of a movement begun in Great Britain in the 1880s, an aesthetic crusade that acted partly as a protest against industrialized manufacturing. The Arts and Crafts movement, ardently embraced in Scandinavia, in no small measure animated Artur Hazelius's nationalist aim of saving, collecting, and celebrating handicraft, or *hemslöjd,* from Sweden's many regions before cheap, factory-produced objects completely took their place. Since the 1870s, Sweden had included crafts as a classroom subject. The ability to knit, sew, and construct large and small objects of wood is still a firmly engrained Swedish educational value and practice. Could the objects that Samzelius was gathering on his Arctic Lapland razzia to be displayed as ethnographic examples of a dying culture also be seen as *hemslöjd*? In some ways Samzelius seemed to acknowledge that Sámi craftwork was in fact a continuing tradition when he commissioned the talented Lars Jonsen Gaidno in Karasjok to create some engraved objects of horn. It can be difficult to sort out the differences among ethnographica, handicraft, and souvenirs. Could a craft object created in the present and sold as a commodity to a passing tourist also be presented as an ethnographic artifact that said something meaningful about Sámi culture?

In 1917 Lilli Zickerman, an influential leader in the Swedish *hemslöjd* movement, left her home in Stockholm to make a tour of every province in Sweden. As the head of the Domestic Handicraft Committee (founded in 1899), she authored most of a 1918 report about the state of *hemslöjd,* along with recommendations for how to protect and promote Swedish arts and crafts in the schools and in society.

Zickerman, a woman of firm opinions, dismissed Sámi craftwork out of hand in her report. Lapp handicrafts did not belong with a study of Swedish *hemslöjd:*

> The Lappish craft objects, limited to primitive material and working methods—reindeer antler, sinew thread, pewter thread, trashy glass pearls and multicolored scraps of fabric—can never be anything but curiosities when removed from their natural milieu. Their craftwork can never be protected on a large scale except as handicrafts for tourists. But if that were the case, there is a risk of it being vulgarized. If that happens its cultural worth disappears and its true worth as outsider-produced craft.[18]

Nothing of the same sort of fate, of course, was envisioned for true Swedish *hemslöjd,* which was seen to promote Swedish cultural worth and provide a living for those who made and sold painted furniture and birch boxes or woven rugs and textiles—thus keeping important traditions alive, even if the products were also sold to tourists.

Although Hugo Samzelius had planned not just to sweep through northern Norway and Finland but to carry his razzia into Russia in search of ethnographica from the Skolt Sámi of the Kola Peninsula, he was foiled by the weather and lack of funds. He was continually taken aback by the sophistication of the Sámi people he encountered. In Karasjok he met Samuel Johanssen Balto, one of two Sámi men hired by the Norwegian explorer Fridtjof Nansen to join an expedition to Greenland. Some years later Balto would depart for Seattle, and eventually Alaska, as part of a group of Norwegian Sámi hired to bring a herd of five hundred reindeer to help transport food and other supplies to the ill-prepared miners stranded in Alaska during the Yukon Gold Rush. Samzelius's guide on the way to Utsjoki was Johannes Persson Karasjok, who spoke several languages, had studied in Vadsø, and had been to Strasbourg and Metz in Germany as a performer at one of the "Lapp exhibitions" popular at the time.

In spite of encountering men who, in fact, were more widely traveled than himself, Samzelius tried to keep to Hazelius's instructions to inquire into "everything that touches on the Lappish ceremonies or worship of gods, their superstitions, anything of that sort." He did manage to collect a certain number of tales of older beliefs, which he would publish in magazines on his return. But the ceremonial drums were long destroyed or had vanished into museums. While Samzelius and his contacts had located a few *sieidis* in Lule and Pite Sápmi in Sweden, he discovered none on his travels in the High North. Instead he continued racking up large numbers of spoons, lasso rings, needle cases, reindeer-skin pouches, woolen caps, and colorful shoe bands.

We might wonder, when the destined home for all this ethnographica was Stockholm, what Hugo Samzelius was doing in Norway and Finland? Of the 1,039 items Samzelius collected on his Arctic Lapland trip, almost 400 items come from Enontekiö, Finland, according to the digital register of objects in the Nordic Museum; another 65 come from Utjoki and 92 from Inari, both in Finland. The total number of Norwegian objects is listed as 385. Allowing for the fact that some of the registry numbers may be off, it's still likely that two-thirds of the objects collected by Samzelius in 1891 did not come from Sweden but from Norway and Finland.

The reasons have as much to do with Artur Hazelius's background as a pan-Scandinavianist as with the wobbling steps of museum formation in the Nordic countries in the late nineteenth century. The complexities were not just limited to the political and cultural geography of the nation-states of the North but involved questions about whether ethnographic collecting included all peoples in a given country or was restricted to primitive peoples abroad and at home. Hazelius came of age in a generation that celebrated the cultural unity of the Scandinavian people, often including Finland, which had been part of Sweden until 1809. Denmark was forced to turn over Norway to Sweden in 1814; the form of government was a union, with the king of Sweden as its head. In the 1870s the dream of a utopian pan-Scandinavia diminished, but many, including Hazelius, still kept it alive in their projects. It was not by mistake that Hazelius's first museum was called the Scandinavian-Ethnographic Collection or that it was renamed the Nordic Museum.[19]

Hazelius's vision was broad; he was less interested in assigning a fixed meaning to his compulsive and eclectic collecting than in just getting on with amassing a terrific amount of stuff. During his lifetime his first museum was sometimes criticized as being too much like an old-fashioned cabinet of curiosities, with objects in glass cases and shelves and even hanging from the walls and ceilings. The lists of objects he bought and the many that were given to the museum included a vast array from many northern countries, including Estonia and Germany: jewelry, costumes, bear traps, medieval weapons, church pews, carved sideboards, silk embroideries, and ballet shoes. From Sweden he collected furniture from multiple periods, medieval to rococo, dozens of painted grandfather clocks, carriages, sculptures, boats, bales of clothing, draperies, linens, toys, tools, and silverware. No wonder he dreamed of a vast structure in which to house all these treasures comfortably, a structure of stone and marble that would stand as a monument to the dream of pan-Scandinavia and to Sweden's preeminent role in the northern countries.

Artur Hazelius died in 1901. He had seen Skansen realized, but the new building that was supposed to hold and display all these collections was far from finished. During his lifetime there were occasional debates about the exact purpose of the Nordic Museum, but after his death, when a commission gathered to discuss the interior design of the museum, a new consensus formed: the aim of the Nordic Museum was to be a national Swedish museum, which would illustrate the development of the Swedish people and emphasize patriotic values. Presumably some of this strong nationalist feeling had to do with the coming separation of Sweden and Norway. The Norwegians, especially those on the left, had long been restive in the union, and in 1905 they managed to force the issue and create a separate state. They imported a Danish prince to become King Haakon VII and turned their attention to creating new institutions of their own, which emphasized *Norwegian* patriotism.

Where were the Sámi collections in all this? As a result of the deposit of Sámi objects by Gustaf von Düben in 1873 and the razzias of 1891 by Artur Samzelius and Henning Nordlund (along with further purchases and gifts), Skansen and the

Nordic Museum now possessed a significant collection of Sámi artifacts, numbering some three thousand by 1910 and far outstripping the few hundred objects held by the State Historical Museum and the Ethnographic Museum in Stockholm. The Historical Museum had inherited the sacred, stolen drums from the Royal Academy of Science. The Ethnographic Museum, once a department of the Natural History Museum, owned about two hundred Sámi artifacts at the turn of the century, along with increasing numbers of objects from other cultures around the world. There were also other ethnographic museums and regional and university museums with Sámi collections in Sweden.

But because of a confluence of factors involving museum formations and shifting definitions of ethnography, Hazelius's Scandinavian-Ethnographic Collection had become the Nordic Museum, which *included* the Sámi from all over Sápmi as a distinct people within Fennoscandia and then, when the public mission of the museum changed, as a distinct people within Sweden. While Hazelius's near contemporary Yngvar Nielsen was occupied trying to get the Scandinavian objects *out* of Oslo's Ethnographic Museum and *into* a new Norwegian folk museum that didn't include the Indigenous people of northern Norway, the Swedish curators who followed Hazelius were content to leave the Sámi collections inside the Nordic Museum and call them, with reservations, part of Swedish culture. The same held true for Skansen. The Lapp Camp was a popular destination—unfamiliar enough to be exotic yet Swedish enough to be part of the open-air museum illustrating all the regions of the country.

By August 1891, the Lapp Camp at Skansen was finished, with Hugo Samzelius on-site to supervise the siting and reassembling of various structures that he had purchased in the Gällivare district in the winter and that had been shipped by steamship down to Djurgården in Stockholm. They included a tent, or *lávvu,* complete with domestic utensils and tools; a turf hut, or *goahti;* a hut for making cheese and other dairy products; and another hut for preserving meat. There was a storehouse on stilts as well, a *njalla.*

In addition to the Lapp Camp, a large selection of all the items collected by Samzelius and Nordlund was displayed in a building nearby. These would eventually go into the Nordic Museum, but at first they were part of the grand opening of Skansen in September 1891. Hazelius had recruited individuals from around Sweden to work at the open-air museum in different buildings and on the grounds. Dressed in regional costumes, they were there to demonstrate crafts like spinning, blacksmithing, baking, and weaving. For the Lapp Camp he hired Sámi families,

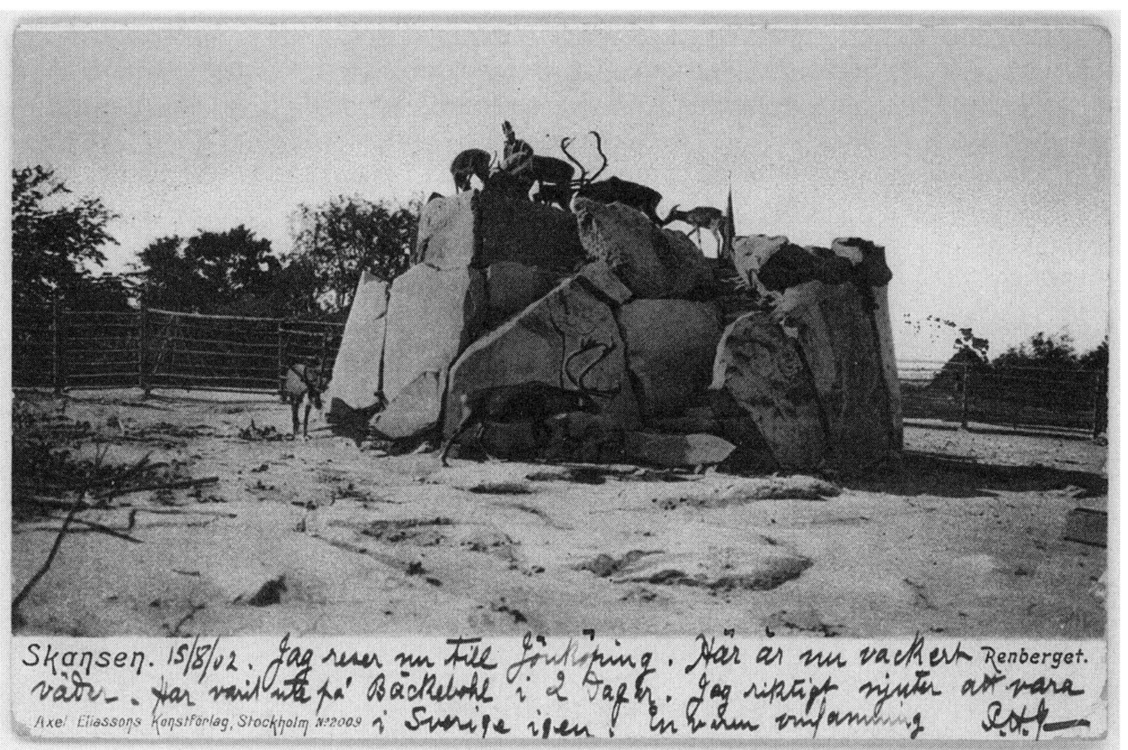

Postcard of Reindeer Mountain at Skansen, Stockholm, 1902. Courtesy of the Skansen collection.

couples and their children, to occupy the camp from spring through the end of September.

Over the coming years the Sámi were regular employees at Skansen, often photographed and the subject of postcards, along with their reindeer and dogs. The so-called Reindeer Mountain was created from blocks of stone; there was a corral and reindeer sled rides in winter. Now tourists didn't need to travel up north to see representative "Lapp life." It was there before them, in the guise of a tent and reindeer corrals. And if they wanted to know more about Sámi religious practices, they could walk to a dammed-up pond nearby and take a rowboat to Sacrifice Isle (Offerholmen), where some of the Sámi *sieidis* collected by Samzelius and Nordlund could be seen, as well as sacrifice stones sent south by collectors such as the teacher H. V. Rosendahl in Gällivare.[20]

There was no Sámi church at Skansen, no mention of Sámi history and culture, and no mention of colonization, of course. One could argue that the Lapp Camp, with its tent and Sámi family boiling coffee on the open fire, at Skansen existed in the same ethnographic present as the old bookbindery or manor house, as performative history. But few of the visitors to Skansen made the mistake of thinking they were anywhere but in a reconstructed, nostalgic representation of Swedish life among the peasants and estate owners of the past. It was different with the Lapp Camp. Most visitors continued to believe and were encouraged to believe that the Sámi lived a primitive, nomadic lifestyle out in the open air, in just the same way as they always had. They might be included in museums about Swedish people, but the way their lives were displayed demonstrated that they were exotic, unchanging, and unalterably different.

The Lappish Department

Ernst Manker was in the attic of the Ethnographic Museum of Göteborg, an enormous eighteenth-century building that had once been the headquarters of the Swedish East India Company. Here, where ethnographic objects from the Congo, Mongolia, and Peru were stored, he was taking rubbings, with black shoe polish and thin paper, of the decorative patterns on iron spears, swords, knives, and other sharp weapons from Africa, lethal objects he had fished out of the packing boxes. It was around 1923, and he was a student, though not a young one. Already thirty, Ernst Manker had gotten a late start. He was born Ernst Olsson in 1893 in a rural village in western Sweden, and only later, after several pen names, did he settle on Manker. After grammar school he worked on the family farm, where he learned everything related to livestock and crops. He could build and repair things, use all manner of tools, and speak the language of ordinary people, a gift that would stand him in good stead as he, improbably, became an ethnographic fieldworker, a museum curator, a well-known photographer, and the author of hundreds of articles and several dozen books, both academic and popular, most of them about the Sámi people and the landscapes of Sápmi.

But on this spring evening Manker was a student, charged by his professor Erland Nordenskiöld, son of the great Arctic explorer Adolf Nordenskiöld, to make rubbings of the African weaponry up in the storage space. In this way he was meant to familiarize himself with the material culture of the Congo, sent back to Sweden from Africa in crate upon crate by Swedish missionaries. It was absorbing work, but eventually he had done enough and came downstairs to find that he was the only one left in the building and the entrance door was locked.

Surely, he wrote many years later in a memoir essay, someone would come; surely the night watchman would arrive and let him out.[1] In the meantime, Manker wandered around the building's many floors, bumping into "spooky" naked statues in the art rooms and "wizards" from New Guinea in another room, festooned with shrunken heads with staring cowrie eyes. Increasingly uneasy and sleepy, he thought about seeking out one of the rococo beds in the historical rooms. Like many museums of the day, the old building held a hodgepodge of art, artifacts, and exotica, all of which Manker generally found appealing. Some years before, when he was still a farmer, he had once seen a notice in a newspaper about a scientific expedition setting off for the South Pacific, which he imagined would require not only scientists to study the zoology and ethnography of the islands but also ordinary fellows—like himself, raised by a father who had been at sea for ten years and had taught him how to tie knots as well as how to use an oar. But when Manker inquired further, he discovered the ship had already sailed.

Now, through ethnography, he would satisfy his wanderlust. Professor Nordenskiöld encouraged him to study up on Africa, to become an Africanist. In two years Manker would leave Göteborg for Stockholm and find employment at the Ethnographic Museum, often called the "Museum of Packing Crates" because in its split from the Natural History Museum it found no secure home for many years and moved from place to place around the city. But Manker didn't plan to be a museum man at first; he dreamed of a larger life, somewhere in the jungle. He wrote a book about the Congo, based on the photographs of Swedish missionaries, even though he never reached the African continent. Just five years after this evening in the closed museum, on the verge of departing for a missionary station that would be his base in the Lower Congo, he went to a doctor to be vaccinated against tropical diseases. He had an X-ray and shortly after was admitted to a tuberculosis sanatorium for over a year.

Ernst Manker was an adventurer who loved a good story and, especially after his brush with serious illness, let very little stand in his way once he discovered that his way led not south to the Congo but north to Sweden's remoter provinces, where in the 1920s and 1930s the reindeer still ran in their thousands and the Sámi people still pitched tents, sat around the fire, and herded the animals on migration. He was carried along not just by professional ambition, though he had plenty of it, but also by a sense of the romance of life and its urgency.[2]

That night around 1923, alone in the museum in Göteborg, he looked for a way out of the locked building and discovered, suddenly, a wall made of slats of plywood that seemed "provisional." Through the slats he could see what appeared to be a normal living room, which could only belong to the watchman and his family. Ernst Manker stood still and listened. The only sound was a clock ticking. He pushed one of the wooden slats to the side and squeezed through. He stood there wondering what he would do if someone appeared. Would he be charged with breaking and entering? There were two rooms and a kitchen, and the kitchen had a window. Out the window was the courtyard of the museum, with plantings, sand paths, and a few garden benches. It was a floor and a half down to the flower beds, though they looked soft enough for a landing. He climbed out the kitchen window of the ordinary little apartment, let go, and landed in the flowers, upright.

There were rooms within rooms in museums and windows to the world as well.

Manker's life has a fairy-tale aspect—a dreamy but hard-working farm lad becomes a gifted student and apprentice. Another of his adventures, one that would lead eventually to his position as a powerful museum curator, began around 1930, when the ancient bearded wizard of Lappology, K. B. Wiklund, who had been the professor of Finno-Ugric at Uppsala University for twenty-five years and was on the verge of retiring, called the young man to his large, book-lined study up a stairway in a venerable old building in Uppsala.

> He had an urgent task to give me, and he wanted to explain it. It had to do with the Lappish magic drums, the Lapps' own picture documents from pre-Christian times. I was to scout out the specimens that were once saved in the past, when the Lapps were Christianized and their drums taken from them and burned. Around thirty or so were found in Swedish museums, some belonged to private parties in the country, and others were spread out in the world. A Lappish magic drum had been in its time a sought-after object for princes and other aristocrats who occupied themselves with curiosity cabinets and Wonderkammers.[3]

Professor Wiklund explained to Ernst Manker, who had seen drums in the State Historical Museum and the Nordic Museum, the basics of how the "sorcery tool" worked, along with the unknown mysteries of the figures and symbols painted with alder-bark ink on the surface. Over the years, scholars had attempted to understand the meaning of the symbols, most recently Bishop Edgar Reuterskiöld, author of *The Religion of the Northern Lapps,* in 1912. Wiklund and Reuterskiöld had together authored a paper on Linnæus's drum and its travels, from Pite Sápmi to Holland, Uppsala, and Paris and then back to Sweden again.[4] But scholars could only go so far, given the lack of organized source material. To collect images and information about these drums, said Wiklund that day in his Uppsala study, was "one of the most important tasks" of ethnographic and religion scholars.[5]

The professor handed over old sources and his own notes, and Manker undertook to carry out the quest for magic drums, using the notes as a treasure map, a guide to where many of the last drums were seen or heard from. Forty-two remained in Sweden in public and private collections; only one was known to have survived in Norway, in Trondheim. Copenhagen possessed six, all originally from Norway.

First in 1932 and then with his bride, Lill Jansson, in 1934, Ernst Manker inventoried drums in Scandinavia, on the Continent, and in Britain. There were thirteen sacred drums in Germany, most from the early 1700s, which were found in private collections and public ethnographic museums in Berlin, Leipzig, Dresden, Cologne, Hamburg, and smaller cities. He traveled to Rome, to the Museo preistorico etnografico, where he found a particularly beautiful example, and to Paris, London, and Cambridge. Altogether, he located seventy-one drums that were intact, with their drumskins attached. A few still had their original hammers and/or pointers or dangling metal strings from the back of the drum. Some were signed, while some had a documented provenance; still others were mysterious in their origins. In these foreign museums and libraries, Manker took notes and made reproductions of the drums so they could be studied back in Stockholm. He began his efforts by trying to photograph the drums using fluorescent lighting but didn't get the detail he needed, so he switched over to using tracing paper placed on the surface of the drum.

For several years he and Lill organized the information he had collected, and Manker wrote the first volume ever to detail all seventy-one drums: each one's provenance as far as he knew it, its current location, the condition of the drum, and whether it still had its hammer and pointer. He also documented another ten drums that were not intact or were missing their drumskins. In 1938 he published *The Lappish Magic Drum (Die lappische Zaubertrommel)*. The 900-page volume, which appeared only in German, the academic language of the time in Sweden, was recognized as a landmark study and is still a primary source for information about the origins, whereabouts, and imagery of the drums. A second volume, also only in German, came out in 1950; at 450 pages, it dealt with the spiritual aspects of the drums.[6] By the time the second volume appeared, Manker had been working for ten years at the Nordic Museum, in the Lappish Department (Lapska avdelingen), a museum within a museum, which had reorganized its Sámi collections and attempted to centralize Sápmi in Stockholm

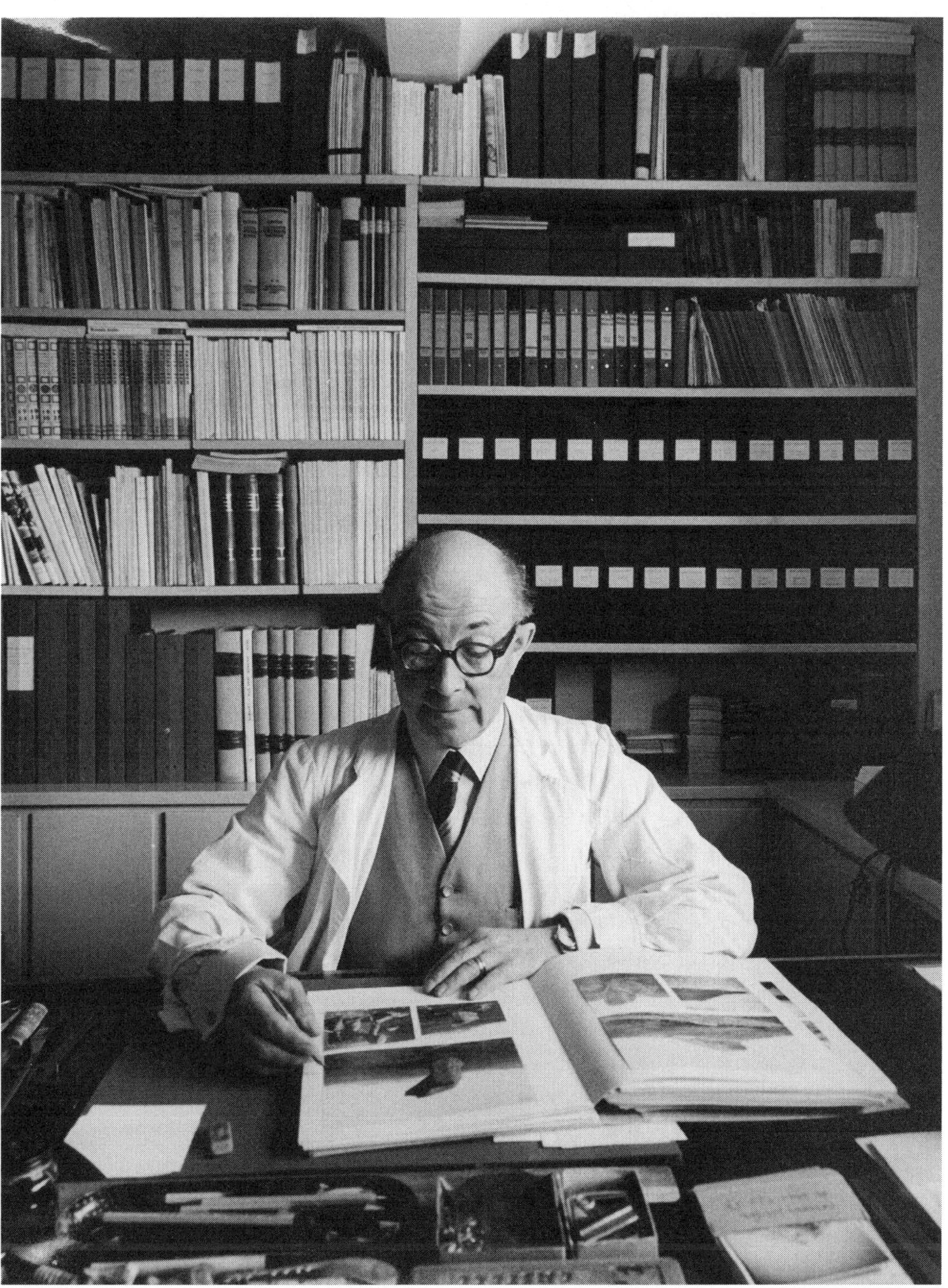

Ernst Manker in his office at the Nordic Museum in Stockholm. Parts of the Lappish Archive were kept here as well as in other areas of the museum. Courtesy of Jan Manker.

through exhibits, publications, archives, and ongoing research. His curatorship was a job he essentially invented rather than one that was offered to him. While he enlarged the role that the Nordic Museum could play in shaping positive perceptions of Sweden's Indigenous people, it also fixed Sápmi in the public eye as the land of the reindeer herders, always living in an ethnographic present that was part memory, part fantasy, and part brushed-up reality.

The idea of an ethnographic museum for Sámi artifacts was raised as early as 1878 when a young man named Fredrik Svenonius wrote in a northern Swedish newspaper that his hometown Luleå should be the site of a museum that would collect and display regional natural history and ethnography. Svenonius was a professional geologist, and as one of the founders of the Swedish Tourist Association, he played an influential role as a popularizer of northern Sweden's rugged natural landscapes and its Sámi inhabitants. That same year, Svenonius contacted Artur Hazelius to ask his opinion on the subject of "an ethnographic memory home, chiefly intended for Lappish possessions," to be built in Luleå.[7] It was the forester Hugo Samzelius who seems to have first used the term "Lappish Central Museum" (Lapskt centralmuseum), in 1890, in a letter to Hazelius, stressing the necessity of a core repository for Sámi ethnographic artifacts. He, like Fredrik Svenonius, suggested Luleå as the best location for this central museum.[8] For Hugo Samzelius, whose forestry work took him all over the Scandinavian north, "central" was likely a geographic term.

On a map, Luleå does appear to be one of the midpoints of Sápmi; it's about five hundred miles from Luleå to Idre, at the southern border of Swedish Sápmi, and another five hundred miles from Luleå north to Vadsø, Norway, on the Barents Sea. But in the opinion of Artur Hazelius, the "center" could only signify Stockholm: the political, cultural, and business fulcrum of Sweden where museums and the crowds to visit them already existed. He dismissed Samzelius's suggestion quickly in a letter, explaining that he didn't believe such a regional museum could find the necessary financing. Already in 1878, Hazelius's vision of Skansen was well underway.

Yet the question of where the Sámi belonged in Sweden, museum-wise, was not fully settled, and not everything collected from Sápmi over the last three hundred years made its way to Stockholm or into Hazelius's collections. Some antiquities were to be found at the University of Lund and in private manors. The Ethnographic Museum in Göteborg also owned examples of Sámi artifacts from the distant past and continued to accept donations from collectors. Stockholm's

State Historical Museum cared for a large number of prehistoric Sámi artifacts, many taken from sacred sites, such as Unna Saivo, near Gällivare, when Swedish archeologists were digging into Nordic and Viking prehistory. The Historical Museum, still lodged through the 1930s in the National Museum, was bursting at the seams, and in 1943, it moved into reconstructed quarters in an area that had once been the naval yards, not far from the Nordic Museum.

The Historical Museum was not the only institution seeking a new physical home. About two hundred ethnographic artifacts from Sápmi had been housed in the Natural History Museum in Stockholm, but in 1900 these Sámi objects, along with a good deal of other ethnographic material from around the world, including large collections from Siberia, Mongolia, and the Congo, were moved into the custody of Stockholm's new Ethnographic Museum, which was still in search of a permanent location. The Ethnographic Museum finally landed in 1930 in a former barracks in the green belt of Djurgården. This was where Ernst Manker had his desk and workspace and where he worked to catalog the sacred drums he'd researched, where he considered his future, and where his interests truly lay.

In the early 1930s a new debate ignited over the idea of a Lappish Central Museum. This time the discussion of whether the Sámi were to be classed with the circumpolar people of the Northern Hemisphere (such as the Greenlandic Inuit and the Tungas of Siberia) or whether the Sámi were to be considered Swedish (though still exotic) was carried out openly in Swedish and Sámi media. The first public mention of a Lappish Central Museum appeared in *Svenska Dagbladet,* in the autumn of 1934, in an article written by Torsten Boberg, the author of several travel and hiking guides for the Swedish Tourist Association. He worried about the loss of "Lappish culture" and suggested that it was necessary to protect "Lappish ethnography" through "a purposeful working alliance between the Sámi people and knowledgeable Swedes."[9] His article included supportive comments by several of these "knowledgeable Swedes" and by Torkel Tomasson, the editor of the newspaper *Samefolkets egen tidning,* or *SET.* Two months later Tomasson printed a double-page spread, titled "The Question Regarding the Sámi Cultural Heritage Has Arisen: Voices for a Sámi Central Museum," with contributions by himself, Ernst Manker, and Björn Collinder, who had taken Wiklund's job as professor of Finno–Ugric at Uppsala University.[10]

Torkel Tomasson was born in Anundsjö parish in Västerbotten in 1881 and from an early age was a key player in the first political wave of Sámi activists in the early twentieth century. He studied law in Uppsala. With the young firebrand

Elsa Laula he founded the Central Sámi Association in 1904. That same year Laula published a thirty-page pamphlet, *Do We Face Life or Death? Words of Truth about the Lappish Situation,* strongly setting out Sámi demands for political recognition.[11] Also in 1904 Tomasson started the weekly newspaper *Lapparnes egen tidning* (The Lapps' Own Newspaper). The paper's original run was brief—only five issues were published—but Tomasson relaunched it as *Samefolkets egen tidning* in 1918. Elsa Laula was relentlessly mocked and persecuted in Sweden, but she continued her activism, organizing women's groups in Sámi districts and giving stirring speeches in Sweden and Norway, where she married a reindeer herder. She and her husband changed their last name to Renberg, and they raised a family. Elsa Laula Renberg, Torkel Tomasson, and others organized the first pan-Sámi assembly in Trondheim in 1917, which began another period of Sámi activism.[12]

Torkel Tomasson stayed in Sweden. Slight of build, calm, and dignified, he was the editor of *SET* for over twenty years and steered the newspaper through financial crises and many changes in Sápmi brought on by industrial development. *SET,* written in Swedish, covered Sámi politics and culture, and it is still in publication a hundred years later, one of the oldest Indigenous newspapers in the world. Tomasson's backing for the idea of a Lappish Central Museum was significant. Even though the Sámi had relatively little governmental influence in the early 1930s, they were on the verge of coalescing through that decade into a stronger political force that, after World War II, would only grow. Ernst Manker saw Tomasson as an ally, and from 1934 Manker began to publish articles in *SET.* Some of the first were about Sámi material culture and the necessity of preserving it from destruction.

Rarely one to waste time, Manker wrote up a "Plan for a Lappish Central Museum" in February 1935, where he laid out an initial vision for what such a museum would look like. Its mission was to be more than just inventorying and dusting ethnographic artifacts. The Lappish Central Museum would offer exhibits for the public but would also be a home for scholarly research. Ideally the museum would sponsor well-financed field research, scientific studies, and public programs. Manker also was clear that the collections of the museum should be part of a network of museums and that research and programs should be coordinated and organized "with the Lapp administration men and—before all—the Lapps themselves."[13]

He circulated this plan along with recent newspaper articles about the need for such a museum and a cover letter. In the spring of 1935, the newspaper *Social Demokraten* joined the discussion and urged haste. Modernity was changing tra-

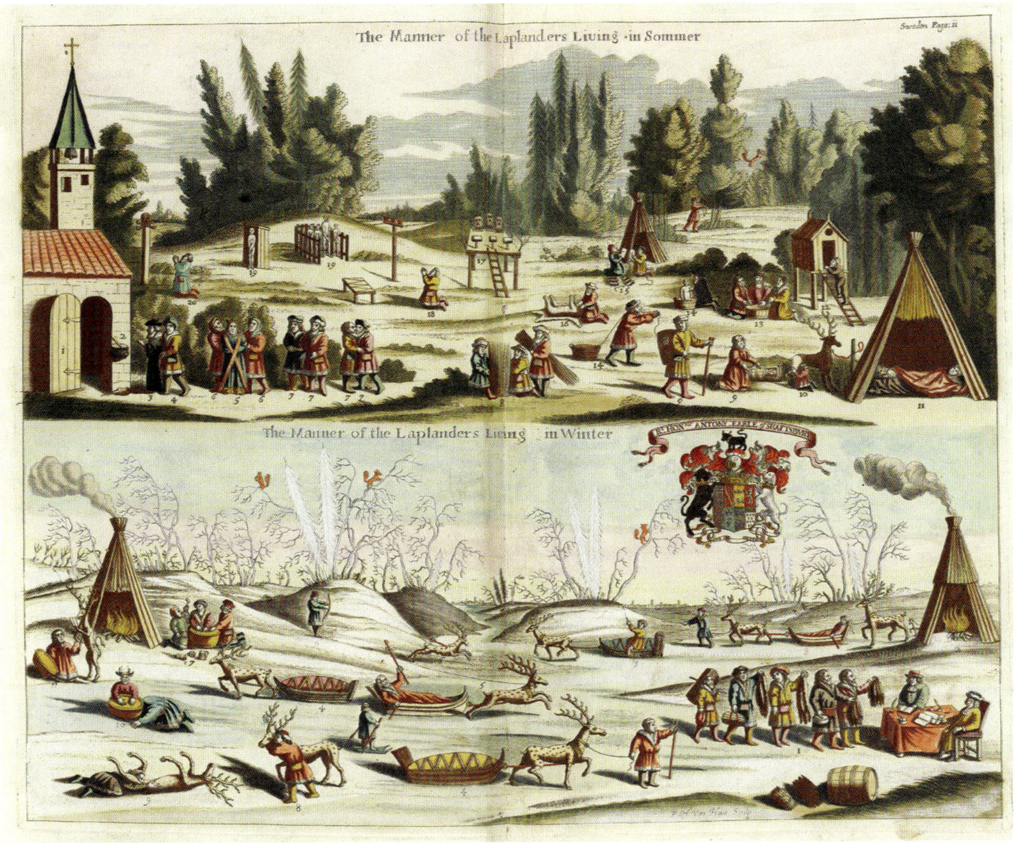

Plate 1. Images of Sápmi circulated in Europe during the seventeenth century in books and atlases. This hand-colored illustration, originally etched in copperplate by F. H. von Houe, was published in England in 1680 in the first volume of Moses Pitt's *English Atlas,* based on earlier atlases by Jan Janssonius of Amsterdam. Photograph by Børre Høstland. Courtesy of the National Museum of Art, Architecture, and Design, Oslo.

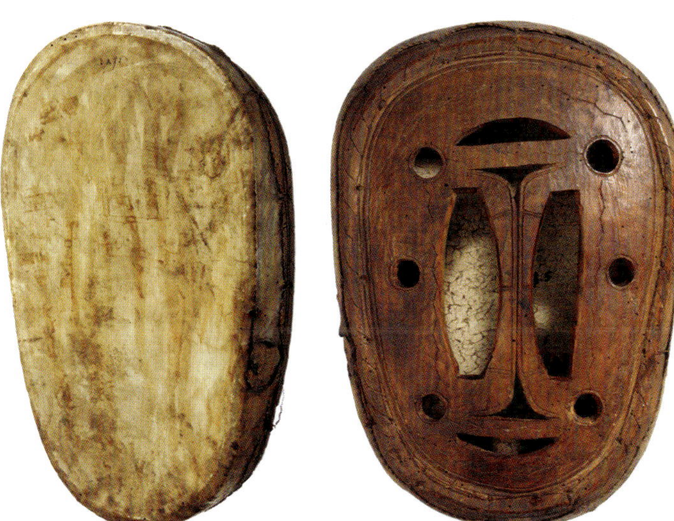

Plate 2. A bowl-shaped drum from the seventeenth century, probably from Ume Sápmi. It was once part of the Museum Wormianum in Copenhagen. The collection was sold to the Royal Kunstkammer in 1655, after Ole Worm's death. Its drumskin faded, it is now displayed at the National Museum of Denmark with other Sámi objects. Photographs by John Lee. Courtesy of the National Museum of Denmark.

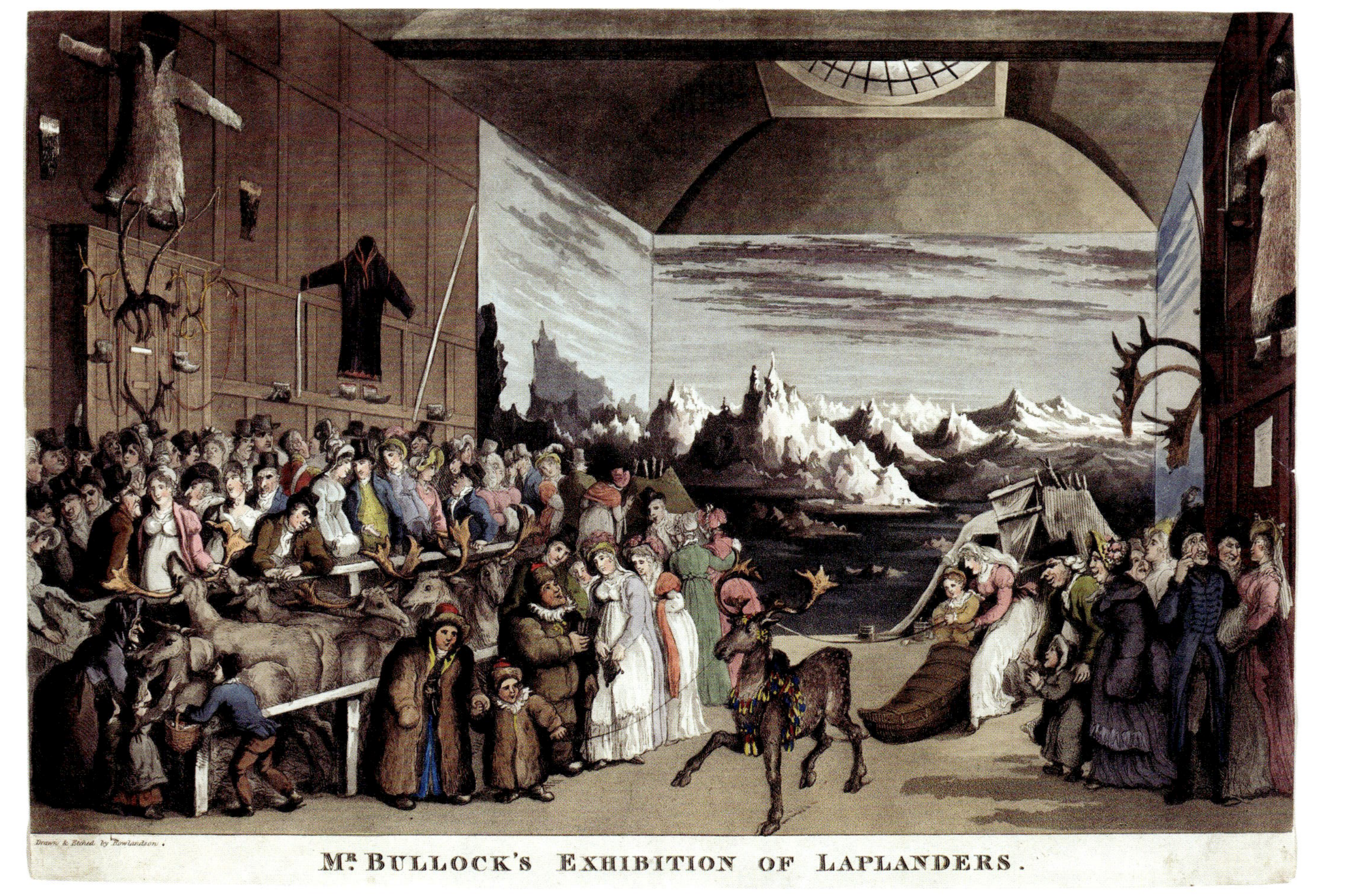

Plate 3. Thomas Rowlandson, *Mr. Bullock's Exhibition of Laplanders,* 1822. Jens Thomassen Holm, Karen Christiansdatter, and their young son, Thomas (in furs), traveled from Norway to London to appear at the Egyptian Hall in Piccadilly in 1822. Thousands flocked to see them, the reindeer, and the objects representing Sámi life. Courtesy of the Rosenwald Collection, National Gallery of Art, Washington, DC.

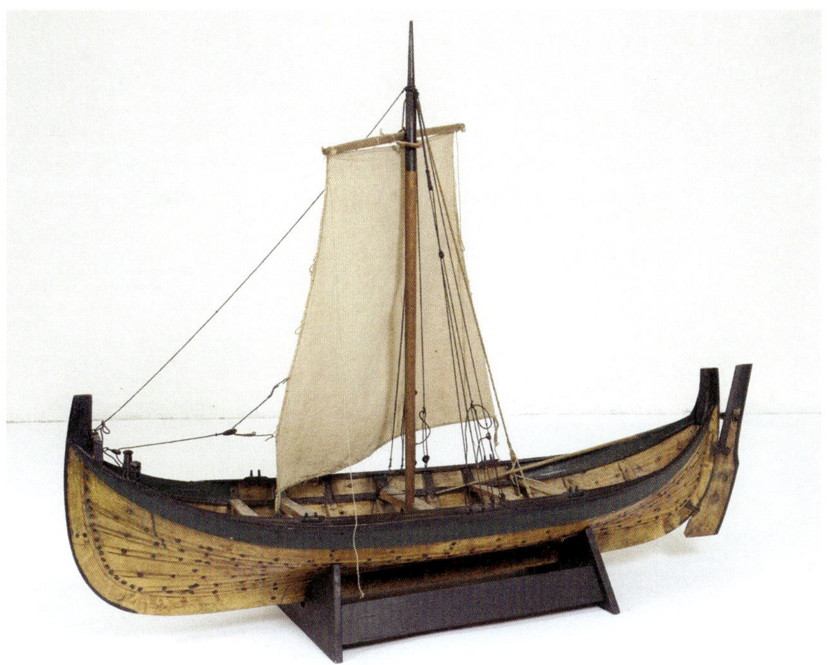

Plate 4. Model of an open, clinker-built "Nordland" boat, of the type used for fishing in the coastal north of Norway, built by a Sámi and a Norwegian. The model was acquired and originally displayed at the Tromsø Exposition of 1870 by District Sheriff Abraham Brun from Nesseby on the Varanger Fjord. Brun's collection was purchased in 1873 by Ludwig Daa for the new Ethnographic Museum in Oslo. Photograph by Anne-Lise Reinsfelt. Courtesy of the Norwegian Museum of Cultural History.

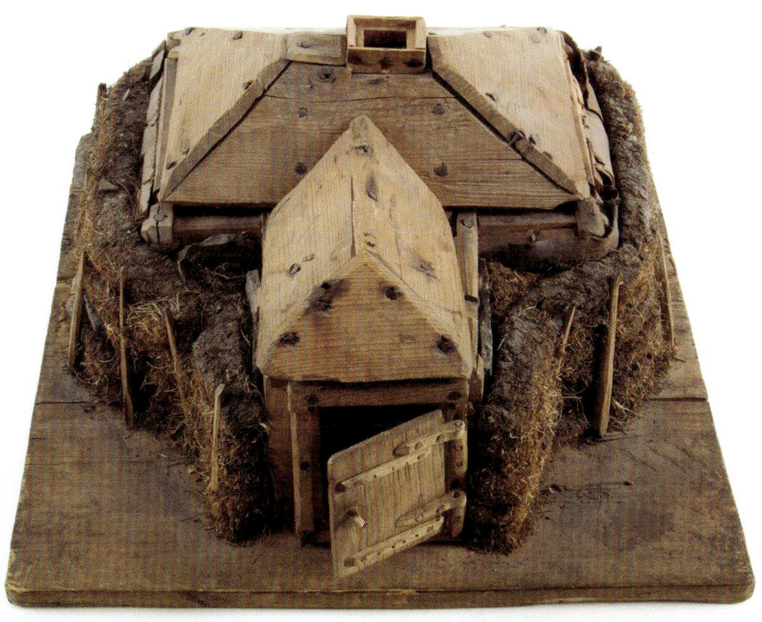

Plate 5. Model of a two-room Sea Sámi turf hut in wood, stone, and peat moss. Made in the Sámi village of Talvik, near Alta, Norway, by fisherman–farmer Sjur Olsen for the Tromsø Exposition of 1870. Residents of northern Norway were invited to send their products to the exposition for display. Courtesy of the Arctic University Museum of Norway.

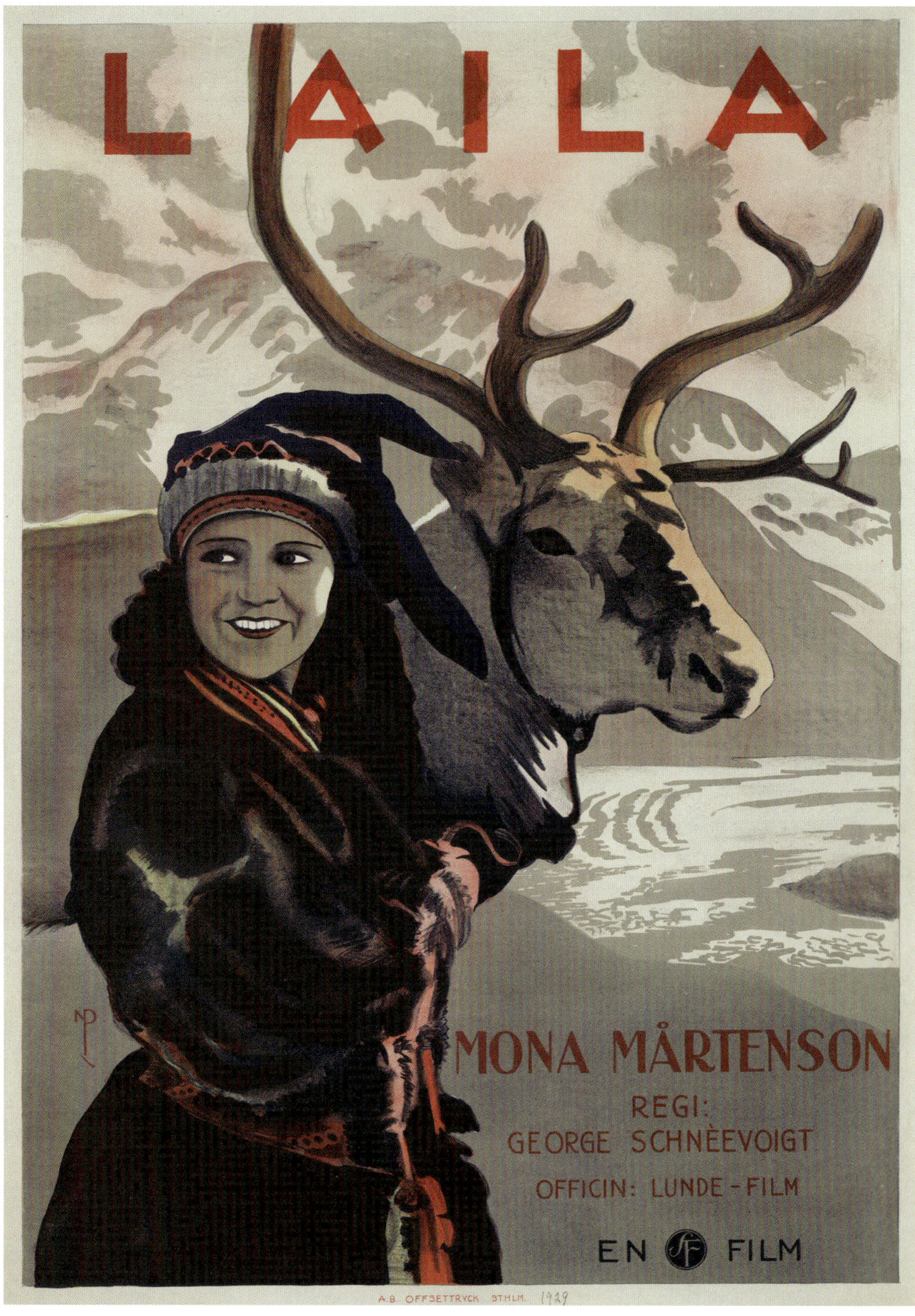

Plate 6. Norwegian poster for the Scandinavian film *Laila* (1929), directed by George Schnéevoigt from the novel by J. A. Friis and filmed in Denmark and Norway. Art by Niels P. Røhder. Courtesy of the National Library of Norway. Copyright 2021 Artists Rights Society (ARS), New York / BONO, Oslo.

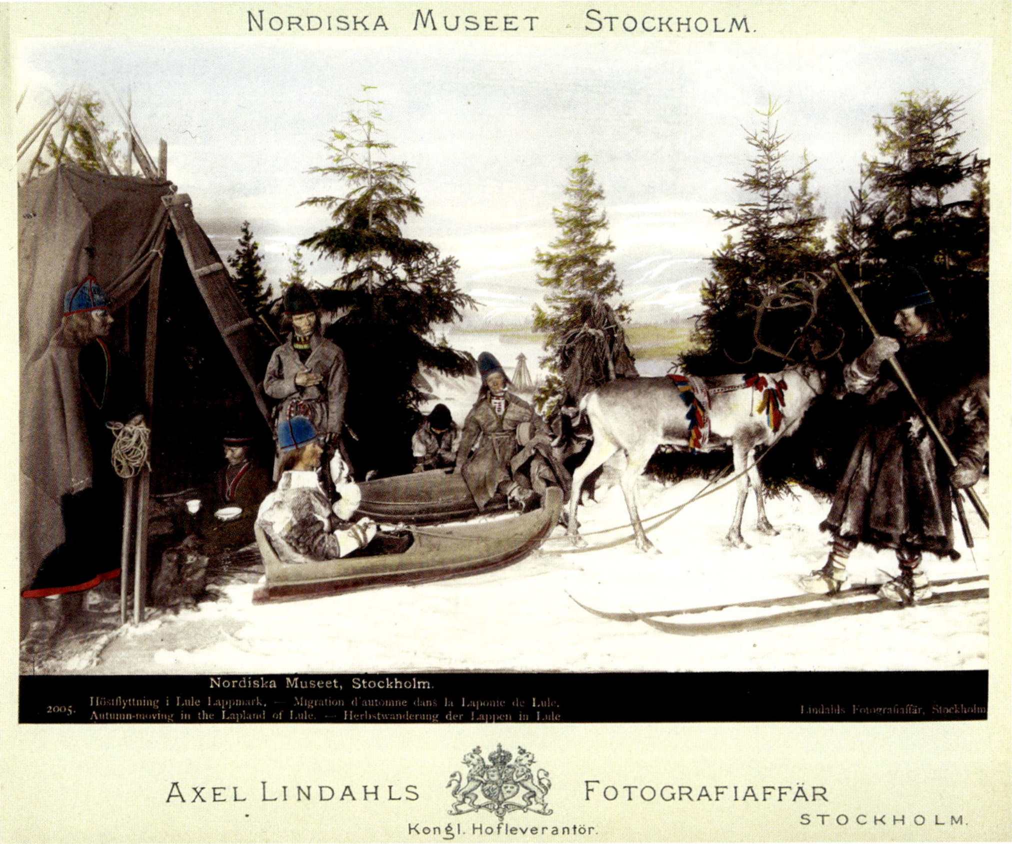

Plate 7. *Autumn in Lule Lappmark* diorama, Scandinavian-Ethnographic Collection, Stockholm, 1874. The models for the exhibit were based on younger members of Gustaf von Düben's family; they wear traditional shoes and hats but newly made tunics and dresses. Photograph by Axel Lindahl. Courtesy of the Nordic Museum, Stockholm.

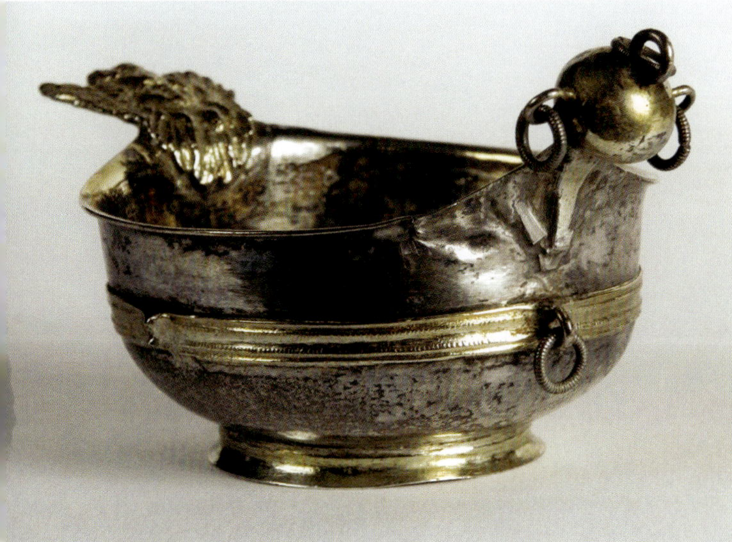

Plate 8. Sámi cup cast in silver in the workshop of Olof Löfvander in Luleå, Sweden, in the late eighteenth century. Silver spoons, jewelry, cups, and bowls from Sámi designs were commissioned from urban silversmiths for use as gifts, dowries, trade, and savings in Sápmi for centuries. Today, a number of Sámi *duojárs* work with silver. Photograph by Anne-Lise Reinsfelt. Courtesy of the Norwegian Museum of Cultural History.

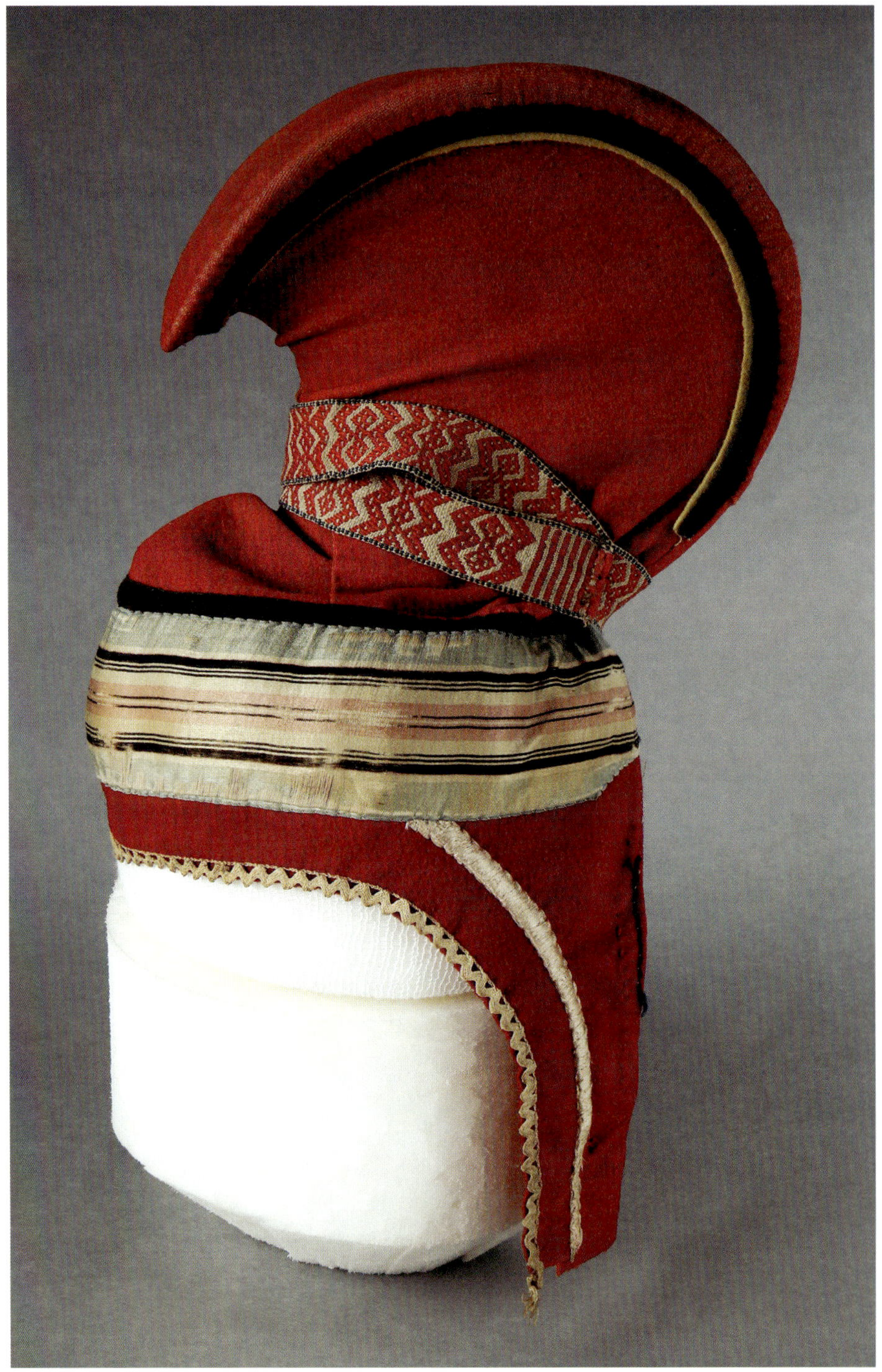

Plate 9. A well-preserved women's hat, or *ládjogahpir,* worn until the late nineteenth century in North Sápmi, fitted over a horn-shaped wooden mold, made by Beret Persdatter and Beret Isaksdatter of Karasjok, Norway. Few original hats of this type remain. This one was collected by Hugo Samzelius in 1891. Photograph by Thomas Adolfsson. Courtesy of the Nordic Museum, Stockholm.

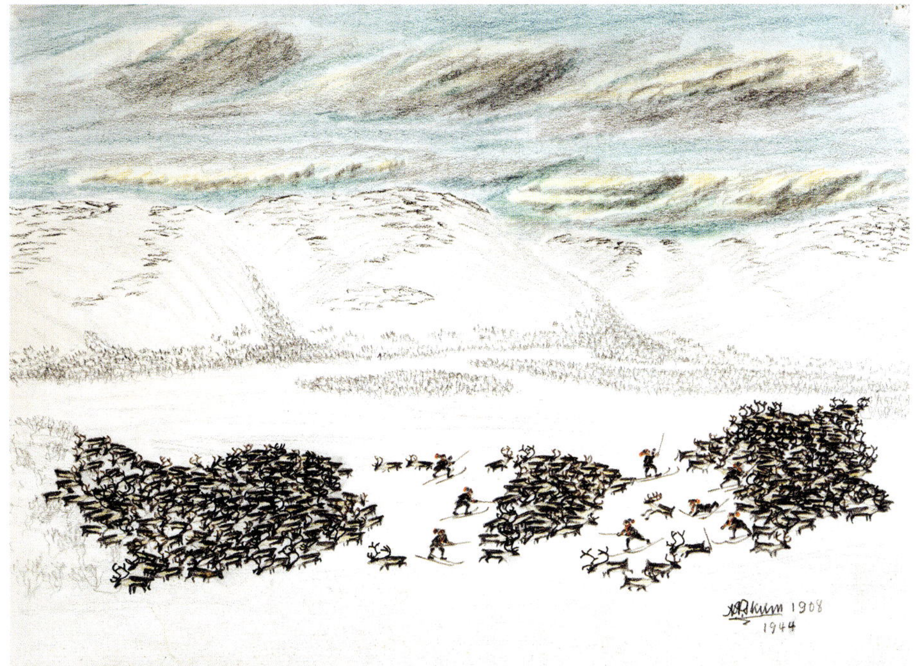

Plate 10. Nils Nilsson Skum, *Reindeer Herd,* 1908/1944. Pencil and crayon on paper. This drawing is similar to many in Skum's book *Herding Reindeer,* which illustrate memories of herding life. He often recorded the date of his memory as well as the date he drew the picture. Courtesy of the Gothenburg Museum of Art, Sweden.

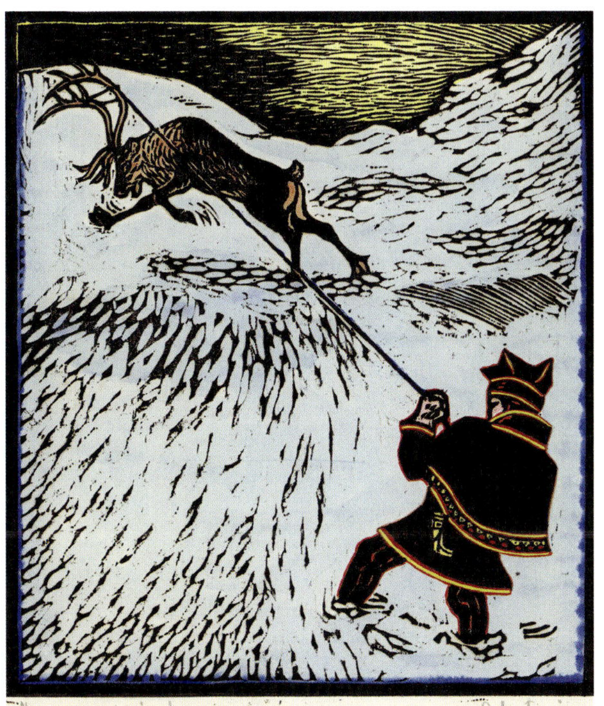

Plate 11. John Andreas Savio, *Man with Bull Reindeer,* circa 1920s. Hand-colored woodcut. Photograph by Børre Høstland. Courtesy of the National Museum of Art, Architecture, and Design, Oslo.

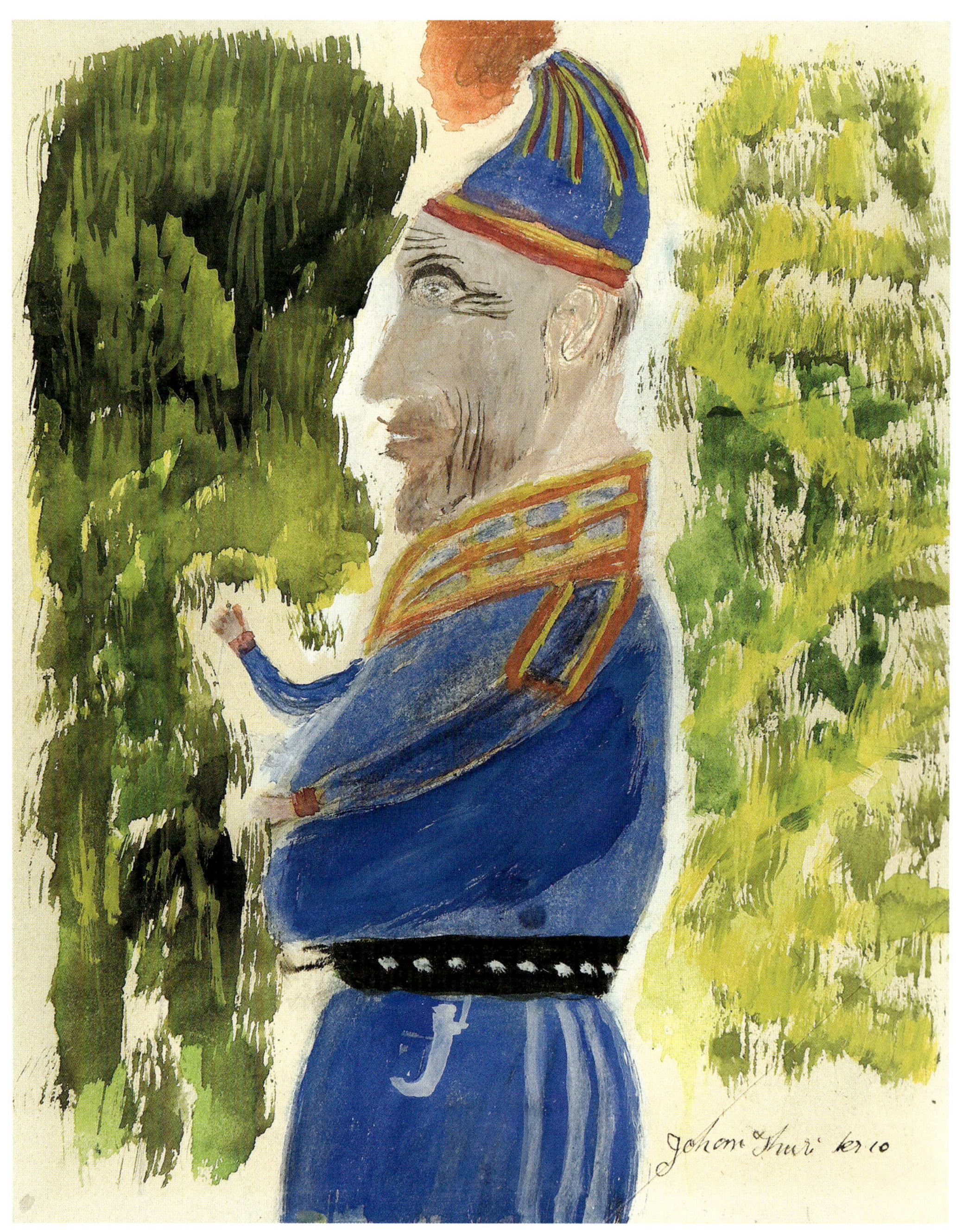

Plate 12. Johan Turi, figure of a Sámi man, 1920s. Gouache/watercolor on paper. Johan Turi was an artist and the author of *Muitalus sámiid birra*. Photograph by Peter Segemark. Courtesy of the Nordic Museum, Stockholm.

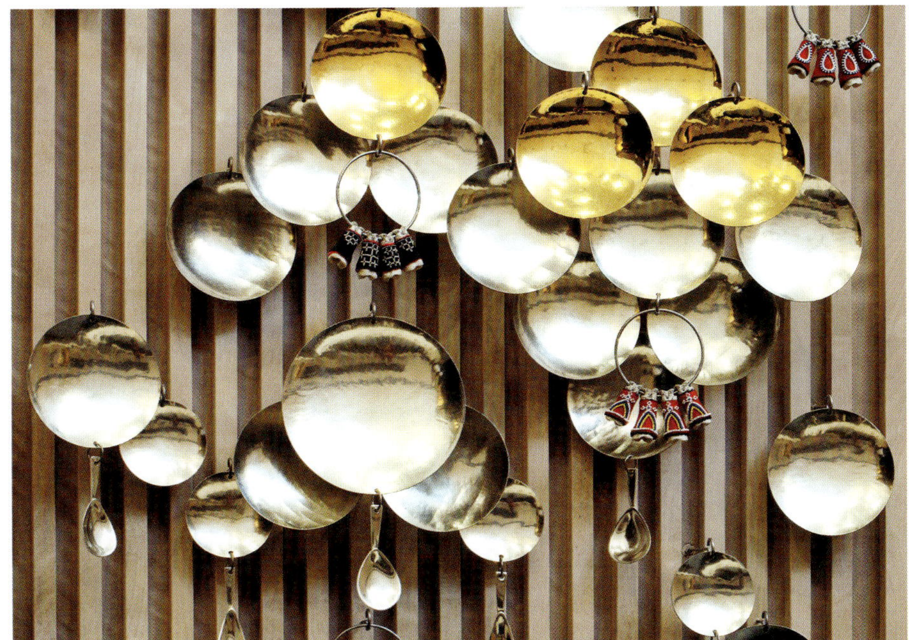

Plate 13. Outi Pieski, *Eatnu, Eadni, Eana—Stream, Mother, Ground,* 2012 (detail). Wall relief in gilded stainless steel, ceramic, bone, and *duodji* in the Sámi Parliament Hall, Sámi Cultural Centre Sajos, Aanaar (Inari), Finland. Photograph by Marja Helander, the Finnish State Art Collection. Courtesy of the artist.

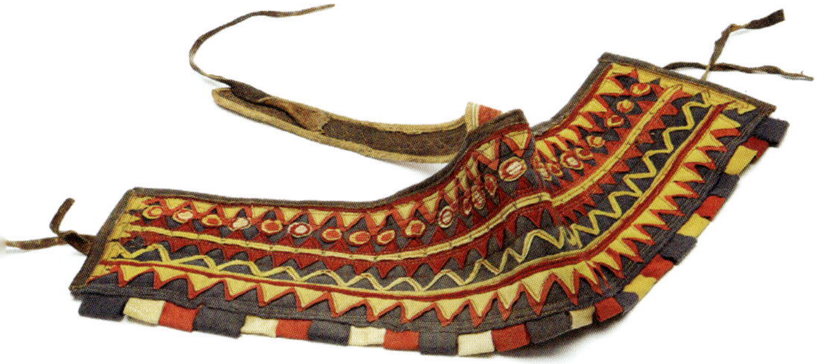

Plate 14. A pair of winter boots made from the leg skin of a white reindeer, with woven wool shoe bands and a colorful wool saddlecloth for pack reindeer. Emilie Demant Hatt collected these objects and many others from the Talma Sámi in summer 1916. Photographs from National Museum of Denmark.

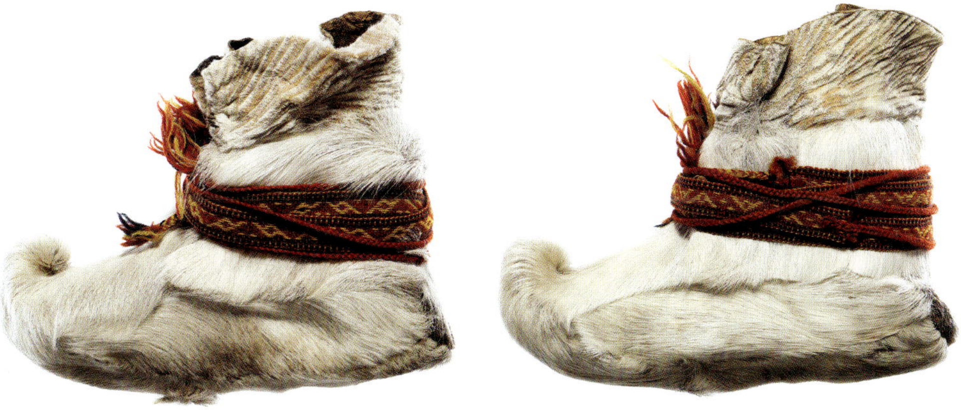

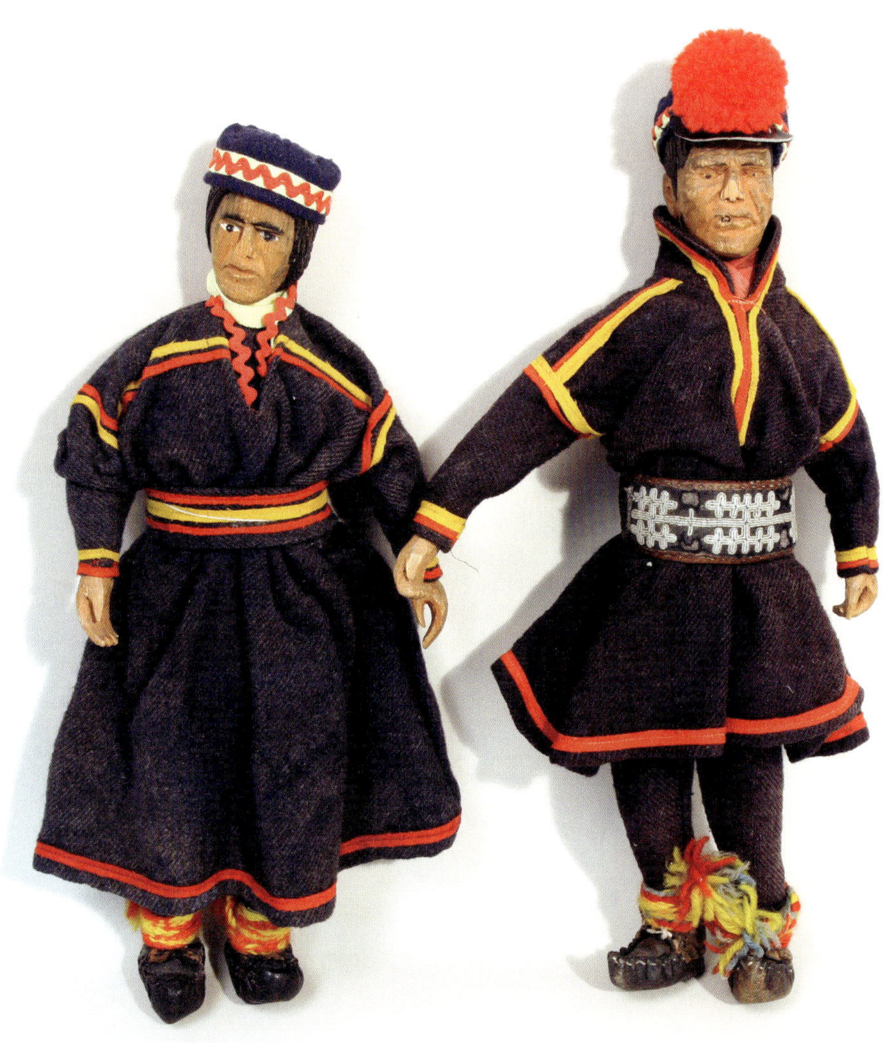

Plate 15. Dolls in Karesuando dress, with wooden faces and hands. Maker unknown, from 1890, originally collected by Birger Nordin. The male doll wears a belt sewn with pewter thread. Photograph from the Forest and Saami Museum, Lycksele, Sweden.

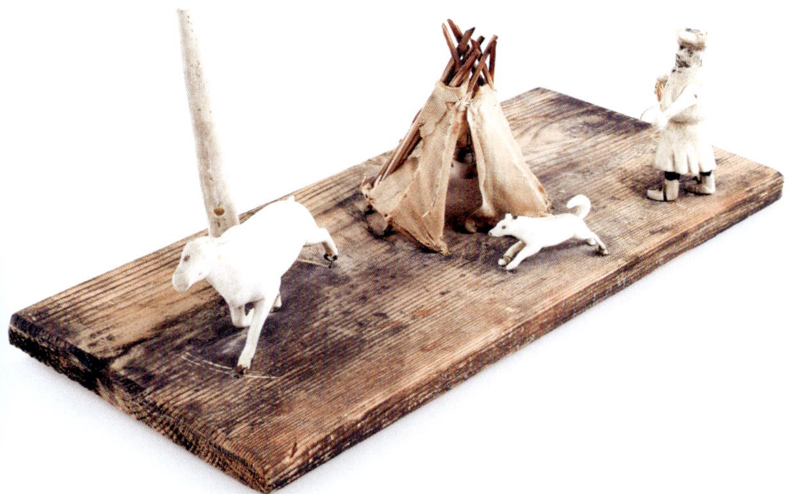

Plate 16. Lars Hætta, *Siida,* a model of carved and painted wood, cloth, and string. Acquired in 2014 by Kautokeino Municipal Museum, Norway. Photograph by Ellen J. Bals. Courtesy Guovdageainnu Gilišillju / Kautokeino Municipal Museum, Norway.

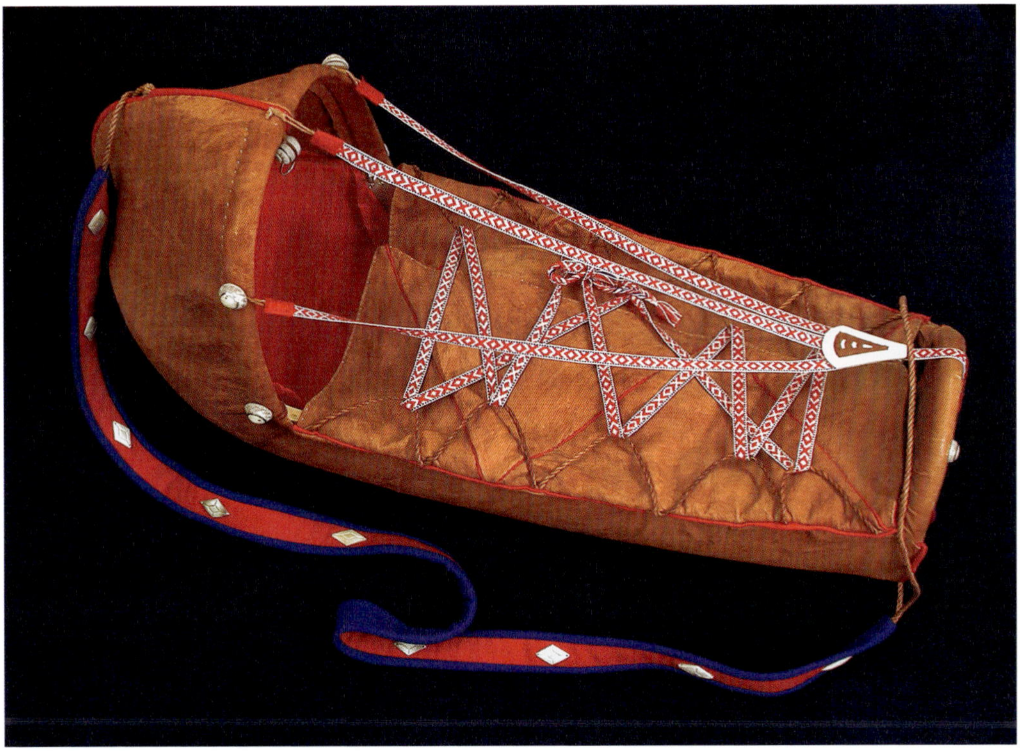

Plate 17. A modern cradle, or *gietkka,* made from traditional materials of wood and tanned reindeer skin, decorated with woven bands and silver buttons, by Gunvor Guttorm, an influential artisan, writer, and professor of *duodji* in Kautokeino, Norway. The cradle is part of a collection of contemporary *duodji* exhibited at the Varanger Sámi Museum in Norway. Courtesy of the Varanger Sámi Museum.

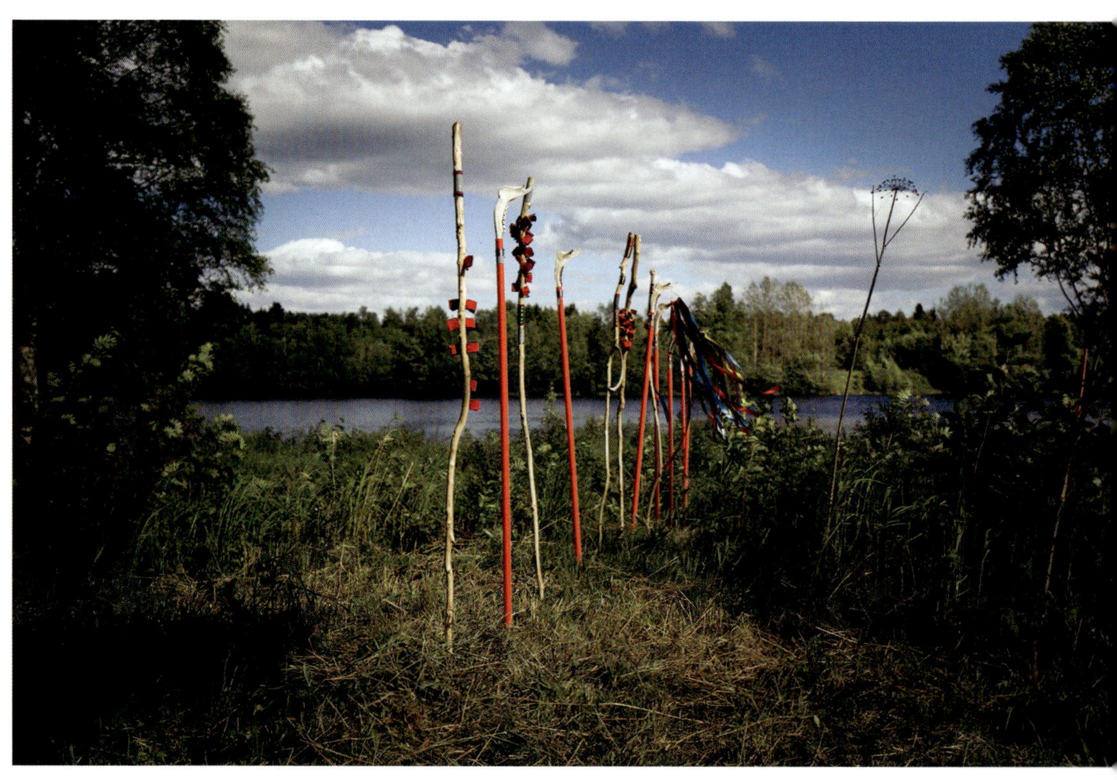

Plate 18. For the 2016 Art Ii Biennial, Sámi artists Outi Pieski and Jenni Laiti created *Ovdavázzit—Forewalkers,* an installation of tall walking sticks ornamented with antler, bone, cloth, yarn, and metal that they placed in a "borderless fence" at the environmental art park near the Iijoki River in Finland. Photograph by Antti J. Leinonen / Art Ii Biennial.

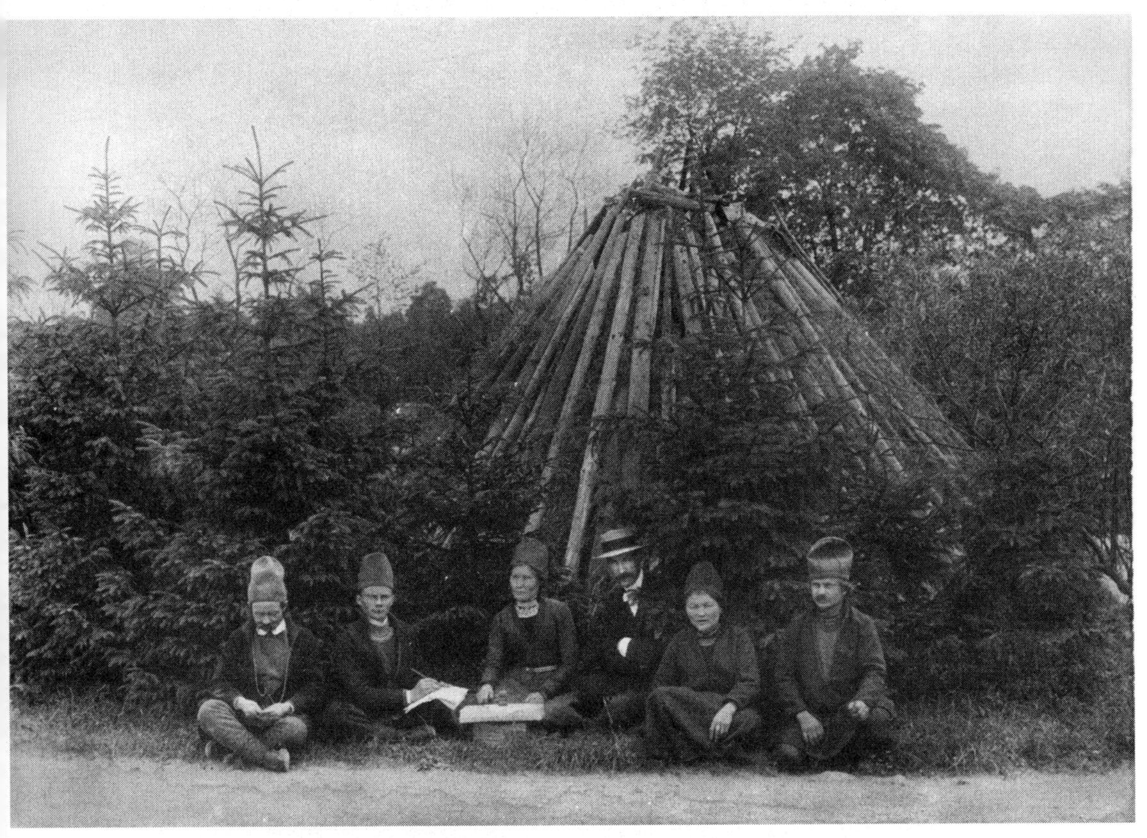

Founding of the Central Sámi Association at Skansen, August 10, 1904. Elsa Laula is at center, with Torkel Tomasson to her immediate left. Courtesy of Örnsköldsviks Museum, Sweden.

ditional Sámi culture—and not for the better. Torsten Boberg, again speaking as one who knew the situation up north, bemoaned the fact that Sámi men were sporting sweaters and golfing pants and that Sámi women were wearing makeup ("Lapp Ladies Are Now Powdering: The Plan Is Ready, but the Funds Are Lacking," read the headline).[14] Little happened in 1936, but the following spring Manker, who by now was angling to become the curator of a Lappish Central Museum, wherever it landed, put together a proposal for the Nordic Museum's director, Andreas Lindblom, with specific details about how it would work to have a museum within the museum. The Nordic, though a private foundation, also received funds from the state, and Manker suggested that Lindblom add a request for ten thousand kronor for the 1938 budget, for a salary and travel expenses for the director of this specialized department. To the budget request Manker appended a briefly worded petition to the state, signed by almost fifty supporters, including Sámi artists and writers, academics, and public intellectuals.

The idea of an actual Lappish Central Museum within another institution was quietly put aside, and the Nordic Museum's existing Sámi collection and research activities associated with it became a museum department in 1939, with Manker its sole paid employee, a multifaceted position he would hold until 1961.

Although the Nordic Museum eventually ended up with the largest number of Sámi objects in one place, it would not be correct to say that the Lappish Department fully dominated the field, much as Manker tried his best to steer donations to Stockholm and continued to collect throughout his twenty plus years at the museum. There were other forces in Sweden that resisted the centrifugal energy that brought Sámi objects south.

Unlike Norway, where the Tromsø Museum housed major collections of Sámi material culture and was a more important site of Sámi studies than Oslo, in the mid-twentieth century Sweden had only two significant centers of Sámi studies, Uppsala University and the Nordic Museum, both in the South. All the same, private collectors in central and northern Sweden managed to amass a sizeable number of Sámi objects, which eventually ended up in museums in Arjeplog, Jokkmokk, Luleå, and Umeå. Most of these collectors either were from these areas or had taken jobs in Sápmi as sheriffs, doctors, clergymen, or engineers. One of the earliest collectors of this sort was the engineer and surveyor H. Hampusson Huldt, who gave some two hundred objects to the regional Västerbottens Museum in Umeå. Many of them are domestic items and embroidered clothing, but some are of silver, including spoons, belt buckles, and other ornaments.[15] Huldt took an interest in ornamentation and in 1920 published a book titled *Patterns for Lappish Handicraft in Västerbotten,* which featured detailed drawings of patterns found on objects in his collection.[16]

Nordic metalsmiths had been active since the days of the Vikings, and jewelry and ornaments were used in trade from the Baltic to the Barents, initially in bronze and imported gold and later in copper and silver that came from mines in Sweden and Norway and were worked by goldsmiths in Bergen for the Hansa merchants and along the Norwegian coast. Goldsmiths were also to be found in Luleå, Tornio and other towns along the upper Gulf of Bothnia. It was common for wealthier Sámi families to take their bone spoons and salt shakers to these smiths and commission silver versions that replicated the shape and some of the etched images, as well as to buy other kinds of silver objects for ornament and investment. Silver objects acted as savings accounts against hard times and usually stayed in families or related families; they were portable on migration and could be buried in case of raids from outsiders. The silver objects were not ethnographica in the way that some collectors, such as Hazelius, had conceived of it, when the idea was to gather everything to do with pagan religion, along with domestic items made by hand by nomadic herders. But later private collectors took a strong interest in silver, particularly two different men in Sweden in the first half of the twentieth century.

Dr. Einar Wallquist was just twenty-six when he arrived in Arjeplog in 1922 to begin a forty-year practice as the district's only doctor. During that time, he treated many Sámi patients. He collected a variety of things over the years, but his obsession was silver, some of it dating back to medieval times and some of it of more recent vintage. His house became an informal gallery of artifacts, and, on his retirement, he created the Silver Museum in Arjeplog, with a vault containing some seven hundred silver objects, as well as other items from around the region. Two hundred kilometers northeast of Arjeplog, in Jokkmokk, the county sheriff Erland Ström also began to take an interest in Sámi ethnography and silver in the 1930s and 1940s, eventually amassing about a thousand artifacts. Ernst Manker hoped that Ström, upon his retirement, might be persuaded to donate his collection to the Nordic Museum, but Ström preferred to keep his treasures in the North, reasoning that since Jokkmokk's Sámi Folk High School had become a center for students to learn the Lule Sámi language and handicrafts, they could use his collection to study. At the time there was no museum of note in Jokkmokk, so he provisionally turned everything over to Norrbottens Museum in Luleå, until a museum was eventually built in Jokkmokk in the 1960s, with a special vault for the silver. This remodeled museum in turn became Ájtte, the Swedish Mountain and Sámi Museum, in 1989.

Although Artur Hazelius had pooh-poohed the idea of a Lappish Central Museum in the north of Sweden, in fact by the end of the twentieth century, many small museums and several larger museums with Sámi collections were located in northern and central Sweden, particularly Östersund, Jokkmokk, Arjeplog, Umeå, Lycksele, and Luleå. Their combined inventories number close to twenty thousand objects, far above what the Nordic Museum cares for today. Yet for many years, nothing surpassed what Ernst Manker was able to pull off, largely on his own but also with a significant network of political allies, wealthy backers, Sámi collaborators, and museal colleagues.

The material collection of Sámi artifacts at the Nordic Museum grew under Manker's tenure as curator but remained essentially consistent in the sorts of physical objects that were gifted or acquired. In 1943, during the process of moving into its new building, the State Historical Museum transferred in a formal deposition twenty-four Sámi drums to the Nordic Museum, almost its entire collection, many of which had been collected at the Åsele assembly in 1725; this brought the Nordic Museum's collection to around forty, the largest collection of Sámi drums in the world. Aside from the drums and *sieidis*—a few of which were moved inside the museum from Sacrifice Isle on Skansen—the material objects were utilitarian though often beautifully decorated and engraved. Domestic items used by herding families, handicrafts, and Sámi clothing privileged the current nomadic and formerly nomadic life. Modernity was not admitted into the museum. Very few factory-made or imported products that Sámi people used in the 1940s and 1950s became part of the Nordic Museum's Sámi collection.

Just like other Swedes of the time, many Sámi people in the northern provinces wore leather boots and woolen jackets, drove trucks, flew in airplanes, and used sewing machines and power tools. As more and more Sámi young people moved to Stockholm and other cities, studied at universities, lived in apartments, and took work in varied sectors of the economy, little of their daily lives was reflected in either the exhibits or the museum's storerooms. The Lappish Department became, during the course of Manker's two decades as its director, a historical collection, organized and interpreted by a man who had first fallen in love with the world of the reindeer herders in the 1920s and found it useful to keep the paradigm of the ethnographic present on view in the museum, even as that present receded further into the past.

The audience for Manker's books, genially written with dozens of black-and-white photographs, was largely the same Swedish public that Artur Hazelius had catered to, though Manker reached many inside and outside Sweden who had rarely visited the Stockholm museum. Beginning in 1928 with his first travelogue about a visit to Lule Sápmi and continuing through a posthumously published essay and photo collection in 1978, Manker left a fifty-year account—a warm, personal, selective, and biased account—of the Sámi communities of Sweden. Not only were his popular literary works the entry point for most Swedes to inform themselves about Sámi culture and history, but they helped enshrine the Sámi

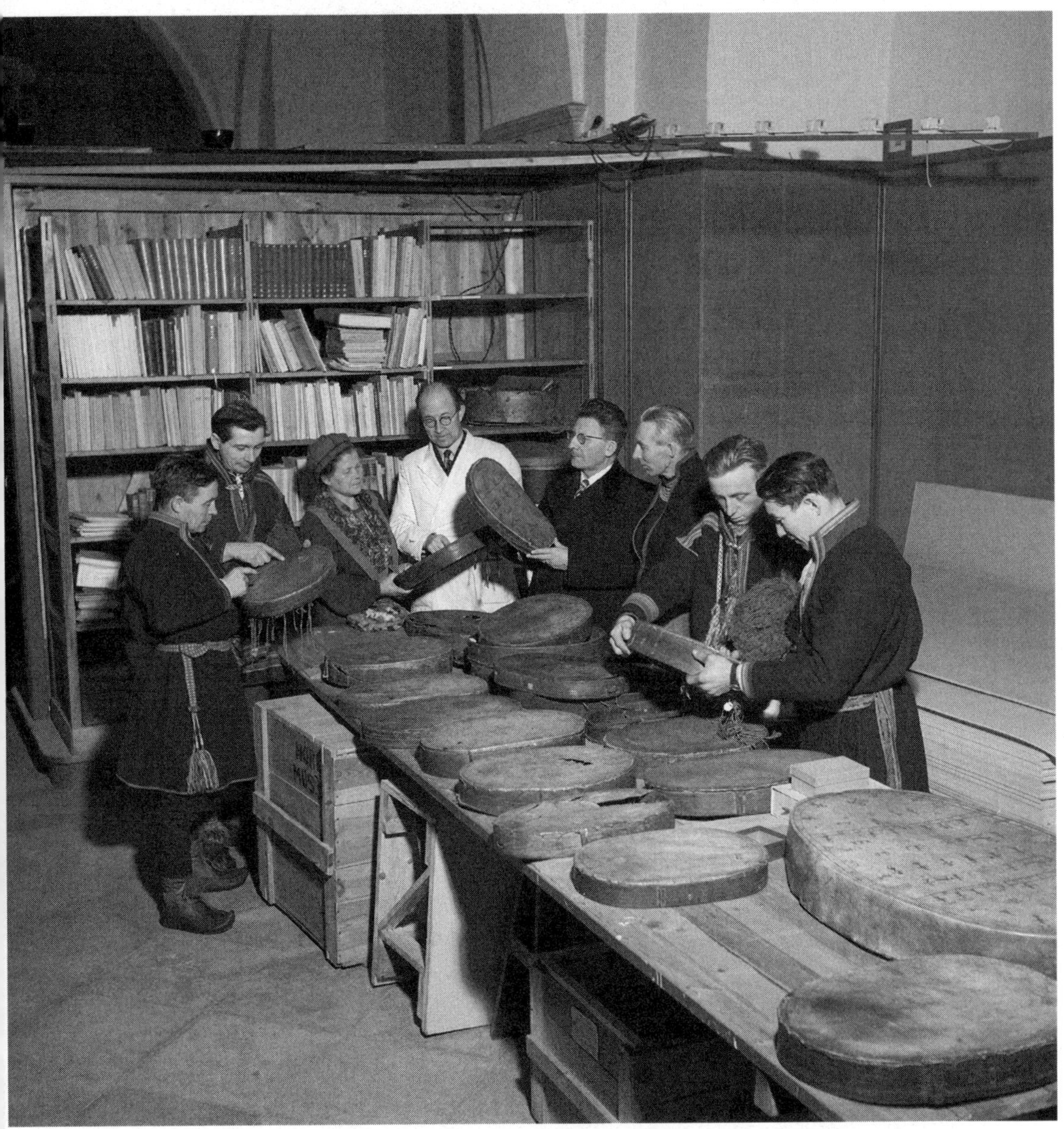

Ernst Manker with a Sámi delegation studies the Nordic Museum's drum collection in 1945. Left to right: Mattias Kuoljok, John Utsi, Anna Gustafsson, Ernst Manker, Gustav Park, Petrus Gustafsson, Isak Parffa, and Nils Erik Kuoljok. Courtesy of the Nordic Museum, Stockholm.

as nomads of the North, conveniently ignoring the urban Sámi and rarely addressing awkward questions about social prejudice and institutionalized discrimination against the Sámi in matters of education, language, and civil rights. He preferred to look at culture through the lens of the past, even though he also acknowledged challenges that the Sámi people faced.

In two books in the early 1940s, one popular and one scholarly, he documented in both photographs and text the building of a hydroelectric plant at Porjus, a project that flooded Sámi houses near the Lule River and tributaries. In that time period, Manker took no political position on the displacement of the Sámi and the destruction of their way of life. Hydropower was endorsed by all parties in Sweden as in the national interest. Later, in the 1950s and 1960s, he spoke out more forcefully against discrimination against the Sámi in articles and speeches. But in the prewar and immediate postwar years, Manker shared some of the biases of most Swedes and the government. Although the days of "Lapps should be Lapps" were nominally over, and the racial biology movement had lost its respectability and its minimal scientific credibility in Sweden as Hitler came to power, the Sámi were by no means seen as fully equal to Swedish citizens, and racist policies against them continued.

Manker was hardly ignorant of the concerns of the reindeer herders. One of his first acts when he was hired in 1939 to run the Lappish Department was to send out questionnaires to the heads of all fifty-one Sámi districts in Sweden. Eight separate questionnaires, largely related to reindeer biology and herding, aimed to create a more complete picture of how many herders there were, where they migrated, and whom they were related to. Using this information and field trips to Sápmi, in 1947 Manker published *De svenska fjällapparna* (The Swedish Mountain Lapps).[17] During the war, the Nordic Museum was only closed for a few months in 1940 to evacuate certain valuable collections. But a rethinking and remaking of the old Sámi exhibition space had to be postponed, as did the idea of programs and temporary exhibits. Manker used those wartime years to create a "Lapland Inventory" not only of all the Sámi objects in the collection but of archaeological sites and structures around Sápmi. The work went on after the war, as Manker continued annual field tours to the Sámi districts in Sweden, accompanied by colleagues. This ongoing documentary work and inventorying was in addition to his efforts to establish the Lappish Archive (LA), composed of documents and images already possessed by the Nordic Museum, as well as new acquisitions. The Lappish Archive still exists in the initials "LA" appended to many hundreds of boxes in the current Nordic Museum Archive and includes Manker's own manuscripts, field notes, and photographs.

While Manker's literary and scholarly publications were prodigious, we only have to look at the catalog of the LA to see the hidden nine-tenths of the iceberg that supported his public presentations. His correspondence was vast, and he kept it organized in ring binders, usually with carbons of letters he sent as well as those he received. As a former newspaper man who knew the value of publicity, he preserved original clippings of anything that mentioned the Lappish Department: its activities, publications, and exhibits. There are printed pamphlets and posters, offprints of journal articles, and a trove of material connected to the scholarly series *Acta Lapponica,* which published books about the Sámi. The LA came to include material by a variety of scholars and authors who had written about the Sámi, as Manker avidly hunted down and charmed away correspondence and personal archives, field notebooks and journals, photographs, manuscripts of published and unpublished books and articles, ephemera, and even artworks on paper. In these efforts to centralize all things Sámi in Stockholm and to establish the Nordic Museum as a scholarly center, he competed at times with Professor Björn Collinder of the Finno–Ugric Department at Uppsala, who managed to hold on to the papers of K. B. Wiklund. But Manker proved patient, persuasive, and persistent, and ultimately the LA became the home of many collections that Manker particularly wanted.

As early as 1939 Ernst Manker was in touch with Emilie Demant Hatt, the Danish ethnographer and artist who had translated and edited Johan Turi's *Muitalus sámiid birra (An Account of the Sámi)* and a second bilingual Sámi–English volume of Sámi narratives written by Turi and his nephew Per, *Lappish Texts.*[18] Demant Hatt and Turi met in improbable circumstances when she was visiting Sápmi as a tourist with her sister in 1904 and encountered him on the iron ore train. An immediate connection sprang up between the thirty-one-year-old Danish artist, who said she had dreamed of living with Sámi nomads since childhood, and this Sámi trapper and hunter of fifty years, who confided to Demant Hatt that his dream was someday to write a book about his people. In 1907, after studying North Sámi at the University of Copenhagen, Demant Hatt moved to Sápmi for eighteen months, living with Johan's brother and sister-in-law and their children in a tent among the Talma Sámi near Lake Torneträsk and participating in the spring migration to Norway with the Könkämä Sámi. She also encouraged Turi to write his book in the Sámi language, and when she returned to Denmark in the fall of 1908, she took his notebooks with her to translate and edit.[19]

With the backing of the wealthy Hjalmar Lundbohm, manager of the LKAB mine in Kiruna, a North Sámi–Danish bilingual edition of *Muitalus sámiid birra / En bog om lappernes liv* was published in 1910 and ultimately translated into several languages. The first edition included an "atlas" of pen-and-ink illustrations by Turi of Sámi nomadic life. Demant Hatt herself returned to Sweden almost every summer from 1910 to 1916, at first alone and then with her husband, the archaeologist and cultural geography professor Gudmund Hatt, to do fieldwork in South, North, and Pite Sápmi. She published two books, *With the Lapps in the High Mountains* and *By the Fire,* a collection of folktales she illustrated with her own linoleum cuts.[20]

The relationship between Turi and Demant Hatt was the subject of some speculation, and he was certainly crushed that she married in 1911. They were in touch until 1936, when Johan Turi died, by then a well-known figure in Scandinavia. Now in her late sixties and living in Copenhagen, Demant Hatt had not been to Sweden since 1916 and had largely focused on painting since the 1920s. Inspired by Expressionism to create vivid landscapes of Sápmi, she was part of a group of interwar women painters in Denmark. Manker ascertained that she still had the original notebooks in which Johan Turi had written *Muitalus* in 1908, as well as years of correspondence from Turi and some of his artworks on paper left from an exhibition she had helped arrange for him in 1922 in Copenhagen.

Manker courted Demant Hatt by letter from 1939 onward, inviting her to Stockholm to receive the Silver Hazelius Award for her work with Turi and showing great interest in her art and ethnographic work. Later Manker wrote about her with sexist nonchalance as "Turi's housekeeper and inspiring genius," but at the time, Manker's encouragement was important to Demant Hatt.[21] It helped her focus, during the long German occupation of Denmark, on typing up all her field notebooks and writing a partial manuscript about her summer in 1910 with two Sámi elders in South Sápmi. In letters throughout the war years, Manker hinted that he wanted to publish her correspondence with Turi and suggested she write a short biography of her old friend. He mentioned other publishing projects, which came to nothing for lack of funds. But what he really wanted was to get his hands on Turi's original journals, which Demant Hatt was reluctant to send him by mail, given the war. It was not until 1950 that Manker made a special trip to Copenhagen and took possession of the journals on behalf of the LA, along with

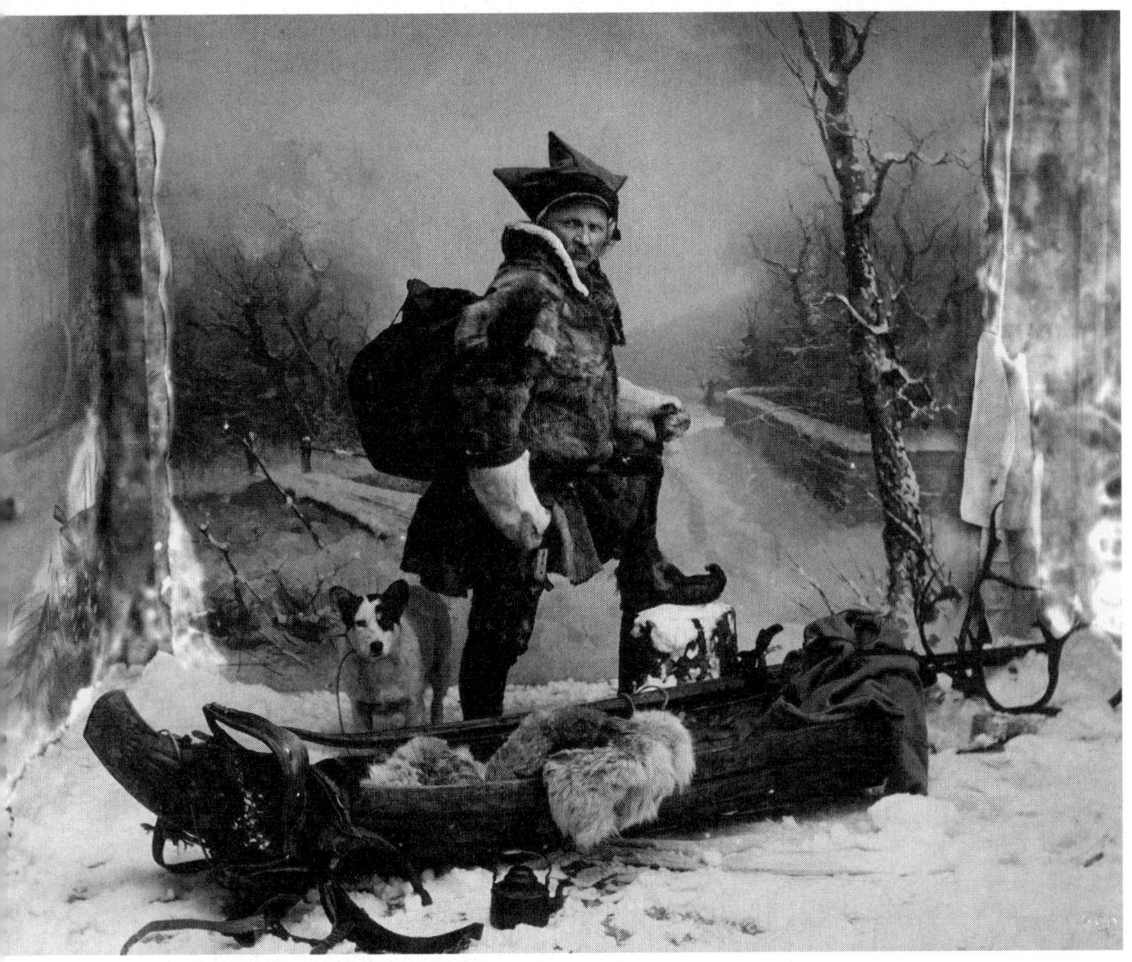

Johan Turi photographed in the studio of Borg Mesch, Kiruna, Sweden, circa 1910. Courtesy of the Nordic Museum, Stockholm.

artwork created by Turi for an exhibit in Copenhagen in the 1920s. In 1953 she also gave fifty oil paintings to the Nordic Museum, all with motifs from Sápmi.

Although Demant Hatt was to donate or leave behind a good deal of archival material in Copenhagen, Manker obtained all her original and typed field journals from 1910 to 1916, in addition to other unpublished material relating to Sápmi and her photograph albums of Sámi people she'd known. She translated and typed up Turi's letters from 1904 to 1936, which she presented along with her explanatory notes on their complex friendship and the originals in their envelopes. She gave the LA her letters from Hjalmar Lundbohm, the mining director of LKAB, regarding all the production details of translating and publishing *Muitalus sámiid birra*. As Manker suspected, the papers of Emilie Demant Hatt and Johan Turi would become touchstone collections in the LA. Turi is now regarded as a central figure in Sámi literary history, and both his words and his drawings are widely spread over Sápmi.

Manker tried to collect not only Turi's papers but his last effects as well. In 1943, during his peripatetic "Lapland Inventory," he had himself rowed across Lake Torneträsk to Johan Turi's old cabin at Lattilahti, situated idyllically along the lakeside surrounded by birches and now owned by Turi's nephew, Tomas Turi. In an atmospheric essay, Manker set the scene for his readers by describing a room in the cabin with Johan's simple furniture—a sleeping bench, a chair, and a table—and some objects he'd made from horn and wood. Together, Manker and Tomas opened a chest Turi had left: "There we had letters, manuscripts, and notebooks, along with drawn and stamped pictures, and the whole stamp block collection, 29 of them."[22] Turi had made the stamp blocks himself, carving small figures of reindeer and tents in low relief at one end of a piece of polished wood. He had also made stencils, figures carved out of slices of horn, also of reindeer. His highly original idea, which Manker found endearing and amusing, was to be able to create artworks quickly for tourists who stopped at the Abisko train station, where there was a large hostel operated by the Swedish Tourist Association. "Pictures with a few reindeer drawn with a pen were 10 kronor, while those that represented a reindeer separation and corral and had a mass of reindeer were priced higher, at 22 kronor."[23]

Manker spent several days up at Lake Torneträsk with the Turi family and returned to Stockholm with a few pictures. Tomas Turi was willing to sell almost everything that had belonged to his uncle to the Nordic Museum. Manker, as so often, had to scramble to find financial support. He wrote, for instance, to Anna Bielke, a countess who had befriended Turi in his later years and had translated one of Turi's books to Swedish, to ask for funding. In the end, some papers did end up in Uppsala due to Professor Collinder's efforts, but most of the artwork came to the Nordic Museum to become part of the LA, along with around forty-five objects, everything from Turi's sled and snow shovel to handmade knives and handsewn calfskin bags. The Nordic Museum even holds a small number of personal effects, including Johan Turi's now hardened reindeer-skin trousers, tunic, and blue cloth cap with a red tassel. The collection of items connected with

Turi is rounded out by gifts he gave Emilie Demant Hatt that she donated to the Nordic Museum.

Manker wasn't an unusual collector for his time in chasing the stories behind the objects and being fascinated by the lives of the people they'd once belonged to—other private connoisseurs in northern Sweden enjoyed accumulating Sámi things and learning about their history and owners—but he was an unusual curator compared to some of his predecessors who stockpiled objects from Sápmi in order to create typological hordes of spoons and needle cases. As a former journalist and photographer, Manker saw the world of ethnography in terms of people and their stories. Manker's evident delight in the outdoor life imbues his essays and book chapters—illustrated with photos of grizzled old reindeer herders, young ladies decked with silver, and kids happily playing by the lakeshore or showing off their reindeer skills—with a sense that northern Sweden was peopled, that Sápmi was not just an empty space on a government map, and that the Sámi had cultural and emotional ties to the landscape.

Relationships and networks were crucial to Manker's work as a curator and promoter of Sámi culture. But few of his relationships with Sámi people were as significant as the one he developed with Nils Nilsson Skum, a Sámi herder, artist, and memoirist who appeared in Manker's life at the very point when he was arguing for the creation of a Lappish Central Museum.

Making Histories

One summer day in 1936, a train from the North pulled into Stockholm's Central Station. The man Ernst Manker was meeting for the first time descended to the platform, unmistakable in majestic girth, a red-tasseled hat, and a blue *gákti* with a wide leather belt from which hung a knife and bone sheath of his own making. Under his arm was a portfolio of drawings of reindeer herds in mountain landscapes, delicate but firm renderings in pen-and-ink and pencil, part of a manuscript he was creating of his own words and images about nomadic Sámi life, a book that Manker in one of his many roles, this time as publisher and art impresario, would publish two years later.

The sixty-four-year-old former reindeer herder and artist from the hamlet of Sjisjka, a dozen miles south of Kiruna on the train line, was not unknown to Manker. Nils Nilsson Skum and Manker had been corresponding since 1934, when Skum wrote a letter to the Stockholm department store Nordiska Kompaniet (the Nordic Company, or NK). His Swedish was dicey, but his meaning was clear; he wanted support for a book of drawings and texts about Sámi herding life. NK was a multifaceted business that, in addition to selling good-quality items, played a cultural role in the city. The letter was passed on to the director of the Ethnographic Museum and from there to Ernst Manker.

Even before they met, Manker was intrigued by Skum and decided to do all he could to make his project possible. As it turned out, the two men would forge a friendship. Manker was fascinated by Skum and wrote about him often over the years. In 1956, four years after Skum's death, Manker published *The Book of Skum* with his version of Skum's life and work.[1] Skum suited Manker down to the ground: the herder–artist was colorful but dignified, eccentric but creative, and authoritative on all things nomadic. Skum's life story was a gift to interviewers.

His art was not only documentary but attractive and collectible, and it fit into Manker's own theories about how Sámi art developed from Paleolithic rock paintings, to the designs on drums and knife sheaths, to contemporary Sámi drawings and paintings that yet retained primitive motifs and energy. For Manker, Skum was an ethnographic embodiment of the Sámi.

Nils Nilsson Skum was born in 1872 to a reindeer-herding family in Kauotokeino. That was twenty years after the uprising, in which some members of the Skum family were involved, but his life was dramatically different than Lars Hætta's and others who had been imprisoned and had lost everything. For economic reasons—a search for better pasturage—his family moved from Norway to Sweden when he was still very young to the Sámi herding district of Norrkaitum (now Girjas) between Gällivare and Kiruna. Skum never attended school but picked up the rudiments of reading and writing in Finnish and Swedish from an uncle. He made art with charcoal sticks from an early age; a relative gave him an ink pen when he was nine, and he used it to draw reindeer and landscapes. A visiting English tourist impressed by his talent sent him art materials on his return to London and even wanted to bring him to England to study, something Skum's father forbade. After his marriage to Helena Kuhmunen, the daughter of wealthy reindeer owners, and while working as the owner of a substantial herd, Skum went on to draw illustrations for several texts, including the cover of Johan Turi's book *Muitalus sámiid birra* and a series of "Nomad School Readers," or schoolbooks specifically for the children of reindeer herders that were produced by K. B. Wiklund in the 1920s. But Skum, who had a large family and the job of "Lapp policeman" in the district, had little time for art for quite a few years.

In his articles and books about Skum, Manker told the story of Skum's gradual loss of his reindeer and his resulting depression, a story that left out the political and social context in which herding became more difficult for almost all Sámi in Sweden in the first half of the twentieth century. Instead, Manker preferred to narrate how a tall, muscular, active man who once shot and killed a reindeer thief gradually put on so much weight that he could no longer herd. According to stories Manker had picked up but couldn't verify, Skum went through a troubled time when he sold more and more of his reindeer and was often found drinking in dives in local towns. But in 1934, Skum, at age sixty-two, gave up herding and began once more to find his way, this time as a *duojár* and fine artist.

In 1937, the summer after Skum's first visit to Stockholm, Ernst Manker went up to stay with the Skum family in their large turf hut in Sjisjka so that he and Nils could make final decisions on which illustrations to include in the book that would be titled *Same sita—Lappbyn (Sámi Siida—Lapp Village).* That same year, in conjunction with an international congress of folklore in Paris, the Nordic Museum contributed an exhibit of Swedish folklore to Musée de l'Homme. *Folklore de Suède* consisted of a variety of objects, clothing, and art from Sápmi, including a selection of original art from *Sámi Siida* "small, exquisite drawings from the snowlands of the Borealis," by Nils Nilsson Skum. When Andreas Lindblom, an art historian and the director of the Nordic Museum, returned to Stockholm and was asked by a reporter what the French had been most struck by in the exhibit, he answered without hesitation, "The Lapps, the Lapps of course, and foremost, Skum."[2]

Manker himself tended to see Nils Nilsson Skum first as a Sámi and then as an artist. He enjoyed the easy-going mood of the Skum household and described the setting where Skum drew reindeer after reindeer on sheets of white paper, in herds crossing rivers or pouring through mountain gaps, while "Mother Elli," Skum's wife, Helena, made coffee and grandchildren and dogs dashed in and out. Later, in remembering these happy days with Skum and his family, Manker would ask himself, "What did I notice about Skum as an artist?" He decided that Skum had passed the "purely primitive stage, where one draws things the way one thinks they are and not as the artistic eye sees them." Yet he had not reached the stage of artistry where he could draw anything "for the sake of the composition or aesthetic effect—that all for him was an unknown concept." All the same, Skum created both life and perspective in his finished pieces "and often a wonderful, gracious charm."[3]

At the time, Manker was winding up the results of his visits to museums and collections in Europe and Scandinavia to examine as many drums as possible. The following year the first volume of *The Lappish Magic Drum* would appear, with its many descriptions of the images on the drumskins. Manker saw Skum's artwork as later manifestations of this "ancient drawing tradition. The hunters of the Stone Age drew and painted reindeer and moose on the mountain walls, the *noaidis* drew the same figures on the skin of the magic drum, and now Skum put them on paper, canvas, and panels. He had the Paleolithic artist's feeling for animal forms and elevated that hunting-magic naturalism to art."[4]

Though Manker often categorizes Skum's art as documentary, he seems to miss the point that Skum, like Turi before him, created his art to share experience and knowledge, not to display himself as a relic of the ethnographic past or a continuation of the Paleolithic. But Skum, whose texts in *Same sita* appeared in both North Sámi and Swedish (translated by Israel Ruong), was clear about the

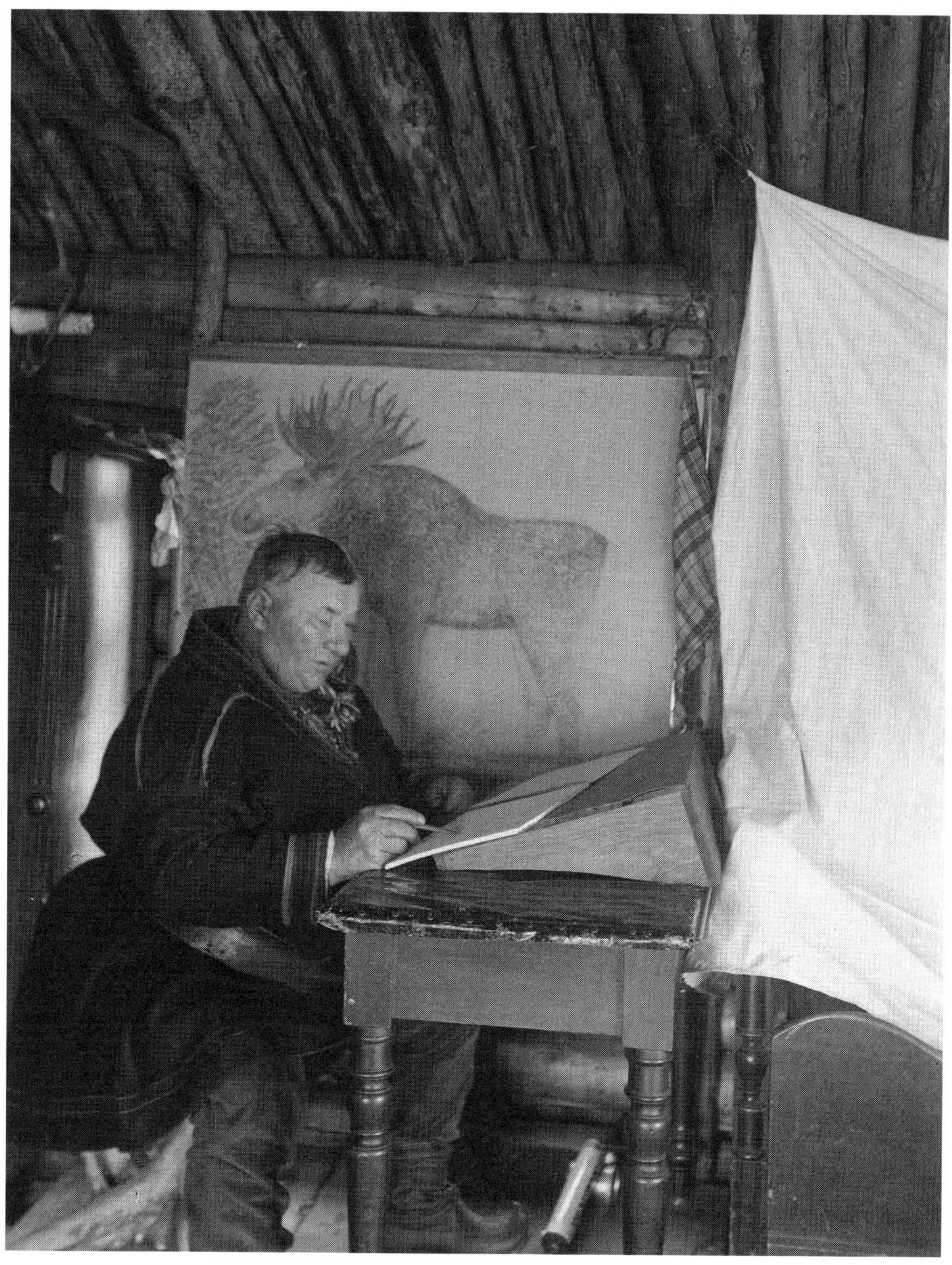

Nils Nilsson Skum at home in Sjisjka, Sweden, circa 1937. Photograph by Ernst Manker. Courtesy of the Nordic Museum, Stockholm.

intention of his project, writing in his foreword: "In the 1880s, when I was growing up and learning to take care of reindeer, this is the way that reindeer herding was managed, as I have attempted to describe in this book." He had done this, in words and pictures, so that knowledge could be saved "for the young people who find it difficult to handle the reindeer, so they can see and learn how the elders managed it."[5]

Sámi Siida—Lapp Village was a different sort of *muitalus,* a narrative or account, from Johan Turi's *Muitalus sámiid birra.* Turi's book ranged freely and poetically over subjects he knew well from observation and experience, topics as varied as herding, wolf trapping and hunting, courtship customs, childbirth, and health remedies. But Turi's words also carried a message to the Swedish government in a powerful, plangent voice, urging them to listen to the Sámi and not treat them so heedlessly. Skum's voice was more conversational, more straightforward and explanatory: this is how reindeer feed and where; this is when they come into rut; this is how they fight off wolves. Even the more fantastical facts, accompanied by a picture, were laid out in a calm tone. For instance, next to a pencil drawing of a mass of reindeer apparently in a body of water, in a dark maelstrom with only antlers showing at the farthest edges, Skum tells this story:

> Once a herd was being driven over a deep section of a river. The front of the herd was frightened and turned back into the water. . . . They began to swim around, as if they were circling in a corral, and it didn't take long before a funnel-like deepening formed in the middle. The reindeer were being swept down; it was as if the whole herd was being dragged down into this sucking vortex. . . . For certain the whole herd would have drowned if the herders had not quickly pulled them out.[6]

In Turi's *Muitalus* the prose was primary. His beguiling drawings, collected at the end of the long book in glossier paper that in some instances folded out, were originally an afterthought suggested by Emilie Demant Hatt, who wrote the captions herself, based on Turi's explanations. They illustrate single lines of reindeer crossing rivers and going up and coming down mountains in annual migrations and scenes of life in the *siida* or church village of Jukkasjärvi. The figures of people and animals are simplified, a step up from stick drawings. The Sámi scholar Harald Gaski describes Turi's lack of conventional perspective as a complex use of time and geography. For instance, Turi shows reindeer both going to Norway on the spring migration and returning in autumn on the same page. His

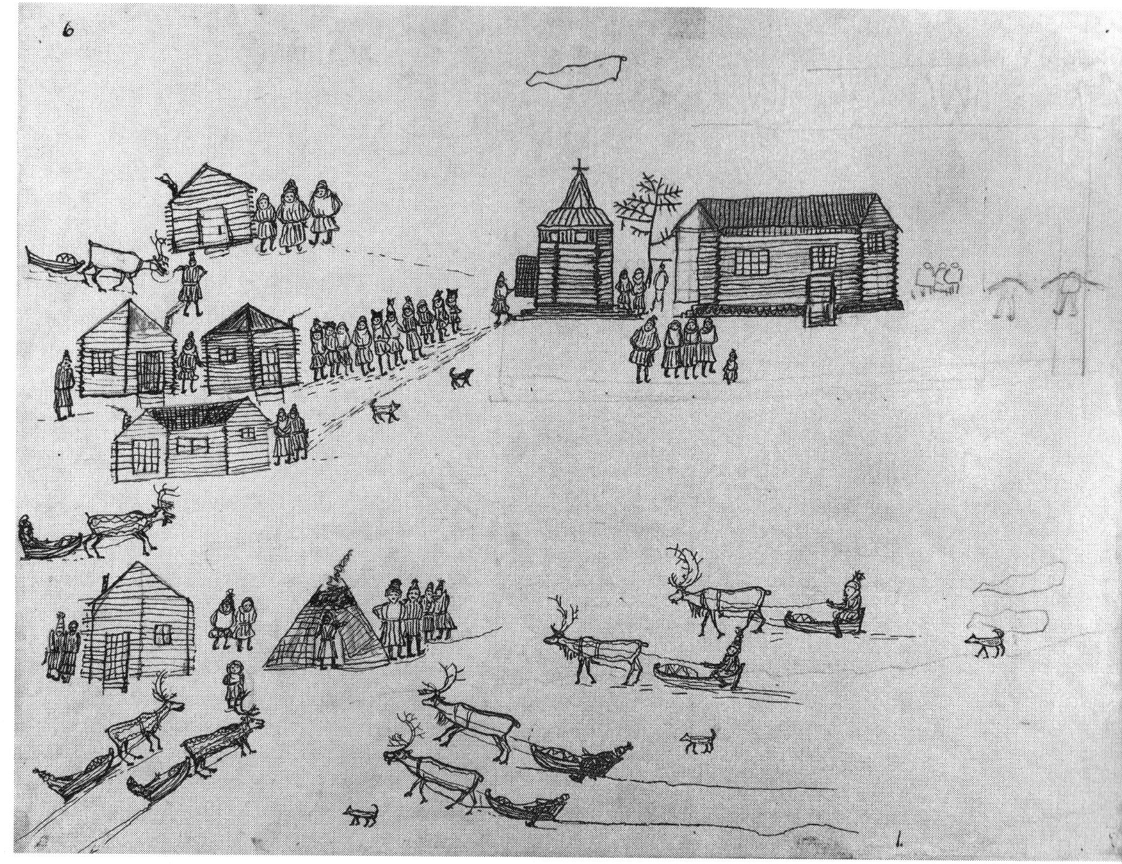

Johan Turi's illustration of the church and village of Jukkasjärvi, Sweden, from his book *Muitalus sámiid birra*, ink on paper, 1910. Courtesy of the Nordic Museum, Stockholm.

scenes can seem observed from above, as if he were watching from a hillside. His drawings in *Muitalus sámiid birra* are "sophisticated contemplations that tread a fine line between realism and expressionism, depicting . . . more than would be possible from a single vantage point."[7]

By contrast, in *Sámi Siida* and in Skum's later style, the pictures have both a foreground and a background, and he is clearly at ease with drawing three-dimensionally, though without shadows or an obvious light source. But the use of white space is different than Turi's, more akin to the way space is used in Asian art. The snow is radiant and ever present—herds of reindeer run through and over plains, drifts, and mountains, over ground that is often barely indicated.

Skum is a master of suggestion whether he uses pencil, pen, or light strokes of crayon (he also worked occasionally in oil and watercolors, but fewer of those pictures appear in his books). Together the artistic drawings and the prose work to create stories, a form of *muitalus* that is both written and pictured.

Sámi Siida came out in 1938, the year before Manker assumed his position as director and sole employee of the Lappish Department, under whose aegis he not only collected and displayed Sámi objects but published a book series, *Acta Lapponica*. *Sámi Siida* was the second title in the series, the first being Manker's own volume on sacred drums. Again, Skum came south to Stockholm, and Manker arranged publicity for him and the book, as well as documented the visit with his own photographs of Skum at the zoo, in a café overlooking the harbor, and on the steps of a stately building. The publication of *Sámi Siida* had been supported by the Humanities Fund, whose patron was the crown prince, and Manker arranged for a visit with this member of the royal family. Later, one of Manker's favorite anecdotes was that the unflappable Skum asked the crown prince how "Papa" was doing. The crown prince answered just as easily that his father, the king of Sweden, was "healthy for his age." Ernst Manker made sure that all the newshounds in the city got the story that Nils Nilsson Skum had been to the palace.[8]

But there were also serious reviews from art critics in major papers in Sweden, Norway, and Denmark. The minimalist drawings drew comparisons with Japanese art and attention from the art world, both pleasing and surprising Manker, who noted that "*Sámi Siida* was not treated as a curiosity, in the usual condescending way, but with the respect due it."[9] Still, there were those who did not understand either Skum's background or his skill. One critic asked, How could a "primitive man, who has seen nothing of art and is entirely self-taught, have such a developed sense of composition, balance and rhythm?"[10] When this critic spoke of Skum as a primitive man, he was not suggesting that Skum was a Swedish Primitivist artist.

In the 1920s and 1930s Stockholm had a flourishing art scene, with room for a variety of modernist painters, including those who experimented with Surrealism, Expressionism, and Primitivism. Some of them had traveled to Africa and the Near East, others merely to ethnographic museums in Paris and Göteborg. Many were, in spite of experimentation, also narrative artists. The curator of a 2007 retrospective exhibit, *10 Stories*, at Stockholm's Moderna Museet, focusing on Swedish modernists from the first half of the twentieth century, highlighted the strong narrative strain in Swedish art: "The narrators of the 1920s and 1930s art are often not contented with merely documenting an event; instead the event seems to merge with the narrator's life. The essential point was to stop differentiating between life and fiction."[11] While Nils Nilsson Skum's work wasn't included in this exhibit featuring Siri Dekert, Nils Dardel, Sigrid Hjertén, and others (only one of his paintings, an oil from 1943 acquired in 1976, is held by the Moderna), this could well be a description of his work from the 1930s. He was not just documenting a general Sámi way of life; he was telling his *own* story through words and pictures.

Manker, while well acquainted with the art scene in Stockholm in the 1930s and the burgeoning interest in primitive art based on ethnographic items from Africa and the South Pacific, didn't see Skum in the tradition of European painters who used ethnography as a springboard for modernist interpretations, nor did he see him as an innovator recalling his memories through the lens of art. Manker saw Nils Nilsson Skum as a talented true primitive, someone who, in creating ethnographic drawings and paintings that expressed a personal style in the manner of all artists, still drew heavily on figurative motifs that went back thousands of years. For Manker as an ethnographer, Skum's work always needed to be put in context, not with other Swedish artists but with the Paleolithic hunter–gatherers making ritual art. For Manker as a writer, Skum was a vivid human-interest story. For Manker as a connoisseur and self-proclaimed interpreter of Sámi arts and crafts, Skum exemplified the continuation of Sámi pictorial drawing over thousands of years.

After the publication of *Sámi Siida,* Skum's artistic star rose quickly, along with sales of his work. He had already been selling some of his artwork and his handcrafted knives at the Wennberg tourist shop in central Kiruna. By the 1930s the original owner of the dry goods store, F. G. Wennberg, had died and his son, Carl, with his wife, Greta, had taken over the shop. They carried *duodji* made by many Sámi artisans in the area, and their home next door to the shop, where their personal collection of Sámi art and handicraft was displayed, would become a center for tourists and collectors looking for choice examples of art from Lapland. The Wennbergs began to collect Skum's work, and Greta acted as an agent for him as well as arranged social events with those who wanted to meet the man himself. She took Skum to Göteborg in 1944 to attend an event in honor of an exhibit of his work there. Carl Wennberg also issued postcards of Skum at the Wennbergs' house, including one with a background of knives, flasks, and bowls artistically arranged on the wall, and sold them in the shop. Prices for Skum's *duodji* and drawings went up as demand soared.

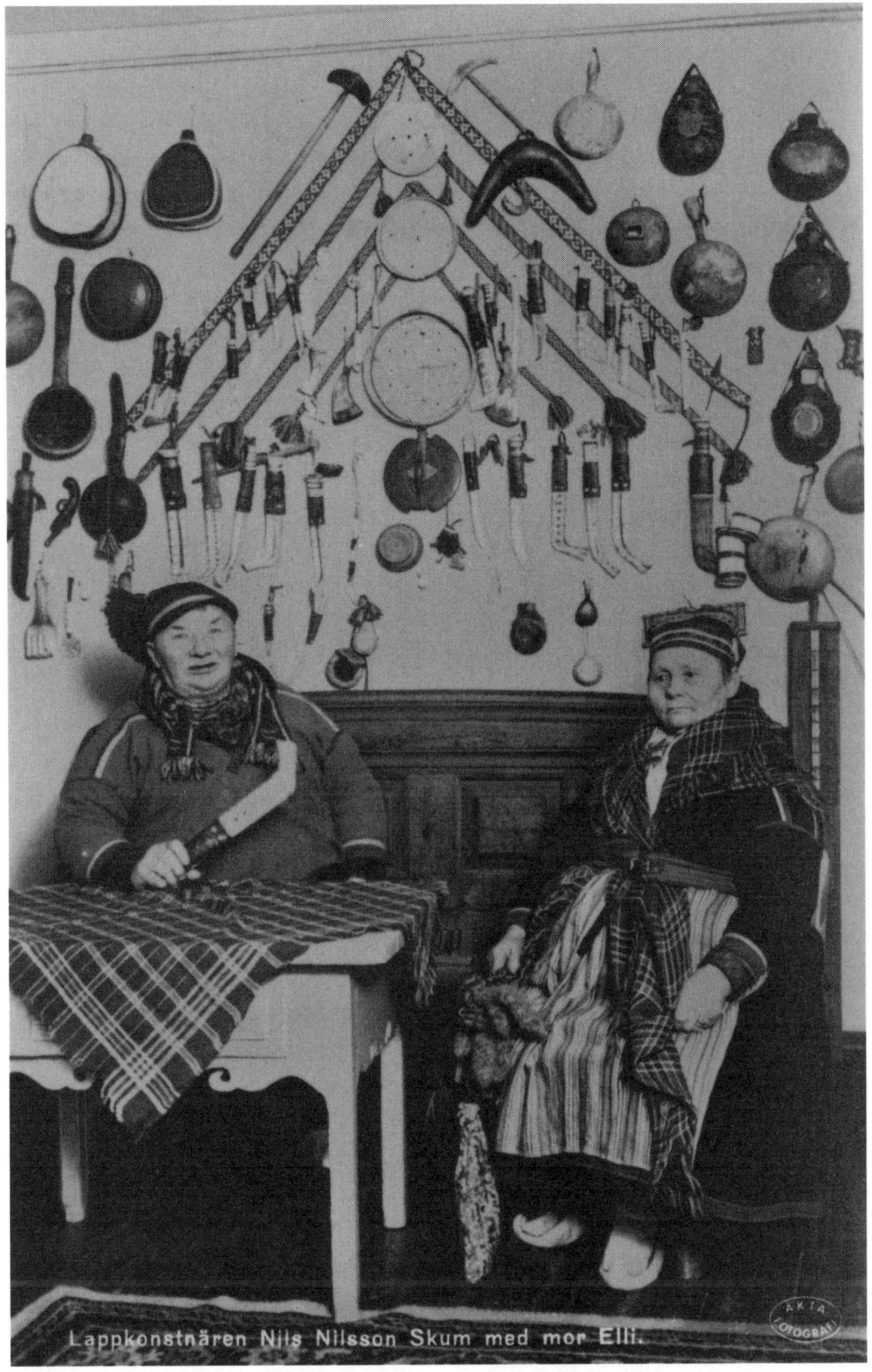

Nils Nilsson and Helena (Elli) Skum at the home of Carl and Greta Wennberg, Kiruna, Sweden, circa 1940s. This image was sold as a postcard at the Wennberg shop. Courtesy of the Arctic University Museum of Norway.

In 1940 the Stockholm gallery Färg och Form (Color and Form) showed some of Skum's work, together with two well-known, but by then deceased, late nineteenth-century Swedish painters: Carl Fredrik Hill and Ernst Josephson. Hill was a landscape painter who developed a mental illness in his twenties and created a series of fantastical drawings. Josephson was a realist whose work grew distorted and primitive after an advancing case of syphilis brought on paranoid episodes. Both spent periods in mental institutions. Manker was somewhat perplexed by the decision to exhibit Skum's Japanese-like drawings in pencil, ink, and crayon with "a pair of sick geniuses," but the show did boost Skum's sales and brought him critical recognition.[12]

Other shows and sales followed. The department store NK exhibited his work in the foyer in 1940 and sold everything. The National Museum of Sweden bought two of his drawings in 1939. A pair of art agents got into the game, setting up exhibits of Skum's work all around Sweden. One of the places they showed Skum's work was the city of Eksjö in the province of Småland. A retired high school teacher, Adolf Hörlén, was so enamored of Skum's art that he bought the whole show, more than a hundred pieces. After the war, at his own expense, he shipped nine crates of Skum's art to New York for an exhibition at the Museum of Natural History. *TIME* magazine reviewed the show, noting that "the Museum had found a primitive of the likes of upstate New York's octogenarian painter 'Grandma Moses.'"[13] Unfortunately for Hörlén, not a single painting sold, and the artwork came back again to find buyers in Sweden and the rest of Europe, with ever rising attention and prices. By the time he died, Skum was a celebrated figure not only in Sweden but internationally. The *New York Times* published his obituary in 1951, enthusing that "Nils Nilsson Skum's career as an artist was little short of fabulous."[14]

In 1944, Skum approached Manker about another project that would combine text and image, *Valla renar (Herding Reindeer).* He wanted to write the text in Finnish and then have it translated into Swedish. Although he signed a publishing contract with *Acta Lapponica,* he did not initially want Manker to be as involved as he had been with his first book. Even more than *Sámi Siida, Herding Reindeer* was meant to pass on Indigenous knowledge to current and future generations, particularly about methods of herding as they had been carried out in the late nineteenth and early twentieth centuries. Skum was explicit in his ending remarks that his narrative about herding would contribute to its continuation. Yet it was also a book of memories, of his parents and the *siidas* that had once existed in Kautokeino and in Norrkaitum. About half of the almost fifty illustrations placed after the chapters had two different dates: one was the date of execution, 1944 through 1946, and the other was a date from the time of the memory, beginning with 1874, when Nils was four and his family arrived in the Gällivare area (Plate 10).

According to Manker, one of the reasons the manuscript didn't progress more swiftly was problems with the translators; another was that instead of holding onto the artwork, Skum "had been unable to resist those who wanted to buy his work, so the originals had largely been sold." Skum had made photographs of all the work, however, and in the end Manker used these reproductions for publication. The entire project took about ten years, with Manker in the end assuming full responsibility after Skum's death in 1951. It is a smaller book in format and ambition, and Manker in his foreword to the book acknowledges that the technical aspects of using photographs rather than originals weaken its presentation. Still, he calls *Herding Reindeer* the "testament" of Skum, the "genius of the wilderness."[15] The year after *Herding Reindeer* was published, in 1955, Manker put out his own narrative about Skum, full of anecdotes and assessments. Although Skum produced two books under his own name, it was Manker who claimed the right to present Skum's life and work under a title with a definite article, *The Book of Skum.*

Parallel to his work with and without Skum on *Herding Reindeer,* the ever-active Manker was occupied with half a dozen projects, from putting the final touches on a new exhibit about the Sámi at the museum; to traveling and documenting Sámi life in Sweden; to writing scholarly articles, journalism, and more books; to fundraising and buying and cajoling ever more objects for the museum and ever more documents for the archives. But he also was occupied with thoughts of the Sámi as artists and with developing his ideas about ethnographic arts and crafts, primitive art, and the line from the Paleolithic to the contemporary Sámi artists.

In 1947, the book *Primitive Art: Art and Artistic Craft among Primitive People,* an oversize, beautifully designed publication with heavy pages and dozens of glossy black-and-white and color photographs, was jointly published by Sweden's two ethnographic museums in Stockholm and Göteborg. The editors' definition of primitive art referred not to the modernist paintings of the twentieth century influenced by African artists but to folk arts and rarities produced by people around the globe.

The preface acknowledged that museal exhibitions of these riches would have been preferable to a book but that physical circumstances, especially the lack of space at the Ethnographic Museum in Stockholm (which was still housed in the old barracks on Djurgården), made that impossible. Instead, the volume aimed to showcase an impressive array of artistic ethnographica, largely housed in the two museums. The illustrated chapters on Asia, Australia and the South Pacific, North and South America, and Africa detailed how the objects had come to Sweden and from which countries; they highlighted with pride the Swedish expedition leaders and collectors who had packed them home.

Beginning with objects brought by some of Carl Linnæus's students who had set off on botanical excursions in the 1700s and continuing with donations from Swedish merchants, sea captains, and missionaries, the museums had become the repositories of North American Indian tomahawks, Chinese ivories, Balinese musical instruments, Amazonian feather headdresses, and much, much more. In 1843–45, Count Armand Fouché d'Orante visited the Blackfoot Indians in Montana and snapped up artifacts as cheaply as he could. In the summer of 1877, the Swedish–Finnish explorer Adolf Nordenskiöld set off north on the *Vega* on a scientific expedition to find the Northeast Passage to Asia. The two-year voyage was the first to circumnavigate Eurasia. Adolf Nordenskiöld returned a hero. The *Vega* also carried home artifacts from the people of Siberia and North Asia, from Alaska, Japan, and China.

In the early twentieth century. Adolf's son Erland Nordenskiöld made South America his specialty, and he encouraged many of his students to travel to Central and South America. The daring Sven Hedin organized expeditions to Mongolia, China, and Tibet from 1927 to 1935 and sent back crates of artifacts for the Ethnographic Museum in Stockholm. The Ethnographic Museum in Göteborg accepted donations from seamen and missionaries. Its African collection grew to be substantial, overshadowed only by the huge number of textiles, pottery items, baskets, sculptures, and carvings gathered from the American Southwest, Mexico, Central America, Peru, and the Amazon.

With all this fanfare around global exotica, it was curious that *Primitive Art* began with a chapter by Ernst Manker, "The Lapps as Artists."[16] Here there was nothing about the heroic expeditions of Swedish explorers who returned to Stockholm and Göteborg with crates of ethnographic loot from Sápmi. The Arctic Lapp-ethnographic Expedition to the Lappmarks of Sweden, Norway, Finland, and Russia, made by Hugo Samzelius, wasn't mentioned, nor were the summer expeditions of the von Dübens or indeed any of the smaller razzias of the twentieth century, including those by Manker. Instead, as in Manker's other writings about drums, *sieidis,* and Sámi *duodji,* the objects were presented as having had a presence elsewhere in some other time yet as having somehow always been in museums, ferried there by noninvasive means.

However the Sámi came to be included in *Primitive Art,* Ernst Manker took on the task of interpreting Sámi material and spiritual culture, largely related to reindeer herding. He structured his contribution to the subject in a way that would become recognizable in a variety of his overview books about Sápmi in Swedish and English over the next fifteen years, from *The Swedish Mountain Lapps (De svenska fjällapparna)* of 1947 to *Sámi Art (Samefolkets konst)* of 1971. He always began with the prehistoric rock carvings in the Nordic countries, many to be found on the Arctic Norwegian coast and others in interior Sweden and along the coasts of the Gulf of Bothnia. The rock carvings were at least six thousand years old and were created by hunting peoples who inhabited the North after the end of the Ice Age. Manker then jumped to similar images of reindeer and hunters on the "magic drums" and then to images etched on bone-handled knives in the Nordic Museum's collections. Finally, he discussed in ethnographic terms the work of three visual artists: Johan Turi, Nils Nilsson Skum, and John Andreas Savio, a younger artist from northern Norway.

Over the years that Manker described Sámi art and crafts, there were both consistencies and changes in his writing. Sometimes Manker included *sieidis* as religious sculpture; sometimes he spoke first about Turi, Skum, and Savio and then moved on to fine handicraft. His interpretations rarely vary, but occasionally the classifications do. In an English-language book from the 1960s, *Lapp Life and Customs,* cowritten with the Norwegian museum curator and scholar Ørnulv Vorren, Manker writes about the drum imagery in the chapter "Intellectual Culture" and shifts his discussion of ornamented or particularly attractive objects once used in daily life to the chapter "Art and Decoration."[17] By the time he published *Sámi Art* in 1971, all he addressed was ethnographic art or artisanship, even though the book took the same path from rock paintings, to drums, to ethnographic objects, to renderings on paper and canvas. These artworks were alternatively and simultaneously described as ethnographic and artistic. The subject matter could be considered ethnographic (men and reindeer), but their execution was stylistically individual, one of the distinguishing hallmarks of fine art. Manker appreciated art, but while he knew many contemporary Swedish artists, he did not attempt to situate the work of the Sámi visual artists within the canon of Scandinavian or European tradition.

In Norway another cultural arbiter wavered over what constituted ethnographica, handicraft, and fine art and how and when to separate them. Harry Fett, head of the Norwegian Directorate for Cultural Heritage and founder of the journal *Kunst og Kultur* (Art and Culture), also grappled with how to situate Sámi artists in Nordic art history. In 1940, during the first months of German occupation and before he was ousted from *Kunst og Kultur* as someone with Jewish heritage, he wrote an influential article in the journal about Scandinavian and foreign artists who had depicted Sápmi, beginning with Olaus Magnus's illustrations in the sixteenth century, and about John Andreas Savio, an artist he identified with the Finnmark region in North Norway. Like Manker, Harry Fett saw an unbroken artistic line from the rock carvings of early hunters in the North to the simple imagery of Johan Turi and Nils Nilsson Skum, which so often depicted reindeer in herds, and the more sophisticated graphic art of John Andreas Savio.

Savio, who died at the age of thirty-six, was born of mixed Sámi and Kven background in the South Varanger region in 1902. His father had accompanied a polar expedition to Antarctica. His mother died of tuberculosis when he was a baby, and his father drowned in the river on the way to purchase a coffin for her. He was raised by his well-off grandparents and showed an early aptitude for art. At age eighteen he moved to Oslo to study English and take classes at the State College of Crafts and Design. It was there he was diagnosed with tuberculosis and had a lung removed. In spite of ongoing poor health, he studied art history on his own and became particularly interested in woodcuts and other graphic art, from Dürer to Edvard Munch. After leaving Oslo, Savio went back to Finnmark, hoping to make a living from his art. Finding that option difficult, he returned to Oslo and then began years of travel, around Norway, England, and the Continent. In the mid-1930s he lived and studied in Paris and held a solo exhibition there during the summer of 1936. His career was cut short by the return of his tuberculosis, and he died in 1938, leaving behind hundreds of drawings and woodcuts, many of which featured Sámi motifs, expressed in powerful lines and shapes (Plate 11).

Fett, in championing John Andreas Savio, never suggested that the young artist belonged to the history of Norwegian art, which had followed predictable European paths from classical mannerism to National Romanticism, from realism to Impressionism to Expressionism. Early Norwegian artists studied in Copenhagen, Munich, and Rome; later artists went to Paris. Sámi artists, insofar as they existed, were a group apart. They documented Sámi life, especially nomadic life, with charm and naivety. Their art and *duodji* were never included in either the National Gallery in Oslo, which first opened its doors in 1842, or the Decorative Arts and Design Museum, founded in 1876. In describing Savio's contemporary woodcuts, Fett fell back often on terms that placed his work both in the ethnographic present and in a prehistoric tradition that went back to the Paleolithic. Savio's woodcuts—though influenced by Edvard Munch—were at the same time "a strange mix of Lappish artistic sensibility filtered through Parisian artistic experiences."[18]

Both Skum and Savio had memorable life stories, often embellished when repeated. All the same, both were gifted, serious, and productive artists, whose work was purchased as early as the mid-1930s. One collector alone, Anthony Biddle Jr., the American ambassador to Norway in 1935–37, bought hundreds of Savio woodcuts for himself and his friends. Savio may have died young and in poverty, but his work is now in the collections of the National Museum in Oslo (formerly the National Gallery), the Arctic University Museum of Norway (formerly Tromsø Museum), and the Savio Museum in Kirkenes, Norway. Artworks and *duodji* made by Skum, once owned by the Wennberg family in Kiruna, who were early dealers in his work, would be sold to the mining company LKAB for exhibition in the company hotel. Although a few public museums hold his works, in large measure they are owned privately, bought and sold at auction.

After John Savio and Nils Nilsson Skum, no other Sámi artist would capture public attention in quite the same exotic and unchallenging way. In the closing few pages of *Sámi Art,* published twenty years after Skum's death, Manker cities only a handful of male visual artists from Sápmi, several of whom were also artisans and most of whom, like Nicolaus Skum (Nils's nephew) and Lars Pirak, worked with the familiar Sámi motifs of reindeer and northern landscapes. In passing, Manker mentions the Sámi *duojár* and sculptor Iver Jåks of Karasjok, who would become a highly regarded artist in his own right as well as a bridge to a younger generation of Sámi artists. Manker doesn't, however, add the name of Nils-Aslak Valkeapää, born in 1943 and known as Áillohaš in North Sámi.

Valkeapää, a multimedia artist from Finland with ties to Norway, upended received ideas of what Sámi art looked like. Already in the 1960s he had put out recordings of joik; he was a poet, a writer, a painter, and a political activist. In 1975 he participated with other Sámi activists in the first meeting of the World Council of Indigenous Peoples, which took place in Port Alberni, British Columbia. This was a watershed moment for the Sámi in the Nordic countries, who increasingly saw the importance of allying with Indigenous peoples around the world, in part to strengthen and support identity but also to pressure their separate governments in Sweden, Norway, and Finland to recognize their rights. The list of what Valkeapää accomplished before his death in 2001 is enormous. He produced albums, gave concerts, organized photo and art exhibits, and published books that combined his pictorial art with poetry. In 1991, he was awarded the Nordic Council's Literature Prize for *Beaivi, áhčážan (The Sun, My Father),* a collection of art and poetry.[19]

Valkeapää's influence is clear in Sámi art, music, and literature today, but he was not the only socially engaged artist to emerge in the 1960s and 1970s in Sápmi. In 1978, a group of eight young artists, seven Norwegians and one Swede, converged on the Sámi village of Máze (Masi), between Alta and Kautokeino, to live and work in a building offered to them by the local council. Most members of the Máze Artists' Group, or Mázejoavku, were from northern Norway and did not come from herding families but had Sea Sámi or settled Sámi ties. Many were products of the boarding school system in Norway in the postwar years, which emphasized "Norwegianization," that is, assimilation. Most did not speak a Sámi language, and only a few had been raised learning traditional crafts. A number had gone south to universities and art colleges in Oslo or Trondheim during the political activism of the late 1960s. They brought back to Sápmi a more confrontational attitude and a desire to explore and express Sámi identity through art, graphic design, and social activism.

The Máze artists were involved in the Alta dam protests, which began in 1979 as a local resistance movement. The Norwegian government wanted to dam the Alta River and create a hydropower plant; the initial plans called for the complete submersion of Máze. The movement eventually brought thousands of people from the Nordic countries and Europe to protest at the construction site. At first the focus was environmental; but soon it became identified with the nascent Sámi movement, ČSV. Although, ultimately, the dam was built, the resistance movement succeeded in drawing attention to the Sámi and inspiring a generation of activists, not only in Norway but also in Sweden and Finland. "Alta" in Sápmi is a word on par with "Selma" and "Stonewall." The Máze artists' building became one of the main headquarters of the resistance, and the artists designed posters and pamphlets as well as attended demonstrations in Alta and in Oslo.[20]

The Máze group went their separate ways after five years, but their informal association led to the organization of the Daiddačehpiid Searvi, the Sámi Artists

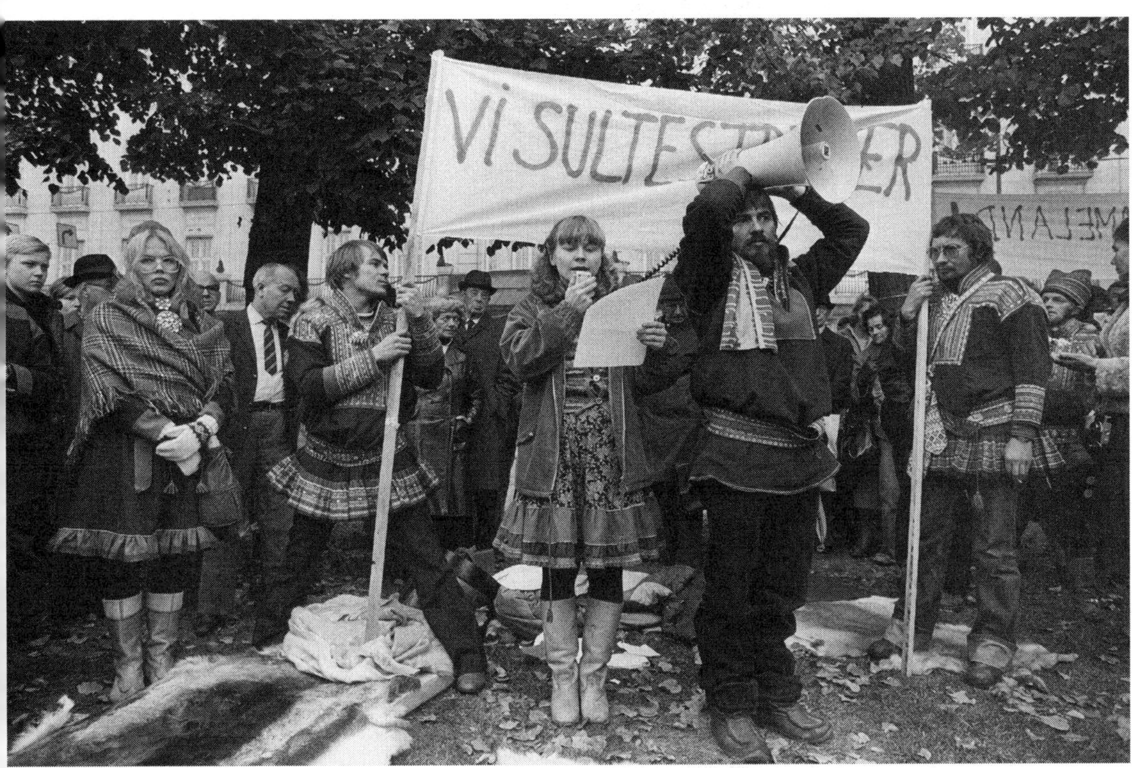

A hunger strike demonstration in central Oslo, October 1979, to create awareness of the Alta conflict and Sámi rights. Left to right: Synnøve Persen, Ánte Gaup, Jorunn Eikjok, Niillas Somby, and Mikkel Gaup. Persen, a poet and artist, was a member of the Máze artists' group. Photograph by Bernt Eide / Samfoto / NTB scanpix / Sipa USA.

Association, in 1979 and to the founding in 1986 of Sámi Daiddaguovddáš (SDG, Sámi Center for Contemporary Art) in Karasjok. The Sámi Museum, established in Karasjok in 1972 to conserve and display Sámi material culture, began to build a collection of Sámi art that today includes thirteen hundred works of fine art and *duodji*.[21] These artworks are regularly circulated throughout Sápmi in museums and galleries and around the country and abroad. Meanwhile, the Sámi Contemporary Art Centre puts on exhibits of avant-garde and contemporary works on a regular basis.

The Sámi Artists Association played a crucial role in integrating Sámi artists into the Norwegian art scene and securing grants for artists and funding for exhibits and installations. Before the 1970s, the Sámi languages had no word for "art." The new word *dáidda* (a loan from the Finnish *taide*) offered a way out from the stereotypes attached to paintings of reindeer and to *duodji* that was associated with handicrafts sold to tourists. It allowed the artists both to draw on the techniques of *duodji,* for instance, embroidery and clothes design, and to embrace the possibilities of contemporary art.[22]

The now well-known abstract artist Synnøve Persen said in an interview, "We wanted to destroy the ethnographic picture of Sámi art."[23] But other artists took traditional *duodji* in new directions, such as Britta Marakatt-Labba, whose embroidered cloth panels of Sámi figures, animals, and other motifs are displayed in public settings and used as details in books (including the cover of this book) and other media. Over a five-year period, Marakatt-Labba embroidered a work titled *Historjá* that narrates in pictorial form the myths and history of Sápmi. The artwork, finished in 2007, stretches for seventy-seven feet along a wall at one of the buildings at the University of Tromsø. It begins with snow and trees and then continues with the emergence of different animals and of hunters and herders on foot and on skis. Marakatt-Labba, who lives in northern Sweden in Ovre-Sopporo, near Kiruna, also included some political history, in particular the Kautokeino Uprising.[24]

Marakatt-Labba's storytelling artistry exemplifies an older concept in Sámi art but a newer word, *muitalandáidda,* which combines the terms for storytelling and art. Both Johan Turi and Nils Nilsson Skum were seen as primitive artists. While Skum had an international following and Turi sold his paintings on paper for a few kronor at railway stations, both produced vividly personal artwork that captured the world they inhabited (Plate 12). We might better describe them as writers and narrative artists, who created *muitalandáidda,* documenting their lives as Sámi and the lives of the people around them and reflecting their determination to pass on Indigenous knowledge to Sámi people in the future. Yet the narratives created in new works by Sámi artists from the late twentieth century onward have not only been focused on memories and past narratives. These works have actively interrogated and reimagined Sámi history, personal and political. *Dáidda* has become a powerful expression of Sámi resistance to stories that have been told about them and histories from which they've been excluded, such as the history of art in the Nordic countries.

Just as contemporary *dáidda,* narrative or abstract or conceptual, sometimes embraced long-standing methods of *duodji,* with its emphasis on natural materials carefully gathered and worked by hand, so did *duodji* begin to shift from only replicating traditional forms to becoming personal expressions identified and valued in a new market for Sámi fine handicraft that took off in the 1970s. In both cases, these emerging forms, definitions, and markets complicated older ways of seeing, valuing, and displaying Sámi "ethnographic objects" and "handicrafts" in museums in the Nordic countries. In his articles and books about Sámi art and craft, Ernst Manker struggled to classify the thousands of objects once scooped up as ethnographica in the Nordic Museum's collections.

It was all ethnographic, but was some of it art?

Roots and Spirals

It had long been Ernst Manker's intention to mount a new exhibit about the Sámi at the Nordic Museum that would modernize the displays created in 1908. He wanted to build on the knowledge he'd assiduously collected and to find ways to reintroduce the Sámi population of Sweden to the public in an engaging and more personal manner. *Lapparna* (The Lapps) opened in 1947. Manker had decided on a mix of displays, both chronological and typological, which included crowd-pleasing mannequins: a "Lapp shaman" on one knee, "soothsaying" on a drum; a woman glimpsed in a tent, busy with domestic work; a man and his dog during a reindeer roundup, cutting an identifying mark into the ear of a calf; and a long "caravan" with several stuffed reindeer, pack sleds, and a man and a woman guiding the reindeer. There were also informational panels with photographs of drums and *sieidis* and displays of some of the beautifully crafted objects in the museum's collection, presented in glass vitrines by type but also placed selectively on exhibit walls and in related assemblages on floor platforms with an eye to form as well as function.[1]

In addition to being organized by use and material, the objects Manker had chosen to showcase were arranged within a geographical context and along a gender divide. In *The Lapps,* an English-language booklet guide to the Sámi exhibits at the Nordic Museum and Skansen's open-air museum, Manker discusses both "handicrafts" and "fine handicrafts" in terms of gender. For everyday use, he wrote, Sámi men created sleds and skis, cradles and chests, and wooden cheese molds and butter containers—all things to do with wood and metal. Sámi women made root baskets and leather bags; they sewed clothing and wove decorative shoe bands with a hand loom. Fine handicrafts were also divided: the exhibit featured one case for "men's handicraft in wood and bone" and another for "women's handicraft in soft materials," with items laid out in patterns for comparison. In the category of fine handicraft made by men was a long row of knives with etched bone handles and sheaths, another row of horn spoons, and further examples of needle cases and two-holed lasso rings. Female "soft handicraft," both ordinary and fine, included embroidered breast cloths, silver collars, and calfskin bags decorated with pewter thread.[2]

These gendered categories were not so strict as Manker indicated in the vitrines and texts. Most Sámi men, in addition to cooking the daily main meal, had sewing kits and used them to repair clothing and gear. Johan Turi, for one, knew how to use a heddle for weaving yarn into shoe bands. Both women and men had made root baskets and sewed with pewter thread in the past, as noted by the Sámi church sexton and informant for Johannes Schefferus, Nicolas Lundius, in the seventeenth century: "Some of the Lapps make much better baskets than the women do. . . . I know a Lapp in Umeå Lappmark, who sews better with pewter thread than any female person."[3] And although root basketry may have been associated with women, roots were scarcely soft. Harvesting them in the forest was arduous work, as was soaking them and stripping them of bark and preparing them for weaving.

The Sámi word for handicraft, *duodji,* which would become pervasive by the end of the twentieth century, wasn't mentioned in the exhibit, nor had a guide been printed in one of the Sámi languages. Yet a variety of Sámi people, through loans and gifts as well as practical advice, contributed to the exhibit. Sigga and Mattias Kuoljok, a married couple from Jokkmokk, for instance, came to Stockholm to explain the correct way of arranging some of the mannequins shown with objects in the tent or on migration with sleds pulled by reindeer. Aside from the "soothsayer" tapping on his drum, all the life-size scenes were described as ongoing aspects of Sámi life, something that contributed to the ethnographic-present shaping of the exhibit. To complement the mannequins, Sámi people were also represented in photographs by Manker or others, in action or in repose, in mountain landscapes, and in traditional dress. Some photographs showed well-known artists and writers, such as Johan Turi and Nils Nilsson Skum. As the curator of the Lappish Department, Manker often worked with Sámi individuals and solicited their input in multiple ways for his project, yet he probably wouldn't have considered the Sámi as the main public for the interpretative displays in the museum. The exhibit viewers were imagined as schoolchildren, Stockholmers, and visitors from inside and outside the Nordic countries. The intention of the exhibit was largely pedagogic. At the same time,

Manker made a case throughout for Sámi arts and crafts, displaying drawings by Skum and Turi and drawing attention to traditional forms of *duodji*.

One of the exhibit's typological displays of form and function demonstrated Manker's aesthetic sensibility. A spiral of twelve shallow baskets used as cheese molds and made from birch roots was arranged clockwise on a wall, beginning with the largest basket and curling inward to the smallest. Several tightly-woven baskets with fitted lids were placed on a low platform below the spiral of cheese molds. Such birch-root basketry had been part of Sámi craft traditions for a very long time. An illustrated page in Schefferus's *Lapponia* shows a lidded basket along with other examples of Sámi handicraft, and he wrote admiringly of the baskets:

> This art is particular to the Lapps, is known everywhere, and nothing can compete with them. The baskets are made of tree roots, which are soaked and cleaved into long threads, so they can be wrapped around rootstocks and bound together. . . . Such baskets are used not only by the Lapps but also by the Swedes. They are also shipped out of the country because of their durability and trimness.[4]

Manker claimed in his guide to the exhibit that "the art of basketwork, in which the Lapps were past masters, is now almost extinct," yet that wasn't quite the case.[5] Beginning in the 1940s, working on her own, Asa Kitok, a widow with six children, had revived and strengthened the craft of binding birch roots into baskets and taught two of her daughters how to find the roots, prepare them, and make smaller and larger containers in the traditional style. Asa Kitok's two daughters, Ellen and Margit, would not only go on in the 1960s to become professional *duojárs* like their mother but take root basketry in the direction of artistry.

But even before Asa Kitok began to work with birch roots, an interest in Sápmi in teaching and learning artisan crafts had been growing, connected to the Sámi people's efforts to chart an economic course forward that would provide a livelihood and honor their cultural heritage at a time when fewer were able to make a living solely on reindeer herding.

Emma Bergström-Andelius, born in the south of Sweden in 1862, was a teacher who worked with others interested in the Swedish handicraft, or *hemslöjd*, movement in Stockholm. At the age of forty-four she married and moved with her husband to Umeå, where she soon founded the Umeå Handicraft Association, in part

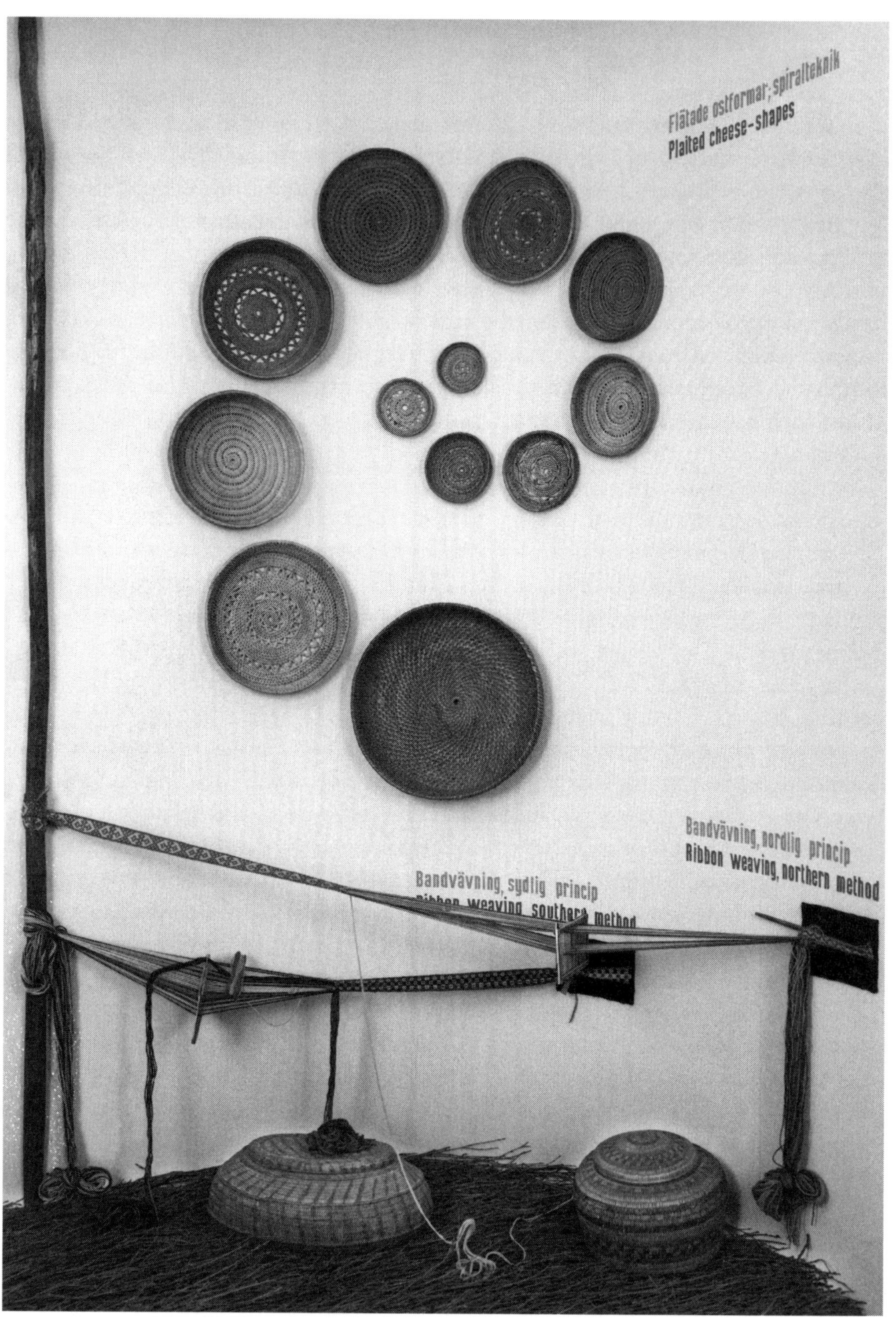

Root baskets and cheese molds displayed at the Nordic Museum's permanent *Lapparna* exhibition, opened in 1947. Photograph by Lennart Nenkler. Courtesy of the Nordic Museum, Stockholm.

as a way of organizing artisans to make and sell their work in a region that struggled with poverty.[6] Her interests included Sámi crafts. Bergström-Andelius was one of the contributors, in 1920, to an influential pattern book of Sámi designs published under the name of the Swedish engineer and collector H. Hampusson Huldt and was likely to have been the first to describe in print some of the techniques used in creating Sámi root basketry.[7] Her small pamphlet, *On Lappish Root Baskets and Their Bindings,* published in 1932, details with simple black-and-white illustrations how a basket is created, beginning with finding and harvesting roots from spruce or birch trees, soaking them in water, and scraping them in preparation for "binding," a method of wrapping thin roots around a heavier rootstock and weaving it into a tight spiral.[8]

Although anyone interested in the art of basketry could have learned from the pamphlet, a line under the title on the first page suggests one audience in particular: "For Nomad Schools and Workshops." The pamphlet was probably created for teachers at these schools to give the children of reindeer herders traditional skills appropriate to their position in Swedish society as a distinct minority to be protected.

In 1913 the Nomad Schools Act was passed in Sweden. Previously, many Sámi families in Sápmi, both settled and nomadic, had learned to read and write from traveling teachers, who were often Sámi. By the early twentieth century, some Sámi families, especially in the South, were sending their children to Swedish schools for a more formal education. What the Nomad Schools Act did was establish a division between families who owned reindeer and the growing majority of Sámi who no longer herded or only kept a few reindeer. In line with other government laws, the nomadic, reindeer-herding Sámi were to be separated from settled Sámi. The settled Sámi were to be assimilated and their children sent to Swedish schools, where they would not be allowed to speak any language but Swedish or learn anything about Sápmi. The reindeer-herding Sámi were to be protected from outside influences and modern life so that they would continue their traditional way of life.

It was a peculiarly destructive idea right from the beginning, given that in Sápmi people had for millennia practiced many sorts of occupations along with herding. Separating Sámi people with similar histories and cultural traditions, who spoke the same or similar languages, into two groups—one of which would be made to become more Swedish and the other of which would be allowed to remain Sámi only as long as they could hold on to their herds—made no sense. Some Sámi activists, including the activist clergyman Gustav Park, protested the

Bindning av rotkorgar med tät vägg

1. Bindningen av en korg kan börja på olika sätt men utgår alltid från *mitten av botten.*

En eller flera kluvna eller runda rottåger läggas kring spetsen av prylen (textfig. 3). Tag så bort prylen och linda över den i ring lagda stödjetågen en finare, kluven eller hel tåg, bindetågen (textfig. 4), tills den lilla ringen är fast och jämn.

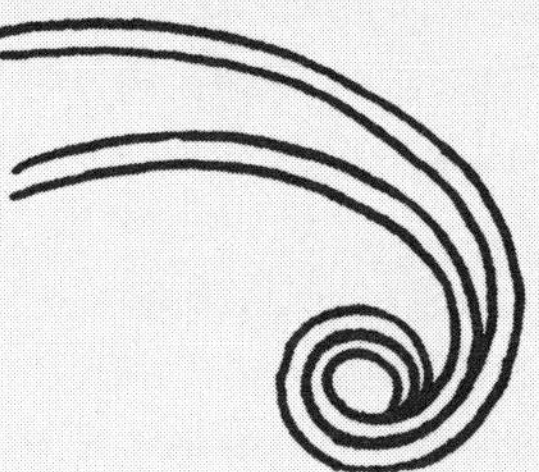

Fig. 3. Bindningen börjar.

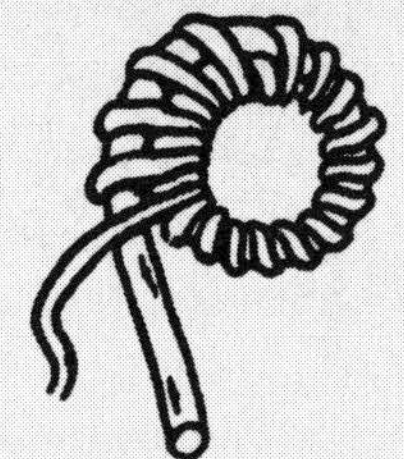

Fig. 4. Bindetågen lindas över stödjetågen.

Ett annat sätt är att över en grövre, avspetsad, rak stödjetåg linda den finare bindetågen ett par centimeter (textfig. 5 a), böja den sålunda omlindade stödjetågen till en ring, ju mindre desto bättre, och sedan fortsätta lindningen. En liten förtjockning brukar gärna uppstå över fogen, men denna kan lämpligen jämnas ut medelst den platta tången. De gamla korgbinderskorna brukade använda sig av tänderna.

2. Stödjetågen fortsätter och bildar *nästa varv,* som fästes vid det föregående på så sätt, att bindetågen lägges över första och andra varvets stödjetåger tillsammans; bindningen sker alltså över två stödjetåger på en gång (textfig. 6).

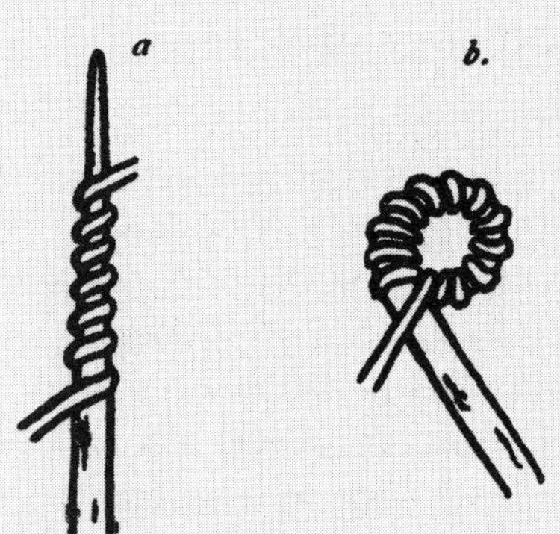

Fig. 5. Lindning kring rak stödjetåg.
a. Lindningen börjar.
b. Stödjetågen böjes därefter.

I den mån ytterkanten vidgas, följer man med vid bindningen genom att på

A page from *On Lappish Root Baskets and Their Bindings* by Emma Bergström-Andelius, 1932. Courtesy of Archives and Special Collections, University of Minnesota Duluth.

artificial division between Swedish Sámi people and called for a Sámi educational system that was equal to the Swedish system. In 1918, at the second pan-Sápmi assembly held in Östersund, Sweden, Park spoke forcefully against the state's handling of Sámi education and followed it up with newspaper opinions and speeches. He wrote articles for the Sámi newspaper *SET* on the subject; in 1940, on Torkel Tomasson's death, Gustav Park took over *SET*'s editorship and continued his political work.[9]

In spite of resistance, after 1913 the nomad schools were put in place very quickly in many districts in Sápmi. The classes, often taught by Swedes, were initially held in the summer, often in the high mountains when the Sámi stayed in one place for a month or more. Later, winter classes took place in larger tents or buildings, and finally, boarding schools were built for the children of nomadic herders. Professor K. B. Wiklund produced three *Nomad School Readers* in the 1920s, in Swedish, with information and illustrations of everything that the nomadic children would need to know to continue the herding life. Handicraft instruction wasn't covered in the books, but in the photographs that illustrated the third *Reader* from 1929, the Sámi were occasionally shown in traditional dress, inside or near tents, with evidence of bentwood chests, wooden bowls, and other handmade objects.[10]

As Emma Bergström-Andelius well knew, *hemslöjd* had not died out in rural Sweden, even though the need for basketry in all communities, Sámi and non-Sámi, had declined with the advent of machine-made containers. She noted that some Swedish basket crafters remembered a Sámi friend from their youth who taught them root craft or a Sámi elder who passed on their expertise. Ninety-year-old Eva Nyberg told Bergström-Andelius in 1932 that, when she was only seven, she and a Sámi girl the same age used to compete over who could make the finest basket. "What became of the Lapp girl I don't know," wrote Bergström-Andelius, "but we have many proofs that Eva became a skilled basket weaver throughout her life."[11]

It's unclear whether Bergström-Andelius, who appreciated the difficult art of root basketry and wished to see its survival, fully understood the nature of the racial ideology behind the treatment of Sámi children or whether she was aware of the economic stresses and physical dislocations that almost all Sámi except those who already lived in urban settings were undergoing in Sweden in the twentieth century. Logging and mining operations had begun the previous century, as well as railway construction, but the era of grand hydropower schemes only took off in the 1950s, as the government pressed forward with damming

Sweden's vast river systems in the North to power sawmills and factories, light new towns, and send electricity southward. The Lule River, which had long been a pristine salmon river, ran through a core area of Swedish Sápmi, where many *siidas* lived and migrated. The first hydropower plant on the Lule River was built as early as 1915; two more power plants came in the 1950s, followed by a dozen more in the 1960s and 1970s, including the massive hydropower complex at Porjus. The Pite River was also dammed, and the Kalix. Lakes were created, fish runs halted, and Sámi villages gradually submerged. The Sámi saw their traditional lands desecrated by mines and logging and severed by roads and railways. They protested and organized, but most of their protests were ignored. Some reindeer herders hung on, but many found themselves forced out of traditional nomadism. They settled by lakes and fished; they sold fish, berries, and ptarmigans at markets, as well as handmade knives, bowls, and other *duodji*; their children went to school and moved to towns or cities where they found other kinds of occupations than herding. The Sámi didn't give up easily, but the industrialization of Sweden increasingly made the old ways of life more and more challenging.

The life of Asa Kitok reflects many of the forces shaping Swedish Sámi life from the turn of the century through the 1950s. She was born into a reindeer-herding family in the Lule Sámi district of Sörkaitum (today Unna Tjerusj) in 1893. Not long after her birth during the autumn migration, members of the *siida* were crossing a lake with all their goods, when a sudden storm blew up and most of the boats overturned, including one with infant Asa in her cradle. She floated and was saved, along with lighter chests and baskets; the heavier objects sank to the bottom. As a child, she had little education: a nomad school in a tent in the mountains for four or six weeks in summer and visits from a traveling teacher in winter for two or three weeks at the beginning of winter. She learned to read the psalms in Lule Sámi and picked up Finnish as well. Her Swedish was minimal; unlike Nils Nilsson Skum, born around the same time, she rarely found a need for it in the communities where she lived. She never learned to write in any language, and she escaped the boarding school life that marred the childhoods of many Sámi children. Instead, most of her memories of childhood and young adulthood involved herding and religion. Her parents were strong adherents of the Læstadian religion; no one went to the Swedish Church or ever saw a Lutheran pastor. Instead, prayer meetings were held in homes with lay pastors.[12]

She married in 1922, into a family of five brothers, who formed a *siida* of their own. Her husband, Anders Kitok, became ill and unable to do the heavy work of herding around 1929, and most of the *siida* gave up herding reindeer and moved that year to Sjaunja, a hamlet that the Kitoks knew from passing through during their migrations. On one side of the river were ten Finnish-speaking households; they farmed and milked cows. On the other side three Sámi families built permanent turf huts and a few outbuildings; there they raised their families, fished, and kept goats for milking and some reindeer for slaughter. The two communities got on well, particularly in matters of religion. Asa and Anders had six children; he died in 1933, when the youngest child, Ellen, was just a year old. From then on, Asa had to support the family. In warmer months, her day began at four o'clock in the morning when she pulled twenty fishing nets from the river. She removed the fish and hung the nets to dry. She milked the goats and drove them to pasture and then returned to rinse the fish and salt them into barrels. She made goat cheese and sold it. She picked cloudberries and set traps. She also built turf huts and made her own nets. She went twice a year to Gällivare to sell and buy at the markets. Gradually what she sold came to include not just barrels of fish and berries but her own creations of root basketry, for which she was paid much better. As her children grew, they helped much more with the household tasks, leaving Asa freer to spend more time with root craft.

Asa Kitok had originally learned something about basketry as a child from helping her mother and other women gather roots in the forest, particularly among the windfallen birch trees, and from watching how the roots were prepared and then used to make cheese molds, small chests with lids, and salt cellars. Having not made baskets for many decades, she had to start again at the beginning and taught herself through doing. It meant something important to her, as a Sámi woman, to express her culture in creating traditional wares and to share that knowledge with her daughters first and her students later. Selling her handicraft also provided an income. She began by offering some items at the Gällivare market twice a year. Word got out about her basketry, and soon she had orders. She worked in traditional forms, though few people used the baskets as they had originally been designed for. The cheese molds, for instance—shallow, wide baskets with open work at the bottom to drain the cheese and make a pattern—became bread baskets for the table or ornamental wall hangings. Baskets with lids could still be used to carry things, but usually they were only decorative, as were the salt flasks, once so important in the task of preserving meat and fish.

By 1953, Asa Kitok was working full-time with root basketry, the first person to make a professional living from it. She was fortunate in that her interest in this particular craft coincided with the rise of interest in the economics of handicraft and in new, concerted attempts by Sámi educational institutions and craft associations to preserve heritage culture and to create new models for identifying and promoting Sámi *duodji* in the marketplace.

On February 3, 1945, a new organization, Same Ätnam, was founded in Jokkmokk, Sweden. A black-and-white photograph taken that day shows about a hundred men and women standing on a snowy street; most are in Sámi *gákti,* and many of them were artisans. One of the women in the photograph was Karin Stenberg, by then in her sixties, a former schoolteacher and longtime activist in Sámi politics and culture. She was born in 1888 into the Forest Sámi community in Arvidsjaur; she would spend her career working as a teacher there and promoting Sámi heritage and education. Stenberg had traveled to Stockholm in 1905 to take part in an education course specifically for Sámi people. Throughout the 1920s and 1930s, Stenberg wrote and organized on behalf of the Sámi. She coauthored a manifesto, *This Is Our Wish: An Appeal to the Swedish Nation from the Sámi People,* that boldly laid out a plan concerning rights related to reindeer herding and other matters. She helped save Arvidsjaur's Lappstan (Lapp Village), a neighborhood of wooden huts constructed near the church, from destruction. In the 1940s she, along with Gustav Park and others, began working to create a Sámi Folk High School, which first opened in Sorsele in 1942. This was the same area that more than two hundred years before had been the site of assemblies where the Sámi had been stripped of their dignity and their drums. During the 1940s, the school was reorganized and moved to Jokkmokk, where it was inaugurated in its new form in 1949. There it became a crucial link in teaching the Lule Sámi language, saving craft traditions, and fostering a new generation of Sámi craftspeople.[13]

Same Ätnam played a significant role in the postwar organizing of the Swedish Sámi. The group worked to educate and pass on craft skills to younger people and to create a quality mark that would identify Sámi *duodji* in the marketplace. There was a need, which only grew more urgent, to protect Sámi-made objects from knockoffs sold for the tourist trade that began to flourish again after the war. *Duodji* came to be seen as vitally important for maintaining Sámi identity in the face of modernization and assimilation, particularly for the 90 percent of Sámi people who no longer practiced reindeer herding.

Stenberg also collected *duodji,* and by the time she died in 1969, she had amassed around four hundred objects and examples of craftwork, which went to the regional museum in Arvidsjaur. There were other Sámi collectors, including Stenberg's political colleague Gustav Park, who donated to Norrbottens Museum, and Lars-Erik Ruong from the district of Luokta-Mavas, who deposited some seven

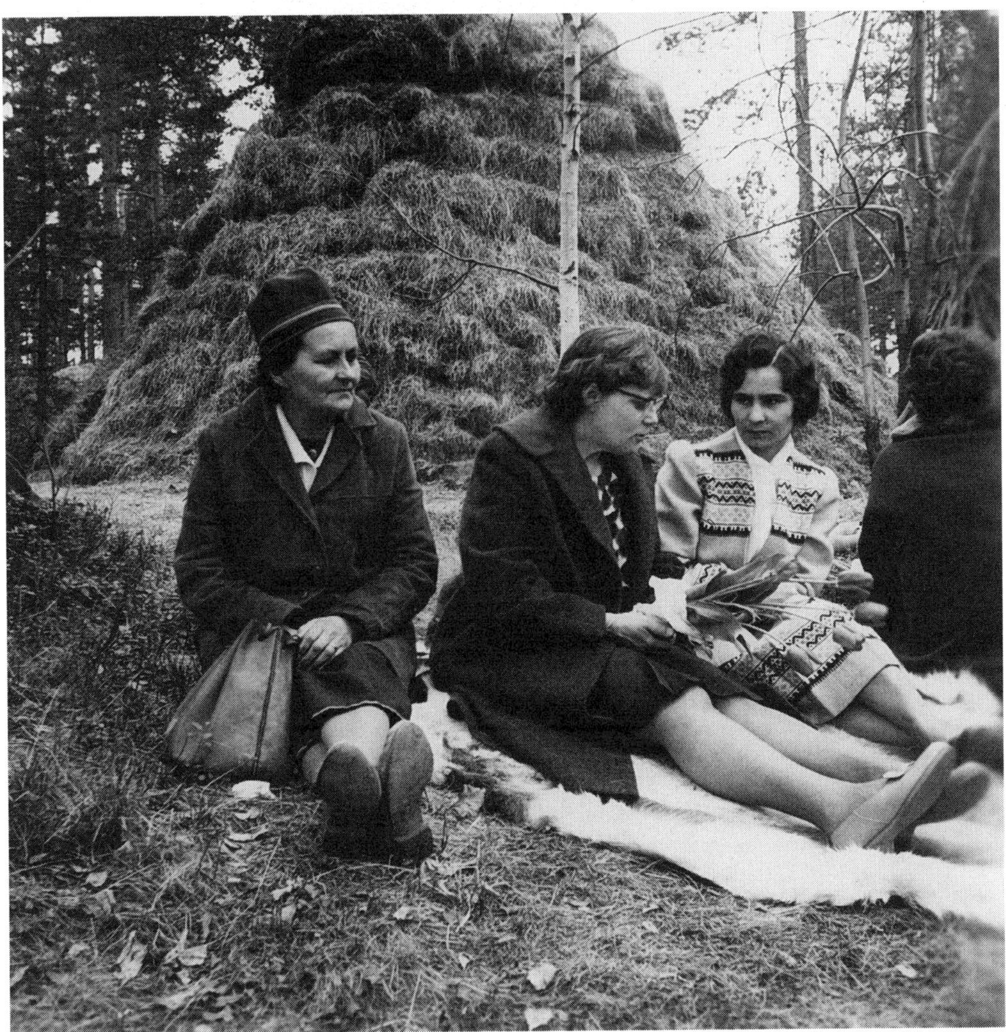

Asa Kitok's daughter Ellen Kitok Andersson (left) with students from the Sámi Folk High School in Jokkmokk, 1963. Photograph by Lennart Wallmark. Courtesy of Ájtte Swedish Mountain and Sami Museum.

hundred objects in the Silver Museum in Arjeplog.[14] Karin Stenberg's collection is notable in that she gathered women's handicrafts in particular. One of her acquisitions was the first basket made by Asa Kitok's daughter Ellen Kitok Andersson.

In 1962 Asa Kitok was invited to teach a two-week workshop at the Jokkmokk school. By this time, the high school had become a hub for Sámi *duojárs*, who worked in different forms of *duodji*: sewing and embroidering pewter thread on cloth or leather; etching on bone and knife making; and creating bowls, spoons, and chests in wood, often with bone inlays. Jewelry making was popular, in part because it sold easily at markets, and other forms of silverwork were coming into vogue. One of Asa's students was Ellen.

At age thirty, Ellen had already learned almost everything necessary to make root basketry, but the course gave her the chance to meet other students and teachers of *duodji,* often in other mediums. Many women were learning to embroider with pewter thread, for instance; most considered root craft too arduous. Ellen understood that. She had gone out with her mother every summer from the time she was around twelve to collect roots. She saw the hours that went into searching for and gathering the roots, which must not be crooked or knobby; she understood firsthand the painstaking labor of debarking, soaking, and splitting the roots carefully, as well as the devotion and effort that went into shaping the baskets, which could take several weeks or more. But she loved the work. Ellen had begun to make her first baskets in 1950, when she was eighteen.

"For me," she told an interviewer, "the desire to become a root crafter was very strong, and I never thought of training for any other sort of profession. I knew the whole time that I wanted to work in a field to do with Sámi culture. But to start root basketry requires orderly planning; it was for that reason that I continued so long with weaving alongside root basketry. Weaving secured me economically while I worked up to being a root crafter."[15]

Her mother's work was fundamental to her:

> What I received from my mother was a precious education. I was able to see her working and to be with her out in the forest. She gave me the inspiration for my future; she's my frame of reference. That is why I have this collection of her handicraft, so that now and then I can look at it. Sometimes I can feel a little tired and have sat a long time at the craft table, then I can sit down and look at my mother's handicraft, caress these objects, and it awakens something special in me. It probably has to do with me admiring her so much for taking this up. That a woman of her generation, who worked so hard and so often lived in such difficult circumstances, could take up root craft again and turn it into something she could market; this was something special.[16]

At the same time as Ellen revered her mother's work, she, like her older sister, Margit Kitok Åström, wanted to take the craft further. They began with the same

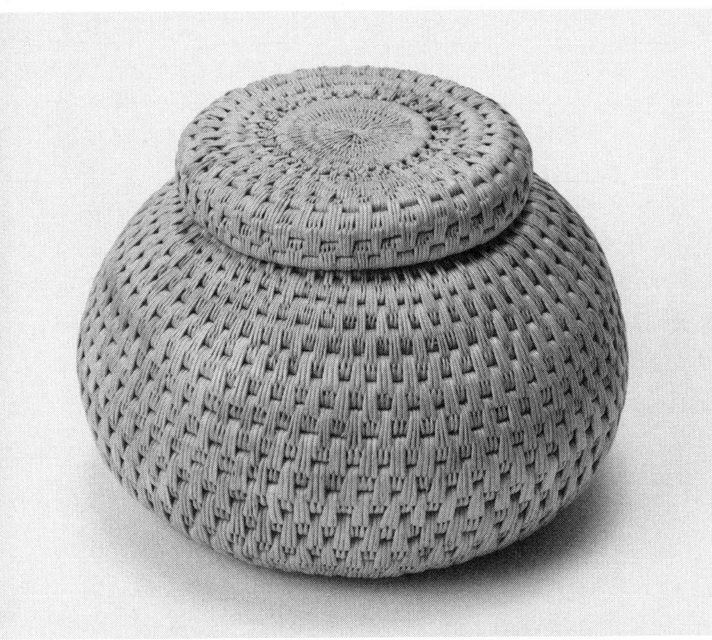

Ellen Kitok Andersson, root basket with lid, 1972. Photograph by V. Cullshed. Courtesy of Ájtte Swedish Mountain and Sami Museum.

forms—the cheese mold, the lidded basket, the salt flask, the sugar bowl, and the milking bowl—but developed them into artistry. Margit often worked with large objects; one of her big shallow bowls was commissioned by a hotel in Kiruna to be hung prominently in the lobby. Her trademark was often a horn button on the lid of her baskets. Ellen enjoyed working with superfine roots and close weaves, using different binding techniques in the same object for variation. She also liked to vary the colors of roots, for contrast, and occasionally leave bark on some roots. Ellen combined basketry with leather and wood, but not with horn.

By the 1980s, the Kitok sisters, now married with children, Ellen living in Jokkmokk and Margit in Malmberget, sold their work to non-Sámi collectors for increasingly higher prices that reflected the artistry and amount of time that the objects took. Some of their work was collected by museums—the Nordic Museum has two pieces by each woman, and Ájtte Museum in Jokkmokk also has representative works by the Kitok sisters, as well as half a dozen by Asa, some of which are on permanent display. Others are in the Sámi Art Collections in Karasjok. The sisters were part of a new generation of *duojárs* who were active professionals, teaching and giving workshops while devoting long hours to their craft. They felt fortunate that they could work in an atmosphere of collaboration and support within a community of like-minded artisans, something that their mother had lacked.

In 1972 Tom G. Svensson, a Swedish anthropologist employed at the Ethnographic Museum in Oslo, traveled to Lule Sápmi to begin a case study on Asa Kitok and her daughters. Asa was almost eighty at that point. At the same time, Svensson ordered from her two *kahpa korja* (baskets for keeping coffee cups), one for himself and one for the Ethnographic Museum, the first order she'd ever had from a museum. Svensson's monograph *Asa Kitok and Her Daughters* was published in Swedish in 1985, as the final title in the Nordic Museum's *Acta Lapponica* series. Asa Kitok died the following year, at age ninety-two.

Ellen Kitok Andersson told Tom Svensson:

> I have a message with everything I do: it is very important! I want to tell the story of the Sámi's hard lives and how they have striven. With my thin roots I will tell about this and that we will defend culture that belongs to us. . . . I am bound to the traditional forms, at the same time I'm excited about new shapes that fit them. Along with the artisans who work in wood I want to speak through my craft. It is better to speak through things than to speak with words; things are my most important speech. There are no limits to what one can express with the objects one creates. What one can say with ordinary words is very limited.[17]

The winter market in Jokkmokk takes place every February. The market has been in existence for over four hundred years, since it was established by King Charles IX as a place for the state to begin to regulate the Sámi population of Sweden and collect taxes. The festival atmosphere would be unrecognizable to those who came in the 1600s with sleds piled with furs. Nowadays, thousands of people, Sámi and non-Sámi, with increasing numbers from around the world, attend the market for the music performances and dances, the lectures and readings, and the chance to see old acquaintances and family. But one of the major draws is the work of makers and sellers of northern Swedish handicrafts and Sámi *duodji*. Display booths line the snowy streets; other tables are inside classrooms and cafeterias of the former Sámi Folk High School, now called the Sámi Education Center. There is always an exhibit of *duodji* made by the students. Other exhibits take place within the museum, the library, and various shops

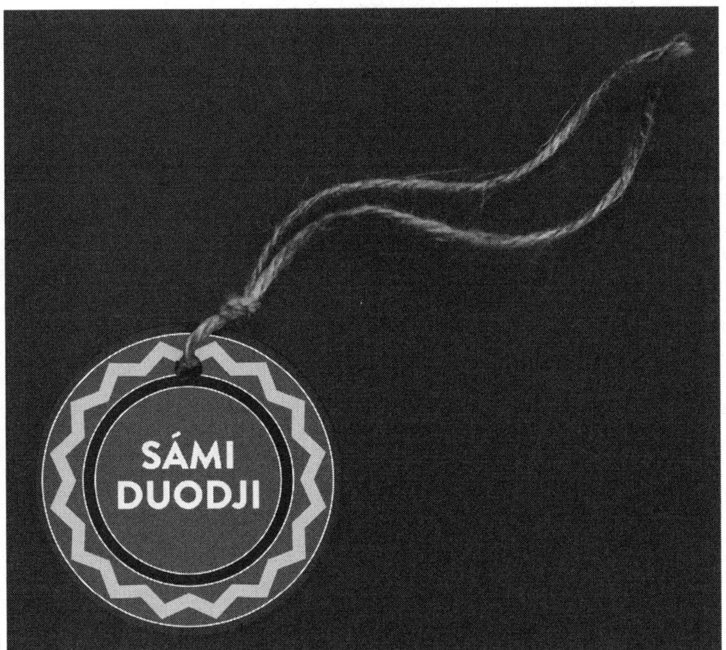

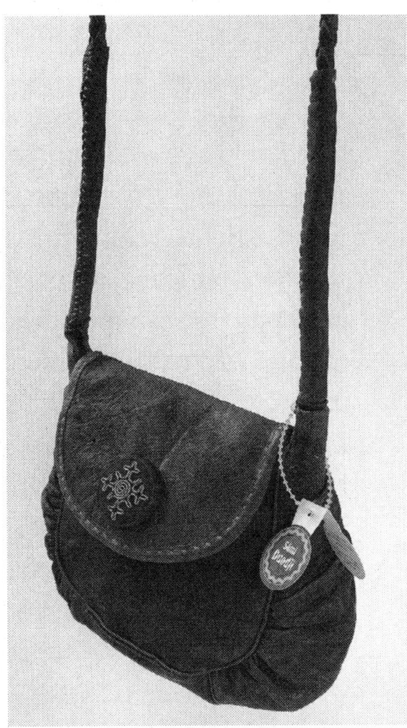

The *duodji* trademark label was introduced in the late 1980s in Sápmi. A purse made by *duojár* Katarina Bergdahl with the label was for sale at the Sámi Duodji shop in Jokkmokk, Sweden. Photograph of the label from the Saami Council / Piera Heaika Muotka; photograph of the purse from Sámi Duodji Sameslöjdstiftelsen.

around town. In a wooden building a few streets away from the complex is the gallery of Same Duodji, the Sámi craft organization, which became independent of Same Ätnam and moved to Jokkmokk in the late 1980s. It was at the beginning of that decade that the Saami Council (Sámiráđđi), working with Sámi organizations in all four countries (Norway, Sweden, Finland, and Russia), introduced the trademark "Sámi Duodji" to distinguish Sámi-made handicrafts from cheap, imported souvenirs and from similar handicrafts made by non-Sámi people. Further definitions specified that the item must use traditional materials and have been created using traditional methods and techniques. The purpose of the trademark is to assure the consumer that the object is created by a Sámi *duojár* and to strengthen Sámi-produced handicrafts in the marketplace. The trademark is authorized by Sámi *duodji* organizations in Sápmi to qualified *duojárs* and is attached to various objects for sale to the public.

Yet a distinctive trademark label was not the end of it. Discussions of what *duodji* was and is and could be continued to be debated even as the demand for it grew, fueled by interest from private collectors and museum curators. An active proponent of Sámi handicraft in Sweden was Kurt Kihlberg, who began to publish large-format books about Sámi *duodji* in the 1980s. With texts in Swedish and English and a smattering of Sámi words, lavishly illustrated with color photographs of exquisitely crafted objects, the main focus was the *duojárs,* often pictured in their homes and workshops, in the process of creation or holding up examples of their work. Kihlberg also included artwork by those who worked in both areas, graphic art and easel paintings, such as Lars Pirak, an all-round painter, *duojár,* and storyteller. The texts of Kilhberg's books, with quotes from the *duojárs,* have a celebratory tone as they recognize individuals and their devotion to making and sharing their craft.

The celebration of *duodji* also brought discussions of continuity and innovation to the fore, especially at a time when new forms of Sámi art, *dáidda,* were emerging. Some makers of *duodji* bridled at the distinction between craft and art. Old definitions of artisan and artist were breaking down, and more and more *duodji* expressed the personality of the *duojár* or took an object only as a point of departure. *Duodji* had by this time moved far from its origins in the useful. No one used a *náhppi* or milking bowl any longer, and yet the form lived on in a *náhppi* still made in the traditional way, from a birch tree bole, but polished to a high gleam and with the handle inlaid with etched and polished horn. Some *duojárs* wanted to incorporate less traditional materials in new ways: Anna-Stina Svakko, living in Porjus, near Jokkmokk, produced a beautiful bag at the request of the Nordic Museum for its new permanent exhibit, *Sápmi,* in 2007, using wool, fish skin, and Plexiglas. She called it *Light Travel*:

> The white bag is entirely a white sheet like watercolor paper. I can make it into a Sámi shape but it does not need to be the traditional colors. It does not need to be brown leather. It does not need to be anything of the old style if I don't choose it. I feel that I don't know what I am doing but I can combine my knowledge about the old craft, the techniques, with the new materials, with natural materials. I can choose totally by myself and that's so fascinating!
> I know even if I turn the page, nothing there is pre-decided. I myself decide and that's why the Plexiglas shapes came in where there had been antler before.[18]

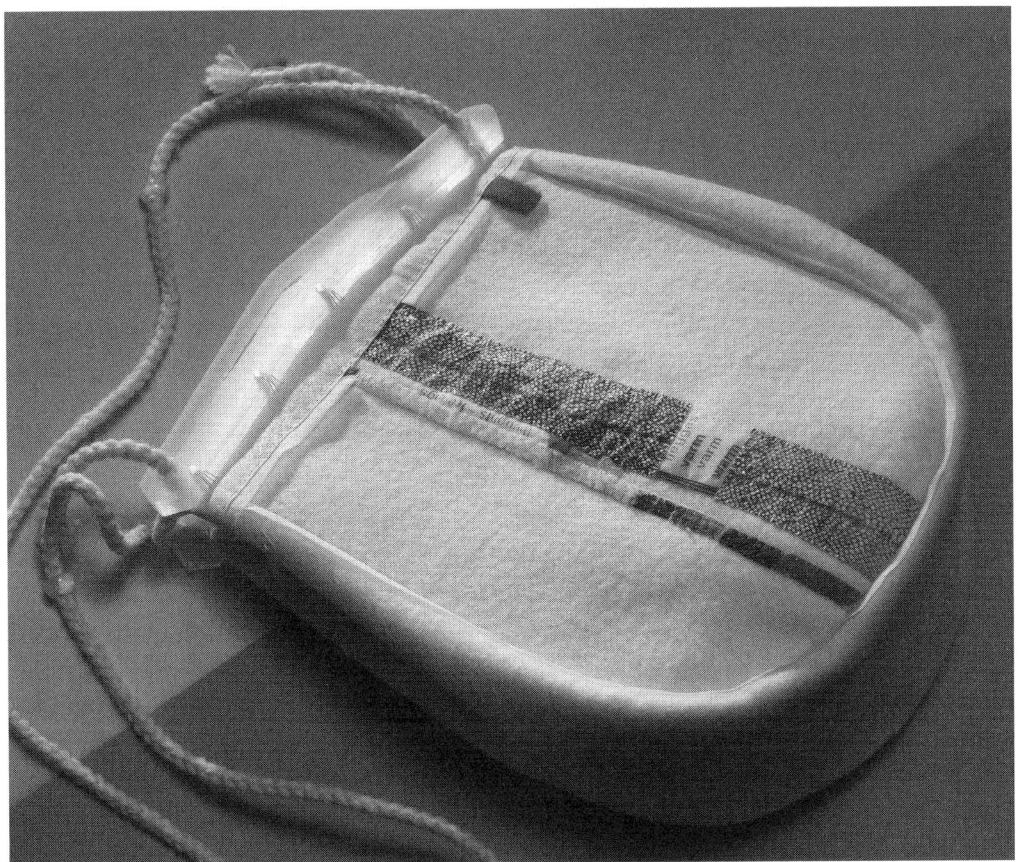

Light Travel, by Anna-Stina Svakko, a purse created of wool, silk, salmon skin, reindeer skin, and Plexiglas, displayed at the Nordic Museum's Sápmi exhibit from 2007 until 2022. Photograph by Birgit Brånvall. Courtesy of the Nordic Museum, Stockholm.

Other Sámi creators intentionally developed techniques and aesthetics that had one foot in *duodji* and another foot in *dáidda*. This had begun as early as the 1960s, when Ivar Jåks, the Karasjok painter and sculptor who had studied graphic art in Copenhagen and brought a modernist aesthetic to his artwork, began to create works that were based on traditional *duodji* with elements of mythology, such as the polished wood door handles at the Sámi Museum in Karasjok. The Sámi artist Lars Levi Sunna comes from a *duodji*-making family (his brothers Thore and Helge Sunna are also well-known *duojárs*, with work in Swedish museums). As a practicing Læstadian, he has fused his interest in pre-Christian mythology with Christian images, creating art and installations for churches and public spaces. Working in wood, often curly birch, he has carved figures of Sámi goddesses and created a sculpture of a Sámi drum split open by a cross, images that are meant not to shock but to heal. Some of his artworks have been funded by the Swedish Church.[19]

Modern *duodji* is often the starting point for many Sámi artists, who use their understanding of materials and storytelling connected with *duodji* to create powerful, original pieces. Rose-Marie Huuva, born in 1943 in Rensjön, Gabna district, near Kiruna, is a poet and multimedia artist who works with textiles, reindeer hide, and metal and stone to tell stories. Some of her work is displayed in the new museum of contemporary art in Kiruna (Konstmuseet i Norr), and other work is in Tromsø at the North Norwegian Art Museum (Nordnorsk Kunstmuseum). One of her installations, *Object of Research—How Long?,* from 1999, explores the past history of racial biology research carried out in Sámi communities in Sweden. Around a pyramid of dirt is a circle of transparent boxes, each holding the model of a human head, faceup, overlaid with reindeer skin. One box is empty.[20]

The Finnish–Sámi artist Outi Pieski created an assemblage for the Sámi Parliament in Inari, titled *Eatnu, Eadni, Eana—Stream, Mother, Ground.* This wall relief consists of slightly cupped steel discs in various sizes, gilded or plated with white gold, suggesting a *risku* or *solju* brooch worn by Sámi women in traditional dress (similar to a *sølje* brooch in Norway) (Plate 13). Pieski, born in 1973, with degrees from Finnish art academies, is a prolific artist whose work is frequently exhibited in the Nordic countries.

Like increasing numbers of female *duojárs* and artists, Huuva and Pieski have moved away from the gender-defined materials of "hard" and "soft" handicraft. The number of men working with leather, yarn, and cloth has grown as well. The Scottish–Sámi writer Johan Sandberg McGuinne has described his interest in weaving bands with rigid heddles in the traditional way:

> Weaving, both as a necessary task to produce bands for belts, backpacks and details on Saami dresses as well as an art form, has traditionally speaking been seen as a woman's task. Until I started weaving, this was also the case in my family; whereas my aajja *(grandfather)* focused on passing on traditional skills related to hunting, fishing and the making of knives, my aahka *(grandmother)* and tjidtjie *(mother)* were always the ones who worked with textiles and woven bands. But while this division between men and women

> as far as our traditional handicrafts go to a certain degree still remains today, I am far from the first Saami man to weave bands and I hope that I will not be the last one to do so.[21]

In recent years, changing gender roles and the emergence of a new generation of multimedia artists and writers—many of them women, some of them openly queer, many of them activists as well and connected to Indigenous movements elsewhere—have put a new stamp on *duodji* and *dáidda*. This burst of creativity rooted in and spiraling out from traditional Sámi cultural practices, from handicraft to storytelling, has also taken place in the musical sphere in the language and sounds of the joik.

Wax Cylinders, Sámi Voices

Maria Persson's attic room was packed. Outside on the single, snowy main street of Arjeplog, a village in the heart of Swedish Sápmi, booths offered silver jewelry, brass vessels, tools, reindeer harnesses, and brightly colored, skillfully sewn and embroidered clothing and shoes. Reindeer pelts and frozen reindeer meat were being sold out of open wagons, while reindeer antlers, with dried blood at the root, lay in bundles on the glittering snow. Swedish locals and a few traders or tourists from more distant parts walked the street, but most of those gathered at Arjeplog's annual winter market over several days in February 1913 were Sámi families from a wide surrounding area. In addition to buying and selling, they were there to celebrate weddings and christen children in the local church. "A cozy and quiet scene," wrote the Swedish author Karl-Erik Forsslund about the street lined on both sides with stalls, "no great throng of people, no hubbub."[1]

The hubbub was up in Maria Persson's attic: laughter and music and coffee and intense listening. Karl Tirén, a tall, fat Swede with a short beard and a beaming, benevolent expression, a fiddler, a maker of violins, a painter, and a state railway employee, had joined Maria and her sister Greta Persson in inviting friends and relatives to share their repertoire of short, rhythmic songs—a *vuolle* or *vuelie* in Lule and South Sámi or a *luohti* in North Sámi, songs commonly known now as joiks, from the verb "to joik."[2] For this occasion the folk music collector and ethnomusicologist Tirén had brought something never seen before in Arjeplog: a phonograph able to record voices on wax cylinders and play them back. His new acquaintance, Karl-Erik Forsslund, a Swede not quite as burly as Tirén but also warmly bearded and equally eager and appreciative, wrote down names with brief descriptions: Sara Enarsson: "a thin, lined face with a pair of deep, dream-warm eyes"; Paul Norsa: "a lithe military type with a blond moustache."

He scribbled the words of the melodies, translated into Swedish, complete with vocables when there were no words: "lo, lo, lo; na, na, na." His journalism might have been embroidered with flourishes, but the article "When the Lapps Joik," which he published a few weeks later in *Dagens Nyheter,* one of the main Stockholm papers, overflowed with on-the-spot details that still resonate when read today. The writer is wholeheartedly experiencing something that much of Sweden has no idea exists and that is "exalted, fine." Forsslund echoes his friend Tirén when he declares, "An enormously rich treasure room has been opened, a whole new world."[3]

It's the lively, even joyous mood of the attic room that Forsslund keeps returning to, the evident merriment when the phonograph sings the songs back to the crowd, "when they hear their own voices and melodies come out of the horn. . . . Everyone can sing, old and young. Some have a repertoire of a couple of hundred *vuoleh.* A fourteen-year-old boy keeps a record of all the joiks he knows, around eighty. And the majority allow their joiks to be listened to, somewhat unwillingly at first, but increasingly inclined, the more they get going." The repertoire describes personal joiks that have been with individuals since babyhood; joiks to other people; joiks to lakes, rivers, and mountains; joiks to Norway and to ocean liners, including the *Titanic*; joiks of sorrow and loss; joiks of love and marriage; joiks that skewer sheriffs and politicians; and joiks to wolves, swans, and especially reindeer.

The Sámi joik is sung using a particular set of throat muscles, which gives the music its deep, vibrating, sometimes haunting sound, though it can also be high and light at times. In the distant past, joiking was part of a religious ritual, with drum beats as accompaniment, a rhythmic chanting designed to help the *noaidi* travel to the other worlds. But there are thousands of other joiks, spontaneous to memorized, which conjure up the world's multitude of beings and feelings. A joik tends to the concrete. It's not a song about something; it is the thing itself, and joiking is the human action of singing, shaping, and recalling.

> They sing to the reindeer grazing lands north of [Lake] Tjäggelvas, to the herd, swarming with a frightened gait. This is superbly recreated in the rhythm, to the reindeer calves, to the leader, a white cow reindeer. "With beautiful lowered horns she runs, lu-lu-lu—and the snow, and the snow it whirls—lu-lu-lu-lu-lu-lu." "Straight into the wind she dashes, the fine silk nose." They sing to one of the dogs killed by wolves, to living moose and dead moose, the latter song plaintive and full of warmth and tender sympathy; to the

> woodpecker, Siberian jay, scoter, fox—to the swan, hare, squirrel, lemming. In a staccato voice how the woodpecker cracks and drums. The swan's *vuolle* is one of the most beautiful, with the rhythm of the wing beat and soaring flight. The hare's melody is a faithful translation of its tracks in the snow, and here are the squirrel's verses: "May the boy child die, but the girl child live, she who doesn't do me any harm so that I can hop from tree to tree in peace." The melody creates the illusion of its springy, daring leap. In the same way the lemming's song sounds like how it scrabbles and takes small hops while at the same time the song has a ring of the high mountain plateaus.

Maria Persson sang "a *vuolle* to the ptarmigan with precise mimicry of the bird's melody—kábau-kábau-njao-njao—the beautiful, particular rejoicing." She had a repertoire of dozens of joiks, some seventy of which have survived in Tirén's notations, with twenty-three of those on wax cylinders that have since been re-recorded on tapes and now digitized. Over three days in Arjepolog, Karl Tirén, with the help of Maria Persson and her sister Greta, captured over a hundred joiks, each a minute, more or less, from around twelve people on seventy-five black hard-wax cylinders. The mood and setting of the recordings were important, and that was largely due to Maria Persson's influence in her community, her desire to share, and her willingness to open her room to strangers and friends alike. Over the course of his long life as a joik collector and enthusiast for Sámi music, Tirén would speak repeatedly of his gratitude to Maria Persson. "In the realm of song, she proved to be one of the most knowledgeable of all the Lapps I subsequently came to know."[4]

In 1913, Maria Persson was thirty-six years old, as yet unmarried, dark haired under her embroidered cap, with a round, cheerful face and gregarious smile. She's splendidly dressed in all photographs, often with crafted tools of bone, brass, and steel hanging from her belt: a knife, needle case, scissors, and spoon. According to Forsslund, during the winter market in 1913 she wore a *gákti* the blue color of "shadows on snow on a sunny day." The dress was edged in decorative bands of yellow and red, but its glory was the collar insert, with its "stars of silk and glass pearls and the most elegant pewter-thread embroidery." She had made it herself, for she was a professional seamstress and embroiderer. Her specialty was festival attire, and many of those in Arjeplog that year would wear one of her embroidered collars or square chest cloths fastened around the neck, sewn with pearls or fine pewter thread in geometric patterns. She made objects as well; in his article about the 1913 market, Forsslund includes a photograph of two little dolls in Sámi *gákti* she had made and a delighted description of them: "a small old fellow with bushy gray hair and beard and a small old lady with two long braids, both in sky-blue tunics with pearls and embroidered bands at wrist and hem."

Maria Persson was born in the mountain district of Luokta-Malvas, just south of the Arctic Circle, one of fifty-one districts carved out of Swedish Sápmi during the Reindeer Herding Act of 1886. Luokta-Malvas stretches west to the once porous Norwegian border; the reindeer had been accustomed to cross back and forth in spring and autumn, and there were marriages and relatives among the Sámi on both sides. After Norway became independent from Sweden in 1905, the border questions grew fraught. Many Sámi, unable to make a living without traditional lands, gave up and sold or killed their reindeer during this time.

Maria's parents were nomadic herders, and she grew up in a traditional *siida*, a community that still actively recalled and passed on stories and joiks. Her parents gave up the migratory life in the 1890s, and like many Sámi of the period, they became smallholders, with a farm outside Arjeplog; they raised goats and sheep, along with a few reindeer. In her teens Maria suffered an accident to her hip or back and was sent to the town of Piteå on the coast, where she lay in hospital for two years "in a plaster cradle," according to her daughter in an interview years later.[5] She never fully recovered and was somewhat disabled the rest of her life. In the absence of detail, we can imagine that it was here in the hospital where Maria may have begun to focus on sewing and making crafts, such as dolls dressed in Sámi clothes, in order to find a means of support. In Piteå she would have spoken Swedish nearly all the time; her fluency put her in the position of being able to negotiate the borders of Sápmi and Sweden. Perhaps it was for that reason she was asked to go to Stockholm in 1909 for the Industrial Arts Exhibition to help represent the large province of Norrbotten.

This exhibition followed on the world's fair held in the city in 1897, an extravaganza that introduced Stockholm's culture and industrial products to the world and that coincided with Artur Hazelius's founding of Skansen and plans for the Nordic Museum. In the midst of "the summer city," as the Industrial Arts Exhibition came to be called, a Sámi couple were invited to display themselves and their belongings as an example of nomadic life in northern Sweden. In the Norrbotten rooms they set up their tent and lit a campfire to boil coffee and make food. The fire created a ruckus with the managers of the exposition. Maria Persson stood up for the Sámi couple. A tent without a fire was not a home at

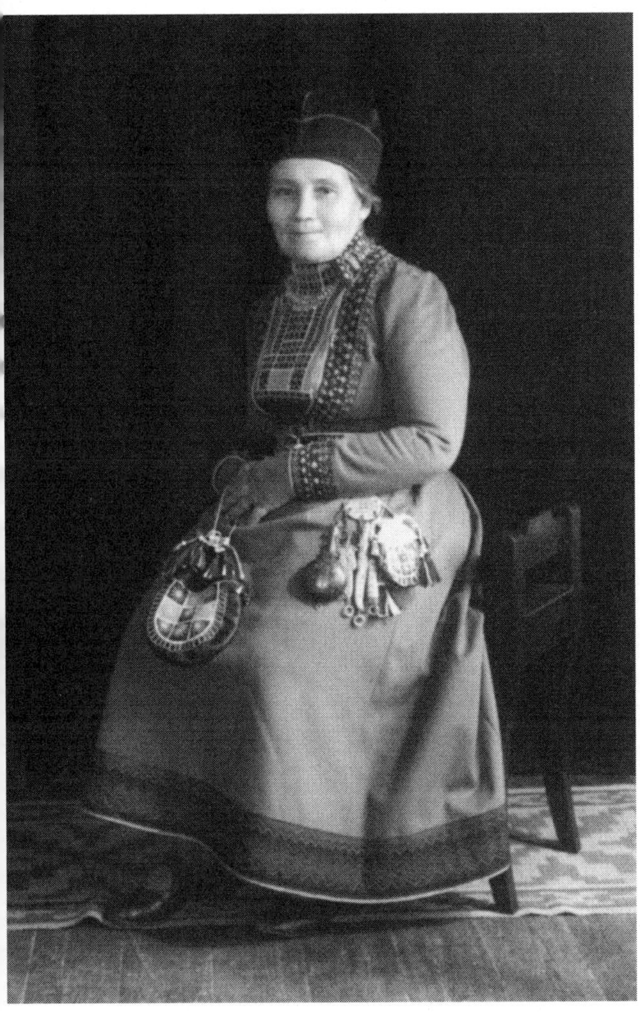

Maria Persson, undated studio portrait. Courtesy of NOMAD, Umeå Municipal Archives, Umeå, Sweden.

all. Surprisingly, she was joined in her protest by a big Swede with a short beard whom she had met at the exposition. Karl Tirén was in Stockholm to show his paintings over in the Jämtland rooms. He too argued with the directors over the importance of the campfire.

He spoke as someone with firsthand knowledge; he'd been born in 1869 in South Sápmi, near Östersund, into a family who was friendly with many local Sámi. His father and his brother, both named Olof, were pastors with Sámi congregants. His much older brother, Johan Tirén, was a well-known painter whose

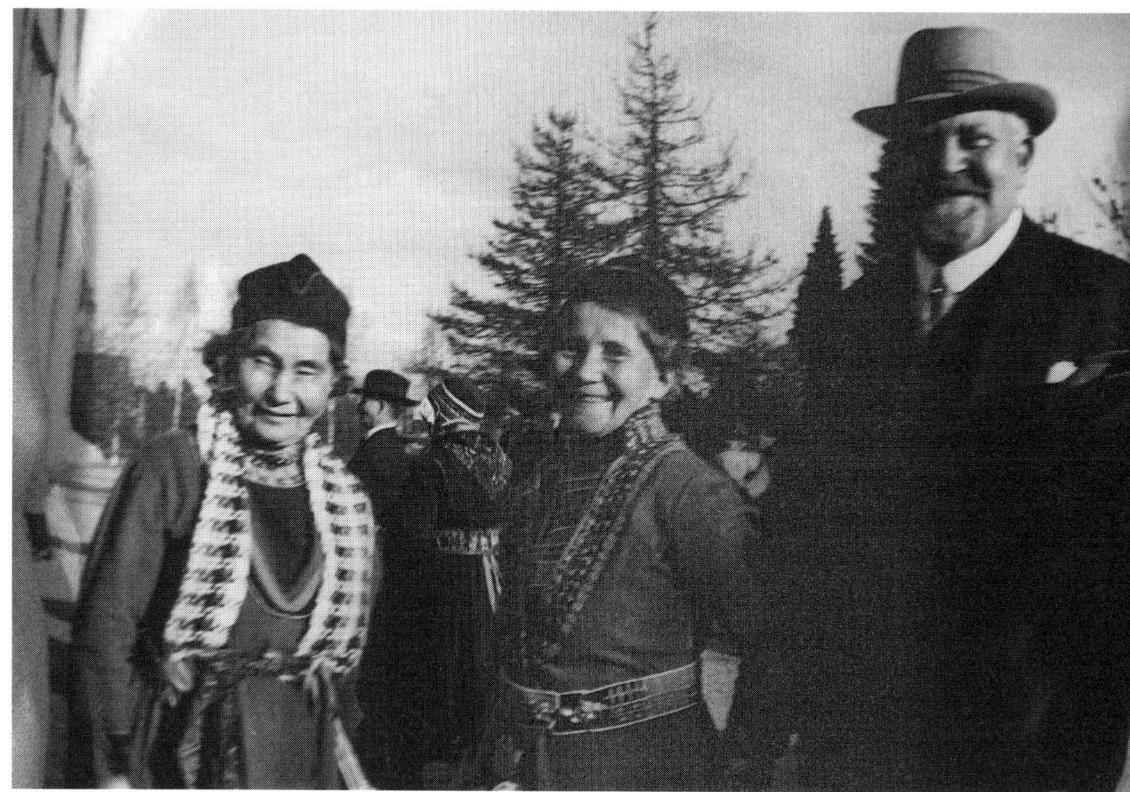

Greta Persson, Maria Persson, and Karl Tirén, 1930s. Courtesy of NOMAD, Umeå Municipal Archives, Umeå, Sweden.

subjects often featured the people, animals, and landscape of Sápmi and whose art had played a role in the national debate about discrimination against the Sámi and theft of their traditional lands. Karl had wavered over a career choice, studying in England, taking art classes in Stockholm, and fiddling and painting. Eventually he joined the state railway system as a way of providing for his family while continuing to develop his interests in music and Sámi culture. As a railway employee, Karl Tirén chose to take posts in the north of Sweden, including Umeå and Kiruna. Since 1907 he'd been working from Boden, near Luleå.

When the Sámi couple decided to pack up and leave the Stockholm exposition, Maria went with them, and so did Karl Tirén. A short time later, Maria arrived as an invited guest to the home that Karl shared with his wife, Karen, and their five children in Boden. Tirén had long wished to hear true joiking and to learn more about the Sámi's musical traditions. Over the course of a few days, Maria Persson shared joiks and explanations, and he noted down her words and melodies as best he could. In letters at the time and later in his published work, he emphasized the importance of his meeting with her: "What I learned from Maria Persson . . . in the form of both tones and information on the character and concept of Lapp song greatly increased my interest and evoked the idea of making journeys to collect and research in this field."[6]

A hundred years ago, when Karl Tirén began to plot how to collect joiks around Sweden, the music was little understood by outsiders, few of whom had ever heard it outside the annual winter markets or tourist camps, where it was occasionally performed in an exaggerated way by men who had had too much to drink. Joiking was often mocked and reviled, even by segments of the Sámi population, particularly those in northern Sápmi, who were some of the most fervent followers of Læstadianism. For these Sámi, the tonal sounds of joiking were connected with drunkenness and Devil worship; they preferred psalms. Still, many individuals and families in Sápmi kept this musical tradition alive. They tended to joik only at home and outdoors in the wilderness, and almost never in front of outsiders, which is why the abundance of material came as a surprise even to someone like Karl Tirén.

Few outsiders and travelers in Sápmi before the twentieth century seem to have had anything positive to say about joiking. Guiseppe Acerbi, an Italian who journeyed to the North Cape in 1799 and published a book about his experiences, was one of the first foreigners to attempt to write down some joik verses. Sometimes he was "obliged to stop my ears with my fingers." He concluded, "Their music was without meaning and without measure, time, or rhythm."[7] Gustaf von Düben shared his opinion, writing in *On Lapland and the Lapps* that "all other civilized men who heard that singing, found it unpleasant."[8] Even K. B. Wiklund, the ubiquitous Swedish Lappologist who wrote one of the first serious descriptions of joiking in his 1906 booklet *Song and Poetry of the Lapps* and urged the collecting of joik music while it could still be saved, didn't seem to enjoy listening to the actual sound: "Joiking does not make a pleasant impression on Swedish ears."[9]

One of the few outsiders who experienced the joik not as performance but as part of daily life was the Danish artist and ethnographer Emilie Demant Hatt. In her field notes, unpublished manuscripts, and ethnographic travel narrative *With the Lapps in the High Mountains* about her months living with the Sámi, she threads references to joiking through the pages, sometimes in passing and sometimes connected with specific individuals. She writes particularly about the storyteller and joiker Anni Rasti in 1908 and about Märta Nilsson, a woman in her seventies with whom Demant Hatt lived for six weeks in the summer of 1910. Märta told her younger friend about joiking as a girl when she was out herding the reindeer and when she was unable to sleep. In the old days, Märta said, they had all joiked, about "everything possible: very often they improvise joiks in an instant."[10] Demant Hatt associated the joik with nature:

> The Lapps' joiking sounds as if it were learned from nature itself; it resembles the wind moving in withered grass and shrubs. It reminds you of water babbling and insects buzzing, when there's quiet joiking, barely audible, during handiwork. But it can also be hoarse and violent in its expression, like a gale in a forest, like ravens croaking and storms howling. I have not heard joiking so often but I have heard both sorts, and always it's made me think of the sounds that are heard in the forests and mountains.[11]

Unlike Tirén, Demant Hatt left only her own impressions of joiking, rather than examples of specific verses or melodies, yet she was one of the first to give the context for joiking as well as to sound the alarm that the tradition was on the way out. This fear was simultaneously real and overblown: just because outsiders didn't hear joiking didn't mean that it was dying out. Although Karl Tirén's collecting was based on the notion of salvage ethnography, it also illustrated his sincere desire to be of service to the Sámi. Unlike some ethnographers of the first half of the twentieth century who only took and did not give back, Tirén had the idea that the Sámi could be encouraged to see joiking as a contribution to world musical culture, to find pride in their music, and to carry the tradition onward.

Tirén would never have an academic position; he received only limited financial support from such organizations as the Swedish Folk Music Commission and the Royal Swedish Academy of Music for his collecting work, but he brushed past difficulties. In fact, his distance from academia and his easygoing relationships with the Sámi joikers were advantages. He used his postings to several different stations in the North to explore the landscapes around Abisko, where he was given permission to build a small house inside the national park. His boundless energy and ability to get along with people made it possible for him to undertake a remarkable series of adventures and excursions around Swedish Sápmi and just across the border along the Norwegian coast from 1910 through 1915.

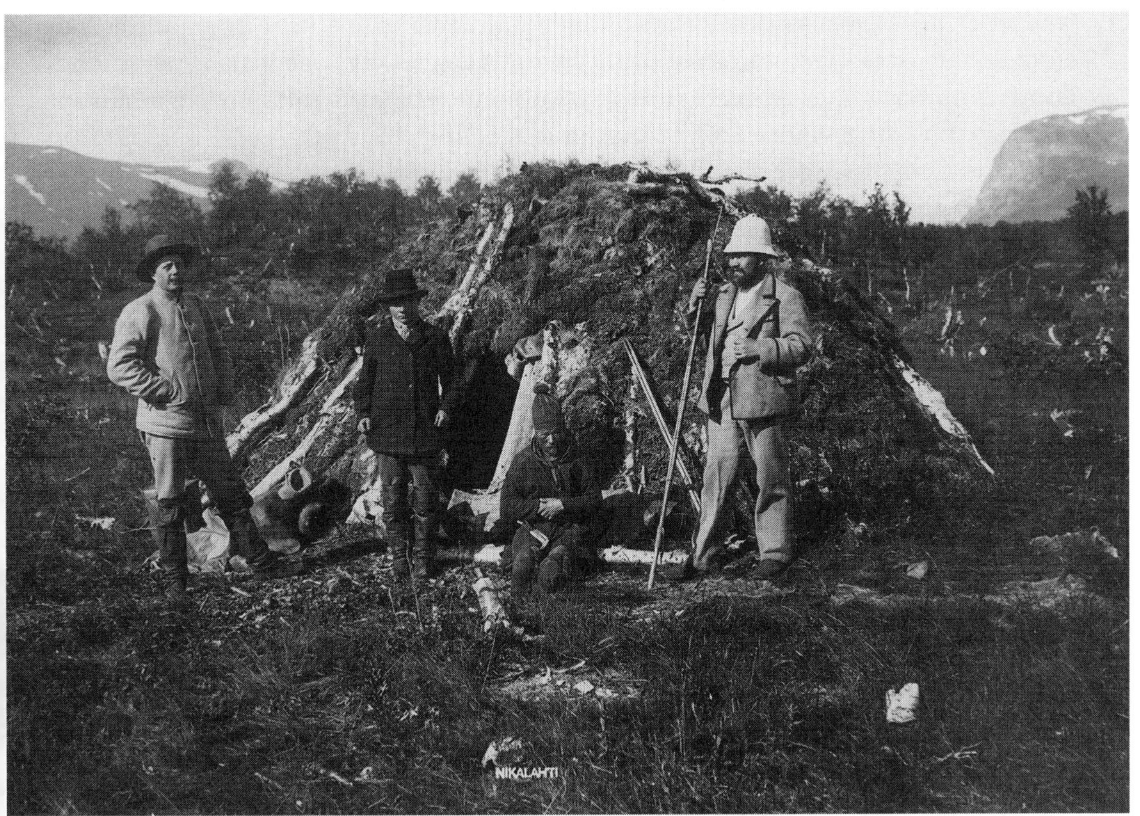

Karl Tirén, far right, in the northern Swedish mountains near Nikkaluokta, circa 1900–1919. The group stands by a turf hut, or *goahti,* constructed of wood and peat moss, an alternative to the tents, or *lávvus,* used in warmer weather or on migration. Photograph by Borg Mesch. Courtesy of the Swedish Railway Museum.

The accounts of his strenuous journeys are replete with miles of hiking over mountains and nights of sleeping rough, of storms and flooded valleys, of missed opportunities, exhausted porters, and "fanatical Læstadians" who warned their *siidas,* "Those who joik for Tirén will also joik in hell."[12] Nevertheless, beginning in 1911, he traveled to the winter market at Lycksele and wrote down in musical notations ten *vuoleh* from nine Sámi people, young and old. In the summer of 1911, with leave granted from the railway, he set off on a much longer and dramatic trip in the north of Sweden, beginning around Lake Torneträsk, and up to areas around Tromsø, where he looked for and encountered Sámi migrating with their herds from Sweden to the Norwegian fjords and coast. Over the following year, Tirén collected examples of joiking from Sámi in the vicinity of his home near Boden, but in the summer of 1912 he was back on the road, this time farther south from Narvik. Once again he was allowed to take leave from his job and was supported by the Swedish Folk Music Commission.

Most of the travel he undertook was in summer; he went by foot, wagon, coastal steamer, and inland motorboat, since there were few train lines in the North. In the winter he covered snowy ground in a horse-driven sleigh. By 1911, he had hired an assistant, a woman teacher from the South with a yen for adventure, Maja Wickbom. She could rustle up a fire and make a meal from little or nothing, sleep on the ground, and whip out rain gear in an instant. She was a tireless walker and never complained. She helped defuse worries from Sámi women that the large Swede had designs on them when he approached, seemingly out of nowhere, on a mountain plateau. Maja Wickbom was crucial in the collecting of joiks from women, who were equal bearers of the musical heritage in Sápmi.

Maria Himmelstrand, a journalist from Stockholm, ran into Karl Tirén in Abisko in 1912 and wrote about the experience in a travel article for the Swedish Tourist Association's yearbook:

> In Abisko we met the station inspector Karl Tirén, painter, musician, inventor, mountain climber, a person known all over Norrbotten. If we mentioned his name among Lapps and settlers, their eyes lit up and the words rushed out: Someone had heard him play the violin; another had even played the violin with him; a third had walked—no, run with him in the mountains. He was a man who jumped off a train going full speed, who sprang into bogs and dashed over mountains and swamps straight to Kebnekaise [Lapland's highest mountain], scorning all paths. "And they say, Miss, that he can put a spell on the violin."
>
> During the summer, Tirén wanders on a mission for the folk music society among the Lapps to study and note down their national melodies and songs, and he told us a variety of interesting things about that. For us, who were going to travel into the interior of Lapland, it was of course doubly interesting to get a glimpse into one aspect of the Lapps' spiritual life. Among other things he described his first visit to a Lapp camp. The Lapps were, to begin with, quite reserved. They were very unwilling even to confess that they had their own songs with their own melodies, partly from distrust and partly from religious reasons. A large number of Lapps in Norrbotten are in fact strict Læstadians.

A significant portion of their verses are old pagan songs and such devilish abominations they don't want anyone to hear about.

They were extraordinary melodies that Mr. Tirén sang for us, small, short stanzas often only within a range of 4–5 tones. The rhythm was singular, quite unlike our usual musical rhythms; it would probably have been very difficult to devise any sort of accurate classification of the measures. There were formal stanzas to the spirits of the air, earth, and water. There were humorous stanzas. There were tonal pictures from surrounding nature. "How the reindeer runs" was a quick little melody, where the rhythm really brilliantly expresses a reindeer herd's swift, light, measured race over the snow. "How the white snowflakes fall" was a masterpiece about the melancholy mood of nature.

One time Tirén came to a Lapp camp, where the Lapps were markedly reserved. Then an old granny had spoken up and strongly rebuked them. "It's shameful," she'd said, "that my family's young men forget their father's songs!" And the granny was plainly a figure of authority, because after that the Lapps didn't need any encouragement to recite one song after the next. Among the Lapps Mr. Tirén has found magnificent voices, really gifted singers, both women and men.[13]

Until the winter market of 1913, Tirén's collecting work was all in the form of musical notations by hand. He was helped by his excellent ear and his skill with the violin. Back at home in Boden, between trips, he would play joiks on his violin from his growing pile of notations. He was occasionally visited in his home by different Sámi acquaintances. A few would joik for him. As his collection of songs grew into the hundreds, he began to group them into categories, some of which Karl-Erik Forsslund mentions in his 1913 article:

Three main groups: *lauloh* or religious songs, *noaidi* songs and defensive songs *(nåite-lauloh),* psalms—and this includes strangely but meaningful enough, trekking songs and walking tunes (*jåttem* and *sirtem-lauloh*). Further luotte: love songs (*rakis-luotte,* in the south *kieresvuota-vuoleh*), wedding and betrothal songs *(suogno-luotte),* hate and pain songs *(vasje-luotte),* mourning songs, meetings and greetings, and farewell songs *(arro-luotte)*—songs to the underground people *(halte-luotte),* along with reindeer-guarding songs *(reina-luotte).* Herding songs are probably the nearest Swedish equivalent to Sámi

> joik. Some songs to a mountain or to reindeer are strongly reminiscent of a song on a birchbark trumpet or a cow horn; they have the same loud ring and heavy, but strong long-distance range.
>
> And to end, the remaining bunch of *vuoleh*. Songs to lands and nations, villages, towns, and cities, relatives and fellow beings, to the king, governor, pastor, and sheriff (generally a lampooning song); to natural phenomena—the sky, the sun, the moon, thunder, the Northern lights, the storm, the snow, the mist, the smoke, the fire, the sparks ("Sparks rise with the smoke—out of the tent—the sparks fly into space and go out")—the tone goes up and then down, an unusually expressive melody and rhythm, to the mountains, the lakes, rivers, ocean, bogs, forests, reindeer grazing lands; to the reindeer, dogs, all kinds of wild animals, uldra songs *(katniha-vuoleh)*; songs to the dead and to the heroes of the sagas—and to the train, steamboat, the motorboat! Humorous stories (*hauskeh*, pleasantries, this extends to animal imitations); lullabies *(tulle lulle mana)*, often small gems; songs to sewing and other work, which even includes a pearlfisher's song. And finally there are epic songs, those mentioned by Fellman but now mostly forgotten.[14]

But the joik is not easy to notate on paper. Aside from the fact that Tirén's knowledge of different Sámi languages was weak to begin with, the shifting pitches and rhythms of different joiks don't fit the standard five lines of Western music. The notations were no substitute for the subtle and unusual rhythms. For that reason he was offered the use of a cylinder phonograph by the Ethnographic Department of the Natural History Museum in Stockholm, and it was this phonograph with its wax cylinders he used for the first time at the winter market in Arvidsjaur and a week later in Arjeplog. The phonograph had been purchased in Berlin just a few years before. Yngve Laurell, a young man who worked at the museum, was sent to learn how to operate the device at the Berliner Phonogramm-Arkiv, a pioneering organization in audio recording, and Laurell in turn taught Tirén and remained his contact at the museum through 1914.

By the time Tirén toted the museum's phonograph to the winter markets of Arvidsjaur and Arjeplog, the apparatus had been in existence for some years. The original hand-cranked model was invented as a curiosity by Thomas Edison in 1877 using hollow cylinders covered in tinfoil. This was followed by a wax cylinder version created by the Bell Studios. By the 1890s, the phonograph with its distinctive horn was widespread; new all-wax cylinders were sold with prerecorded songs and instrumental music in their grooves. They generally played for about three minutes and could wear out after only a few dozen times. The black, hard-wax American Edison cylinders used by Karl Tirén, in contrast, were far sturdier and are still playable today. By the 1910s the cylinders had competition from the flat discs we now call records. But the cylinder had an advantage over the disc, one that anthropologists and musicologists would make use of: the cylinder phonograph had an attachment that made it possible to record music and voices.[15]

Fieldworkers from different disciplines had been using the cylinder phonograph for at least a decade before Sweden took it up. The Finnish musicologist and composer Armas Launis traveled in the High North of Finland and Norway in 1904 and 1905, documenting and recording joiks, and in 1908 he published a German language collection, *Lappische Juoigos-Melodien*. Although Karl Tirén eventually became aware of Launis's work, he did not find in the Finnish musicologist's work any of the songs he had recorded on his own, and the two men never met. As a musician himself, Tirén shared his efforts with composer friends such as Wilhelm Peterson-Berger, who would create a symphony based on Sámi melodies titled *Same-Ätnam*. But Tirén's real collaborators were the Sámi joikers themselves, particularly when the recording cylinder phonograph was introduced into the mix. Although Tirén, while recording the joiks in Maria Persson's attic, manned the phonograph himself and maintained control of the way each joik was presented, with his voice announcing in Swedish the name of the singer and the joik's subject at the beginning of each recording, the Sámi played a role in the decisions about the content. They chose what to sing from their own repertoire and what to hold back. They felt freer to joik the personal melody of visitors to the attic. Forsslund writes:

> When new guests arrive one of the previously arrived whispers with a glint in his eye, "Now I'm going to sing his or her *vuolle*!" And out it comes and everyone listens with recognition and laughter, not least the subject of the joik.
>
> Thus, Lars Eriksson Steggo—tall, trim, and powerful, a true reindeer herder. Great delight when his hardships are sung about in the mountains, how he toils in storms and bad weather, how the wind blows out his cooking fire or turns over his coffee pot, so the coffee runs out![16]

There are more joiks to people in the phonograph recordings than in Tirén's written notations, and there's other evidence in Forsslund's description that the Sámi were active participants in the process, especially as they heard the recordings played back. Some joiks were requested often, some were corrected, and some sparked memories of other joiks. Everyone who was there remembered those days in Maria's attic, and some of that energy and enjoyment remains in the faint grooves of the wax cylinders.

The last time that Karl Tirén seems to have used the borrowed phonograph was at Maria Persson's wedding in Arjeplog in 1915, when she married Johan Johansson. Maria's new husband was originally from Norway. He had spent most of his life as a seaman, working thirty years as a machinist on large ships in ports around the globe. He too came from a family that knew and respected the art of the joik; his brother, Abraham Johansson, and his sister, Sara Johansson, had both joiked for Tirén. Abraham and Sara were both traveling teachers and were bearers of stories and joiks, some of which were recorded by Tirén. Sara married Lars Ruong and settled in Luokta-Malvas to herd. One of Lars and Sara's children was Israel Ruong, Maria Persson-Johansson's nephew, who would come to play a significant role in Sámi cultural history as an inspector of nomad schools, a joik collector, an author, and a professor of linguistics at Uppsala University.

The wedding celebration that Karl Tirén attended and described so jovially in his diaries was not the last time Karl and Maria were in contact, but their lives went in different directions. Soon after their marriage, Maria and Johan Johansson moved to his family home in Norway with their baby daughter. On their return to Sweden a few years later, Johan had an accident. He fell through thin lake ice and drowned. Maria continued supporting herself as a *duojár*. Like many who made clothing for the Sámi community, her skills were highly valued, though evidence of her work is confined to a few pieces that people donated to museums. Ájtte Museum in Jokkmokk conserves two of her chest cloths, the rectangular pieces of flannel with stand-up collars fastened at the back of the neck. Sewn of traditional Sámi colors, green, blue, red, and yellow, they're artfully embroidered and decorated with small stars and pearls.

Karl Tirén moved with his family to the village of Bergvik, outside Söderhamn on the Baltic coast, where he became the stationmaster. His work as a civil servant was modestly paid, but he continued to have a rich inner and outer life, meeting many of the era's celebrities, including Greta Garbo and, it's said, Vladimir Lenin. As one of the few experts in Sámi musical traditions outside the Sámi community, he corresponded with musicians and scholars, lectured on Sámi joiking, and performed joiks on his violin. His passionate personality earned him the volcanic name "Stromboli."[17] In the 1930s, he finally finished his opus on Sámi music.

Written in Swedish, it was translated to German, the scientific language of the time, and published in 1942; *Die Lappische Volkmusik* became the third volume of Ernst Manker's series *Acta Lapponica*. In this substantial book were notations for around five hundred joiks. Tirén also developed his comparison of the way that Sámi joiks functioned as musical leitmotifs, not unsimilar to those found in the work of Richard Wagner. Today Tirén's notations are seen as too simplified, and more than one scholar has pointed out that the Sámi joik bears no resemblance to *Parsifal*. But part of what Tirén was grasping for was a recognizable analogy for the way that joiking embodies the unique materiality of creation. He understood that the titles he gave the joiks—"To Greta Persson" or "To the Ocean Liner"—were not odes but concrete poems. Beingness itself, recreated in sound.

More important for the popular spread of Tirén's impressions and research on joiking than the hefty volume in German were articles written about him and by him in the Sámi weekly newspaper *Samefolkets egen tidning*. As early as 1919, its editor, Torkel Tomasson, praised Tirén's work. Again in 1926, Tomasson described how Tirén gathered and saved "the last remnants of the singular tones of the Sámi. . . . Karl Tirén has accordingly made a contribution which cannot be appreciated enough—for what is a people without music?"[18]

Most of the recordings, some seven hundred examples of joik captured on approximately three hundred cylinders in their original labeled cardboard tubes and original boxes, went to the Natural History Museum in Stockholm for safekeeping. Gunnar Ternhag, who has written about Tirén's collecting expeditions from 1910 to 1915, says that because of the way his notes, manuscripts, and cylinders were dispersed in several storage locations, it can be difficult to know for certain how many of Tirén's recordings and notations still exist. The bulk of the wax cylinders, the core collection of 287, was transferred from the Natural History Museum to the Nordic Museum in 1946, while others went to the Institute for Language and Folklore in Umeå or stayed with the family. In the late 1960s, the cylinder collection was moved again, this time to Stockholm's Music Museum.

Karl Tirén died in 1955. But that was not the end of the story for his collection of cylinders or for the collecting of joik material. In 1953 and 1954, Swedish Radio had sent out two field collectors, Matts Arnberg and Håkan Unsgaard, on two recording journeys with the aim of creating a comprehensive inventory of the country's joik traditions and finding material to broadcast. The two musicologists were, fortunately for the project, accompanied by Israel Ruong, Maria Persson-Johansson's nephew. Ruong, in addition to speaking several Sámi languages, had a network of friends and family to draw on, not only in his native

Pite Sápmi but also north of Jokkmokk to Karesuando. When the collection of 195 joiks was released on seven albums in 1969, ten of the songs were joiked by Ruong himself. A book was released with the recordings that included words to the joiks translated into Swedish by Ruong. The book includes an introductory essay by Israel Ruong, "Remembering, Feeling, and Yoiking."[19]

Here he speaks of the joik's ability to conjure up the past. During the course of a few weeks during the winter of 1920, at the age of seventeen, Ruong lost his parents, Sara and Lars Ruong, and his two younger siblings to the Spanish flu. He was left in charge of the other siblings, and it was only with great determination that he finished a correspondence course and then began teaching in local nomad schools before going on to study and eventually gaining a doctorate in Uppsala. Some of the joiks that Israel Ruong had learned as a child were from his mother, Sara. One he had learned was a joik to the "old man of the wind," the *Biegga-galles*. Its words tell the story of how no birch or pine can resist the gale. They are all uprooted. Only the rocks and the mountains can withstand the storm. Ruong's essay has a melancholy tone not found in Tirén or Forsslund, who tend to emphasize the good cheer and liveliness of the musical gatherings they experienced. To Ruong, who recorded his own joiks to his parents and siblings, change and regret and bitterness and loss were central elements.

The recasting of joik as public performance began around 1966, when the multimedia artist Nils-Aslak Valkeapää began to organize large concerts with other joikers. As a poet, musician, and visual artist, Valkeapää was a key figure in introducing the joik to world music and in strengthening the joik as a signifier of Sámi identity. His first album, *Joikuja*, in 1968 was followed by others that fused traditional vocal joik with instrumentals and ambient sound. Soundscapes with reindeer, wind, and water underlying the joik were also employed by the Finnish Sámi musician Wimme and the Norwegian Sámi musician and composer Frode Fjellheim. The revival of joik performance and recordings continued in all parts of Sápmi and gradually found audiences in the cities of the Nordic countries and beyond. Mari Boine, raised in a strict Læstadian family in Norway, sought personal freedom as a woman and musician in her performances in the 1980s. Boine's breakthrough album, *Gula gula!* (Listen, Listen!), in 1989 cemented her status abroad as a world musician, and she was not shy about using her platform to speak out for Sámi rights, a tradition that younger female joikers such as Sofi Jannok and Maxida Márek have continued.[20]

Along with audio recordings came new definitions and scholarship about the joik, often undertaken by the Sámi themselves. The Norwegian Sámi musician and law professor Ánde Somby has written that the joik differs from a Western European song in that it has no linear structure: no beginning, no middle, no end. "A yoik . . . starts suddenly and stops just as abruptly. In this respect, a yoik has neither a beginning nor an end, and is therefore circular rather than linear."[21] Frode Fjellheim, on the other hand, finds that the joik does most often have a linear structure and a musical form, "though the performance of the yoik is often not linear in the way that it doesn't always start and stop at the same place. The yoiker repeats the yoik a number of times (circle), but starts and stops often anywhere within what I actually see as a 'linear' musical shape. Most yoikers I interview even tell me where the start and the end of the yoik is. But in a live performance they often don't start at the 'start.'"[22]

With the burgeoning interest in Sámi vocal traditions came the inevitable question about whether traditional joiking, with its emphasis on community and participation, had a place in a more commodified world, where only some people joiked, on stage or in recording studios, and others merely listened and where a single voice, sometimes accompanied by a drum, had begun to give way to joiking against a background of synthesizers. Did changes in how musicians reinterpreted the joik, including young rappers like SlinCraze and Maxida Márek, mean that the old repertoire was consigned to history and the archives? Or could the joik continue to evolve and transform?

Frode Fjellheim was born in 1959 in Mosjøen, Norway, to a Sámi father and a Norwegian mother, both teachers. Eventually, his family moved north to Karasjok, one of the epicenters of Sámi culture. As a teen and young adult, Fjellheim was more interested in rock music and jazz than in Sámi music, though he was very familiar with joiking as performed in Karasjok. In the early 1980s, he began studying classical piano in Trondheim and playing in local bands as a freelance keyboardist. Slowly he turned to trying to find ways to incorporate his South Sámi roots into his performances. Invited to write music for a staged work by the South Sámi Theater (Åarjelhsaemien Teatere), he was given copies of some of Karl Tirén's notations of South Sámi joiks. The woman who provided the material was Anna Jakobsen, a longtime teacher of the South Sámi language who had known some of Tirén's original informants. She had also been a consultant on the project by the Music Museum in Stockholm, which began to transfer the material on Tirén's cylinders to magnetic tape in 1982.[23]

Fjellheim, excited about the idea of doing instrumental arrangements of the joiks with synthesizers and percussion instruments, did not want to reproduce the vocal performances Tirén had notated but instead wished to use the notes as a jumping-off place for something new. The more he studied Tirén's original manuscript, the more interested he became in the possibility of reconnecting with the Sámi culture he had never fully identified with growing up. His first CD was *Sangen vi glemte* (The Song We Forgot), produced in 1991. Ten of the eleven arrangements on the album came from Tirén's collecting efforts. A good portion of the joiks came from Sámi women, including Sara Ruong's joiking of "the old man of the wind," which Tirén heard at Maria Persson-Johansson's wedding in Arjeplog in 1915 and which was remembered and joiked by her son Israel Ruong for Swedish Radio. Fjellheim's arrangement of "Wind God" (Vindguden or Biegkealma) has a lighter touch, with timpani, bassoon, baritone sax, and harp. It's strikingly beautiful in its reinterpretation.

In his notes for the CD, Fjellheim acknowledges the efforts Tirén made to document and record joiking, especially from the South Sápmi areas. After this recording came out, under his own Idut label, Fjellheim created the Jazz Joik Ensemble, which became the group Transjoik, a name he links to trans(formation), trans(global), and trans(pose). His later work, for keyboard and percussion, often incorporated sonic soundscapes and vocal layering of joik rhythms and words, and he continued to use Tirén's notations as a springboard for his compositions. Fjellheim also created choral music for the group Cantus, including the song "Vuelie," used in the animated musical *Frozen*. In 2015 he and Cantus released the album *Spes*, which includes the composition "Njoktje" (The Swan), which reimagines the winged bird in flight with slow, regular beats and soaring vocals. It was originally joiked by the young Kristina Johansson in Lycksele in 1911 to Karl Tirén.[24]

The physical collection of cylinders of Sámi joiking recorded by Karl Tirén bears no resemblance to the collections of hand-crafted spoons, knives, sleds, stuffed reindeer, clothing, kitchen utensils, and the 101 other marvels that scholars, ethnographers, tourists, and other outsiders bought, stole, sold, traded, displayed, and stored from Sápmi. Each paper tube looks like the next; the black wax cylinders inside are sturdy yet fragile, invisibly inscribed with individual voices from the past. On most of the recordings, Tirén's voice can be heard, introducing the joiker and the title of the joik, after which he blows a pitch whistle. Some cylinders feature him playing the fiddle and assaying a bit of joiking himself. The Music Museum released a CD of selections from the Tirén recordings in 2003, *Sámi Röster* (Sámi Voices), with a photograph of Maria Persson smiling on the front.

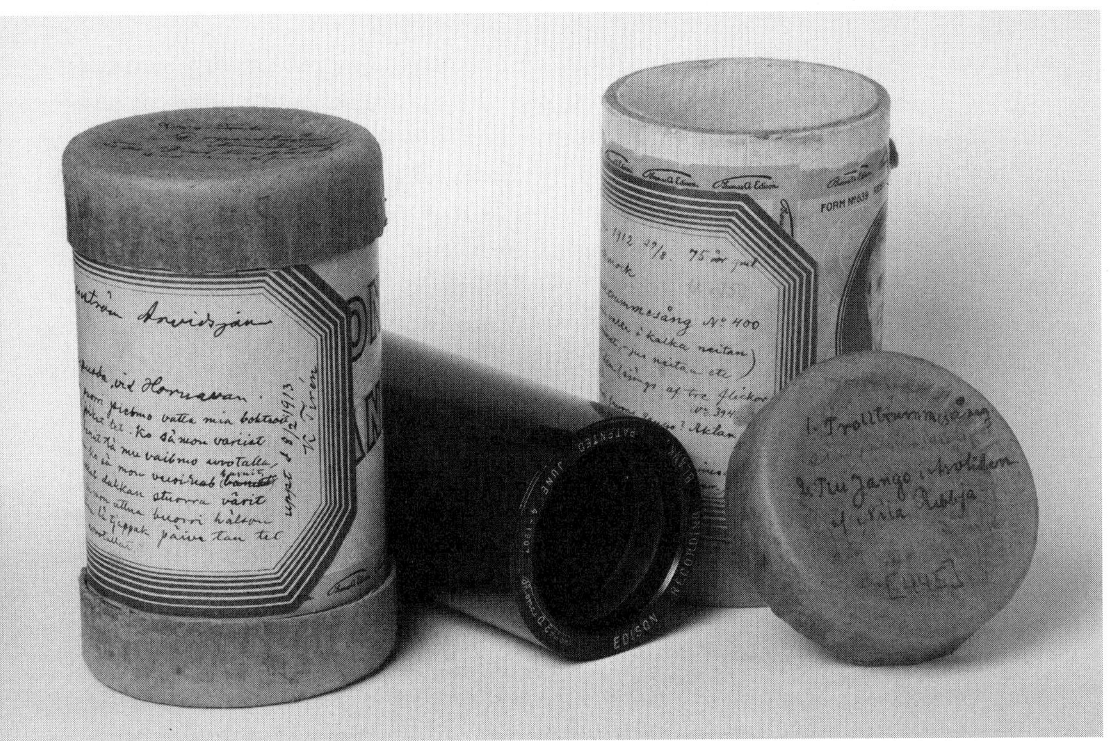

Wax cylinder cases from Karl Tirén's audio recording expeditions, 1913–15. Photograph by Eric Hammarström. Courtesy of Svensk Visarkiv.

In 2003 the cylinders left the Music Museum and were deposited at Svenskt visarkiv, the Centre for Swedish Folk Music and Jazz Research, in Stockholm. Swedish Radio had already digitized the cylinder recordings, but Svenskt visarkiv processed them again. The sound is still fairly crinkly and scratchy, but perhaps it's more alive for that reason. Beginning in early 2019, Svenskt visarkiv released six digital collections of Tirén's recordings under the Caprice Records label and in cooperation with Ájtte Museum in Jokkmokk and the Institute for Language and Folklore in Umeå. The first five collections include almost everything Karl Tirén recorded from 1913 to 1915. The sixth collection records Tirén himself playing and singing. In all, around a hundred men and women are represented in the digitized collections, people from nine years old to seventy-seven.

In 1998, Biret Ristin Sara, a joiker from Karasjok, helped start the Joikers' Association and became its first director. Interviewed by Thomas Hilder for his book on Sámi musical performance, Sara said that the goal of the group was to "look after joik" by passing it on to new generations as well as performing it at events for the public. She and others began to wonder about the many archival recordings, about where they were and how they could be accessed by the Sámi. From 2004 until 2007, the Joik Archive Project compiled a lists of all recordings in the Nordic countries, and Sara visited archives held at Tromsø Museum and the Norwegian Radio Sápmi archives in Karasjok, as well as archives in Sweden and Finland. During the process, Sara told Hilder, she listened to all the recordings:

> Many of the joiks, she explained, seemed to lack feeling, which she surmised was because there was no intended receiver of the joik, that in this context joik ceased to be a form of communication. Indeed, Sara could tell, for example, that the joikers in the recordings were joiking to a strange or unfamiliar person in an artificial situation. Rather, it felt more as though the collections served the purpose of simply compiling as many joiks as possible, whereby quantity was more important than quality.[25]

The notations and recordings that Tirén managed to capture in the early twentieth century are important historically as one of the oldest systematic efforts to collect Sámi voices. Unlike some other collectors of the same time period and later, who often searched out older joikers who might be assumed to know far more songs, Tirén recorded everyone, which means that his collection also includes young people and almost an equal number of women and men. As a whole, the collection has zest and personality. The Sámi participants were not necessarily joiking for the benefit of the likeable Swedish man who expressed such interest in their music. They were often joiking for themselves and to the relatives and friends around them. But the life force of individuals, their particular timbres, rhythms, flows, and stops, is there in the recordings, scratchy as they are sometimes.

If you listen closely, you can hear both who is joiking and who or what is being joiked. You can hear Maria Persson's voice, with its phrasing particular to the *vuolle* of the Lule Sámi, the two or three notes close on the scale, often long notes that conjure up a sense of freedom mixed with longing. In Arjeplog, at the winter market of 1913, she joiks to the sea bird; if you close your eyes you can see the bird flying over the water, low and gliding. She joiks the squirrel scampering—the same squirrel song that Forsslund noted down: "Let the girl child live, she who doesn't do me any harm so that I can hop from tree to tree in peace." Then there's Maria's joik to her sister Greta. It was Greta who joiked in 1913 to the ocean steamer and Hornovan lake; her voice is deeper than Maria's. Maria's joik to Greta is steady and rhythmic, almost a march. As if the sisters are walking steadily over a mountain plateau, over rocks and rivers, small girls with spirit and strength.

And at the end of the joik there's a laugh, Maria's quick laugh, a breath of delight.

Opening the Blue Chest

Made in the winter of 1907–8, the *giisá,* or small oval chest, is somewhat over a foot high and twice as wide, with a rounded, hinged lid. It would have been constructed in the traditional way, by boiling or steaming a thin strip of birch and bending it around a bottom of alder and then securing it with pegs or glue. The chest is painted dark blue, with loose loops of what seem to be green stems and flowers and extra curlicues of red along its sides and lid. A layer of shellac makes it more waterproof. Painted around the keyhole is something resembling a flower's opening. The large key is nickel, of a simple skeleton type, and there's a cloth strap stretching under the key lock for hanging the *giisá* off the saddle, along the flank of a pack reindeer.

The *giisá* was crafted by Johan Turi and was a gift for Emilie Demant, who was living in the tent of Aslak Turi, his wife, Siri, and their four children. Johan made it for Emilie to hold clothes and other personal things, perhaps her journals, her letters from family and friends, and her sketchbook and watercolors. The *giisá* is sturdy and well traveled. It accompanied Emilie when she migrated with the Turi family and their community, the Talma *siida,* from Laimolahti to lower elevations in the autumn of 1907. It came with her on an arduous reindeer migration she undertook with the Könkämä Sámi over the high mountains from the icy plateaus of northern Sweden to the Norwegian coast in May and June 1908. The blue chest returned with her by ship and train from Tromsdalen in Norway to a small house near Törnetrask Station in Sweden, where she and Johan worked on the book he was writing about the Sámi, a book she translated and saw published in a bilingual edition in 1910. Eventually the *giisá,* along with assorted other bags and boxes, was checked as baggage on the long train trip back to Denmark in October 1908, and there it stayed for many years.

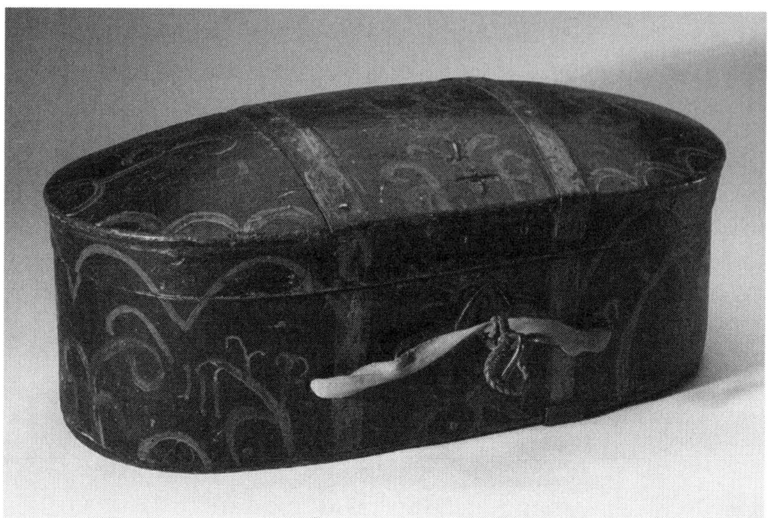

The blue chest, or *giisá*, made by Johan Turi for Emilie Demant (Hatt), winter 1907–8. Courtesy of the Nordic Museum, Stockholm.

In December 1940, the *giisá* returned to neutral Sweden from occupied Denmark by train with Emilie, who was to receive an award and give a lecture at the Nordic Museum in Stockholm. A photograph of the blue chest illustrates an article in the newspaper *Social Demokraten* about her travels in Sápmi years before and her friendship with Johan Turi. The blue chest is described by the journalist as having *mystiska krumelurer,* "mystical squiggles," supposedly taken from the old ceremonial drums, and the flowerlike center around the keyhole shows the sun, "the most important symbol" of the Sámi. Inside the chest is a colorful shawl, "a courtship gift," along with a wolfskin muff with "a large claw."[1]

The blue chest is also the lead in another article the same day, on the "Kultur" pages of the country's largest paper, *Svenska Dagbladet.* In the accompanying photograph, Emilie is presenting the *giisá,* along with the shawl and two amulets that once belonged to Johan, a bear's tooth and a wolf's claw, to Ernst Manker, director of the new Lappish Department at the Nordic Museum. Emilie is also gifting the museum with something that is hers alone, a large Expressionist painting in oil with motifs from Sápmi.[2]

By 1940 Johan Turi was dead and Emilie Demant had been married to Gudmund Hatt for almost thirty years. Before her marriage, when Turi still hoped to persuade her to love him, he gave her other presents. According to Sámi tradition, as Emilie knew well from observation, conversation, and questions, these gifts were freely accepted and just as freely returned if the courtship stalled or the

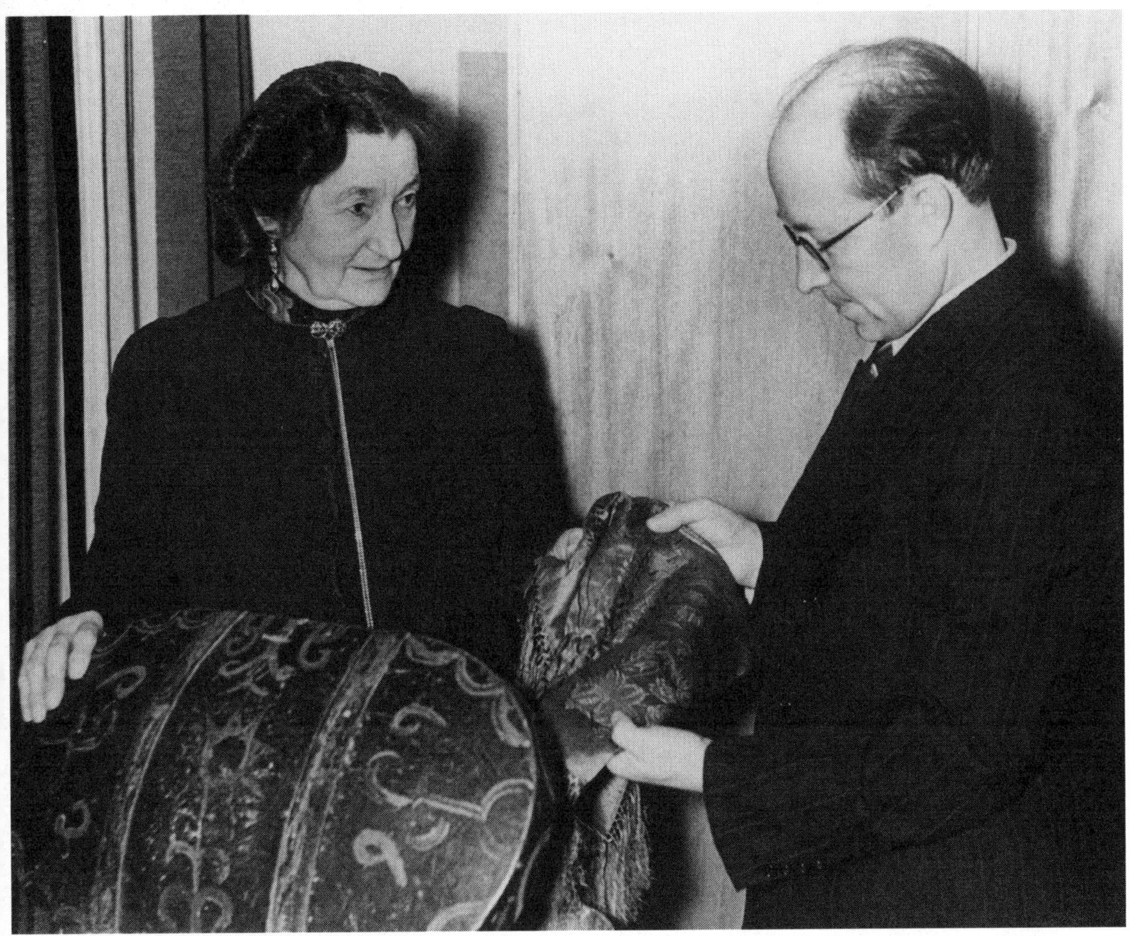

Emilie Demant Hatt in a Swedish newspaper photograph on December 4, 1940, presenting the blue chest made by Johan Turi to Ernst Manker on behalf of the Nordic Museum. Courtesy of the Nordic Museum, Stockholm.

woman decided to wed another. But as Emilie wrote in a letter to her parents in November 1911, two months after her wedding, the only present Johan wanted back, the only thing he would accept, was a large wooden bowl for making bread. This story is also repeated in one of the Swedish newspapers: He wanted only the bread bowl.

There are ninety-one objects said to have belonged to Johan Turi in the current collection of the Nordic Museum. A few were given by Emilie to the museum in 1940, when she came to receive the Hazelius prize: the wolf claw, a red printed shawl or kerchief, and the blue chest. Most of them were purchased in the mid-1940s by Ernst Manker from Johan's nephew Tomas Turi, who inherited his uncle's house on Lake Torneträsk: some clothing, a stool and other household items, and a variety of wooden and bone stamps carved with small reindeer, which Johan used in making some of his works on paper. Among the objects are several wooden bowls made by Johan Turi. I imagine one of these bowls could be the gift Emilie returned to Johan in 1911.

There comes a time in every biographer's life when it's not enough to read about the physical world that the subject of one's study moved through. It's why we travel to a city, a landscape, a school, a house; it's why we want to see our subject's childhood streets or her desk and other precious possessions. We want to touch what she touched, to see what she saw, to understand, through objects and houses and landscapes, what connected her to other people in her life. This impulse had sent me at different times to the Danish village of Selde in Jutland, where Emilie Demant Hatt was born in 1873; to the Royal Academy of Art in Copenhagen, where she and other young women fought to study art in the late nineteenth century; and to Lake Törnetrask in search of the mountain and forest views I could glimpse in her paintings and photographs from the 1930s and 1940s, when Emilie was in the strong grip of memories and visions that she needed to record in vivid colors on canvas.

In 2008, I asked Eva Silvén, a curator at the Nordic Museum, if I might be able to see the blue chest Johan gave to Emilie. Eva agreed to have the *giisá* brought from storage to a viewing room, and together with another colleague of hers at the museum, Cecilia Hammarlund-Larsson, I pulled on thin white gloves. We spent about twenty minutes looking at the blue chest from several angles, and I took photographs. With my white gloves, I stroked the lid and sides of the chest, and then Eva turned the large nickel key and opened the chest. I looked inside. I sniffed. It was unfinished, with light gouges from the hand tools still visible in the steamed birch strips that had been bent or, as the Swedish has it, "swept" around the alder bottom. The blue chest still smelled of wood, perhaps with a tinge of forest and smoke. I imagine it was Johan Turi's intention that every time Emilie Demant opened the *giisá* she would think of him.

I'd first seen this chest reproduced in black and white in *Boares Nauti* (Old Wolf), Nils-Aslak Valkeapää's book about Johan Turi consisting of images, maps, and texts in Danish and North Sámi.[3] This was in 2001, on my initial trip to Sápmi to explore northern Fennoscandia in winter, when I first heard about the friendship of the Old Wolf, Johan Turi, and the Black Fox, Turi's name for Emilie. Since then I'd found references to the blue chest in the newspaper articles from December 1940, when Emilie was invited to the Nordic Museum as part of a "Lapland Evening" to receive the silver Hazelius award and talk about Johan Turi. I felt at the time that the blue chest might offer a key to a relationship that had been lightly investigated, one often summarized in contradictory ways based on assumptions and hearsay (she was his muse, housekeeper, secretary, and possible lover; he was exploited by her to further her own ambitions) and gossiped about for a hundred years.

In 2004 I spent a few days in Stockholm, mostly in the archives of the Nordic Museum reading Emilie's typed transcription in Danish of letters from Johan from 1904 until just before his death in 1936. She had also typed up (in the 1940s) her own notes to clarify some meanings and to dispute for history some of his claims, for instance, that there had ever been anything romantic between them.

I asked a curator if I could see the fifty paintings Emilie had donated to the museum in 1953. Maria Maxén escorted me down to a lower level that held storage rooms, which led off a long corridor and were separated from each other by what I recall as plywood and chicken wire but was probably somewhat more substantial. We passed enclosures of baroque chairs, tall painted clocks, and rolled-up tapestries; the Nordic had vast holdings of everything to do with Sweden's cultural past. Emilie's paintings, in their original frames, leaned up against each other or against the walls. Some were as large as four by six feet; most were painted from the mid-1930s through the 1940s. All were strikingly vivid, radiantly colored depictions—in deep blues and bright greens, frozen whites, and fiery reds and oranges—of mountains, lakes, ice bridges across melting rivers, northern lights, deep green forests; tents blazing with light; Sámi figures in large hats and *gákti*; and lively dogs and strings of pack reindeer.[4]

We pulled out as many canvases as possible so I could take photographs of them. I felt astonished by their power, almost dazed with happiness, as I was in those days, by the discoveries I was making, each a kind of epiphany. These pivotal encounters with Emilie's archives and art, which I recorded with exuberance and awe in my journals, would sustain me for years as I turned to the often painstaking work of documentation and assessment.

Today the paintings, along with almost everything the museum owns that is not on display, are held off-site in a suburb of Stockholm in a vast storage facility, climate controlled and secured by passkeys and overseen by video cameras.

You can also find Emilie's paintings online at the Swedish DigitaltMuseum, with their dates and titles and accession numbers. You can also see the blue chest—*Nomadkisa*. NM.0222574A-B—indexed as "Transport and communication" as well as "Sámi history."

I've been to that suburban storage site. I've seen Emilie's paintings there, mounted high on great pegboard screens so that you can view several dozen at once. The paintings are just as wonderful as I remember them when I had to prop them up on a table to photograph them. But I'm still glad that I saw them in the storage basement once, picked them up by their frames, put my nose up to their surfaces to observe the layering of paint, the gestures and marks, the physical traces of Emilie's arm and hand on the canvas.

And I'm glad that I saw the blue chest, too, that I touched its smooth sides, saw the vines and flowers, smelled the wood, and saw the faint gouges left inside by Johan Turi, imprints of his once living presence.

Emilie would eventually leave many personal possessions related to the Sámi to the Nordic Museum archives, including her original field journals from 1910 through 1916 and the typed copies she made of them; her correspondence from Johan Turi and from the Kiruna mining director Hjalmar Lundbohm, who published Emilie's and Johan's books; her photography scrapbooks and original negatives from pictures taken of the Sámi people she met and knew well; and fifty Expressionist paintings with motifs from Sápmi.

In Denmark, the State Archives in Copenhagen has several dozen boxes of written material, manuscripts, and photographs. The Skive Art Museum in Jutland has a selection of her canvases, her student and early works on paper, and her sketchbooks with watercolor landscapes of the Jutland heaths and the Limfjord. The Ethnographic Collection at the National Museum of Denmark was given sketchbooks and other papers some years after Emilie's death, a total of eight boxes.

The largest part of her collection of Sámi material culture went to the National Museum of Denmark during her lifetime, in four separate deposits: 1916, 1924, 1938, and 1953.[5] The approximately three hundred items form a large portion of the National Museum's holdings from Sápmi. Aside from a few beautiful items of purchased clothing, including bonnets and *gákti,* the majority of the items donated over this almost forty-year period by Emilie and her husband, Gudmund, are ordinary household objects and reindeer paraphernalia that were owned and used by Sámi herders whom Emilie often knew fairly well or met on her field trips (Plate 14). They include clothing, pack saddles and harnesses, leather bags and wooden boxes, cheese molds, root baskets, toys, and knives and spoons, most of them well used, some patched and mended. Among the objects are also amulets, a bag made from an entire loon skin, and a bearskin with a head and legs that the Hatts purchased from Johan Turi for the National Museum.

Many items originated in the Talma Sámi villages around Lake Torneträsk: Laimolahti; Kattovuoma; and Salmi, a settlement on Lake Stallujárvi, a site of many stories about the ogre Stallo.[6] Others Emilie picked up in Tromsdalen in Norway and in South Sápmi on the Swedish side of the mountains. A number of them were purchased in July and August 1916, during the Hatts' last visit to Sápmi, when they stayed for several weeks with members of the Turi family on the northeast side of Lake Torneträsk. The money to buy them came from the director of the National Museum in Denmark at the time, Sophus Müller, which is likely why the accession notes for 1916 speak of Gudmund Hatt as the donor. Gudmund was not yet on the staff of the museum, but he had connections there. In 1916, he was working with his wife on her Sámi-related interests as well as following up with the material research that resulted in his PhD dissertation on Arctic skin clothing. In addition to representative items from Sápmi used daily in the tent and on migrations, the Hatts collected reindeer skin gloves and boots, fur tunics, and hats, all items of clothing that Gudmund had written about in his dissertation.

The later deposits, beginning in 1924, are registered only in Emilie Demant Hatt's name, and they include things that she had purchased or been given on earlier solo trips from 1907 until 1911, largely in Laimolahti, Jukkasjärvi, Karesuando, and Tromsdalen, as well as items connected with Johan Turi that she hadn't wanted to part with until then. By 1924, at age fifty-one and immersed in the art world of Copenhagen again, Emilie may have recognized that she would probably not travel again to Sápmi. Gudmund was by that time employed at the National Museum doing archeological research, largely on Iron Age Denmark; soon he would become a professor of cultural geography. The book the Hatts had planned to write about Sámi culture was abandoned as Gudmund instead worked on a four-volume geography textbook, *The Earth and Human Life*. They traveled to the Virgin Islands and the Dominican Republic, to Greenland, England, and France, but never back to Sápmi, though Emilie continued to keep in touch with her friends there for many years.

Many of the objects that Emilie donated in 1924 had personal meaning to her: clothes she had worn on her travels in Sápmi; toys and dolls that had belonged to children she knew, including Anne Turi, the youngest daughter of Siri and Aslak Turi; and around twenty items that had been either made by Johan Turi, owned

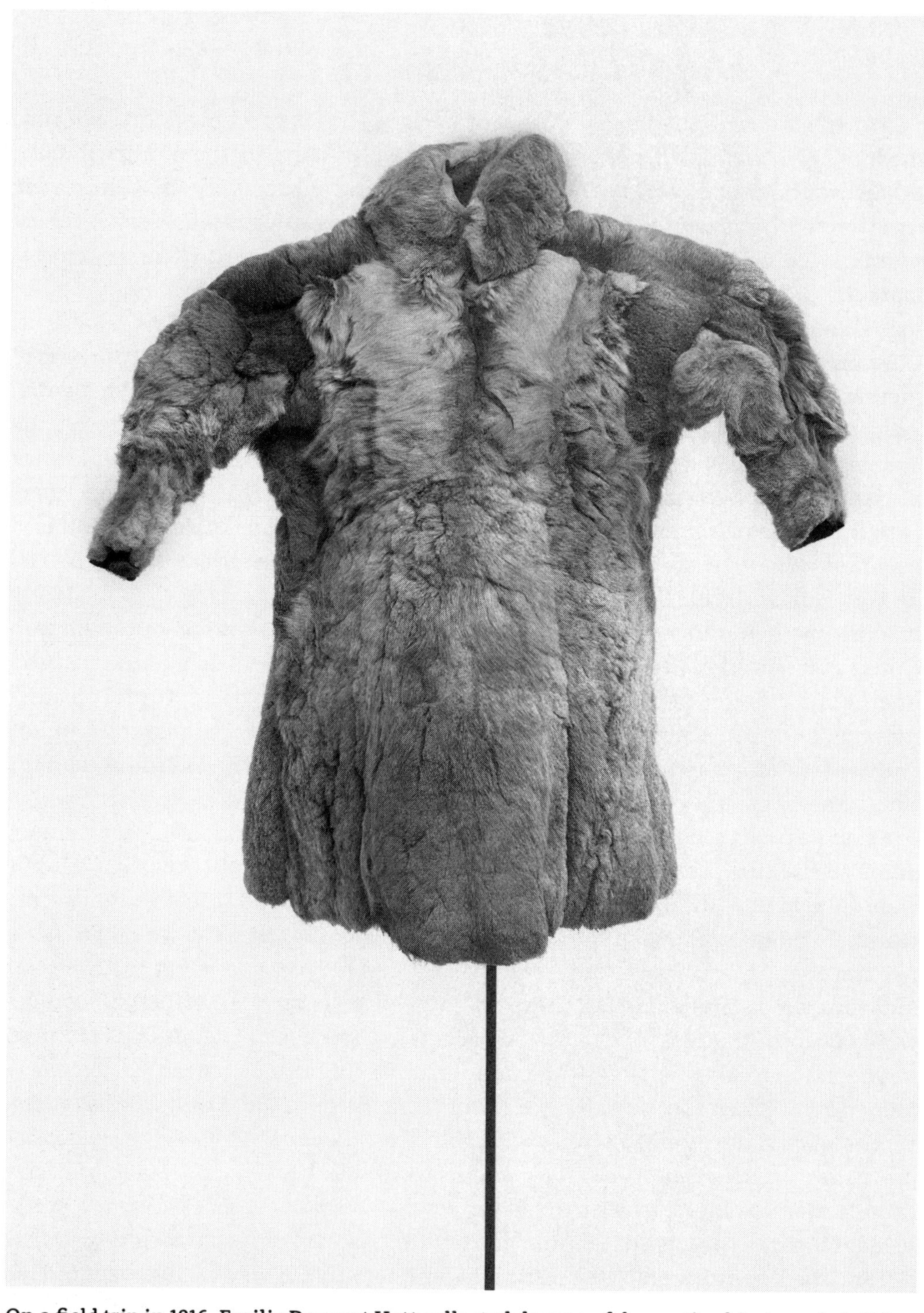

On a field trip in 1916, Emilie Demant Hatt collected dozens of domestic objects and clothing items from the Talma Sámi communities near Lake Torneträsk, Sweden, including this winter coat made from reindeer skins. Photograph by Roberto Fortuna. Courtesy of the National Museum of Denmark.

by him, or gifted to Emilie from him. These included knives, needle cases, and a heddle, all of polished and etched horn or bone, several with the initials J.O.T. and E.D.; a milking bowl; several amulets, including a bear's tooth and a leather string to be worn around the wrist to ward off sprains; the foot of a wolf, said to be from the last wolf that Johan ever hunted; and a silver belt buckle and twelve small rectangular silver plates to be attached to a belt, which Johan gave Emilie during the fall of 1908.

In 1924 she did not donate the blue chest, however, leading me to wonder whether she continued to live with it at home in Copenhagen and to take it with her on trips to the village of Kauslunde on the island of Funen, to a house she had inherited from her sister. She and Gudmund had built a small cabin next to that house in the style of a Sámi turf hut. Perhaps she kept the blue chest with her when she went to Kauslunde to paint. Perhaps the blue chest held Turi's letters and other precious items and was an ongoing part of her life until she brought it to Stockholm in 1940.

A list of the objects connected to Johan and the Turi family and donated to the Ethnographic Collection was compiled in August 2004 by Rolf Gilberg, curator of a wide-ranging department at the National Museum that included material culture and archives from Mongolia and Greenland as well as Sápmi and that was the result of Danish expeditions and colonization in centuries past. Gilberg had also done fieldwork in Inner Mongolia and was a founder of the Danish–Mongolian Society. The Sámi collection was small compared to the thousands of items from Oluf Olufsson's fabled travels to Bokastan in the 1890s and Knut Rasmussen's many adventurous trips to Greenland and other polar destinations, but Rolf Gilberg also had an interest in Sápmi.

I first met him in 2005 when I visited the Ethnographic Collection's archives upstairs in the National Museum. I had tentatively decided to translate Demant Hatt's *With the Lapps in the High Mountains* and hoped to get a better sense of her life by looking at the boxes deposited there of sketchbooks, family photographs, and correspondence. Gilberg brought out the boxes and left me to it. Over the past decade or two he'd had visits from several Sámi writers, including Nils-Aslak Valkeapää, who put together documents about Turi and Demant Hatt for *Boares Nauti* using material from Demant Hatt's archives, and John Gustavsen, a Norwegian Sámi journalist who had also written a play about the first meeting of Emilie and Johan on a train in Lapland in 1904 and had become a personal friend of Gilberg. The material in the Ethnographic Collection was rich but seemed incomplete. I supposed at first that the rest of her archives were all in Stockholm. The State

Archives in Copenhagen had her husband's papers, but I was told that they had nothing more of Emile Demant Hatt's. Even to get permission to see Gudmund Hatt's archives was difficult, because many boxes contained restricted material.

Rolf Gilberg gave me the impression of a man who didn't like to waste time. I'd asked if it was possible to see some of the items that Demant Hatt had donated, and he told me to meet him under the clock at the Central Station one morning. He then rushed me into a commuter train to somewhere outside the city and herded me off to an enormous warehouse ten minutes away, where he waved in the general direction of a large stuffed reindeer with antlers on a shelf high above and then disappeared to chat with colleagues. This warehouse seems in my memory to have been packed with cabinets with pull-out drawers and other shelves. I vaguely remember some Sámi milking bowls and knives and other small objects made of antler or bone. I didn't really know what I was looking at, and before I realized it we were on our return journey to the Central Station.

On the way back he told me a confusing story about an elderly woman, Gerd Smidt, who had some connection with Sápmi and ethnography and had contacted him some years ago, saying she had material belonging to Demant Hatt. I can't recall now whether Gilberg went to her chaotic apartment and rescued the papers or whether someone else did that after Smidt's death in 1988. Later I would find correspondence from Gerd in a box in the State Archives in Copenhagen, including a long and interesting letter from February–March 1958 detailing Gerd's travels in Sweden and Norway the previous summer and her meetings with members of the Turi family and others who knew Emilie in the Torneträsk area. I also had the impression that she had hoped to arrange some sort of exhibition of Emilie's work in Norway or Sweden. This may have been why Gerd Smidt ended up with valuable material, including letters that Emilie wrote her family from her initial stay in Sápmi; letters from various parties about the publication of *Muitalus sámiid birra* in English in 1931; the subsequent problems with royalties stemming from the contract with Jonathan Cape; and other financial conflicts between Emilie and Johan. Gerd Smidt also donated around twenty objects, mainly related to reindeer herding, to the Ethnographic Collection in Copenhagen; many were collected from a Sámi summer camp in Máze, Norway, in 1957.

When I came to Copenhagen on a return visit to the Ethnographic Collection in early 2007, I found Rolf Gilberg packing up his personal possessions and organizing things in what would be his office for only another few days. For budgetary reasons, he had been asked to take early retirement. He told some of his colleagues it was possible that his career had been derailed by the potent curse of a Mongolian shaman angry that Rolf had revealed his secrets. Rolf's position as curator would not be filled, or at least the constellation that included material culture from the Indigenous, often nomadic, people of the Arctic, sub-Arctic, and northern Central Asia was dissolving to be reapportioned differently. Others would take over some of his work with the Mongolian, Arctic, and Greenlandic collections, but he was the last curator fluent in the culture and history of Sápmi.

I would return to the Ethnographic Collection often to look at Emilie's archives, and in 2008 when the State Archives were recataloged according to the searchable online system DAISY, I was able to discover and order (apparently the first person to do so) thirty-two boxes of letters, journals, photographs, and printed material belonging to Emilie, which Gudmund's brother had given the archives in the 1960s. With all this newly available material in hand, I finally felt able to begin the projects that would eventually lead to my biography of Emilie Demant Hatt.

My questions about Emilie Demant Hatt and Johan Turi were ones that I hadn't seen addressed elsewhere, at least to my satisfaction, and that no one else seemed to be much interested in. I wanted details, for instance, about the history of how Johan Turi's book, *Muitalus sámiid birra,* came together as a publishing project. I was intrigued by Johan's letters to Emilie over thirty years, with their expressions of longing, hope, and frustration, as well as by Emilie's letters to Gudmund Hatt before their marriage, in which she talked about her friendship with Johan and her fears that he would throw a fit if she told him she was marrying a young Danish graduate student (he did). I questioned whether one could call what Johan and Emilie managed to do together "collaborative ethnography," as some scholars wrote, or whether it might be something else, less about ethnographer and subject and more about two writers and artists inspiring and influencing each other.

I was curious, of course, whether there had really been a romance at some point, but I was more curious why Emilie had presented herself initially to the reading public as a sort of domestic servant to Johan instead of a cocreator. I was curious why her reputation had become eclipsed by his, since he was now so feted as the forefather of Sámi literature. I was especially curious why all her other ethnographic fieldwork, which often involved notes on women's and children's lives, had been so ignored and forgotten.

During the course of what came to be many years of studying, translating, and writing about Emilie Demant Hatt, I couldn't help but become interested in the objects she had collected in Sápmi and about the meaning of her relationship to Johan and other Sámi people as expressed through the medium of gift giving.

She gave her friends in Sápmi gifts as well. She shared with them things that were sent to her from Denmark, in some cases edible delicacies (chocolates and apples) and in other cases books or art supplies. These gifts were enjoyed, read, or used to create art. They were not preserved in Sámi culture in the same way that their gifts to her took on meaning as examples of a northern Indigenous culture.

The personal gifts that Turi gave her in 1907–8, for instance, were probably not anything she originally imagined would end up in a museum. Johan Turi had no particular status in Sámi society at that time; on the contrary, he was seen as a dreamer, even a figure of fun: a "bald bachelor," he was called. Even after *Muitalus sámiid birra* was translated from Danish to German and English and his renown grew, the people around him still joked about his incompetence as a herder or opined that he should not have shared information and stories about the Sámi. The reverence in which the Sámi began to hold him and the historical and literary significance of his writing largely came after his death in 1936. The scholarly attention given to his work now and the dissemination of the images he drew and painted have created new meaning from anything he touched, including the gifts he made for Emilie, from the initial red kerchief to the blue chest to the various gifts he presented her with over the period of a few years.

The first present that could be construed as a courtship gift might be the red silk kerchief, which was commercially produced and purchased by Johan at a shop in Jukkasjärvi, a village outside Kiruna, Sweden, during the annual St. Andrew's Day market in November 1907. Such silk handkerchiefs were a frequent gift from young men to young women, along with jewelry and watches. In her book *With the Lapps,* Demant Hatt discusses courtship gifts:

> When a young man fancies a girl, he gives her little gifts, betrothal gifts or *gilhi,* which consist mainly of neckerchiefs, often of silk; fancy aprons; a silver spoon (always in the old-fashioned Lappish style, with a short handle, which goldsmiths in cities nearby make especially for the Lapps); a silver ring with leaf bangles.
>
> These days, however, the common gold ring has quite displaced the silver ring. An amorous lover or young husband can give the object of his affection three or four such rings (she only wears one of them though). It's also become quite usual to give a watch as a betrothal gift. One often sees a young, manly Lapp wearing a small ladies' watch, which he uses himself until he gets the chance to give it as a *gilhi.* It's always a good idea to have a gift ready; a mountain Lapp can't go whenever he likes to a watchmaker and purchase

> a watch. But just because a girl accepts the gifts doesn't mean that anything is settled between them. She accepts gifts from all her suitors and is especially coy with some of them. As long as she hasn't chosen one in earnest, a *diettelas irgee* (the recognized lover), she has her complete freedom. Betrothal gifts are hidden very carefully in the girl's colorful little painted chest with iron hardware. She only wears her watch, if she's lucky enough to have received such an expensive gift.
>
> Later, when she's made her final choice and married her chosen one, all the other suitors get their gifts back. The rejected ones try again with the same gifts to other girls. Yet not every rejected suitor takes it so calmly. It's not uncommon to get revenge on a girl and her future husband by killing her reindeer—her dowry. Up to a hundred reindeer can lose their lives in this way. There's no surplus of young girls among the nomad Lapps; it's always considered, therefore, something of a success to find a wife.[7]

Over the next months, other gifts from Turi followed, including a needle case of bone, an item that would generally hang from the brass ring attached to a woman's belt, which also included a knife and scissors. The polished, ivory-white bone is tubular, etched with a diamond pattern and the initials J.O.T. and E.D. Another needle case has the initials E.D. and the date 1908 etched in. The most serious courtship gift of all was the present of a family heirloom, the small silver plates that would have been sewed into a decorative woven belt and perhaps had already been in a belt at one time. The gift is mentioned in a long letter Emilie wrote her family on August 23, 1908, describing the hot, oppressive weather, her adventures with both Swedish and Sámi visitors, and her work encouraging Johan to write down in small notebooks the narratives and observations that would become *Muitalus sámiid birra:*

> [Turi] will soon be finished writing—there could be a good deal more, but that can come later. When he's finished with writing we will go through the whole thing a couple of times and that takes time. Every line must be looked at, and I'll write notes and explanations in many places. If I had time I would translate a little too.[8]

As she does so often in writing to her parents, she emphasizes the necessity of a longer stay in Sápmi and minimizes any worries they may have about her relationship with Johan Turi. Somewhat disingenuously in this letter, she recasts a gift from Johan as one presented in gratitude: "He is incredibly thankful for my help and [gives?] me everything possible. Silver buttons for a belt—inheritance from his mother's father, old Aslak Logje, the richest and most warm-hearted Lapp in his time."[9] This would have been Aslak Logje from Kautokeino in Norway, reputedly the owner of a great number of reindeer, Johan's grandfather, and, incidentally, a fictionalized character in J. A. Friis's novel *Laila*.

Emilie took the gifts home to Denmark with her, along with her clothes, her memories, and Turi's notebooks, which she began transcribing, translating, and eventually shaping into a bilingual Sámi–Danish book, funded by Hjalmar Lundbohm as the first of a series in a new imprint called *The Lapps and Their Land*. She and Johan continued to correspond, but she did not respond to his hints and longings. In the fall of 1909 she met a graduate student, Gudmund Hatt, and two years later she married him.

Two objects given to Emilie by Johan as courtship gifts that eventually ended up in museum collections are separated by several hundred miles and a body of water. One of them is held by the Nordic Museum and is in storage in a Stockholm suburb. This is a knife with a sheath of leather and horn, etched with a design and the initials J.O.T. and E.D. and the date 1909. It was made by Johan the year after Emilie returned home to Denmark from Sápmi, when she was deeply immersed in transcribing, translating, and editing Johan Turi's notebooks into the bilingual edition of *Muitalus*. She had much help during this period from friends and scholars in Sweden and Norway and was constantly in contact with Hjalmar Lundbohm in Kiruna. She was less in contact with Johan, who often wrote her letters of longing and questions: Did she care about him? When was she coming back? Not until the late summer of 1910 did she return to Sápmi, and then most of her time was spent in South Sápmi, with two Sámi elders, Märta and Nils Nilsson. She was redefining herself as an amateur ethnographer at this point, as well as a translator and collector of folklore. She accepted the knife as she had accepted all of Johan's gifts, with no promises.

The other courtship gift, a heddle, is displayed in the ethnographic exhibit at the National Museum in Denmark, along with other examples of Sámi material culture: knives and knife cases, silver spoons, a *giisá,* and a wooden cup. The rectangular handloom, shaped from horn and etched with the initials J.O.T. and E., is still threaded with woolen yarn in bright colors of blue, red, and yellow. This is a band weaving in process; part of it is finished and lies flat on the glass shelf. The accession information in the museum's database says only that

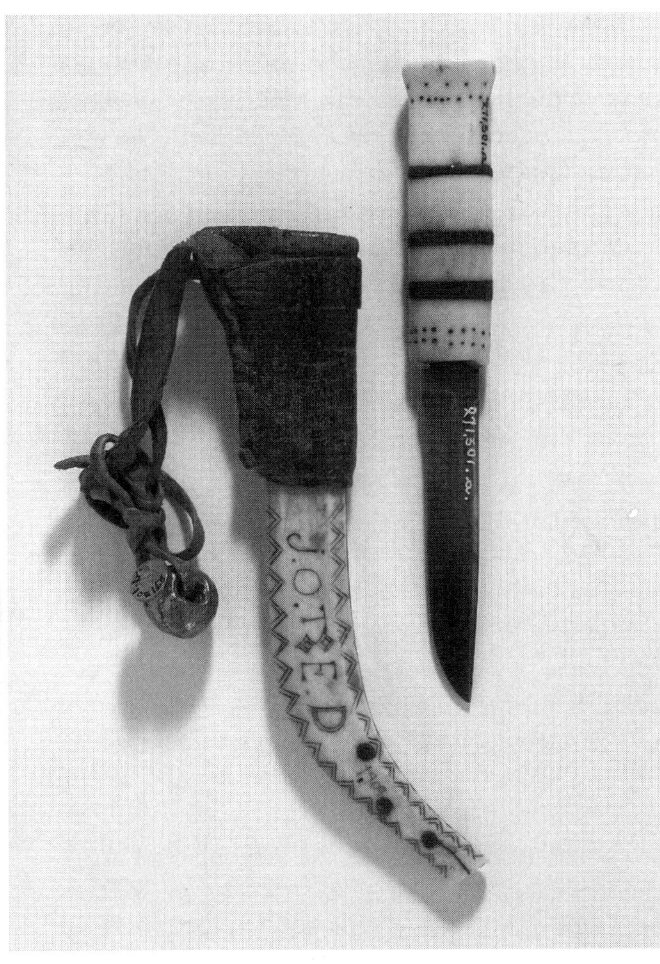

A knife and sheath with the initials J.O.T and E.D., made by Johan Turi, circa 1908–9, given to Emilie Demant (Hatt). Photograph by Bertil Wreting. Courtesy of the Nordic Museum, Stockholm.

the heddle was created in Jukkasjärvi around 1911 and donated by Emilie Demant Hatt in 1924. The typed list created by Rolf Gilberg records that it was made by Johan Turi, listing the initials J.O.T. and E.D. Seeing the initials, Rolf may have reasonably assumed that it was a present to Emilie and erred in adding a "D." to his written record. It's possible Turi had hoped to add a "T." after the "E."

Did Johan intentionally leave the weaving unfinished, as an example of how band weaving was done? Or was his planned gift to her of the heddle and shoe band halted by heartbreak? In the summer of 1911, Emilie went on her last solo trip to Sápmi and spent several weeks in the Kiruna area in July, working with Johan on a new writing project and trying to gear up the courage to tell him that she was about to marry Gudmund Hatt in September. Johan's shaken response is detailed in a letter Emile wrote Gudmund from Kiruna, where she sadly reports Johan's words to her: "I am captured by you like a ptarmigan in a snare, my heart has bound itself tightly to you, and if it's torn away now then all the ligaments and veins will snap and I will bleed to death."[10]

Neither the accession form nor Rolf Gilberg's note about the initials mentions the personal history behind the band weaving. Although the object is displayed in a vitrine in a large national museum, the initials are only visible on one side and are very small. And even if a visitor were to see the initials, they'd likely make no sense without a story.

The knife that Johan gave Emilie in 1909 has never been publicly displayed, but it is visible through Sweden's DigitaltMuseum. Here, online, the Old Wolf and the Black Fox are merely separated by a few clicks. The knife appears in searches of both Emilie Demant Hatt and Johan Turi. But the only clue to some part of their story is in the object's registry, which tells us that the knife came to the Nordic Museum only in 1966, donated by H. Hatt. This is Harald Hatt, Gudmund's brother and the executor of their estate, who spent years sorting through their effects and dividing papers, artwork, and objects for various museums and archives. Emilie had died in 1958, and Gudmund only a bare year later.

Imagination does its guesswork: Emilie never gave up this gift from Johan while she lived.

Museum collections are often stories of relationships among the objects themselves, reflected by their placement together in a vitrine, on a shelf, or in a diorama and by the details found in notes and registries with the stories of who collected them and from whom and when and why. Sometimes the relationships are intensely personal, though not always to the extent of the Turi–Demant gifted objects. I've heard it said that Emilie never fully understood or that she pretended not to understand the meaning of the gifts that Johan made for her and gave to her in 1907, 1908, and 1911.

I think she understood very well, yet she didn't always act in a way that would clarify matters. Out of friendship, interest in his work, and a desire to learn from him, she remained close to him, while also trying to set limits. Beginning in 1907 and for the next four years, she told him that she did not want to get married, that she was too old to get married, and finally that she *was* getting married but to someone in Denmark. She complained to her friends and family

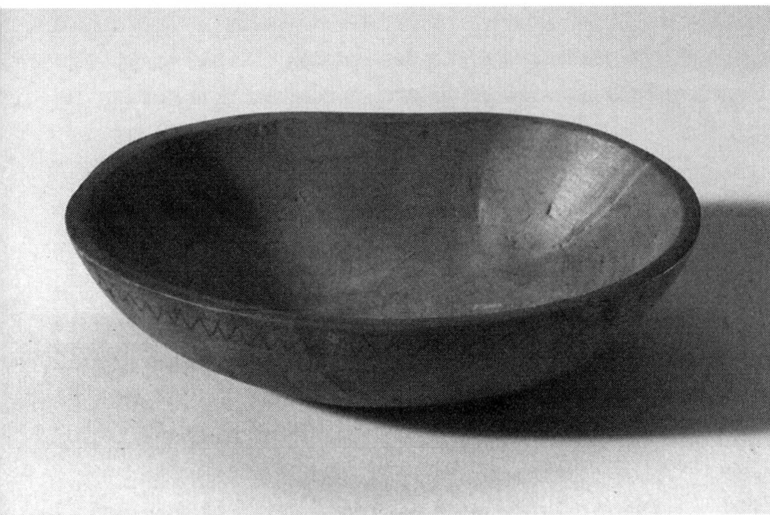

Bread bowl made by Johan Turi, circa 1910–11, given to Emilie Demant (Hatt). Courtesy of the Nordic Museum, Stockholm.

that Turi didn't believe her, that he kept waiting and hoping. But until she told Johan Turi about Gudmund Hatt in the summer of 1911, he didn't fully believe her. And until she was actually married several months later, she didn't try to give his gifts back.

By then all Turi wanted back was his bread bowl. Eventually he also wanted the notebooks with the original manuscript of *Muitalus sámiid birra*. She gave him the bowl but—wrongly, in my opinion—not the notebooks, which she seemed to fear could be lost, destroyed, or sold to a private individual. She waited until Turi had died and then, in 1950, gave his letters and his notebooks to Ernst Manker of the Nordic Museum, who traveled especially to Copenhagen to receive them by hand.

Compared to the Ethnographic Collection at the National Museum of Denmark, the Nordic Museum has only a few physical objects of Johan Turi's that once belonged to Emilie. Most of the rest of the Demant Hatt holdings in Stockholm are papers, photographs, and paintings in the archives and in storage. Her relatively small contribution to the thousands of Sámi objects at the museum is significant mainly in terms of Johan Turi and their relationship. In Denmark, however, the Hatt collections are extensive and make up almost half of the Sámi holdings. Collected as they were between 1907 and 1916 directly from people who used the objects, they have both historical and personal interest. Some items (a fur tunic, a bonnet, shoes) were ones she'd worn. There's a dress she sewed for herself from tanned reindeer calfskin in the summer of 1907, under the expert tutelage of Siri Turi, which she writes about in her travel narrative *With the Lapps.* She is wearing the dress in an oil portrait from 1911 executed by her friend the Danish painter Olga Lau.

Other items are associated with people she spent time with during extended periods in Sweden and Norway. Still other material objects and clothing, many of them well-used domestic items of no particular aesthetic value, were owned by Sámi people who came from particular *siidas* in areas she knew well in Tromsdalen or around Lake Torneträsk. Other objects were deliberately collected for Gudmund's 1914 dissertation, *Arctic Skin Clothing in Eurasia and America,* and correspond to Emilie's pen-and-ink illustrations in that published dissertation.[11] Taken together, these objects form a collection of some integrity, as an aspect of Demant Hatt's ethnography and her working partnership with Gudmund Hatt.

Now that Johan Turi has become such a key figure in Sámi literary history, it seems fitting that some if not all of the objects that he made deserve an exhibit of their own, with detailed backstories that include his desire to make Emilie his companion. Yet rarely are their two names mentioned together in museum exhibits or public texts. A few objects (the wooden stamp blocks he used to make prints of tents and reindeer on paper, a photograph of him, a reproduction of a page from *Muitalus*) were for some years on display in the Nordic Museum's exhibit *Sápmi.* In Denmark, aside from the bone heddle with its hardly noticeable initials in the ethnographic exhibition at the National Museum, the rest is in permanent storage. Should the objects made by Johan and gifted to Emilie and now held by national museums in both Sweden and Denmark be returned to Sápmi? The Danish government, pressured by Greenlanders, played a decisive role in bringing thousands of Indigenous objects back to Greenland, while Danish ties with Norway are far back in history now and Denmark has no significant Sámi population.

Yet physical repatriation is complex in its own way. Assuming that things can only be in one place at a time in our material world, how is that place chosen? Whose story is told by that choice, and whose story is obscured or lost? Whose story does the handloom tell, or the bread bowl, or the blue chest? Is it the maker's story or the recipient's? Are the gifts hers or his or theirs together? And if these objects are seen as connected, both hers and his, where do they belong?

Which criteria is useful and which criteria is lasting? If the intent is to show the breadth of Emilie Demant Hatt's career as an ethnographer, artist, and collector, should all or most of her holdings be in the same place? Isn't her working relationship with her husband, Gudmund, as important as her work with Johan Turi? Where does Gudmund belong if not in Denmark? Where does Johan Turi belong if not in Sápmi? And where does Emilie Demant Hatt belong if not in both?

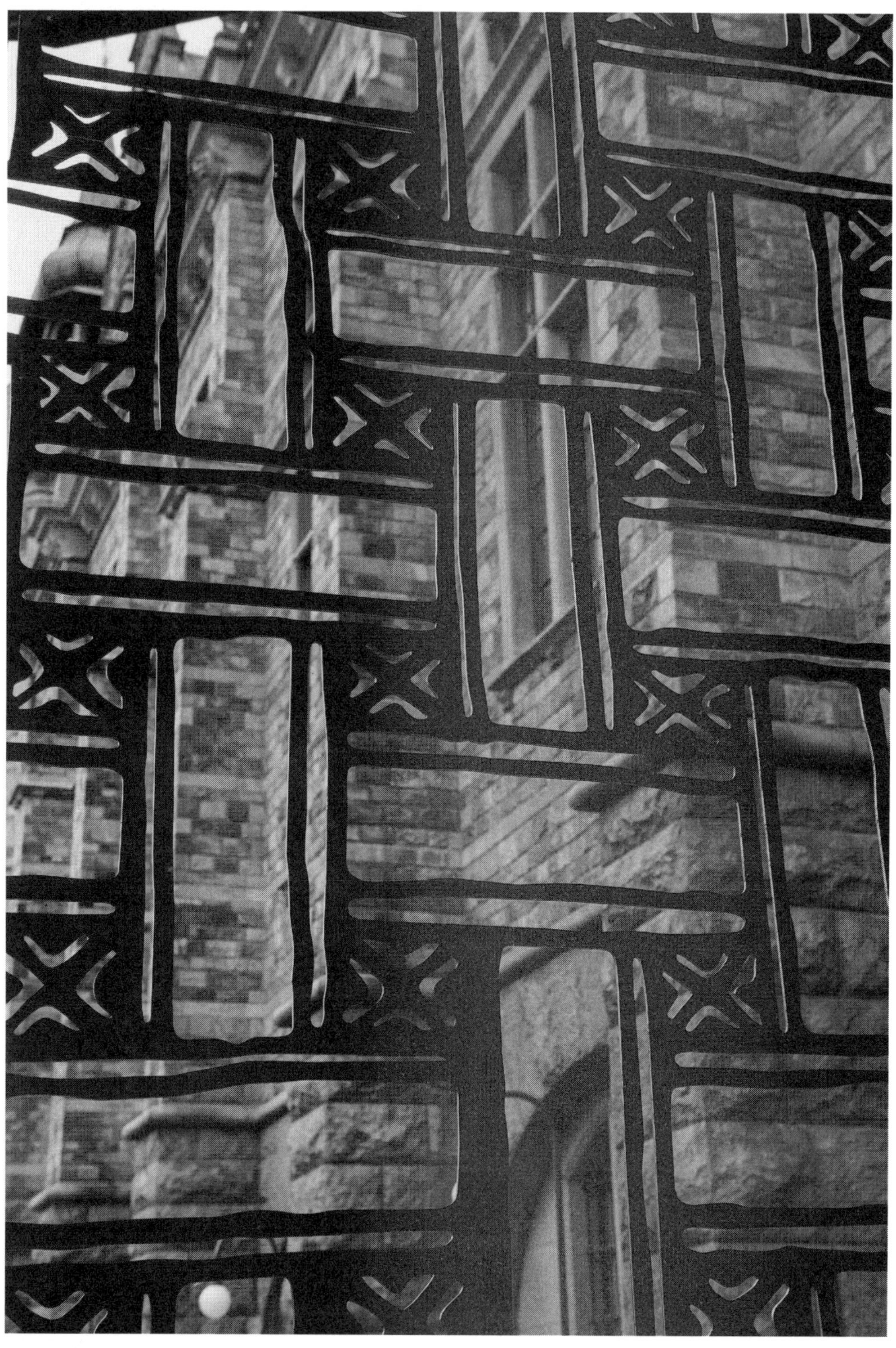

Outti Pieski, *Guektien bïegkese—Guovtte biggii—Two Directions,* 2020 (detail), at the entrance to the Nordic Museum in Stockholm. Photograph by Helena Bonnevier, Nordic Museum. Courtesy of the artist.

PART III
Two Directions

Recentering

Sweden

In May 1980, two Sámi women set out on a mission to visit almost every museum with known Sámi collections—national, regional, and local—and make an inventory of Indigenous heritage in Sweden. Marianne Nilsson, born in Ammarnäs in South Sápmi and a longtime *duojár,* was at the time the *duodji* consultant for Same Ätnam, the political organization founded in 1944 to strengthen Sámi culture, particularly handicrafts. Nilsson would later become the head of the Sámi duodji association in Jokkmokk. Inga-Maria Mulk, from Lule Sápmi, was working on a doctorate in archeology, based on fieldwork on prehistoric Sámi sites. The two of them hit the road in a razzia very different from Hugo Samzelius's Arctic Lapland Expedition in 1891; they were not collecting ethnographica, only information about the location and number of objects around Sápmi and the general conditions in which they were publicly displayed and stored.[1]

Nilsson and Mulk drove to Arjeplog in Pite Sápmi, where Maria Persson had gathered friends and family to joik into Karl Tirén's recording machine and where a Swedish provincial doctor, Einar Wallquist, built the Silver Museum, which now contained three thousand Sámi objects. Seven hundred of them were on deposit from Lars-Erik Ruong, a local Sámi collector. The two women traveled to the Linnæus Museum in Uppsala, where they viewed the famous portrait of Carl Linnæus and his drum. They saw the actual drum that the botanist was given in 1734 and nine other objects from Sápmi. Nilsson and Mulk went to the ethnographic museums in Göteborg and Stockholm. They visited small open-air collections of wooden buildings sited on old farms or parsonages; these homesteads *(hembygdsgårdar)* are widespread attractions in the Swedish countryside, meant to show how life was lived before industrialization. Those with Sámi

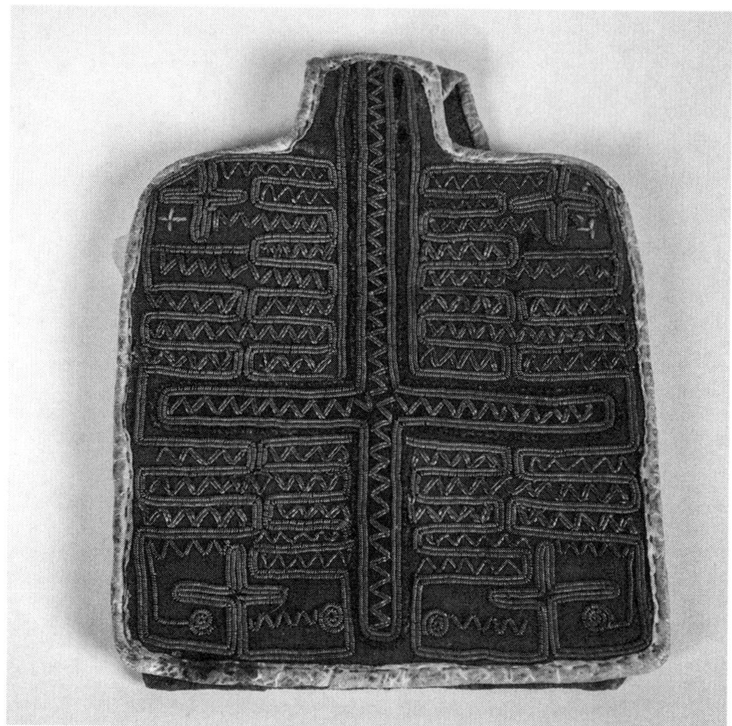

A man's small bag, possibly for a pipe, made of reindeer skin and red and blue cloth, embroidered with pewter thread in different cross, wave, and spiral patterns, from Storuman in Ume Sápmi, nineteenth century. From H. Hampusson Huldt's collection at Västerbotten Museum in Umeå, Sweden. A drawing of this bag was included in Huldt's book *Patterns for Lappish Handicraft in Västerbotten*, 1920. Courtesy of Västerbotten Museum.

collections were often found in core Sámi church villages like Arvidsjaur and Jukkasjärvi, villages that had been important meeting places for Sámi and non-Sámi since at least the seventeenth century. Inga-Maria Mulk and Marianne Nilsson visited smaller Sámi associations *(sameföreninger)* in Kiruna, Tärna, and elsewhere to discover what objects they owned and larger regional institutions like Norrbottens Museum in Luleå, the city Hugo Samzelius had proposed for a Lappish Central Museum. In 1980 Nörrbottens Museum had a fine collection of objects, and the two women noted that "the collection of root handicraft is impressive."[2]

They traveled to Umeå, where Pastor Nils Grubb and Anna Charlotta Adelcrantz had lived in the early eighteenth century. Umeå was, since 1965, the home of a large university, as well as Västerbottens Museum, with a substantial collection from Sápmi, particularly Ume Sápmi. Their holdings included root baskets and other handicrafts left to the museum by Emma Bergström-Andelius and around two hundred objects from the districts of Sorsele, Tärna, and Vilhelmina from the collection of the engineer and surveyor H. Hampusson Huldt. The pair described the textile collections in Umeå as "well conserved." They could not say the same of the Nordic Museum, which was said to have the largest number of Sámi objects in the world but whose textiles were cared for in a "substandard" way and difficult to obtain access to "for lack of personnel."[3]

Mulk and Nilsson listed between eighteen thousand and nineteenth thousand Sámi objects in museums in Sweden, with a further twenty-three hundred in private collections, some of which were open to the public. They had undertaken this inventory on behalf of the cultural arm of the Nordic Sámi Council with funds from the Swedish state, but the project had a larger agenda: to create "a future central Sámi museum" in Jokkmokk.[4] Their typed report on the inventory included figures, descriptions, and a summary at the end of their findings. But it also explained the reasons for making the inventory and the background. In 1976 a small conference of museum workers in Sápmi had taken place in Inari, Finland. From that had come a cross-border Sámi Museum Group, led by Marit Teigmo, who was at the time the director of the first Sámi museum in Sápmi, located in Karasjok, Norway. Teigmo issued a memorandum that had lasting impact: Sweden, Finland, and Norway should each create its own national Sámi museum, and each museum should be built in a region where Sámi people lived. The memorandum listed five criteria necessary for such a museum:

- Sámi people or Sámi organizations should be the majority of the board.
- Sámi people will be in charge of the administrative and professional work.
- Sámi culture will be the main theme of the museum, though there may also be large natural history collections.
- The museum will carry out a policy where traditional Sámi culture is respected and Sámi traditions are studied from a Sámi perspective.
- The museum will be located in a core Sámi region.[5]

When Inga-Maria Mulk and Marianne Nilsson were traveling the highways and byways of Sweden in the long bright days of late spring in 1980, collecting data and investigating the storage rooms and glass cases of all these large and small museums, they couldn't have known how timely their report would be by the time it was typed up and disseminated in December 1980, in the midst of an escalating conflict between two Sámi organizations and the Nordic Museum. The museum had chosen October 1980 as the opening date of its new permanent Sámi exhibit, *Samer,* to finally replace Ernst Manker's *Lapparna,* which had been taken down a few years before. The old Lappish Department was no more; the ethnographer and curator Rolf Kjellström was responsible for the new exhibit, and his aims were largely educational. By systematically displaying traditional Sámi life, largely focused on reindeer herding, along with exhibits on geography, history, handicraft, religion, and spirituality, he wanted to give visitors, Swedish or international, a sense of Sámi occupations and the Sámi relationship to nature.[6]

Unlike Ernst Manker, who had collaborated with several Sámi people from Jokkmokk and Arvidsjaur for the 1947 *Lapparna* exhibit, Kjellström and his project group did not involve Sámi experts in shaping the exhibition. The texts that were to accompany the displays were sent to the Swedish Sámi Association (SSR) and Same Ätnam (SA) only a month before the scheduled opening in October 1980. The negative response so surprised the museum that the exhibit was postponed six months to address the problems; a working group of four representatives from SSR and SA was convened, and Kjellström made some changes. Yet by the time *Samer* opened in March 1981, the conflicts were still far from resolved. As one of the Sámi representatives, Inga-Britt Blind, explained, "If only the [Nordic] Museum had been more interested in collaborating from the beginning, it would have been a completely different exhibition. . . . But there is so much work to do that it would take a Sámi person full-time involvement before the exhibition has an acceptable form for the Sámi people."[7]

It wasn't just that the members of the working group wanted to change the wording of some texts and correct factual inaccuracies; they also wanted written mention of the Alta River conflict currently in process and related struggles over natural resources in Sápmi. Some of the exhibits were deemed stereotypical and offensive, for instance, the figure of a Sámi man in furs threatening a stuffed bear with an upraised spear. They also objected to the general lack of respect for their culture shown by the Nordic Museum in the way that the exhibit was created. In an issue of *Samefolket* (previously *SET*) that was published soon after the opening, the Sámi politician and researcher Lars Thomasson lambasted the museum for not living up to its responsibilities as the most prominent disseminator of information about the Sámi in Sweden: "The museum can now either enable a real and active Sámi participation in that information, or leave the Sámi to their previous passive role when, essentially, others speak about them and their culture. The choice should not be too difficult in 1981."[8]

Unfortunately, the Nordic Museum at this time made the wrong choice. Another twenty-six years would go by before the *Samer* exhibit was replaced. By that time the national Sámi museum, Ájtte, had long been up and running in Jokkmokk.[9]

In their report of 1980, Inga-Maria Mulk and Marianne Nilsson had already identified Jokkmokk as the obvious place for a central Sámi museum, given that there was already a Jokkmokk Museum, built in 1966, which cared for a collection of two thousand Sámi objects. There had already been discussions regionally of remodeling the museum to add a natural history component, given that Jokkmokk was a main gateway to some of Sweden's most beautiful national parks, with a long Sámi history. In the Lule Sámi language, Jokkmokk is Jåhkåmåhkke, meaning River's Curve. Nearby Vuollerim has been inhabited since the end of the Ice Age, and the whole area in the confluence of the Lule River and the Lesser Lule River has been the habitat of reindeer herds and Sámi *siidas* for many centuries. Jokkmokk has a long history of colonization as well. In 1605, King Charles IX decreed the establishment of a winter market there. Originally established as a place to control trade and collect taxes from the Sámi, the market has continued as a cultural meeting place for more than four hundred years.

Swedish Sápmi has other hubs. The Sámi Parliament has long had its headquarters in Kiruna in a renovated school. Now a decision has been made to locate the long-planned new parliament building in Östersund, five hundred miles south. Östersund is the home of the South Sámi cultural and research center Gaaltije. Umeå University offers an academic program in Sámi languages and culture and hosts the Centre for Sámi Research, Várdduo. But Jokkmokk has played an important role in education and heritage protection since 1942, when the Sámi Folk High School was established in Jokkmokk to offer a Christian education as well as classes in the Lule Sámi language and in Sámi culture and history. Its substantial programs in arts and crafts led to the establishment in the 1950s and 1960s of a teaching and practicing community of artists, writers, and craftspeople. Eventually the folk high school became the Sámi Education Center (Sámij Åhpadusguovdásj / Samernas Utbildningscentrum) and is now led by Sámi. It is still a center for language studies and craft, but it also includes classes in filmmaking, joik, and fashion.

Opened in 1989, Ájtte ("storage hut" in Lule Sámi) has both a natural history section and exhibits on Sámi cultural history. It stands on the same site as the old Jokkmokk Museum but has been enlarged and remodeled with a theater, a restaurant, a performance space, and a large giftshop, along with an information desk for hikers and campers. An adjacent building holds a modern archive and library called Ája ("river"). While Jokkmokk turns into a hive of activity each February, visited by thousands of people, with outdoor and indoor craft booths, pop-up cafés, concerts, lectures, films, and storytelling events, the library and museum provide community space all year round and host conferences, literary workshops, films, and readings. It's what American anthropologist James Clifford calls a "museum as contact zone," in the literal sense of people coming together, but also as a place where "their organizing structure as a *collection* becomes an ongoing historical, political, moral *relationship*—a power-charged set of exchanges, of push and pull."[10]

The exhibits created within Ájtte echo old-fashioned dioramas showing how life was in older times in Sápmi, pre- and post-contact. Yet the reconstructed scenes and displays of objects also tell an alternative history, one that doesn't use the passive tense, for instance, in describing the church assembly in Åsele in 1725, where the authorities forced Sámi parishioners to hand over twenty-two drums.

For some critics, the museum's representations of Sámi and reindeer only reinforce stereotypes of the Sámi as living in the ethnographic present; others see the exhibits as acts of reclaiming traditional Sámi culture. Some postcolonial theorists have seen such exhibits and such museums as "strategic essentialism," used with success by Indigenous people worldwide as a way of uniting communities, claiming identities, and focusing attention on an unbroken occupation of landscapes that could strengthen claims for land and water rights. Ájtte's texts often imply or are explicit about a "we" represented by the exhibits. In a world where Sámi identity has often been trivialized and punished, that "we" is important.[11]

Today, Ájtte cares for approximately forty-five hundred Sámi objects, which include the original two thousand that belonged to the Jokkmokk Museum, many others donated by individuals or other museums, and still other objects on long-term loan. In 1988, on the request of Ájtte, the Ethnographic Museum in Stockholm made the decision to transfer its collection of several hundred Sámi objects. Ájtte also requested from the cultural geography department at Uppsala University the deposition of seventy objects collected by Gerd Enequist in the Lule River valley in the 1930s; this collection came to Ájtte in 1988. These two transfers were the first acts of partial repatriation from museums in the South back to the traditional Sámi homelands of the North. Ájtte has a number of objects on long-term loan from the Nordic Museum, including ten drums. Most of these drums are, in fact, on deposit to the Nordic museum from the State Historical Museum, when the two museums divided up their collections in 1943.

Repatriation is a tangled question among the various museums in Sweden;

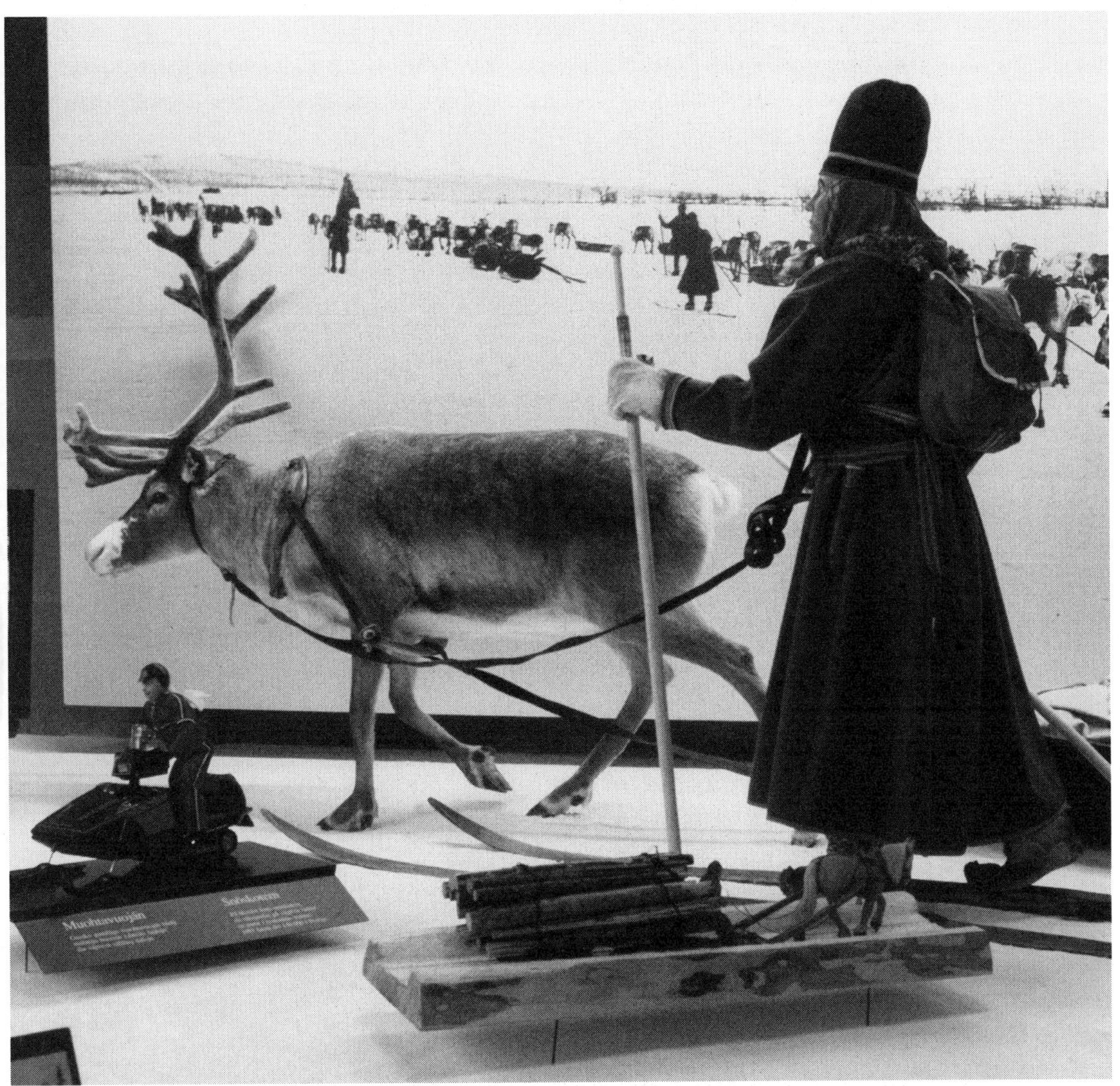

Diorama, Ájtte exhibit, Jokkmokk, Sweden. Photograph by Jan Gustavsson. Courtesy of Ájtte Swedish Mountain and Sami Museum.

loans only partially solve the problem of who should own what and how it should be displayed. Beginning in 1989 and continuing until the present, the curators at Ájtte chose a style of representation—dioramas—that the Nordic Museum later tried to free itself from. *Sápmi,* the exhibit created for the Stockholm museum in 2007, would take a radically different form and attempt to create a different kind of contact zone, which looked at the reciprocal and conflicted historical and contemporary relationship between Sápmi and Sweden and for the first time made more explicit the museum's role in shaping images of the Sámi people and their cultural artifacts.

> *Sápmi deals with encounters between people. How have the Sámi shaped Swedish-ness and how have Swedes shaped Sámi-ness? The intention is not to provide a chronological narrative about an ethnic group but to focus on borderlands, meeting places, conflict zones, mixed forms and traces.*[12]
>
> —From the catalog to *Sápmi* (2007)

Sápmi: On Being Sámi in Sweden was designed very differently from the 1981 exhibit *Samer.* It did not presume to interpret the long and complex history of the Indigenous people of Swedish Sápmi only in terms of the objects that they had produced and that the Nordic Museum had collected. Although the exhibit did have glass cases, that wasn't what visitors noticed first upon entering the large open area on the fourth floor of the museum, which overlooked the center hall below. Instead, the space was dominated by big hanging photographs of Sámi people from different parts of Sweden, with quotations from them underneath. To the question of how they defined themselves as Sámi, they answered in a variety of ways: "Sámi-ness is something I carry inside me. It's me, and I take it with me wherever I am" (Sylvia Simma). "You should be able to be a Sámi in many different ways" (Lars-Marcus Kuhmunen). "Is *that* what it means to be Sámi? That you get interviewed?" (Lotta Willborg Stoor).[13]

Questions were at the postcolonialist heart of the *Sápmi* exhibit. In addition to the photographs, posters on the walls above the exhibits asked, in North Sámi, Swedish, and English: *Who is what? Who is Sámi? Who is Swedish? Why do you want to know? Whose rights? Whose land? Who was first? Does it matter?*

The exhibit didn't shy away from controversial subjects like Lappology and racial biology, though they were handled in a manner that perhaps understated some of the traumas of the past: the boarding schools and punishments for speaking Sámi as well as the skull and body measurements and photographs taken by racial biologists like Hermann Lundborg of nude children and adults and published in books meant to show the inferiority of the "Lappish race." Yet the exhibit also made space for a booth, a "black box," where a video was played of Sámi ethnologist Lis-Mari Hjortfors talking about her upsetting discovery that a photograph she assumed was an ordinary group portrait of family members was in truth taken by a racial biologist for purposes of research. That video, along with extended audio interviews of the six Sámi individuals in the large hanging photographs, brought emotional depth to the cleanly designed exhibit space.

Sápmi displayed only a fraction of all those spoons, knives, bowls, sleds, and articles of clothing amassed in the collecting expeditions before and after the turn of the twentieth century. The items were shown, often thematically and further illustrated with watercolor catalog cards, as assemblages in vitrines, sometimes with photographs and written material from the Lappish Archive, such as Karl Tirén's notations of joiks or Johan Túri's notebooks, which became the basis for *Muitalus sámiid birra*.

Within the larger exhibit was another smaller collection consisting of seven objects, each displayed in its own vitrine. These were chosen in collaboration with members of the Sámi reference group, with whom the designers of *Sápmi* had worked to create the exhibit.[14] The objects included a belt embroidered with pewter thread; a red silk collar decorated with ornaments of silver, worn by a woman on ceremonial occasions; a milking bowl; a *sieidi* from Ailesjokk; a "Noaidi drum" from the seventeenth century, one of those known to have been illustrated in Johannes Schefferus's *Lapponia*; and another drum, created in 1890 by Anders Pirkit in Kvikkjokk and sold to Hugo Samzelius's colleague Henning Nordlund, who haggled unmercifully over the price. The last object was a miniature white reindeer, made by Jöns Paulus Mikkelsson Hatta sometime in the early twentieth century in the Forest Sámi district of Gällivare. The story went that Hatta lost all his reindeer and was left impoverished. He began to make reindeer figurines of fur and leather and sold so many that he was able to build up his own herd again.[15]

Often museum objects are divided into categories of greater and lesser significance. Certainly the rare Sámi drums carry the weight of their fraught past, while other objects are abundant and continue to be made and used today, like belts and purses. But in the exhibit *Sápmi* these seven objects are treated equally, and the comments of some of the Sámi people who contributed to choosing them add meaning to their display.

Ájtte and the Nordic Museum's *Sápmi* both constructed imaginative, carefully designed spaces, with sometimes parallel, sometimes contradictory ways of looking at Sámi history, culture, and identity. However, they presented two different ways of conceiving the museum as a contact zone. Ájtte has research staff and ongoing

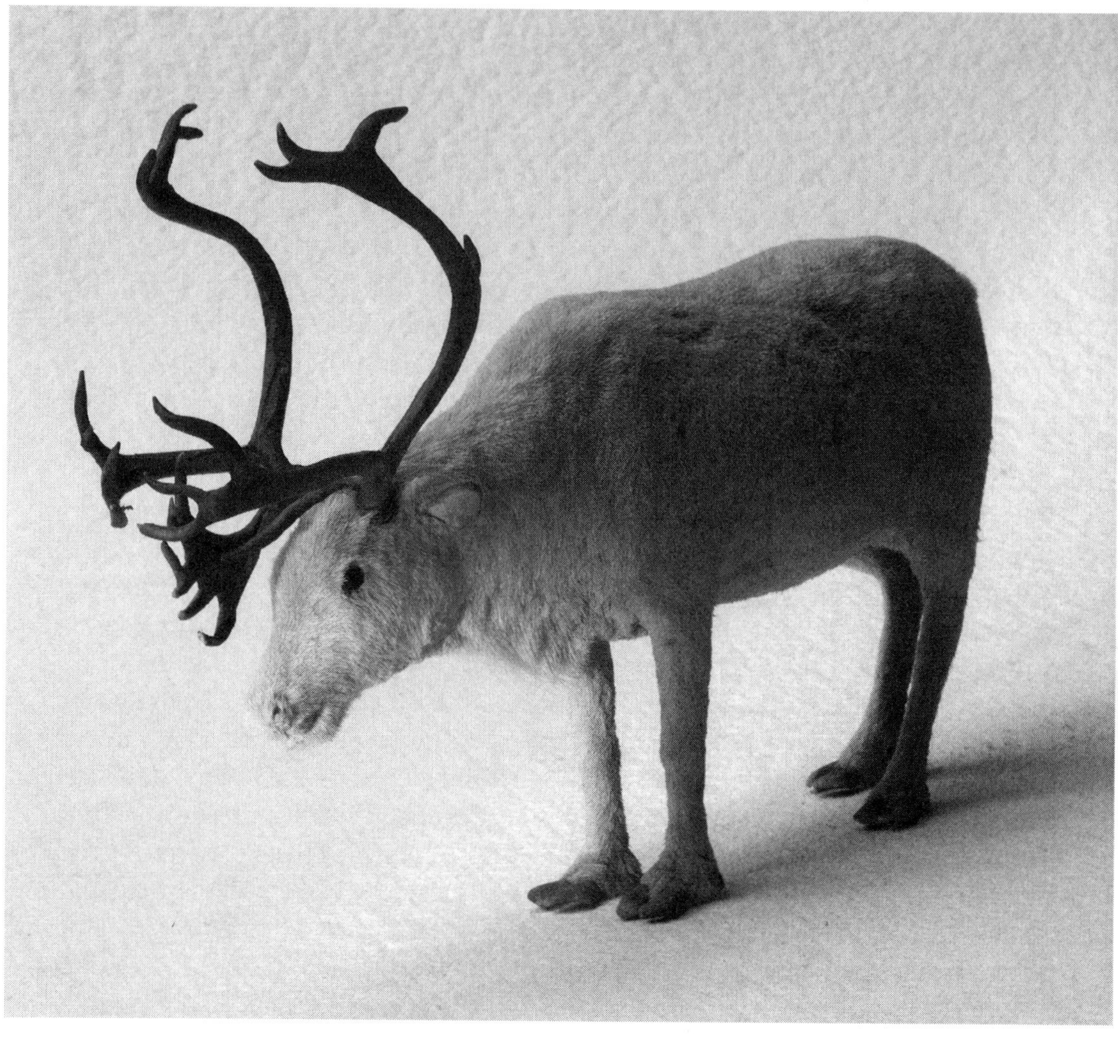

White reindeer model by Jöns Paulus Mikkelsson Hatta, Gällivare, Sweden, early twentieth century. Chosen by Victoria Harnesk as one of the seven objects with stories displayed in the *Sápmi* exhibit at the Nordic Museum. Photograph by Mats Landin. Courtesy of the Nordic Museum, Stockholm.

projects; the giftshop offers a wide assortment of books relating to Sápmi; it holds regular conferences, festivals, and cultural events in conjunction with the library and the folk high school. The Nordic Museum's efforts have tended to preserving and describing the collections of Sámi objects it cares for. With state funding, a few years after the *Sápmi* exhibit was installed, the museum went through the entire collection of Sámi objects to have them photographed and to make everything available on a national digital museum registry, under the new subject category "Sámi History." Importantly, the museum's staff added to the information known about the objects and removed discriminatory language in earlier catalog records, such as *trolltrumma* (magic drum). After this, almost all of the objects were transferred to a state-of-the-art storage building in a Stockholm suburb, along with thousands and thousands of objects from the museum's other collections.

The Nordic Museum's website also links to related sites, including one with Lotten von Düben's photographs and another about Sweden's recognized national minorities. These include not just the Indigenous Sámi but also Jews, the Roma, the Tornedalen Swedes (Finns who, to a lesser extent, were subjected to the same racial biological research as the Sámi), and the Sweden Finns (a Finnish-speaking minority), with short videos of representatives from each group discussing objects in the Nordic Museum's collection. Berit Inga, at the time a curator at Ájtte, speaks in Swedish about four objects from Sápmi: a bound volume of early issues of the newspaper *Samefolkets egen tidning;* a winter boat-shaped sled; a photograph of Sámi children in a nomad school tent; and a small handloom.[16]

Whose things? Whose cultural heritage? Whose history? Robbery or rescue? The Nordic Museum asks more questions—in the catalog, in posters in the exhibit, and on the website—than it can answer, and that is intentional on the part of the curators. The questions are largely focused on identity and the right to a cultural heritage. The exhibit's perspective is that the Sámi are a distinct Indigenous people in the Nordic countries, yet questions about identity still remain and are interspersed with questions about Sweden's heritage and relationship with Sápmi. What does it mean to be Sámi after centuries of oppression, persecution, loss of language, intermarriage, forgetting, and reclaiming? Is Sámi social history a narrative unto itself, or is it so deeply intermingled with Sweden's social history that it's not easy to sort out, only to ask provocatively and perhaps a little plaintively, *Whose things? Whose cultural heritage?*

The curators at Ájtte, along with many Sámi people, would probably have no difficulty answering: *Ours.*[17]

Lycksele, a small inland city on the banks of the Ume River, hardly noticeable on the map in the midst of Sweden's vast boreal forests, isn't very different from many Swedish municipal centers, with its hospital, high school, transit station, sports halls, and local traditions, like the giant ice cone constructed every winter and the weeklong motorcar celebration every summer. Its main industry for decades was, unsurprisingly, logging.

But one thing makes Lycksele stand out: it is also the oldest continuing Sámi settlement in Swedish Sápmi. For centuries, the region was occupied mainly by seminomadic Forest Sámi *siidas,* hunters and fishers who kept small herds of reindeer; it was later colonized by Finns who used slash-and-burn methods to clear the land. The twice annual markets were established by the Swedish Crown for purposes of trade, taxation, and control. The first church was built in 1607; the first Swedish Sámi school in 1632. It was at Lycksele that Pastor Nils Grubb arrived in 1723 to oversee one of the assemblies where Sámi parishioners were forced to turn over drums. Grubb probably left with at least one drum in his baggage, the same one that may well have turned up in Hans Sloane's collection in London ten years later. Carl Linnæus attended high mass in the Lycksele church on his botanical journey in the 1730s, and Lotten and Gustaf von Düben passed through Lycksele in the 1860s, picking up ethnographica to send back to Stockholm.

Yet for all its centrality in Sámi history, until the twentieth-first century, almost no Sámi artifacts were on view in Lycksele. In 1980 when Marianne Nilsson and Inga-Maria Mulk inventoried Sámi artifacts all over Sweden, Lycksele was not even mentioned in their final report. The world of the Forest Sámi on the Ume River was a world that seemed to have vanished with few traces. When a new museum was built in 1984 on a small round peninsula jutting out into the river, it was called the Forestry Museum (Skogsmuseet), and its primary attractions were logging equipment, from handsaws to diesel-drive machines, that showed the growth of the industry in the region. A permanent exhibit on the Forest Sámi was limited initially to a small section of one of the buildings. Outside the museum were various structures, which also included a Sámi turf hut.

In recent years, that has all changed. The exhibits *Era of Axes* and *Era of Logging Machines* are still there and still highly popular, but the museum, which underwent a name change in early 2022 to the Forest and Saami Museum, now cares for three significant Sámi historical collections and has become an important repository of Sámi material culture and heritage. Each of the collections of Sámi material culture, artwork, and archives was gathered with intention. Separately and together, the collections constitute an unexpected recentering of Sápmi in Sweden.

Birger Nordin, now in his mideighties, decided to begin collecting objects of Sámi origin in 1982.[18] He originally came from northern Sweden, before moving to Sundsvall on the southeast coast to work at a large forest products company, eventually as CFO. He had always been interested in reindeer and Sámi culture, he told me, but did not expect that his casual collecting would become such a far-reaching passion. From the beginning, he was clear on his criteria: he would collect all kinds of objects, from everywhere in Sápmi. He focused on older artifacts, those crafted until the mid-twentieth century, some for use and some for sale. His interests included not only knives with etched handles and needle cases of horn and leather but also carvings of people and animals as well as dolls in Sámi *gákti* (Plate 15). Nordin's interests led him to the world of auction houses and antiquarian dealers, largely in Stockholm and elsewhere in the Nordic countries, but also in Britain, Europe, and North America. In Sweden he advertised in local papers ("Sámi objects purchased") and spread the word to colleagues that he was collecting. Over the course of the next thirty years, Nordin built up a unique assemblage of fifteen hundred objects, which included traditional *duodji,* silver, toys, and a further collection of several hundred works of art, including sculptures and paintings by, among other artists, Nils Nilsson Skum and Johan Turi. He also put together a library of five hundred books on Sápmi.

Some finds were accidental. In 1996 Nordin and a friend were visiting one of many antiquarian shops on Kensington Church Street in London, when Nordin spied some small Sámi objects, including a painted reindeer. These turned out to be several models made by Lars Hætta, probably part of the trove brought to London in 1863 by Ludwig Daa to sell or exchange for global exotica. Nordin bought them on the spot. Later he met a Swedish Sámi man, Lars Sikku, at an exhibition in Tokyo and eventually invited him to see his Sámi treasures at home in Sundsvall. Sikku was able to purchase the carved wooden models from Nordin and has displayed them publicly on various occasions.

Birger Nordin loaned his artifacts freely to Sámi organizations, to museums, and for study purposes to *duojárs.* Over the years he was approached by several parties who wished to buy his entire collection, but in the end he decided to sell it to the charitable arm of a bank based in northern Sweden, Sparbanksstiftelsen Norrland, which deposited the collection in 2008 in the Forest and Saami Museum. This collection of Sámi objects has become a featured attraction at the museum, with revolving exhibits of the objects on-site and a fully digitized catalog with detailed information on each artifact. The collection's curator is Mikael Jakobsson, an Ume Sámi who took up museum studies at Umeå University after an earlier career in Lycksele as a car mechanic.

Jakobsson always knew he was Sámi on his mother's side. She came from Malå, the southernmost Forest Sámi village, and had relatives there that the family would visit. After he grew up, Jakobsson began to trace his father's side of the family and eventually discovered a Sámi ancestor who had owned land not far from Lycksele. By the eighteenth century, many of these properties, previously uncontested as Sámi "tax lands," had begun to be seized by the state and sold or given to settlers for farming. Some of the Sámi were able to retain parts of their properties and became farmers. Many of the Sámi families in Lycksele parish were buried in the churchyard; their skeletons were at times dug up and sent south to be sold, including twenty-five skulls exhumed in the 1950s and taken to the State Historical Museum in Stockholm for research. In 2019, these particular skulls were repatriated from the museum's storage and formally reburied in Lycksele, a ceremony that involved the local Sámi association, the Lycksele municipality, the Swedish Church, and the Forest and Saami Museum.

Mikael Jakobsson, who is also the chair of the Swedish Sámi Parliament's ethics council, told a reporter that eleven Swedish state museums, universities, and institutes still have human remains from Sápmi in their collections. "Understanding of the issue has begun to improve, but so far it seems the museums have generally preferred to keep them," he said. "They have been seen as objects, not as the people they once were."[19]

Jakobsson also worked for the return of one of the drums from Lycksele in the Nordic Museum's collection and found the museum amenable to a long-term loan if not yet a full repatriation. Jakobsson wrote to me that it felt like a "great relief" to have both the human remains and the drum back in Lycksele. "I think that the abuse against us has unknowingly harmed us, both as a people and personally. Some say you can inherit grief and shame without knowing it. Maybe that's why I feel this so much."[20]

Birger Nordin's personal collection ended up having something of a catalyzing effect in that once it was installed at the museum, other private donors and organizations began to consider gifts and loans to the Forest and Saami Museum. A significant collection of mid- to late twentieth-century Sámi handicraft was deposited in 2019 by Same Ätnam, the seventy-year-old organization devoted to maintaining standards for Sámi *duodji*. The specimen items include many calf-leather bags and embroidered chest cloths, caps, belts, and jewelry in silver, horn, and leather.

The third collection of substance came to the museum around the same time, as an outright inheritance gift from Ume Sámi collectors and writers Bertil and Valborg Wiinka, who had amassed between five hundred and one thousand do-

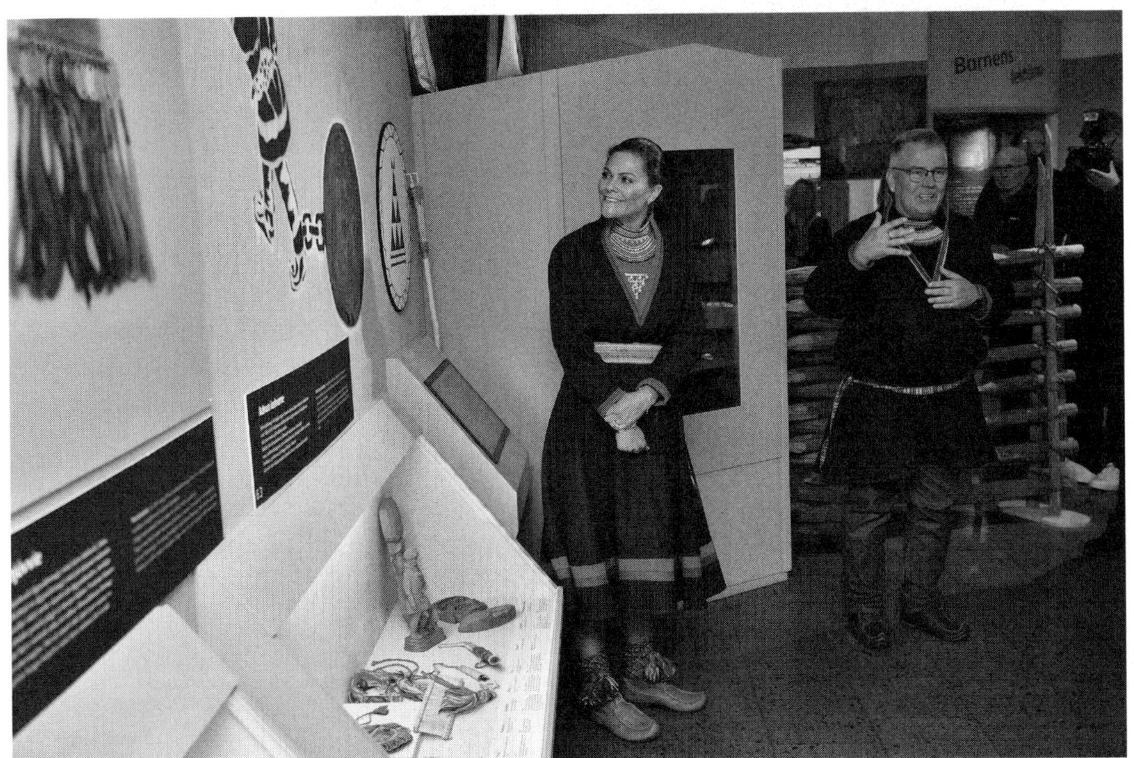

Crown Princess Victoria of Sweden, in Sámi *gákti,* and Mikael Jakobsson, curator of the Sámi collections at the Forest and Saami Museum, in Lycksele, September 1, 2021. Photograph by Jonas Ekströmer / TT News Agency / Alamy.

mestic objects used by farmers and Forest Sámi, which were displayed in two of several buildings on their property not far from Lycksele. The Wiinkas also donated their important archives, which include recordings and notes from interviews with Sámi elders and their research on the Ume Sámi language.

Nordin, after undergoing serious heart surgery in 2009, began collecting again as a way of healing. He now has a new collection of a thousand objects. Some private collectors buy and sell for the money and the thrill of discovery and possession. But while Nordin has made money from his collection, he says that is less important than having had the chance to meet people, to learn, and to share his finds. He speaks at schools and values his connections with Sámi organizations. In a sense, Nordin undertook a long journey to find Sámi objects that had scattered far and wide and consolidated them into a collection that was then returned to the Sámi homeland, in an act of informal repatriation. "My wife and I wanted the collection to come to Lapland," Nordin wrote me simply. In Lycksele, the collections are accessible for Sámi artisans and researchers to study and for the community to take pride in.

The question of where and to whom Sámi objects belong is hardly settled. The scarcity of older Sámi *duodji* is evidenced by bidding wars at auction houses and the difficulties Sámi museums have in competing with private collectors. And yet, as the changing fortunes of Lycksele seem to prove, there are alternatives to a Sámi Central Museum, once confidently proclaimed as only being possible in Stockholm, within the confining embrace of a national Swedish institution like the Nordic Museum or the Ethnographic Museum. Museums in Lycksele and Jokkmokk, far from the urban centers of the South, offer a connection with the physical landscape and the cultural community where objects were first created, not as rarities then but as beloved and necessary things that are also beautiful.

Returning

Norway

One memorable October day in 1997, the king of Norway, Harald V, spoke at the year's first session of the Sámi Parliament, convening in Karasjok. It's likely that no royal had ever addressed the country's Sámi citizens with such a direct admission of regret. "The Norwegian state is founded on the territory of two people—Norwegians and Sámi. Sámi history is closely interwoven with Norwegian history. Today we must apologize for the injustice the Norwegian state has earlier inflicted on the Sámi people through the hard policies of Norwegianization."[1]

We might argue that the phrase "founded on the territory of two people" was an aspirational rewriting of history. Even in 1997, eight years since the Sámi Parliament had been founded, a number of Norwegians still believed that the Sámi were outside Norwegian history. They were either a lesser race that would gradually fade away or a small ethnic group that was culturally exotic but perhaps received special treatment by calling themselves Indigenous. Much of this thinking was ignorance on the part of the public, fostered by the absence of Sámi history in school curriculums for most of the twentieth century, but some of the prejudice was ingrained in long-standing stereotypes about the Sámi rooted in both legislation and habit from centuries past.

The Norwegianization policies that the king referred to had been part of Norway's quasi-official position for about a century, from the nineteenth century through the first decades after World War II, and they had indeed been "hard." Discrimination was daily and legal: it was enshrined in legal codes, property laws, and education. Sámi citizens were not allowed to buy property, for instance, unless they took a Norwegian name; children were forced into boarding schools in many districts in the North, where they were not allowed to speak their language.

Norway, finally independent in 1905 from the disliked union with Sweden, had celebrated nationhood through an intense patriotism that left little room for heterogeneity. Compared to Sweden, where the laws against Sámi people had been more benignly paternalistic, Norwegianization was harsh and repressive.

The occupation of Norway by Germany forces during World War II drew together Sámi and Norwegians in resistance; but it was the North—and much of Sápmi—that was bombed and burned in the scorched-earth retreat of the Nazi soldiers across Finnmark at the end of the occupation. The welfare state established after the war rebuilt northern Norway, but the price was the last vestiges of Sámi independence. Overnight, it seemed, the census figures for Sámi people dropped precipitously—not because the Sámi were mysteriously abducted by aliens after the war but because large numbers of Sámi individuals, especially on the Norwegian coasts, stopped publicly identifying as Sámi. Those who did still feel their Sámi-ness as a crucial aspect of life often kept it quiet. Many experienced internalized shame for how they had been treated and were still seen by government, educational, and church organizations. Others, in the interior of Finnmark, especially those who still owned and managed reindeer herds, carried the burden of constantly demanding their rights to traditional territories and ways of life.[2]

The king's speech was not the first stirring of conscience in the Norwegian body politic, but it was a significant step toward the principles and actions that have guided official Norwegian attitudes toward the Sámi population since. Three years later, in 2000, King Harald returned to Karasjok to dedicate a soaring new Sámi Parliament building, which also contained a library. From being a backwater on the Finnmark plateau, Karasjok became a center for Sámi political and cultural activity. As a signer of the United Nations Declaration on the Rights of Indigenous Peoples in 1990 (ILO Convention 169), Norway went to the top of the Nordic class in acknowledging the rights of its Indigenous people to limited self-determination and fuller management of their cultural heritage, including the return of ceremonial objects and human remains.[3]

In contrast, Sweden has never signed the ILO convention and has not considered itself bound in the same way to respect the UN's guidelines for Indigenous rights for its Sámi citizens, in part fearing the degree to which that would interfere with its continued exploitation of natural resources in the herding lands of Sápmi. Finland, too, has debated and redebated signing ILO Convention 169 and has always decided against it. Like Sweden, Finland has mining interests in its northern provinces that it sells to global investors. Until recently, the Finnish state had also shown enthusiasm for a proposed railway in the Arctic, which would have run from Rovaniemi to Kirkenes in Norway, connecting the European Union with Asia via Russia and bisecting reindeer grazing lands in Finnmark.

Norway, while also involved in these infrastructure proposals, is bound by the ILO convention to consult with its Sámi population. Yet Norwegian business and state interests eagerly eye the Northern Sea Route, which would turn northern cities into super-cargo ports on the increasingly ice-free Arctic Sea. A Norwegian mining company, Nussir ASA, has plans to open a copper mine near Hammerfest on the Repparfjord (Riehpovuotna) in traditional Sámi territories and to dump copper tailings into the pristine waterway, designated a national salmon fjord. A focal point of resistance for the Sámi and many environmental allies, the case is going through the courts.[4]

In these cases and others, the long-standing ILO convention agreements are a roadblock in Norway's economic plans to exploit the Arctic. Yet, simultaneously, the government is pursuing various forms of reconciliation with its Sámi citizens. In parallel, arts and educational institutions have also moved in that direction. One of the results has been the Bååstede project, which was initiated by the Norwegian Museum of Cultural History (Norsk Folkemuseum, or NFM) in Oslo in 2009, for the purpose of discussing and eventually acting on a plan to return Sámi material culture to Sámi museums. Leif Pareli, the past curator of the Sámi collections at the NFM, has written that his participation in the International Council of Museums, where repatriation and restitution were regularly considered, was formative, as was his work with the Sámi Museum Association.[5] An inter-Nordic research project, Recalling Ancestral Voices, charged with identifying all Sámi objects in museums, concluded with a published report and a conference in 2007 in Inari, Finland, as well as a stated commitment by the NFM to pursue possible repatriation of parts of the collection to Sámi museums.[6]

In 2012, a seventy-page report on what the Bååstede project might look like in terms of logistics, mutual agreements, and financing was produced in Norway; in June that year an Agreement of Repatriation was signed in a ceremony at the Sámi Parliament in Karasjok. By 2014 a project manager, Káren Elle Gaup, was appointed, along with various object conservators.[7] The purpose of the transfer of Sámi material objects, according to the report, was based on the rights of the Indigenous Sámi people to manage their cultural heritage. The Ministry of Culture in Norway annually allocates funding of arts and culture to the Sámi Parliament, and since 2007 that has included the National Sámi Museum Association. Bååstede, meaning "the return" in South Sámi, had three partners to begin with:

the NFM, the Sámi Museum Association, and the Sámi Parliament, which had taken over the administration of the Sámi museums in 2002. These parties were later joined in the agreement by the former Ethnographic Museum, now part of the University of Oslo's Museum of Cultural History (Kulturhistorisk Museum, or KHM).

Their inspiration was Utimut, the Danish-Greenlandic joint undertaking, which had continued over a period of around twenty years, from 1979 to 2001, involving the transfer back to Greenland of some thirty-five thousand objects, the majority of which were archeological, obtained by Denmark during the colonialist period and held in the National Museum of Denmark. A new museum in Nuuk was built to house the returned objects, as well as a research center, which were managed jointly by the Greenlandic and Danish governments. Due to the decentralized nature of Norwegian museums, Utimut ("return") could not translate directly to the repatriation of Sámi objects within the borders of Norway, but the Greenlandic–Danish model of formal agreements and professional methodologies demonstrated how the process of return could be carried out collaboratively and respectfully.

Sweden and Finland each have one main Sámi museum, Ájtte in Jokkmokk and Siida in Inari, along with a variety of regional and specialized museums. In the fall of 2021, the National Museum of Finland in Helsinki completed a transfer of most of its twenty-two hundred objects originating in Sápmi to the renovated and expanded museum in Inari. The decision was made relatively quickly and firmly, with an eye to increasing the accessibility of Sámi cultural heritage in the Sámi homeland. The museums signed two agreements, one concerning the physical repatriation of the collection and the other a clarification of responsibilities on the part of each museum to cooperate in the matter of new collecting efforts and no-fee loans. The National Museum of Finland will continue to collect items connected with the history of Sápmi in Finland and the relationship between the Sámi and the Finns, while Siida will display and collect Sámi historical and contemporary material culture. Frequently mentioned in the agreements are the words "cooperation" and "consultation." The process has been helped, no doubt, by the fact that only two museums have been involved and the fact that the National Museum transferred almost all of its Sámi holdings within a relatively brief span of time after making the official decision in 2017.[8]

Norway, by contrast, has twelve Sámi museums, consolidated into six museum organizations.[9] Many of these museums serve multiple important and historic functions as gathering places. Like Ájtte in Sweden and Siida in Finland, Norway's Sámi museums not only provide space for permanent displays and traveling exhibitions but also offer rooms for meetings and events. They are education centers for the local communities where classes in *duodji* and the Sámi languages are offered. Some have preschool facilities. They were not all created to simply house objects but also to create space for Sámi exchange and conversation. Transferring around half of the NFM's collection of forty-two hundred Sámi objects, everything from tiny needle cases to heavy fur coats, has been a long and complex process with many challenges.

In late January 2016, I took a stroll with Bååstede's director, Káren Elle Gaup, through the Sámi exhibits inside the NFM's main building on Bygdøy, just outside central Oslo. Much of the complex is an open-air museum, similar to Skansen in Stockholm and established around the same time, in 1894, with many of the identical aims: NFM was created to demonstrate "how our fathers lived and toiled, how they battled with the unforgiving land and harsh conditions, cultivated the soil, brought home their catch, traded, carried out their craft, lived and dressed, brought up their children; and how their spiritual life was affected by the changing times, what they thought and what they believed."[10]

But while the founder of Skansen, Artur Hazelius, saw Norway and Finland (and thus Sápmi) as part of Swedish history, NFM's founder, Hans Aall, was far more insistent on a separate identity for Norway, one that extended back to Viking and medieval times, when Norway was a seat of wealth and influence. He also wanted to emphasize Norwegian folk arts in all their rich particularity. Like Skansen, the museum reconstructed timber houses, shops, and schools, as well as an authentic stave church from 1200. Some church treasures went back to the early Middle Ages, when Trondheim was a pilgrimage site, but there were also folk altars and pews from later centuries.

In the first year of the NFM's founding, about ninety Sámi objects were also collected, but after that it was decided to keep Sápmi separate from Norway. The Ethnographic Museum in central Oslo was the place for everything to do with the Sámi people. Not until after World War II was there a museal reconsideration of Sápmi's place in Norway's cultural history. In 1951, all twenty-six hundred of the Ethnographic Museum's Sámi objects were transferred to NFM, which then continued to accept further donations.[11] The first overview ethnographic exhibition of Sápmi opened in the NFM's main building in 1958, and it was renewed in 1990; two years later the open-air museum created a Sámi tent site. In 2007, the NFM added more space to the Sámi exhibit, with a focus on contemporary life. After the Sámi Museum in Karasjok opened in the 1970s, the NFM ceased to collect older Sámi artifacts in favor of more contemporary Sámi-made *duodji*. The museum still cared for most of the older objects, a few dating to the 1600s, and some connected with Sámi religion, including several surviving ceremonial drums.[12]

By the time I met with Káren Elle Gaup, the Bååstede project had been going for several years and was originally scheduled to wrap up in 2017, in order to coincide with centennial celebrations around the first pan-Sápmi assembly organized in Trondheim in 1917. However, the repatriation project was far from complete, due, as Gaup explained, to complications. Many of the furs and textiles in the Sámi collection had been treated in the early days with DDT and other toxic conservation methods. Removing toxins is expensive and time-consuming, and funds for that were slow to materialize. Other issues had to do with the fact that early collectors often didn't bother much with provenance. They didn't write down the makers or the owners of clothing, tools, and domestic items or identify the *siida* or village where the object came from. Sometimes the sole identification in the inventory was "Finnmark." Sometimes not even that.

Part of the work of the conservators at the NFM was to identify, with the help of researchers and curators from the receiving museums, the origin of many objects, in order to decide which district of Sápmi they should be returned to. The original 2012 cooperation agreement had specified that objects would not be transferred to the Sámi museums until the institutions were ready to accept them. That meant, among other things, sufficient and secure storage space with climate control and staff trained in conservation techniques. The agreement included a projected budget but was vague on how some of these things would be paid for. The Sámi Parliament is given an annual sum each year from the Norwegian Parliament to spend as they decide, but they have any number of other economic outlays. The Bååstede agreement could only hope that the Norwegian government would be contributing more to this project, something that the government initially balked at.

Gaup, born into a reindeer-herding family in Mierojávri, a ten-minute drive north of Kautokeino, had studied economics, ethnography, and the Sámi language at the University of Oslo. She had previously been the director of RiddoDuottarMuseat (RDM) in Karasjok. Her take on some of these difficulties was expressed with discretion: she understood that it would take patience and persistence to get everyone on board and make this huge undertaking a reality. She has emphasized the bigger picture:

> This collection is the closest concrete, tangible connection that today's Sámi have to their ancestors, and it concerns their struggle for existence, equality

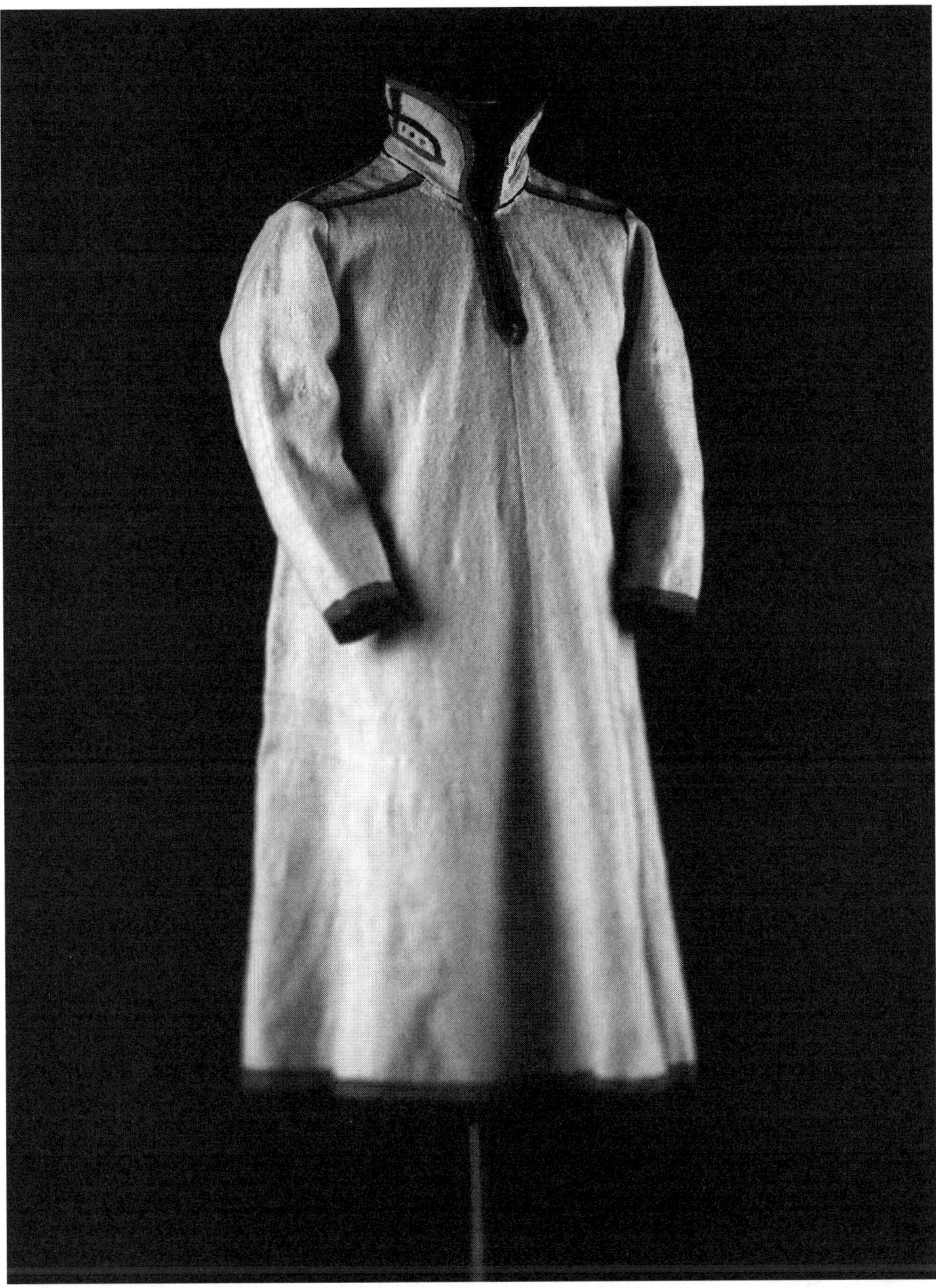

Sámi man's wool tunic, or *gákti*, Kvalsund, Norway; collected by Bertrand Nilsen in 1911. Not all clothing and objects were so easily identified in museum collections in Norway. Photograph by Haakon Michael Harriss. Courtesy of the Norwegian Museum of Cultural History.

> and justice. It is not the number of artefacts that matters but how the transferred artefacts increase the breadth and depth of the individual museums' documentation, research and dissemination related to Sami cultural heritage in the region.[13]

Others, for instance, Lars Magne Andreassen, of Árran Lule Sámi Center (Árran Julevsáme guovdásj), have been outspoken about the economics of repatriation. In a strongly phrased article in *Museum News* in 2015, Andreassen spoke of the gap between well-meant intentions and lack of follow-through, particularly about what was necessary to bring Sámi museums up to the same standards as Norwegian museums. He quoted the then president of the Sámi Parliament, Aili Keskitalo: "Norwegianization and oppression is our common history, and as long as that is made out to be only a Sámi issue, that will make evolution more difficult." Andreassen went on to point out that "Sámi museums are not only for the Sámi. All students should learn about Sámi culture and Sámi museums are important learning centers. . . . The Sámi museums are not only arenas for the Sámi narratives and for an understanding of our common national identity, they are also significant educational and economic players."[14]

The idea that Sámi museums were necessary to tell the story of both Norway and Sápmi, of a people many of whose ancestors were on the Fennoscandian Peninsula *before* the first Norwegians sailed north, *during* the centuries of Danish–Swedish–Norwegian dominance, and are *still here,* seemed to be a radical notion for many in the Norwegian government and for the public. Norwegian academic historians, beginning in the nineteenth century and continuing through the twentieth, had often pushed theories that the Sámi were later arrivals in Norway, particularly to the regions south of Trondheim, in South Sápmi. Although Sámi cultural expressions have become more visible in the last decades, most Norwegian students still study the Sámi as an ethnic group peripheral to Norwegian majority culture and history. Can Sámi museums help to change that? Is it the job of Sámi museums and Sámi exhibits to explain Sámi history to non-Sámi visitors? And what kind of history lesson should these museums and exhibits provide?

For many in the core communities of the Sámi homelands, the point of the Bååstede project is to bring what was created in Sápmi back to Sápmi, so that the Sámi themselves, in coming to the various museums, can see and study the objects made by their ancestors. At the same time, most Sámi are aware of the symbolic power of repatriation as a step in the process of acknowledging and righting historic wrongs. To the former president of the Sámi Parliament Aili Keskitalo, "it is a moral imperative that we own our past, present, and future, and that we can tell our stories."[15]

Repatriation is a physical form of atonement, one of various efforts undertaken in the Nordic countries with Sámi populations in recent years. In 2017 the Norwegian government established a Truth and Reconciliation Commission (TRC) to investigate the consequences for living people and descendants of Sámi and Kven people who suffered under the injustices of the Norwegianization policies that began in the nineteenth century. The Finnish and Swedish governments followed suit, with TRC projects beginning, respectively, in 2019 and 2020 and related only to their Sámi populations. The idea in all three countries is to collect testimony from Sámi individuals about their past and present experiences.

The Swedish cultural minister Amanda Lind said in a press release in 2019, "This is a historical step in the work to make visible the violations and abuses that the Sámi have been exposed to throughout history and which are far too little known."[16] In Norway, there is hope that the TRC will shine a light on injustice, by encouraging those who have been victimized to speak up and to "map the consequences of the Norwegianization policy" not just for the Sámi but for the majority population.[17] This increased emphasis on past wrongs would revise the collective narratives in ways that would allow the Sámi to become visible in Nordic history. But there are consequences to speaking out. Norwegian religious scholar Tore Johnsen writes that "Sámi visibility trigger[s] conspicuously strong resistance in local communities as the Sámi dimension is lifted from the private sphere and given public status."[18]

There is also distrust and fear among the Sámi that there will be no real follow-up to the traumatic disclosures that Sámi people might make. "Of course we want the truth to come out. We want the Norwegian and Sámi society to know what happened in Norway and in Sweden, and in Finland, but in many ways we already know that. So, truth is great . . . but what is the point if it's just another report put into the drawer?" says Christina Henriksen, president of the Saami Council (Sámiráđđi), a nongovernmental, pan-Sápmi organization.[19] Rauna Kuokkanen, a Finnish-Sámi scholar, also has taken a more skeptical view, asking whether such commissions will result in meaningful structural chance: "Settler states often define reconciliation as the venting of individual psychological traumas, rather than the eradication of structural causes of injustice."[20] She noted that Finland's TRC process was taking place at the same time that

Finland was considering plans for an Arctic Railway without soliciting input from the Sámi herders and residents whose traditional territories it would impact (the plan for the railway was cancelled in May 2021). She quotes a Sámi participant in Finland: "It's totally crazy to seek a railway through our lands and at the same time we need to start reconciling. I do not know what is the biggest threat at the moment, is it that the state seeks reconciliation? So that in the future, if something goes wrong with the Sámi, they can say, 'but we have reconciled and apologized.'"[21]

The Lutheran Church in Norway and Sweden has also in the last ten years been making serious efforts in the direction of reconciliation. From 2012 to 2016 the Swedish Church sponsored an extensive white paper study that resulted in over a thousand pages in two volumes of scholarly articles, documenting the Swedish Church's long history of discrimination against the Sámi in Sweden. Several contributors were Norwegian as well. A majority of the steering committee commission was Sámi, and the articles were written by historians and experts in the field.

This project was followed by another volume, in English, which summarized the findings and took a proactive stance, based on Christian theology, not only to acknowledge the past traumas and the Church's role in the colonization of Sápmi but to clarify that the acknowledgment was only the first step. There are, in Tore Johnsen's formulation, three further steps beyond witnessing: repentance, restoration, and forgiveness. Restoration may be the most difficult on a practical level. Centuries ago, the Swedish Church began attaching Sámi-owned lands for the building of churches and vicarages, and some of these appropriations resulted in large tracts of lands and forests that now belong to the Church. Sylvia Sparrock, a member of the Sámi Council in the Swedish Church, writes pointedly about steps the Church can take to make this land available again to the Sámi herders and to support the Sámi in their demands for consultation in all matters involving their lives and livelihoods:

> The Church has been on the side of the authorities and society in general throughout, and has hardly ever been on the side of the Sámi people. They have tacitly observed how Sámi culture and space have been curtailed. The church should take responsibility for this "policy of silence" by now coming down on the side of the Sámi people and defending Sámi rights.[22]

The term "northern Norway" conjures up only the latitude of the country, not the true geography of the Barents coastline, where the Norwegian border tilts far to

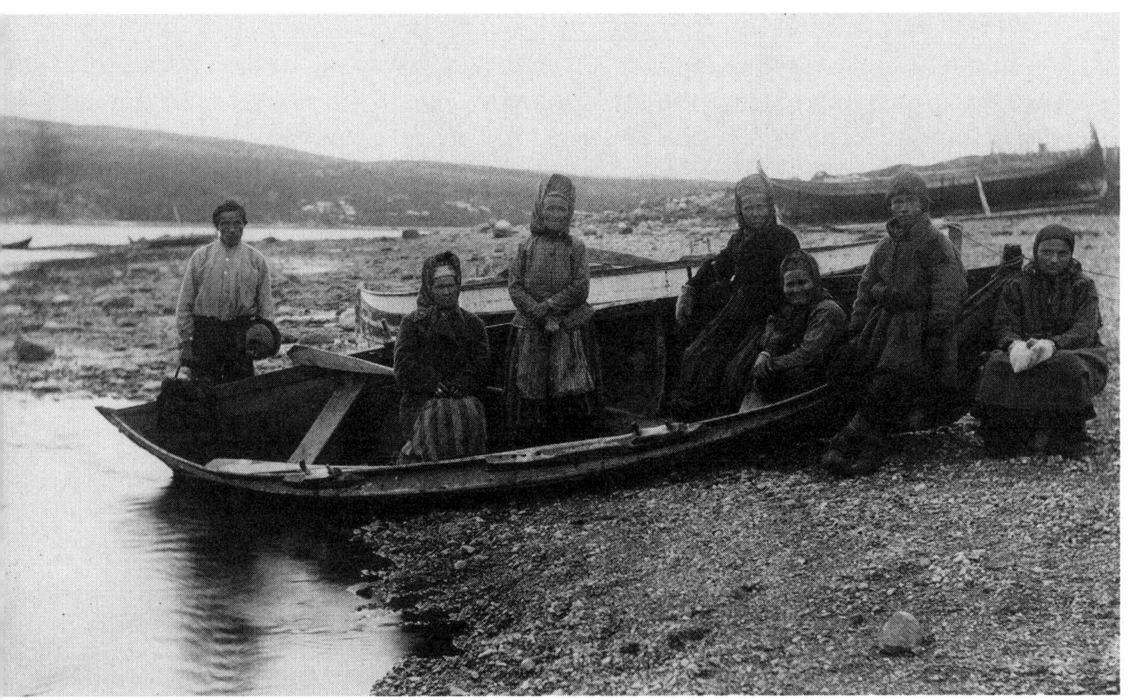

A group of Skolt Sámi from Pasvik prepares to set off in a rowboat for the salmon fishing grounds of Bøkfjord near the Barents Sea, circa 1900. Two Sea Sámi are with them on the right. Photograph by Ellisif Wessel. Courtesy of the Borderland Museum, Kirkenes, Norway.

the east, over Finland, to meet Russia's Murmansk province. The Norwegian border town of Kirkenes is on the southern side of the Varanger Fjord, and the city of Vadsø is on the northern side. The broad Varanger Fjord, more like a sound than one of the narrow inlets that cut deep into the western coast of Norway, is the only fjord in the country with an entrance facing east. Some settlements along the Varanger Fjord have been inhabited continuously for the past ten thousand years. The landscape of scoured headlands, scrub birches and rivers, and teeming fishing grounds isn't often what people think of as typically Scandinavian, and the mix of people—Sámi, Kvens, Finns, Norwegians, and Russians—who live here is distinctive as well. The Sámi population itself consists of two different groups, the majority Norwegian Sea Sámi and the Skolt or Eastern Sámi, whose traditional homelands are in three countries: Finland, Russia, and Norway. For several centuries they moved back and forth across the borders, fishing the rivers and tending their reindeer, until the Cold War put an end to travel patterns. Most Skolt Sámi now live in Finland, with small groups in Norway and Russia.

It's about sixty miles from the Barents Sea to the end of the fjord, where the Várjjat Sámi Musea (Varanger Sámi Museum, or VSM) was first constructed in 1995.[23] The museum was originally founded twelve years earlier, with the aim of displaying the history of the Sea Sámi in this area. It's only one of a number of small museums around the Varanger Fjord that represent the complex history here, some of it archaeological, some of it reflecting centuries of trade between Scandinavia and Russia, some of it the result of twentieth-century politics and war.

VSM, the largest of four Sámi museums around the fjord, will eventually receive around 150 objects from the NFM to add to the approximately two thousand objects it already holds. VSM's exhibits center largely around boats and coastal waters, both the Barents Sea and the river systems in northeast Finnmark, like the Tana River. Here, the traditional picture of the reindeer herder so prevalent in tourist literature gives way to dioramas of prehistoric hunters, sealers, and fishermen. VSM has historical displays that guide the visitor from the retreat of the ice to the first settlements during the Paleolithic. Although reindeer hunting and herding is part of the story of Eastern Finnmark, far more attention is given to fishing and trade, with a diorama, accompanied by sounds of waves and seagulls, of Sea Sámi in boats and on shorelines. There's a final exhibit of a Sámi home in 2000, with an armchair and television and a few Sámi markers—books and magazines in North Sámi on shelves and on a coffee table and clothing hung on pegs.[24]

The objects being repatriated from Oslo to Varanger are abundant with meaning for the residents around the fjord, a region subjected to heavy Norwegianization and to destruction during World War II. "That led to there being few older objects of material culture here and that is reflected in our collections," Ingvild Marie Bjørnå Pettersen wrote me. She is the head of the VSM and spoke for the community when she added, "People in our local society are involved with getting things back; they believe it's a positive step. They look forward to the objects being physically returned so that they can come to their own museum and see them in real life. They perceive it as 'right and reasonable' that Sámi objects belong in Sàpmi and will now return home."[25]

That older artifacts originally made in Sápmi belong back home in remodeled or even newly constructed Sámi museums where Sámi people can regularly visit them is a given for many Sámi communities. Depending on the location of the Sámi museums, it also means that the experience of Bååstede is shared with non-Sámi visitors, including many who have less understanding of Sámi history. VSM, for instance, is not too distant by car or bus from either Kirkenes or

Vadsø, two ports that, particularly in summer, see the visits of thousands of cruise ship passengers. Kirkenes, with its Snow Hotel in winter, also welcomes tourists year-round from Russia, Europe, and Asia. Thus, VSM provides a double function of museum/community center for locals and an educational center for tourists, who learn from the exhibits that the Sámi and their ancestors have long inhabited this part of Northern Europe. VSM also has the opportunity to explore some aspects of Norwegianization and the meaning of Bååstede by displaying the returned objects.

Other Sámi museums are located in regions traditionally Sámi but definitely off the beaten path for many tourists. Várdobáiki Sámi Centre is located in Evenskjer, a village of fewer than a thousand people off the E10 highway from Narvik to Harstad in the northwestern fjord country. Established in 2010, it moved into a new building in 2018 that has climate-controlled storerooms for the approximately fifty objects being returned through Bååstede. But Várdobáiki is more than a museum with exhibit space and storage; it also houses a kindergarten and archives for research. It counts among its resources the "immaterial heritage" of the North Sámi people who engaged in a mixed economy, including herding and fishing. This nonmaterial heritage, as described on the center's website, includes traditional knowledge, oral storytelling, myths and beliefs, and "words, expressions, and traditions connected with objects."[26] From the website we might understand that while Várdobáiki welcomes visitors from elsewhere, its primary purpose is to explore and strengthen Sámi culture.

A few hours' drive south of Evenskjer is Árran Lule Sámi Center in the village of Drag on the Tysfjord.[27] Like Várdobaiki, Árran plays a crucial role in the region, offering classes in *duodji* and the Lule Sámi language and hosting lectures, concerts, and traveling exhibits in its museum space. Additionally, Árran is a media center, publishing an annual popular scientific journal, *Bårjås,* and a series of illustrated children's books in Lule Sámi. Over the past several years Árran has increased and improved its storage space to receive 366 objects through the Bååstede project in October 2022, with an exhibition of some of the objects opening in 2023. By car, neither of these two centers with museums is far from the popular Lofoten Islands, but few cruise passengers make their way to either Vardobaiki or Árran. For most travelers, Norwegian or foreign, Sámi museums outside the urban centers remain invisible and are often seen by the Norwegian public as physically distant, reinforcing the illusion that Sápmi is peripheral within Scandinavia. Their value may be more cherished by the local communities, crucial as a means of keeping the diverse traditions and memories of Sápmi alive.

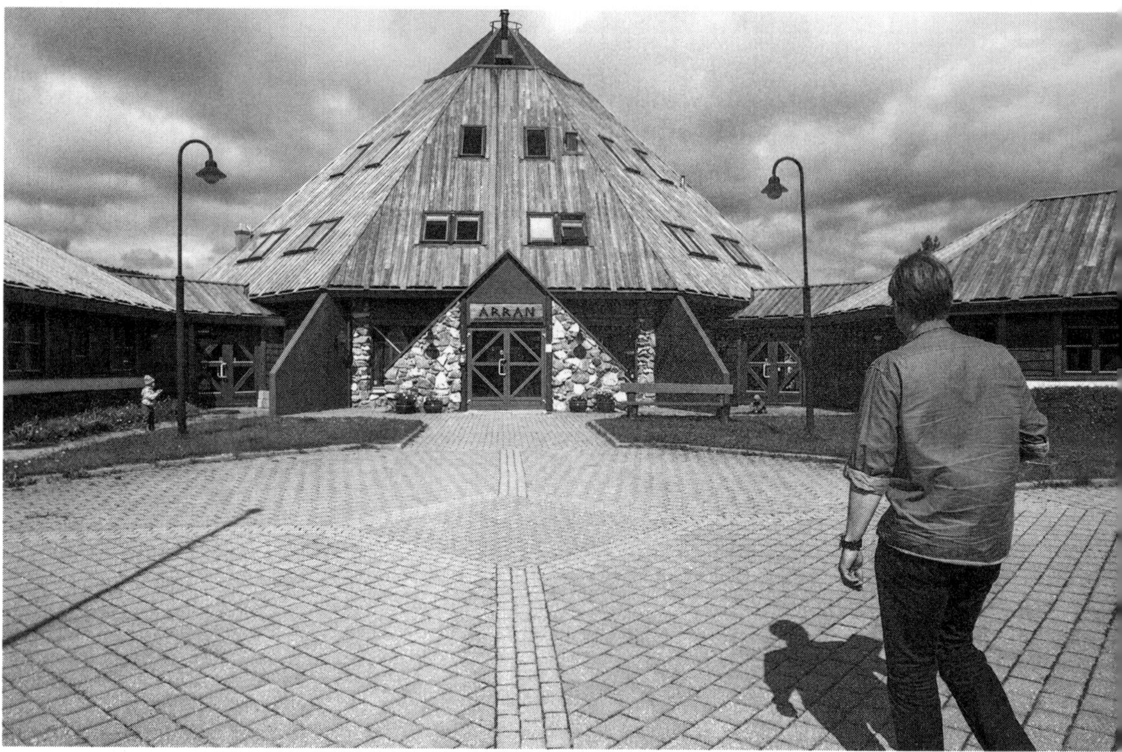

Árran Julevsáme guovdásj / Árran Lule Sámi Center in Drag, Norway. Photograph by Fredrik Forsberg. Courtesy of Árran Lule Sámi Center.

To return to Eastern Finnmark, in the High North, take the case of Ä'vv Saa'mi mu'zei, the Skolt Sámi Museum, in Neiden, Norway, about halfway between Kirkenes and Varangerbotn.[28] This village of 250 people, many of them Sámi or Kven or with a mixed heritage, is inland from the indented coastline of the Barents Sea and not far from the Norwegian–Finnish border. Finland has a village with a Finnish variant of Neiden, Näätämö; the two districts were officially separated in 1852 and suffered further incursions and divisions over the next hundred years. The Skolt Sámi are small in number and, before the borders divided them, ranged with their reindeer across Norway, Finland, and Russia. Russian culture marks the Skolt minority out from the rest of Sápmi, along with their adoption of Eastern Orthodox Christianity in the sixteenth century. The Skolt Sámi language is one of the world's most endangered. It's estimated that only about three to four hundred people still speak it; most of them are not in Norway but in Finland. During World War II, the Nazis built POW and concentration camps in Finnmark, fought the Russians and Norwegian partisans, and on their scorched-earth retreat in 1944 and 1945, bombed and burned all housing and the reindeer grazing lands in the area. Many Skolt Sámi were evacuated or ended up temporarily in refugee camps in Norway; other families were divided by the border with Russia during the Cold War. Arguably, the Skolt Sámi took the brunt of the German occupation and its aftermath in the North.

Given the bloody and contested record of that area, it's hard to believe that any Skolt Sámi are left, but when the Skolt Sámi Museum formally opened in 2017, six hundred people came to celebrate. This museum is for and about the Skolt Sámi, whose possessions were largely destroyed and only restored by gifts, purchases, and, now, different forms of repatriation from museums down south, both in Norway and Helsinki. The Skolt Sámi Museum is part of Bååstede. Whether or not many visitors come through Neiden to see the exhibits on Skolt Sámi heritage, the local community now has a place to gather and to also engage in networking with other Sámi centers and museums in Norway and Finland and to rebuild identity across national boundaries.

Around the Varanger Fjord are also non-Sámi museums in Vardø, Vadsø, and Kirkenes, all of which display aspects of the multicultural North and its complex past of fishing and trade, of intermarriage and war, interwoven together in a unique history. In Kirkenes, for instance, is the Borderland Museum (Grenselandmuseet). Its exhibits and significant archives tell stories about the ways in which Russians, Finns, Kvens, Sámi, and Norwegians lived and worked together. The effects of World War II—the partisan fighting, bombings, and evacuations—are documented in photographs and oral histories, as is the legacy of the Cold War in the 1950s and 1960s. The Borderland Museum displays a Sámi exhibit from their small collection, but as one of the staff members, Camilla Carlsson, told me, "We are dedicated to being a good museum for all the local population, no matter who they are."[29] This is an example, in a small, positive way, of how to present the braided history of the Sámi and the Norwegians with other narratives, those of people with Kven, Finnish, and Russian heritage, woven in as well. The Sámi museums of the Varanger Fjord tell one story, and the regional museums tell another, but in many ways it's the same story—of neglect from the South; of trade among Norway, Finland, and Russia; of resilience in the face of destruction; and of new opportunities and challenges in the future.

Around two hundred miles to the southwest from the Varanger Fjord is the spread-out municipality of Kautokeino, where the majority of the population of three thousand is Sámi and about half of them have an economic connection to reindeer herding. While the Sámi Parliament and several other Sámi institutions are located eighty miles north in Karasjok, Kautokeino has a number of cultural and educational organizations. It's the home of the National Sámi Theater, Beaivváš, which performs all over Sápmi; Sámi University of Applied Sciences (Sámi allaskulva); and the International Sámi Film Institute. Its small municipal museum, Guovdageainnu gilišillju, is part of the administrative RDM group in Karasjok. Although Kautokeino's museum is participating in Bååstede, few objects will be returned until the structure is remodeled or fully rebuilt, with climate-controlled storerooms. According to Johan Aslak Hætta, its director, that is unlikely to happen anytime soon:

> It sounds good on paper, that the Norwegian government wants to give the Sámi people back the things that have meaning for us. But when they set conditions for the return that we have no financial ability to meet, and don't give us the money to create those conditions, that makes it very difficult. But here in Kautokeino we want the models made by Lars Hætta, and we would keep them on exhibit. That is different in Oslo where they are always in storage.[30]

Johan Aslak Hætta is the great-great-grandson of Aslak Hætta, who was tried and executed for his part in the Kautokeino Uprising of 1852. Most people in Kautokeino are very keen to see the museum receive objects from the NFM in Oslo, particularly the miniatures created by Lars Hætta during his time at Akershus. A few years ago, Johan Aslak Hætta acquired another model made by the Bible translator and former prisoner. This is a small scene mounted on a board of a tent, dog, reindeer, and Sámi herder. Bought at auction in Uppsala in 2014, this object is far more than the model of a tent. It is a memory scene of animals and a herder with a lasso, wearing a Four Winds hat, a rare glimpse into a world where models come to life and are seen in relationship to each other (Plate 16). Although its history has taken it far and wide, there's no doubt in Johan Aslak Hætta's mind that the model is home where it belongs again.

The Sámi museums, like museums everywhere, are limited by space. Not everything can be displayed or not all the time. The objects each museum receives through Bååstede will still need to be stored, and climate control and conservation are key. What is happening in Sápmi, nevertheless, is a significant effort on the part of many stakeholders to change the paradigm of Indigenous ownership, of reconciliation and repatriation, of how artifacts are studied and displayed, and even of what a museum might mean. The process of Bååstede is not only a physical act of atonement; it is an ongoing aspect of changing the story of Norwegian history. While Bååstede is limited to Norway, the project has influenced discussions of repatriation throughout the Nordic countries.

Bååstede doesn't extend to international repatriation, yet the initiative has implications for challenging the colonialist narrative that resulted in several thousand Sámi artifacts ending up in ethnographic collections in England and on the Continent. If and when objects of Sámi origin are repatriated from Europe, it is likely they will initially be the ceremonial drums and *sieidis*. How might such a return function? In the region northwest of Trondheim lies the South Sámi Museum, Saemien Sijte, in the town of Snåsa. A new museum building opened in June 2022. Like many of the Sámi museums, it is also a community center, with craft workshop areas for courses in *duodji* and space for individual artisans. Due to the halving of the budget, a hoped-for auditorium for events was not included. The museum in Snåsa has received 163 objects from the NFM in Oslo to add to its own collection of around five hundred items. One of the objects returned is the so-called Bindal drum, or *gievrie*, in South Sámi, which comes from the area of Bindal in Nordland province. The Bindal drum had been used by several generations of *noaidis* (*nåejttie* in South Sámi) and was probably made in the seventeenth or eighteenth century. It is thought to have been in use until around 1900 and then hidden in a mountain cave until 1925, after which it went to the Ethnographic Museum in Oslo and then to the NFM.

Saemien Sijte is also planning to request the formal repatriation from the Meininger Museum in Germany of the *Freavnantjahke gievrie*, "the drum from Frøyning Mountain" that once belonged to Bendix Andersen and was taken from him by Thomas von Westen in 1723. Recall that this drum was part of the Danish Royal Kunstkammer before it was given away by Frederick V and ended up at the Meininger Museum. It was rediscovered in the 1990s when persistent curators from the National Museum of Denmark were attempting to track down all the objects that had once been in the Royal Kunstkammer. In 2017 the *Freavnantjahke gievrie* was hand carried to Trondheim by a curator at the Meininger Museum to be displayed for a few months in an exhibit at the NTNU University Museum (NTNU Vitenskapsmuseet). It will take high-level diplomacy and money to bring the *gievrie* back to Sápmi on a permanent basis, but it may well be the first of several repatriations of drums from Europe.

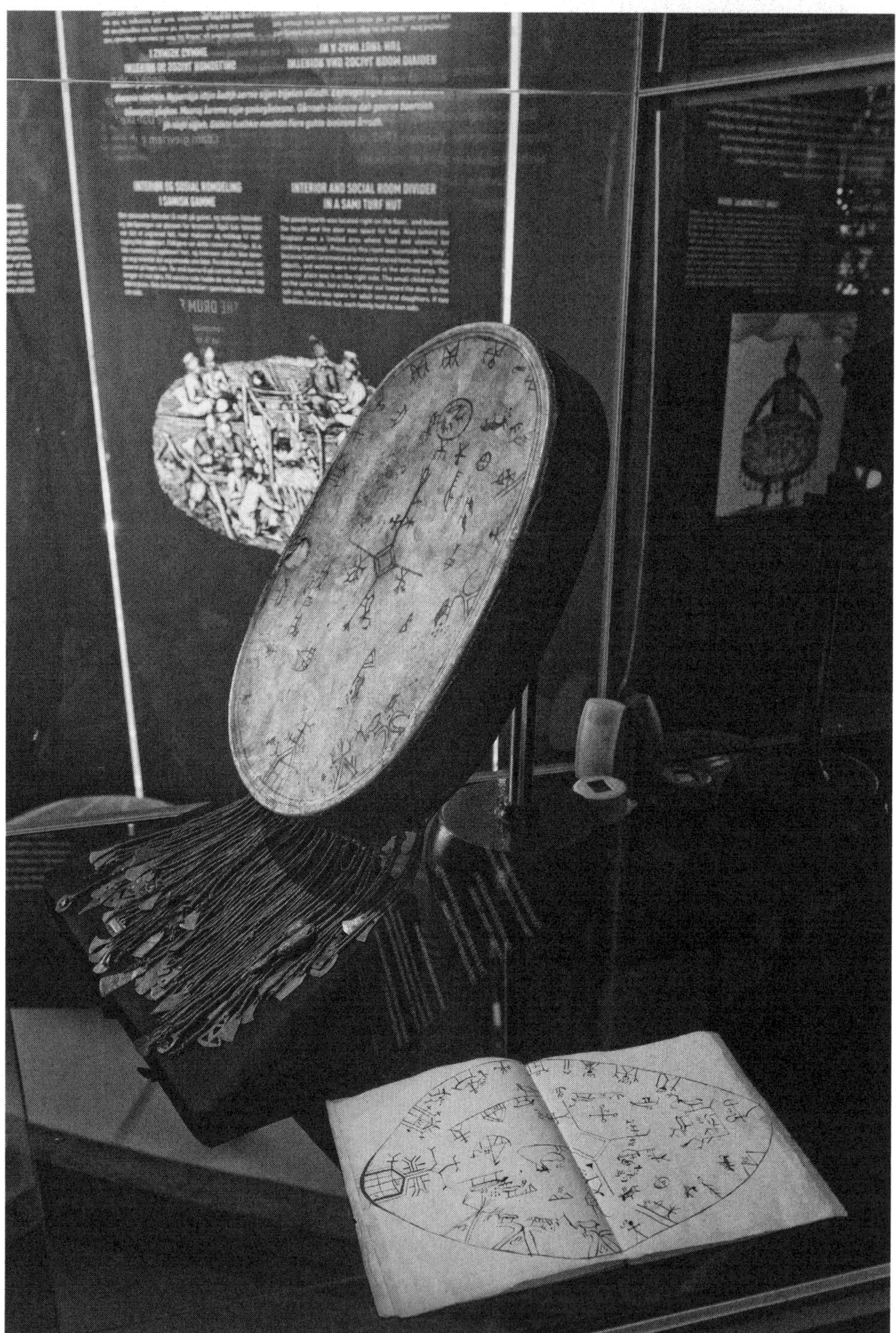

Freavnantjahke gievrie, “the drum from Frøyning Mountain.” Next to the drum is the original description of the meaning of the symbols explained to Thomas von Westen by Bendix Andersen and Jon Torchelsen. Displayed in the NTNU University Museum, Trondheim, Norway, in 2017, by permission of the Meininger Museum in Germany. Photograph copyright Bente Haarstad.

The display of the *Freavnantjahke gievrie* in February 2017 at the NTNU University Museum was only one aspect of the important exhibit *Who Owns the Story?* This exhibit was part of Norway's nationwide acknowledgment of the centenary of the 1917 pan-Sápmi assembly in Trondheim, the first time that Sámi individuals had ever gathered across state boundaries to forge joint statements and create political alliances, and it was fitting that the exhibit took place at NTNU. Norway has seven university museums, most of which are rich in archaeological collections from prehistory, Viking, and medieval times and some of which have significant Sámi collections. The NTNU University Museum cares for four hundred Sámi objects. Some are donations from families in the Trøndelag region of central Norway/southern Sápmi, but many of the objects were purchased in Finnmark by Bertrand M. Nilsen, a clergyman who combined his work as the head of the Norwegian Sámi Mission with a sideline in selling and donating Sámi ethnographica to museums in Oslo, Trondheim, and elsewhere. The University Museum also has some older rarities from earlier missionary days, such as a manuscript by Thomas von Westen, one intact drum, and fragments of other drums from the region nearby. These days the museum is more focused on prehistory and medieval archeology; it no longer collects Sámi ethnography but continues to conserve its various historical collections and use them to acknowledge Sámi history more fully and begin to question long-held assumptions.

This interrogation of Norwegian–Sápmi history played a role in the 2017 exhibit *Who Owns the Story?*, where the *Freavnantjahke gievrie* illustrated the forced Christianization in South Sápmi and the confiscation and destruction of ceremonial objects and altars, along with the appropriation, by questionable legal means, of land used for reindeer grazing. The exhibition also displayed Sámi artifacts created between 600 and 900 CE in South Sápmi. The curators juxtaposed the museum's recent archeological finds in the exhibit with texts explaining nineteenth-century theories taken as fact and promulgated by Yngvar Nielsen.

Yngvar Nielsen, we might recall, was the director of the Ethnographic Museum in Oslo from 1877 to 1907. He chaired the Norwegian Historical Association and edited or coedited historical journals. Not only did he write about geography, ethnography, and history, but he was a great proponent of hiking and tourism in Norway. His travel handbook for Norway, nicknamed *Yngvar,* appeared in a dozen editions and was translated into English and German. Nielsen used his various platforms to write, always condescendingly and often negatively, about the Sámi and to scorn Sámi claims to their own history and ties to the landscape, particularly in South Sápmi. He claimed—dismissing generational memory—that the Sámi had not inhabited the Trøndelag region until reindeer herders moved down from the North in the middle of the 1700s. These theories weren't just suppositions with no weight; they were used as late as the 1990s as the legal basis for rulings between Sámi reindeer herders and Norwegian farmers over who had the right to the grazing lands. It was only in 2001 that the Supreme Court of Norway abandoned Yngvar Nielsen's conjectures.

The exhibit in Trondheim used archeology to explicitly contradict long-accepted ideas about where Sápmi began and ended by effectively proving that generational memory was correct. The wall text explained that a remote mountain lake that had been dammed for hydropower in 1953, Aursjøen, underwent repairs in 2006 that dropped the water level. Archeologists went in to find, date, and document artifacts at a number of ancient Sámi sites that had been inaccessible since the dam was built. Some of these artifacts were on display at NTNU. Some of the wall texts at the University Museum (in South Sámi, Norwegian, and English) acknowledged that the "Greater Society," in the past and perhaps the present, had been indifferent to Sámi realities:

> In the late 1800s, the power and knowledge elite in Norway were preoccupied with nation building towards independence. The result over time has been a very homogenous presentation of Norwegian history. Elements that did not fit the vision of what was "Norwegian" were overlooked and left out.[31]

Several years on, this exhibit moved further south within Trøndelag, to the regional museum of Røros, a much-visited mountain town east of the Aursjøen site. Røros has been a World Heritage Site since 1980. Beginning in 1644, it had a long history as a copper mining center. The town layout and many remaining timber buildings from the 1700s and 1800s invite the tourist to, as the official Norwegian tourism website, Visit Norway, puts it, "travel back in time." But Røros's history is not just copper mining. The region is deeply imbued with Sámi history, too, something that is increasingly reflected in the Røros Museum's exhibits. Sámi reindeer herding went on in most of the surrounding mountains and valleys in Norway and Sweden, as the border is only about thirty miles away.

Jenny Fjellheim, a cultural history consultant at the museum with South Sámi heritage, contributed research to the NTNU exhibit and was instrumental in bringing it to Røros in April 2021 for a year. She wrote me that often in the past the faculty of history at NTNU had held onto a view of history in Trøndelag that reproduced Nielsen's theory of late migration by the Sámi, a view "that had such great consequences for the Sámi community—right up to the new era! I choose to look at this exhibition as a break with the view of history that has previously been communicated." She saw the 2017 exhibit *Who Owns the Story?* as "a big gesture towards the Sámi community—to show the relevant objects in the exhibition."[32]

The king's carefully considered wording in his 1997 speech ("Sámi history is closely interwoven with Norwegian history") is a concept that has yet to fully take hold. It is not only the Sámi museums that bear the responsibility for creating exhibits that show past and present injustices but national, regional, and university museums. In some ways, the reckoning of Norway's historical treatment of the Sámi is best presented in the context of a major urban or regional museum, such as the NFM in Oslo or the Arctic University Museum in Tromsø, where many more visitors are likely to see colonialist history as not just a Sámi problem but a Norwegian one. Yet the Sámi museums are not there solely to demonstrate Sámi historical visibility to other Nordic people. They are centers of community engagement and renewal. The objects in the museums play a vibrant role in identity and education, as well as in the creation and display of new forms of *duodji* and *dáidda*.

Recollecting

Sápmi

In 2017, the Ashmolean Museum in Oxford, England, opened *Spellbound,* an exhibition of exotic and humble items connected with divination and magic, with love, spite, and murder. Many of the objects were from the United Kingdom, while others were from Europe and the Americas; they were largely historic and literary, pointing to Great Britain's long fascination with dark magic. *Spellbound* was accompanied by a handsomely illustrated volume of the same name, introduced by Philip Pullman. One chapter, "The Fear and Loathing of Witches," highlights the crazed witch hunts of the fifteenth through eighteenth centuries with deliciously frightening photographs, like a poppet with a stiletto through its face and an Italian witch garland of feathers from Tuscany. There's also an image of a drumskin said to be a "Finnish shaman's drum . . . an exceptionally rare survival. Painted with magical symbols, perhaps a map of another world, it was used in divination."[1]

We've encountered this drum before, in detailed notes in the British Museum's online catalog and in established Sámi drum research.[2] The drum is not from Finland but from central Sweden, perhaps Pite Sápmi, and it may have formed part of the Museum Schefferianum, in Uppsala in the seventeenth century. Its original maker has never been identified, but it's likely to have been the drum brought to London in 1681 and presented by Johan Heysig-Ridderstjerna to the Royal Society. Whether via Hans Sloane or directly from the Repository of the Royal Society, this drum eventually came into the collection of the British Museum by the end of the eighteenth century. Whatever its true origin, the drum has a long history, along with all the drums that were saved from destruction in Sápmi, as a religious object in the hands of the *noaidi* who used it to move between the worlds of the living and the dead and as a larger symbol of colonialist policy and Sámi resistance.

As it turns out, the actual drum in the British Museum's collection wasn't loaned to the Ashmolean for the *Spellbound* exhibit, nor were the curators able to obtain the loan of an equally old drum housed at the Museum of Archaeology and Anthropology (MAA) in Cambridge. Still, the drum that once perhaps belonged to Johannes Schefferus and Hans Sloane appears in the *Spellbound* catalog, among the dried-up animal hearts stabbed by pins and the glass bottles holding curses, as a northern curiosity, the tool of a sorcerer in the Arctic hinterlands, "an exceptionally rare survival." The British Museum has also displayed this drum outside its political and religious context. From 2003 to 2005, the drum toured South Korea and Japan as part of the exhibit *Treasures of the World,* organized by Asahi Shimbun, a Japanese newspaper that is also one of the British Museum's longstanding supporters. For six weeks in 2008–9, the "Sámi Magic Drum" was also on view in Room 3 of the museum. A journalist at *The Guardian* urged readers to see this "atmospheric recreation of the world of the Sámi people" and to celebrate its place in the British Museum's collection for 250 years. As far as I can tell, the atmospheric recreation consisted of a Sámi tent set up in the room and the background sound of "a Sámi Shaman's chant"—presumably a modern version.[3]

According to the most recent inventories, more than ten thousand Sámi objects are held in museums abroad, with some of the larger collections in Copenhagen, Leiden, Berlin, Munich, and other German museums; there are six thousand artifacts in Russia alone, mainly in the Ethnographic Museum in St. Petersburg.[4] Other Sámi artifacts, including thirty-one of the remaining eighty-odd sacred drums, are scattered around national and regional museums in Britain and on the Continent. Aside from the rare drums, many of the objects in museums are ethnographica, purchased from museum agents or antiquarian dealers in the nineteenth and early twentieth centuries. Some objects were collected more directly by archaeologists, anthropologists, or tourists in the twentieth century. They include clothing, shoes, root baskets, spoons, knives, photographs, and souvenirs like painted plates, drawings, and dolls. Some illuminate certain regions of Sápmi and are well documented in notes on provenance and use; others, scooped up by travelers, could be from almost anywhere in the Nordic countries. In many museums abroad, documented provenance on Sámi objects in their collections is thin to nonexistent. Elsewhere in Europe the Sámi objects, often tagged only "Lapp" or "Lapland," are buried in boxes in storerooms, not yet inventoried or visible in digital catalogs, much less displayed using the expertise of Indigenous specialists from Sápmi.

Berlin's Museum of European Cultures has the most substantial collection outside the Nordic countries and Russia: about a thousand items and six hundred photographs. Most of the purchasing of Sámi objects was originally commissioned by the directors of Berlin's ethnographic museum, the Royal Museum of Ethnology (Museum für Völkerkunde), on the salvage ethnography plan. One agent was Wilhelm Crahmer, who traveled extensively in Sápmi in the first part of the twentieth century and brought back around a hundred representative items. In 2019 a Sámi delegation from Norway, headed by the then president of the Sámi Parliament, Aili Keskitalo, visited Berlin to inspect the collection, none of which was on display except a single hat. The explanation from the curator was that the staff did not have "sufficient knowledge of the various objects, their provenance, utilization, etc. to show them to the public."[5] The holdings in Berlin include two ceremonial drums. One of them dates from the 1700s, when it was probably transported from Ume Sápmi, where the church assemblies around Lycksele and Åsele took place, to the Kunstkammer of the Brandenburg–Prussian rulers. As was the case in other countries, the Kunstkammer's treasures were distributed to other state museums in the nineteenth century, including Berlin's Royal Museum of Ethnology.

The Norwegian minister of culture at the time of the visit to Berlin, Trine Schei Grande, proposed a cooperation agreement between the Sámi museums in Norway and German museums with Sámi collections. Repatriation was not the only subject on the table; the idea was to share knowledge that would encourage the German museums to display their Sámi objects. One of the complicating factors with material culture from Sápmi is that objects often can't be traced definitively to a single country, much less to a specific district or village.

Loans and repatriation of ceremonial drums are handled somewhat differently in Denmark, where several drums in the National Museum date back to the seventeenth and early eighteenth centuries, including Anders Poulsen's drum, confiscated in Vadsø during the witch hunts and trials of the late 1600s and sent south to Copenhagen after he was murdered shortly after his trial in 1691. This historically important drum, once part of the Royal Danish Kunstkammer and then the Ethnographic Collection, was returned on loan in 1979 to the Sámi Museum in Karasjok in an agreement that's been renewed every five years. When the renewal came up once again in December 2021, the question of permanent repatriation to Sápmi was forcefully raised by the Norwegian Sámi Parliament

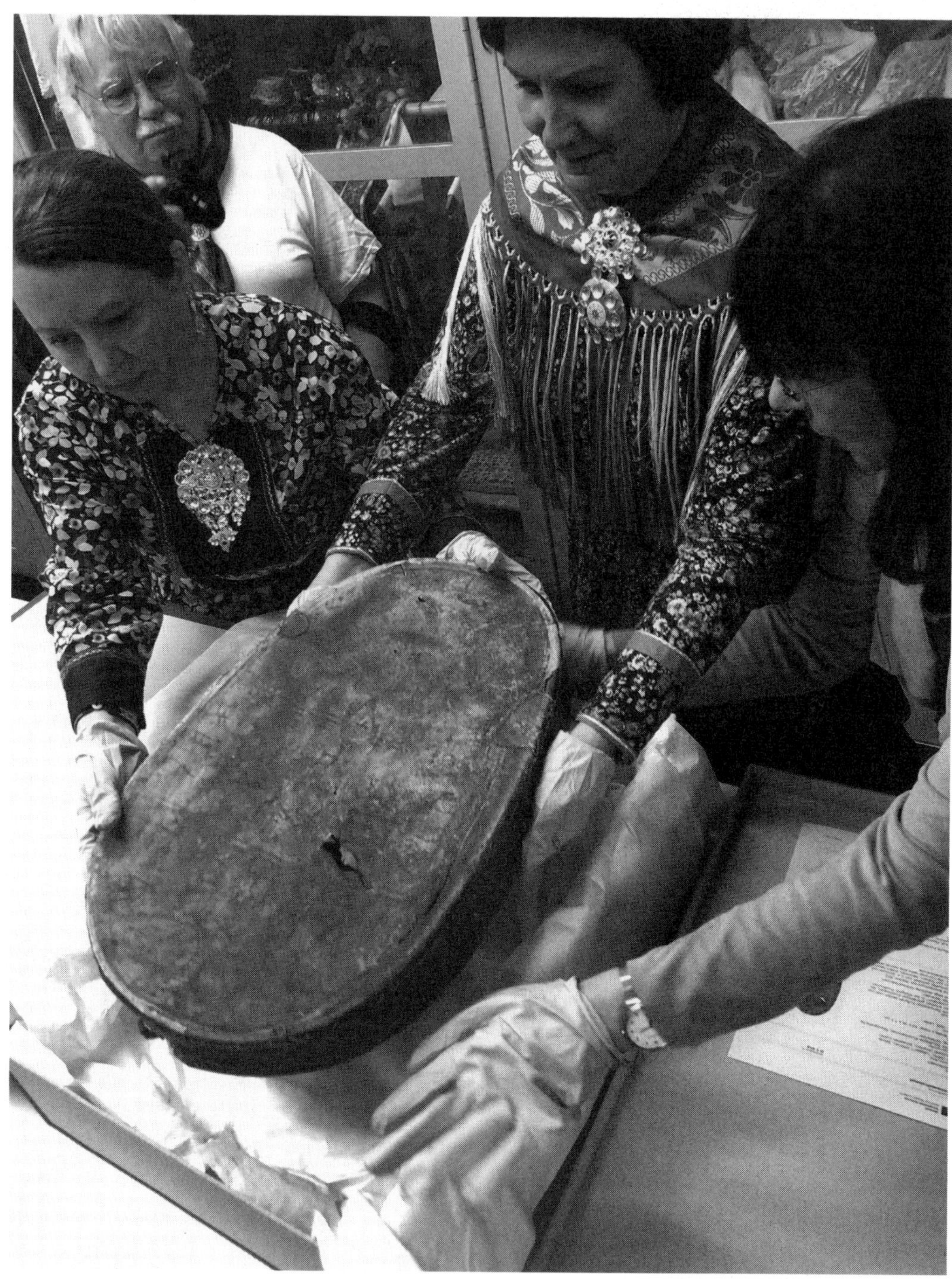

Aili Keskitalo (center), a past president of the Norwegian Sámi Parliament, visits the Museum of European Cultures in Berlin in July 2019. The drum is from Ume Sápmi, collected in the 1700s. Photograph by Siv Eli Vuolab. Courtesy Sámi Parliament/Samediggi, Norway.

to the United Nations and the European Union. The president of the Sámi Parliament even made a public request to the queen of Denmark.

In January 2022, the Danish cultural minister, Ane Halsboe-Jørgensen, announced that the National Museum would remove the Sámi drum from the Danish museum's holdings, stating that it made sense to do so since the Karasjok area had a historical connection to the drum and it had been displayed at the Sámi Museum for so many years. The press release added, however, that "normally, there is no question of removal to museums in other countries, but in this specific case, permission has been granted."[6] The careful language seems designed not to set a precedent, and the word "repatriation" is not mentioned. Meanwhile, in Karasjok, the reaction was jubilant. Sámi Museum director Anne May Olli told a reporter, "It feels good to have formal ownership to something that is already ours. And that our own cultural heritage is recognized. It is important not only for us, but for the whole of Sápmi."[7]

The National Museum of Denmark is one of the few European museums with a permanent display of some of its objects from Sápmi. Another is the MAA in Cambridge, which gives serious space to its modest Sámi collection. This goes back to 1947, when the museum first opened *Lapland,* a permanent exhibit put together from objects and photographs donated by Dr. Ethel John Lindgren, an American-born Cambridge University professor of anthropology, dating from her field expeditions to Lule Sápmi in the mid-1930s, and by her new husband, Mikel Utsi, a reindeer herder born in Karesuando, who became her partner in the effort to bring reindeer herds to Scotland's Cairngorm Mountains. They had originally met when Lindgren, who had degrees from Cambridge and had done her fieldwork on nomadic life in Mongolia and Siberia (her doctoral thesis focused on a female Tungas shaman, Olga Dmitrievna Kudrina, from Siberia), had turned her attention to Swedish nomadic culture. She was married then, with a young son. Mikel Utsi belonged to a *siida* whose summer camp was in Vaisaluokta on the shores of Lake Áhkkajaure, northwest of Jokkmokk.

From 1939 to 1946, Utsi ran restaurants in northern Sweden and played an important role as a regional police officer rescuing Norwegians escaping across the border and getting them to Jokkmokk's refugee camp. For his efforts he received a medal from King Haakon of Norway. Lindgren was busy, too, lecturing in England and raising funds in America. But after the war she visited Sweden again, and she and Mikel Utsi reconnected and married. Utsi became a British citizen in 1955. Together they founded the Reindeer Council of the United

Kingdom. Over the years, they drew on each other's strengths to write articles on herd management and advocate for a wider understanding of Sámi culture in Great Britain.[8]

Utsi was a talented *duojár* as well, who advised the British Museum on its collection and donated a few objects to them and other museums in Great Britain, including the MAA and the Scott Polar Research Institute (SPRI) in Cambridge. For the SPRI, he was also commissioned to craft twenty "specimens" of Sámi objects in wood and horn. Although one or two are models, most aren't miniatures like the items made by Lars Hætta a century before in Norway. Created in the 1960s and 1970s, before the political resurgence of Sápmi but certainly during the time when *duodji* was being made in larger quantities and young people were studying how to update and work with older forms, the SPRI specimen collection has its own integrity. Utsi aimed to recreate the techniques that he had learned from his family and to preserve the outward form of traditional objects: a knife, a salt flask, a needle case, a pipe, a lasso ring, a heddle, a spoon, and a birch-bole cup.[9]

The 1947 *Lapland* exhibit at the MAA was mainly assembled of clothing and domestic *duodji* from Swedish Sápmi, augmented with notes and captions by Lindgren and Utsi and with photographs from the Sámi encampment at Vaisaluokta. But the display also included a few older objects, most notably a seventeenth-century drum on deposit since 1914 from Trinity College Library, likely from Lule Sápmi, maker unknown. Perhaps, as Ernst Manker wrote, it was presented to Trinity College in the 1730s by Daniel Solander or Joseph Banks. It is a frame-style drum, without Christian symbols. The membrane was torn and later repaired, leaving three patches around the rim. A number of surviving Sámi drums show rips and burn marks, whether from careless handling or because they were partially destroyed but saved in time, in the interest of either science or superstition.

In 1998 the drum was hand carried by the college librarian on a plane from England to Sweden to become part of a powerful new exhibit, *Drum-Time,* which Ájtte's staff designed with cooperation from the Nordic Museum in Stockholm, using eight drums from the museum's collection. The exhibit showed both in Stockholm and Jokkmokk, with a booklet in Lule Sámi, Swedish, and English by Anna Westman and John E. Utsi, a nephew of Mikel Utsi. Both the text of the booklet and the four vitrines showcased different aspects of the drums, including their construction, their use by individual families and *noaidis,* and their stories, particularly the fraught histories of Swedish colonization and missionary activities in Sápmi.[10] The loan to Ájtte was renewed in 2003 for another five years, but in 2008 the drum returned to the MAA. The staff at Ájtte took it hard and for some years purposefully left a space for that drum in a vitrine, marked with a card about its appearance in Jokkmokk after centuries and then its disappearance again.

In February 2009, a refreshed exhibition of Sámi artifacts opened at the MAA, entitled *Sápmi: Collections and Connections from Northern Europe* and curated by Mark Elliott of the MAA and Catrine Ayélé Durand, a former PhD student at Cambridge who had done research on both Sámi collections in Sweden and Maori collections at the MAA. The "connections" in the title of the Sápmi exhibit included relationships both older and ongoing—the Lindgren–Utsi collections were newly displayed with more information gathered about the photographs and objects, and the staff at the MAA worked on the display in cooperation with staff at Ájtte. Durand had written in her dissertation about a Sámi drum created by Swedish *duojár* Helge Sunna for the Ethnographic Museum in Stockholm, and the MAA decided to commission Sunna to make a drum for the Sápmi exhibit. This drum, which is displayed in a case near the "Trinity drum," is not a replica model but a new creative work.[11]

Born in Leavas Sameby in Kiruna, Sweden, in 1940, Helge Sunna grew up in a family of *duojárs* and later moved to Stockholm with his wife, Inga Sunna, also an artisan. Innovation has been part of his work from the beginning, particularly with the contemporary images he adds to drumskins but also in his design of bowls and knives. His aim, he's written, is to create "with the hand's skill and the heart's warmth, for the eye's delight."[12] Active in the organization Sámi Duodji, he has been part of a generation dedicated to transmitting the spirit and standards of inherited artisanship as well as showing how to put an individual stamp on traditional forms.

Like Helge Sunna, the Sámi *duojár* Gunvor Guttorm crafts new work based on traditional materials and shapes (Plate 17). She is both a hands-on teacher and a theorist of *duodji*. As a professor of *duodji* and former rector at the Sámi University of Applied Sciences in Kautokeino in Norway, she has written extensively on the role of *duodji* instruction in secondary and higher education. Passing on the cultural context, the specific skills, and the knowledge of natural materials used in Sámi artisanship is an essential aspect of how *duodji* is taught. Guttorm, like many other teachers, curators, and activists, also stresses the role of *duodji* in building Sámi identity and community.[13] *Duodji* may be seen as artistic craft and commodity in auction houses, museum gift stores, souvenir shops, and online sites maintained by artisans themselves, but for master *duojárs* such as Helge Sunna and Gunvor Guttorm the finished product is only part of the process. Practicing and polishing the craft goes along with demonstrating that one way to experience Sámi history and culture is through the hands.

Preserving language, particularly specific terminology for materials and techniques, is another goal of *duojárs* who teach. Ann Solveig Nystad in Karasjok has been one of only a handful of artisans who weave a particular type of belt for both women and men, a *láhppeboagán,* using a rigid heddle loom. In 2020 the Sámi Museum in Karasjok asked Nystad to make detailed descriptions of the belts currently in the collection and engaged her as a teacher. The patterns of imagery in the belt correspond to traditional Sámi worldviews, and there are about thirty unique words connected with the weaving materials and tools. When Nystad and others who know this technique teach, they are passing on not only a skill but a whole vocabulary that could be lost if not renewed and shared. Education in *duodji* that pairs handiwork with language is becoming increasingly common, sometimes within the structure of a "living museum" and sometimes in more informal workshops.[14]

Eeva-Kristiina Harlin is a Finnish scholar whose research and activism focus on the repatriation of material Sámi heritage. Outi Pieski is a Sámi artist born in Finland who works across borders, in various mediums—metal, textiles, and canvas—that combine *duodji* and contemporary art. A few years back Harlin and Pieski began to collaborate on a project centered around the *ládjogahpir,* the horn hat once widely worn by Sámi women across the High North (Plate 9). This form of female headgear—a cloth bonnet, fitted closely around the face, with a dramatic padded horn worn to the back of the head, stuffed with down stretched over a wooden frame *(fierra)*—was in use up until the last decades of the nineteenth century in Finnmark. The French traveler Leonie d'Aunet, who accompanied the La Recherche Expedition in 1838–39 with her artist husband and wrote a book about her experiences, described the hat as giving Sámi women an Athena-like military look. Like the Four Winds cap often worn by Sámi men past and present, the horn hat seems to harken back to medieval times.

The Læstadian revival put an end to its wearing. "The Awakened" were instructed to dress modestly, and many a horn hat and its wooden frame were tossed on the fire after the religious movement took hold in Finnmark. Some claimed that the Devil hid in the horn. It may have also been that the helmet-like hat just wasn't very convenient to wear. Whatever the reason, only about sixty of the horn hats survive. Some of the cloth bonnets and the wooden frames became northern curiosities, which can now be found in the collections of the Museum of European Cultures in Berlin and the Pitt Rivers Museum in Oxford. But a few made their way, via collectors like Hugo Samzelius, who gathered several on his Arctic Lapland Expedition of 1891, or the Norwegian merchant Christian Fandrem, to museums in Stockholm, Helsinki, Bergen, and Oslo.

Over the past few years, the horn hat has become a valued object as part of the Bååstede project and the process of reclaiming and exploring heritage. In Norway, Sámi *duojár* Heidi Persen wrote her master's thesis, "In Our Foremothers' Footsteps," on the horn hat and its place in Sea Sámi culture. In the process, Persen, who lives in her home area of Porsanger and in Alta, created examples of the *ládjogahpir* and the *fierra* in different materials, which have been displayed in exhibitions in northern museums in the past few years.[15] Eva Dagny Johansen is a curator and lecturer at Alta Museum, in Alta, the main city of Western Finnmark. Johansen, with Sea Sámi heritage, is working on a doctoral dissertation based on interviews and collaboration with local Sámi people regarding artifacts in their storerooms. She wrote me:

> It is exciting to see how local knowledge can contribute to the museum's practice and work and how we all learn in this process. For example, a small net needle, *geahpa,* offers the opportunity to explore issues of fishing policy, and a bonnet horn, *ládjofierra,* illuminates the missionaries' view of Sámi culture and belief, and the myths of why the horn-hat stopped being worn. The horn-hat has also been the inspiration for copies. Now it is made and used again by local women. Additionally, we experience how collaborative work contributes to more information about the objects that are already found in the museum storerooms, and contributes so positively to the local museum's management of Sea Sámi objects.[16]

A similar form of collaborative remaking of heritage was spearheaded in northern Norway and Finland by Eeva-Kristiina Harlin and Outi Pieski. One of the hats in the collection of the National Museum of Finland in Helsinki turned out to have belonged to a foremother of Pieski, a wealthy reindeer herder named Golle-Gáddjá from the village of Utsjoki, on the border of Norway and Finland. Using this particular hat as a model, Harlin and Pieski researched it, deconstructed it, and began to hold workshops with Sámi women on how to make both the *fierra*

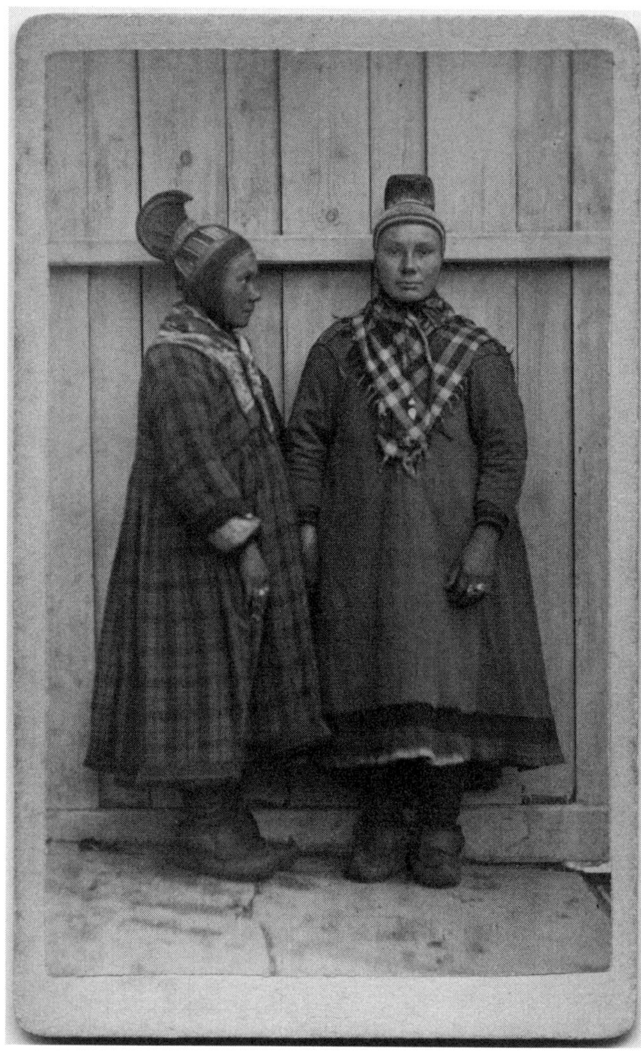

Two Sámi women wear the *ládjogahpir.* Carte de visite, circa 1870s. Photograph copyright Pitt Rivers Museum, University of Oxford, 1941.8.41.

structure and the cloth bonnet that covered it. In the process, they developed an interest in both the hat's ties to earlier matriarchal beliefs and its practices in Sámi history.

Harlin, who has helped compile a digital inventory of the locations of thousands of Sámi artifacts, was able, with Pieski, to trace the history of "the strong-willed matriarch" Golle-Gáddjá. In 1902 the hat and its wooden frame, the *fierra,* were sold to a Russian archeologist, Theodor Schvindt, by Golle-Gáddjá's son and daughter and eventually became part of the Sámi collection at the National

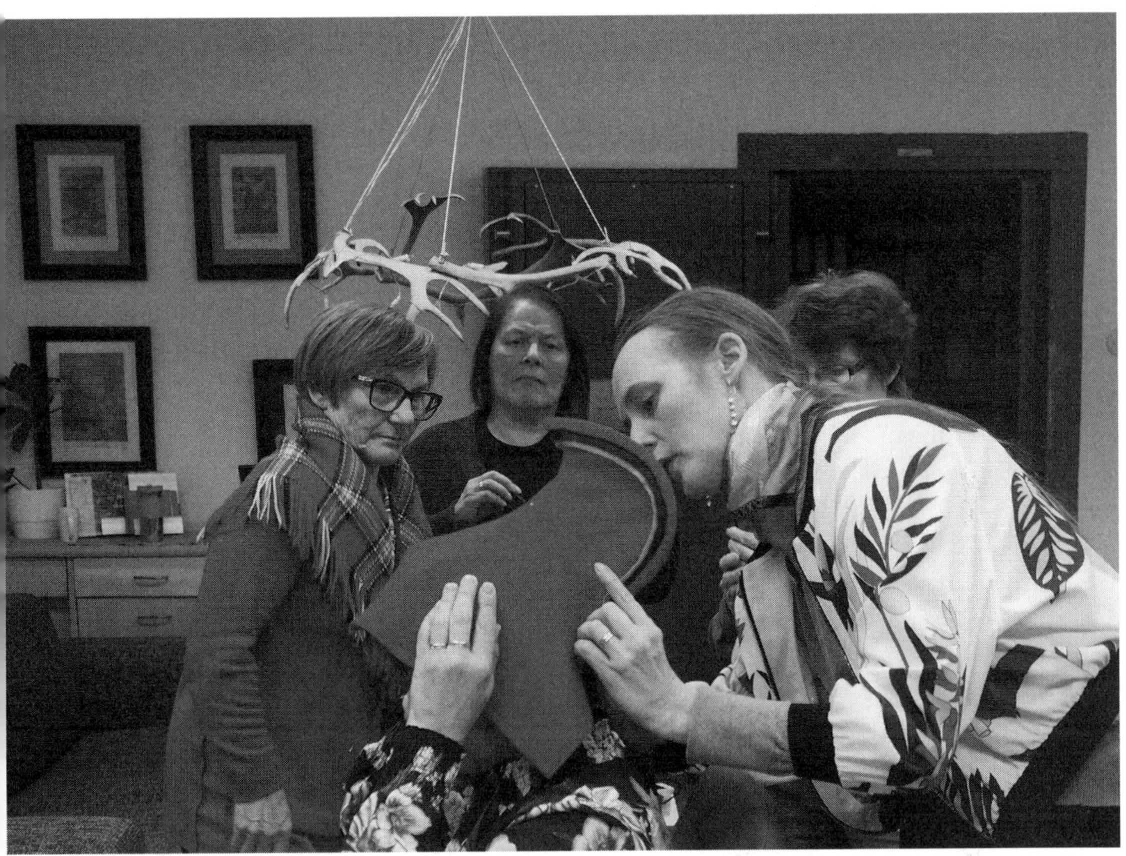

Anne-Bergitte Henriksen and Vivian Johnsen observe how a *ládjogahpir* is fitted to the wearer's head by Outi Pieski during a workshop at Deanu šaldi (Tana bru), Norway, in 2018. Photograph by Eeva-Kristiina Harlin. Courtesy of Outi Pieski.

Museum of Finland, where it was exhibited continuously for decades. For Harlin and Pieski, the *ládjogahpir*'s return to Sápmi is more than simply part of a transfer of property from a national museum to a Sámi museum:

> Repatriation means restoring artefact collections from museums and other institutes to source communities. But it can also mean returning knowledge, so that the knowledge connected to the artefacts is retrieved to the community, by getting to know the production method and the materials of the artefacts in museum collections or the history behind the objects. Repatriation aims to transfer control of the cultural heritage to the source community. By

> exploring the history of collections, their origins, and by sharing this information with the community [*sic*] can, at best, enable objects to be actively involved in empowering and healing processes. A process where numbered objects revert to cultural belongings. These belongings carry the knowledge of the ancestors, they are the database, the language that opens to the descendants and they carry and evoke emotions at both a private and collective level. Like the *ládjogahpir,* the heritage within the objects breaks away from the museum vitrines and flows into the source community to create new meanings in addition to the old ones, thus undergoing a process of rematriation.[17]

In a beautifully designed book that Harlin and Pieski published in 2020 are photographs of the fifty-seven known historic *ládjogahpirs,* most of them in museums in southern Scandinavia and Europe but some repatriated to Sámi museums in Finnmark. But the book also includes photographs of horned hats newly created by Sámi women who participated in the workshops held in three different venues in North Sápmi. The many historic black-and-white photographs of Sámi women wearing this headgear are joined by photographs of contemporary Sámi women in the process of cutting, shaping, and modeling the frames and hats. As Outi Pieski worked with each group, the women talked, laughed, and remembered. It was joyful and sometimes emotional work with hands and hearts.

Eeva-Kristiina Harlin also interviewed many of the women on audio. Later she and Pieski wrote, "The rehabilitation of lost elements of heritage is not an easy process. Collective work helps in this, as well [as] in terms of healing, which for Indigenous societies is an essential part of survival and flourishing." They also noted the challenges inherent in recreating *duodji* based on "lost artefacts. The original symbolism and meaning of the *ládjogahpir,* including the messages its use communicated, is mostly lost and our thoughts on this are speculations."[18]

Equally as important as the book and an exhibit that came from the collective efforts of Harlin, Pieski, and several dozen women *duojárs* was the fact that elsewhere in Sápmi, in Varanger, Tana, and Alta, for instance, women began to pass on the knowledge of how to make the hats and to wear them again. Sometimes their foremothers had worn them, but sometimes it was a new undertaking for Sámi women. The hats are not small, not shy. They are graceful in their shape and colorful in their cloth and embellishments. They are also dramatic and highly visible, especially out of a vitrine and as part of life again.

The ways that Sápmi is represented in museums abroad, with rare exceptions like the MAA in Cambridge, tend to be frozen in time and space. Often the objects are not displayed at all, but when they are it's in a context far from informative and often actively exotic. The objects are historical, some from the seventeenth century and many from the era of museum formation from the late nineteenth century through the first decades of the twentieth century. Most were gathered from wonder and curiosity, or from the ethnographic mission of salvaging remnants of a disappearing culture, or of backing up notions of racial development by collecting so-called primitive artifacts. Like many Indigenous people, the Sámi were and are exhibited in the ethnographic present—which often means they are hardly present at all, except as sorcerers of the North with their magic drums or as nomads crossing the frozen wastes in reindeer caravans. Rarely do the museums include the stories of how the Sámi objects arrived at the museum or make the collecting process and early collectors an integral aspect of the history. This is not always the fault of past curators, who worked with what they had, but it shows a lack of curiosity on the part of present-day curators who have access to new databases and scholarly historical research.

Increasingly in the Nordic countries themselves, however, we can find a multiplicity of styles and methods of collecting and displaying Sápmi, most of which now go beyond older debates about what belongs where in geographic terms. To see some of these complex and contradictory modes of representing Sápmi past and present, we only have to consider several venues in Karasjok, a small town of only twenty-six hundred people, far from the national urban hubs. Yet the town is also an administrative center where the Sámi Parliament is located and only a two-hour drive west of Inari, the seat of the Finnish Sámi Parliament and home of a major museum, Siida. In Karasjok, within walking distance, is the Sámi Museum, Sámiid Vuorká-Dávvirat, and nearby is Sámi Dáiddamagasiidna, the storage rooms of the Sámi Art Collections; a tourist attraction called Sápmi Park; and a cutting-edge art gallery, Sámi Dáiddaguovddáš (Sámi Center for Contemporary Art, or SDG), featuring Sámi art and craft.

Collecting for the Sámi Museum in Karasjok began sometime in the 1930s and was undertaken largely by local people for their community. The collection was made up of donations and housed in a wooden building that was one of many structures burned by the Germans as they retreated through Finnmark in 1945. After the war, collecting resumed, and a large new building opened in 1979. The Sámi Museum and its storerooms hold more than five thousand objects and include over a thousand works by Sápmi's leading artists and artisans. The displays in the main hall are staid and representational, with dioramas and clothed mannequins, but they do a decent job of introducing the history and traditional culture of North Sápmi to visitors. In one vitrine is a replica of Anders

Poulsen's drum, the one seized by the Danish authorities after his trial and death in 1681 (the original is kept in controlled conditions behind the scenes). The Sámi Museum was a milestone in Sámi community strengthening and political activism. Long before the permanent exhibits were in place in the 1980s, the building was in constant use as a space for classes, meetings, and events. It was, as Ole Henrik Magga, the first president of the Sámi Parliament, has said, "the first location where Sámi people didn't have to 'bow and scrape.'"[19]

A five-minute walk from the Sámi Museum, the ceremonial drum is presented in a different, more mystical light in Sápmi Park, a commercial venture cosponsored by the Scandic hotel chain, with a large gift shop, café, and restaurant. Clearly created for tourists, it offers opportunities to throw lassos and to learn to joik. A "reindeer feeding experience" is an extra eight dollars. Visitors can also take in a multimedia visual experience in the Magic Theatre: described as "located literally near the end of the Earth . . . the Sápmi Magic Theatre open[s] a unique window into the ancient mythologies of the reindeer herding people known as the Sámi. In this 30 minute digitally produced show featuring the Northern Lights, a blazing camp fire, tents, white reindeer, with joiking in the background, visitors are encouraged to experience Sápmi through their hearts, via the voice-over from an old Shaman."[20] And lest anyone believe that the invocation of the old Arctic magic is merely a tourist trap at Sápmi Park, the respected Norwegian academic Trude Fonneland could tell you differently. Her ethnographic research on "neo-shamanism" and its rise in Norway in the past decades, involving both Sámi and Norwegian practitioners, offers a view of many of the old rituals re-enlivened for modern seekers, many of whom now own and employ sacred drums.[21]

The Sámi Center for Contemporary Art in Karasjok has been in existence since 1986, but in recent years it has played an increasingly important role in curating retrospectives, organizing seminars, and sustaining artists' careers all over Sápmi. A number of shows organized by SDG also go on tour both in Sápmi and elsewhere in Norway, for instance, a thirty-year retrospective of the work of Rose-Marie Huuva, the Swedish Sámi poet and artist whose work with textiles and natural materials ranges from intimate pieces to large installations. Exhibits at SDG in 2020 included *Sustainable and Lively Root Works,* a display of basketry by well-known past masters of basketry, especially the two Kitok sisters, and newer practitioners of the craft. The exhibit on *ládjogahpir,* arranged by Eeva-Kristiina Harlin and Outi Pieski, took place at SDG, along with a seminar on the political and cultural task of "rematriation," a term increasingly defined as a form of reclaiming ancestral knowledge and spirituality, beyond acts of repatriating objects, and used by Finnish Sámi scholar Rauna Kuokkanen in her work on Indigenous self-determination and governance. Kuokkanen and others see rematriation as a way of bringing traditional women's voices and practices back to the forefront in Sápmi.

The making and using of new vocabulary is part of the artistic practice for many Sámi artists, writers, and scholars. Sometimes the language chosen is English, to bypass Norwegian, Swedish, or Finnish altogether and to connect more readily with an international audience. Increasingly, the vocabulary comes from one of the Sámi languages, as in the use of the word *dalvedh* from South Sámi, for a long-running art and research project initiated by Norwegian–Sámi artist and filmmaker Sissel M. Bergh, with the collaboration of the musician Frode Fjellheim and a variety of historians, archeologists, and other Sámi scholars. *Dalvedh* is a verb meaning "to appear again, after a long absence." Bergh's project, combining installations, photographs, objects in cases, and video and supported by text that explores the history, language, and disappearances of the South Sámi people, began to be exhibited in regional museums and galleries around Norway in 2014. Bergh's intention with the exhibit and the documentary-art film titled *Dalvedh*, along with talks and panels in different communities, was to connect "Indigenous and academic knowledges through the poetic and the sensuous to create a space for reflection around the writing of history and its activation into the present."[22] The artistic-historical Dalvedh project has an explicitly political perspective. Unlike the exhibit originally at NTNU, *Who Owns the Story?*, the Dalvedh project is firmly rooted in a worldview in which Sápmi engages with conventional Nordic history and transcends it. The issues posed go beyond how to make Sámi presence visible in that history, beyond the problem of who owns what. How Sápmi can be recollected and reimagined by the Sámi themselves is at the forefront of art making and exhibiting in contemporary practice.

Beyond Karasjok, contemporary art from Sápmi has begun to make an international impact. Along with Sissel Bergh, artists such as Anders Sunna from Jokkmokk and Máret Ánne Sara from Kautokeino, with degrees from art colleges in Scandinavia and abroad, are explicitly confrontational in their work, which often references environmental degradation and the continued colonization and exploitation of Sápmi. Anders Sunna, a prolific painter, muralist, and multimedia artist, is as outspoken about the class conflict long fostered by the Swedish government between the reindeer-owning Sámi and those who lost their reindeer as he is about making art in Sápmi: "I was looking for inspiration beyond Sámi art while making sure I stayed true to my historical background. If you don't dare to look outside—always with Sámi eyes, of course—there is no development. Sámi culture is no exhibit in a museum. We are a living people, and our culture needs to be alive, develop, and change."[23] Máret Ánne Sara, who studied in the United Kingdom and is also a lauded fantasy writer for young adults, makes provocative installations, such as *Pile o' Sápmi,* which consists in part of a curtain made from reindeer skulls and metal wire. Sara's intention is to shock and to protest the forced slaughter of reindeer herds in northern Norway.

Both these artists, together with Pauliina Feodoroff, a Skolt Sámi from the Finnish and Russian parts of Sápmi, represented Sápmi at the Venice Biennale in 2022. For the event, the Nordic Pavilion became the Sámi Pavilion. It was the first time the Nordic Pavilion was represented solely by Sámi artists. One of the lead commissioners of the pavilion was Katya Garcia-Antón, the director of the Office for Contemporary Art Norway (OCA). In 2017 the OCA put on a far-reaching exhibit in Oslo of Sámi artists, *Let the River Flow,* which included the work of those with long careers as artists, like Synnøve Persen, as well as newcomers. Garcia-Antón has been an outspoken advocate for not just including a few pieces of Sámi art but also actively encouraging Sámi artists to interrogate Scandinavian society.[24] It's a truism to say that artists often are ahead of political change. In Sápmi, it does seem, however, that in spite of the obstacles that the Nordic states have created and continue to create for Sámi self-government and serious consultation, artists are able to articulate frustration and anger and to explore the complexities of contemporary Sámi life, in forms that resonate with regional and international audiences.

Sámi artists, like all Sámi people, live in the modern world, and their lives reflect comforts and certainties unknown to ancestors. At the same time many search for ways, in their art and social life, to reconnect with and stay connected with traditional perspectives and memories. Hyperlocal and yet nomadic in the sense of freely moving over difficult, sometimes inhospitable terrain, in a landscape not familiar to many in Scandinavia, Sámi artists simultaneously challenge stereotypes and reaffirm Sámi identity, while creating works that are influenced by modern art currents.

In 2016 the Art Ii Biennial, which hosts site-specific artworks by international artists in the town center and environmental art park of Ii, Finland, on the Gulf of Bothnia, chose eight Sámi artists and/or *duojárs* to participate in a project titled the Poetics of Material. The thematic intent was to look at environmental art and the use of natural materials. Working in collaboration, Outi Pieski and Jenni Laiti created tall walking sticks from tree branches, ornamented with antler, bone, cloth, and metal, which they placed in a "borderless fence" in the birch and shrub landscape near the Iijoki River (Plate 18). They titled their work *Ovdavázzit/ Forewalkers* to recognize and honor the Sámi ancestors. The *ovdavázzit* echo the way past walkers decorated their personal staffs; some of the materials, such as copper and colorful yarn, point to the fact that the Sámi also used material from other cultures.

Like Outi Pieski, Jenni Laiti was born in Finland. She studied *duodji* and Sámi culture at Umeå University in Sweden. She describes her work as "a mixture of cultural intervention, installations, and performative direct action, dealing with colonialism, decolonialism, climate justice, and the Sámi people's rights to their own culture and land."[25] *Ovdavázzit/Forewalkers* is a simple, beautiful, and powerful installation that recalls the many centuries when Sápmi wasn't divided into separate states and the Sámi moved freely through accustomed landscapes. These landscapes, as Pieski says, were not a wilderness up in the North but a cultural environment.[26] The details of the walking sticks suggest artisanal techniques and materials employed in new ways to provoke memory and emotion at the same time they make a political statement about shifting borders and claiming territories.

The Nordic Museum was built to last. Until recently the vast stone castle has had only one public entrance, up wide, steep stone steps to an imposing set of heavy oak doors. The entrance leads into a foyer on the second floor, with a ticket booth, behind which you can see a giant, seated stone statue of King Gustav Vasa overlooking the Great Hall. But in 2020 the museum broke through the stone to the ground floor on the opposite side of the building. This facade looks toward the inland waterways with boats and ferries and the royal palace. The new ground-floor opening has a different style and feel; it was designed by architect Lone-Pia Bach, with an entrance created by artist Outi Pieski. Pieski was invited into the Sámi collections to look through the ethnographica in order to create the idea that was eventually chosen for the entrance. Selecting an etched horn spoon from South Sápmi as inspiration, she created an airy metal installation titled *Two Directions* that shapes and encloses the new doorway. The ceiling of her installation is based on the braided design of the spoon, carved by Pål Zakrisson from Jämtland around 1862. Outside the building, for the first time, are seating areas under newly planted linden trees and a café created from a small brick building once used to disinfect the many items destined for the collections.

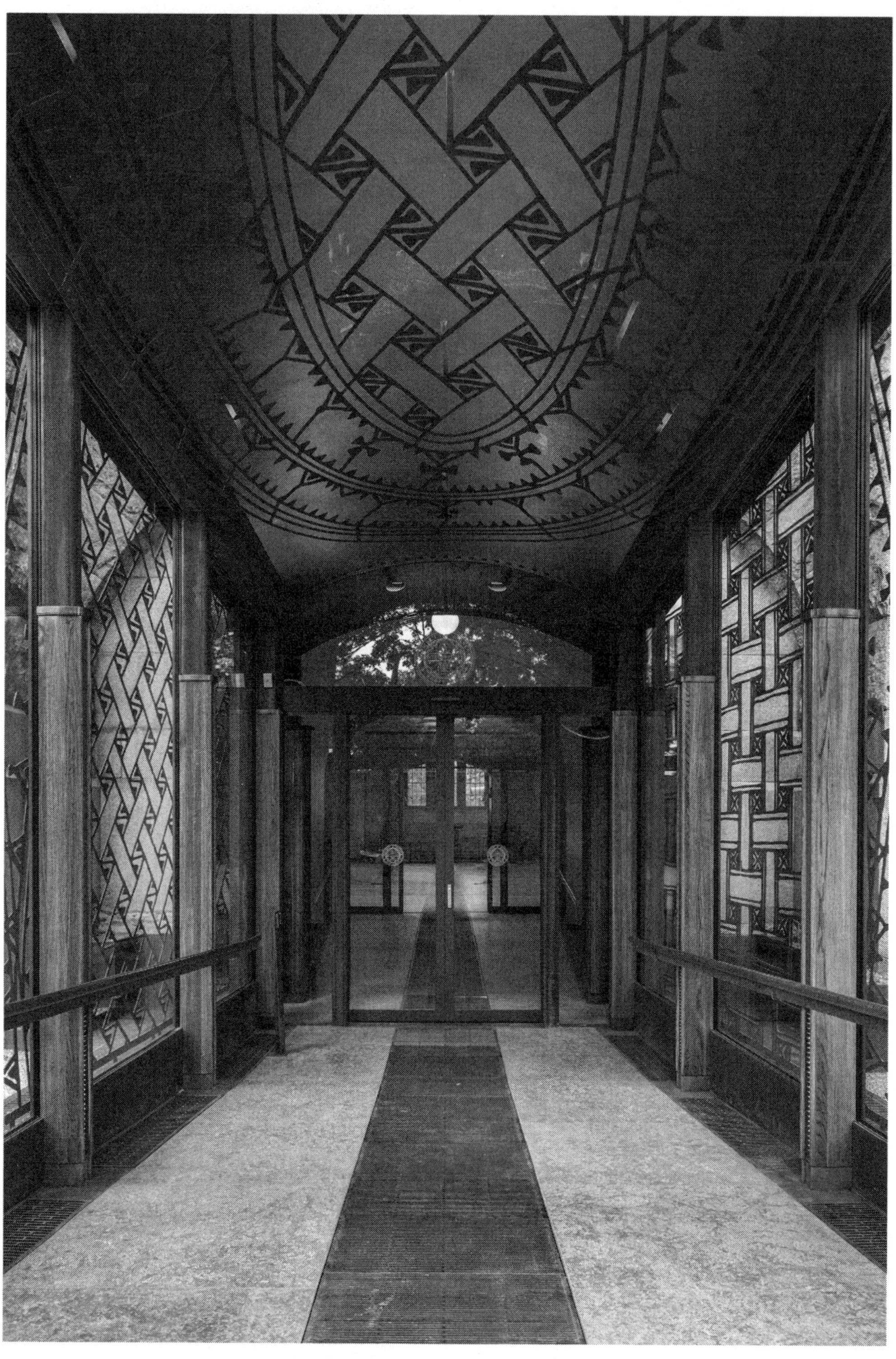

Outi Pieski, *Guektien bïegkese—Guovtte biggii—Two Directions,* 2020 (detail). The new entrance to the water side of the Nordic Museum in Stockholm. Photograph by Helena Bonnevier, Nordic Museum. Courtesy of the artist.

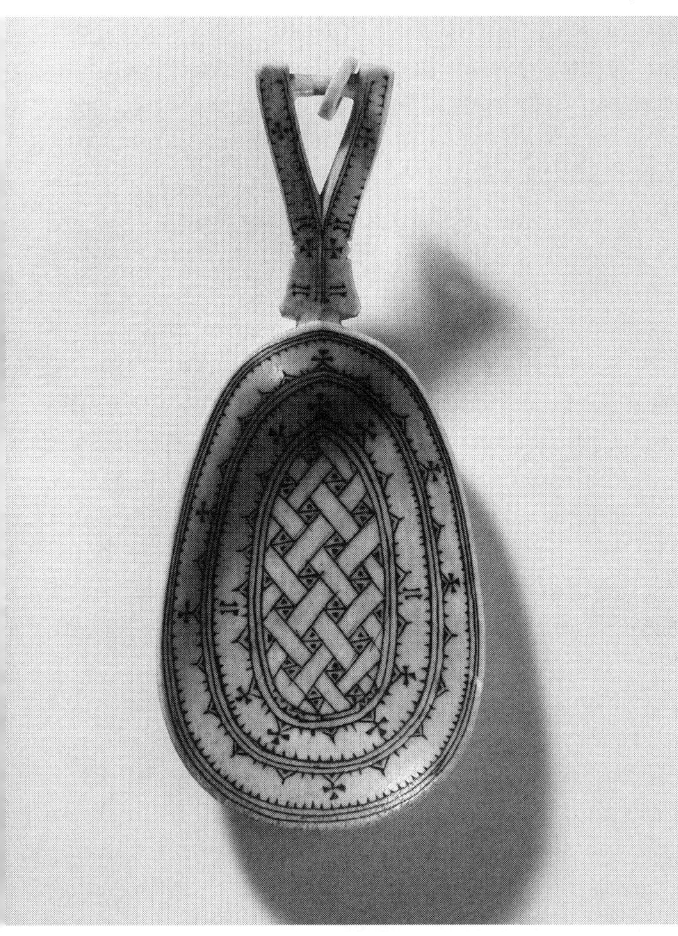

Spoon carved from moose antler by Pål Zakrisson from Jämtland, Sweden, and donated in 1933. Photograph by Bertil Wreting. Courtesy of the Nordic Museum, Stockholm.

I've been to the Nordic Museum many times over the decades, initially as a visitor to Stockholm in the 1980s and many years later to meet with curators, to study in the archives, and once, in 2014, to give a lecture on Emilie Demant Hatt's work in conjunction with a small exhibit of her paintings from the collection. The first time I deliberately came to look at the Sámi objects on display was in 2002, after spending three winter months mostly in Sápmi, traveling around the north of Norway, Sweden, and Finland. The glass vitrines and dioramas were in the old ground-floor rooms of the museum then. It was the basic exhibit, *Samer,* from 1981, quiet and incurious. *These are the Sámi; this is how it was, and how it still is.*

I knew by then that wasn't the whole truth: During my several months of traveling that winter, I'd visited other museums with different takes on Sápmi.

Tromsø Museum still had its older cases and dioramas of tents and reindeer, but it also had a new exhibit across the hall, *Sápmi: Becoming a Nation,* which had been part of my awakening to the political forces of Norwegianization. With photographs and posters, the exhibit gave me an important history lesson and a way of understanding some of what I'd seen and heard from Sámi people during my travels. Inari, with its modern museum, Siida, focusing on the natural history of Sápmi and the lives of the Inari (Aanaar) Sámi around Lake Inari, was another important stop. Two weeks after my first visit to Siida, I flew back north from Helsinki to attend Skábmagovat, the Indigenous People's Film Festival. Every year this film festival pairs the work of Indigenous filmmakers from around the globe with Sámi-directed films for three days; showings are held in the auditorium and outside on a screen made of ice. Here was a museum that was also a vital cultural center for Sámi in the local community and elsewhere in Sápmi, as well as a place where interested outsiders like myself could begin to understand something very different about Sápmi than the stereotypes prevalent elsewhere. Important too was the fact that at the film festival other Indigenous people's lives and art were showcased, proving the point that the Sámi are not and have never been as isolated as they are often made out to be.

One year, in 2008, I returned to Stockholm to work in the Nordic Museum archives and found the new exhibit, *Sápmi,* taking up quarters and questions on the fourth floor of the museum. The new experience was completely different than visiting the staid vitrines of the old exhibit. I was encouraged to think, to ask, to disagree, and to want to know more. Over the past dozen years, several major museums in the Nordic countries have become venues for new discussions, where researchers look at collections with new eyes and write scholarly articles on colonization and representation. Museums can be stodgy and old-fashioned; they can also be renewed and reimagined, as places of continuing curiosity and wonder, as arenas of encounters and understanding.

Not every object that originated in Sápmi can be returned to Sápmi, nor perhaps should it be returned. As Nicholas Thomas has noted, when a major museum keeps all or part of its ethnographic collections, there is incentive for cooperation—incentive that would be lost if everything were repatriated. There are obvious flaws in this argument—a museum could also choose not to display the Sámi objects it houses or not to make the objects in storage easily available for Indigenous scholars and artisans to study. The museum could display the work in a manner that is uninformed or disrespectful. But, as in the case of the Nordic Museum's new entrance with a Sámi motif taken from its holdings, chosen by a Sámi artist and used as the basis for new technology, we can glimpse shifts in how even rock-hard institutions can blast open a new doorway.

Projects like Bååstede, which make possible the physical return of material culture to museums in the source communities, are crucial for many reasons, but perhaps "the Return" can be thought of as a two-way street. The Sámi have often been invisible to the larger public in the Nordic countries, but they have always been there, and not only living in core regions of Sápmi as fishers, herders, and farmers but also thriving in larger cities as students, workers, and creators. The writer Mattias Aikio lived in Oslo, as did the artist John Savio. The activist Elsa Laula studied in Stockholm, as did the journalist Torkel Tomasson. Israel Ruong was a professor in Uppsala. Frode Fjellheim composes and teaches in Trondheim. Any number of Sámi musicians, artists, and writers live, teach, and work full-time or part-time in Oslo, Trondheim, Tromsø, Stockholm, Kiruna, Helsinki, and Rovaniemi, as well as travel frequently abroad. Creators and artisans are as vital to Sámi life as they have always been. That they are seen now in ways that they were not before is an important part of this story of "the Return." While political resistance and moral acknowledgment and reconciliation play a role in the resurgence of Sámi visibility and agency in the Nordic countries and on the world stage, the fact is that the Sámi people never disappeared. They have remained. They've continued to make objects, tell stories, travel through new and traditional homelands, celebrate, pray, and joik landscape, animals, weather, and loved ones.

Dalvedh is a verb often used as a noun, meaning "what has long been missing, until it appears again." Historical and contemporary literature about objects that were collected from Sápmi as curiosities to be marveled at includes stories not only of appropriations but of collaborations, not only of loss but of reclaiming, repatriation, and rematriation. It's true that objects disappeared and were destroyed, but some were saved and have reappeared in hundreds of forms. Many more objects have been remade as *duodji* and reimagined as *dáidda*.

These objects to be marveled at are still being created, just like Sápmi itself.

Acknowledgments

From Lapland to Sápmi rests on a foundation of research undertaken by many writers and scholars, both Indigenous and non-Indigenous, over many decades. Of greatest importance to my understanding of the subjects in this book has been the traditional knowledge and the lived experience of Sámi educators, curators, scholars, artists, and artisans, from whom I have learned much and continue to learn. *Ollu giitu.*

This book began to take shape some years ago while I was working on a biography of Emilie Demant Hatt and often visiting archives and museums in the Nordic countries. I have particularly benefited from the generosity and expertise of Eva Silvén, formerly of the Nordic Museum in Stockholm, who has written about Ernst Manker and about Sámi exhibitions in a museum setting; Eva has long been a good friend and an inspiring colleague, sharing her own work, reading mine, and putting me in touch with other researchers and curators. I was fortunate to have already visited many of the museums I describe here, in Norway, Sweden, Finland, Denmark, and the United Kingdom, before the pandemic arrived and made further travel from the United States impossible. Much of my research then had to be completed through books and correspondence. I can't thank sufficiently the many scholars, librarians, archivists, and curators who kindly answered questions and sent copies of material I needed.

Many thanks to Inge Damm of the Ethnographic Collection at the National Museum of Denmark for making copies of the detailed registers of Demant Hatt's donations of Sámi material culture to the museum and for later reading and commenting on the chapter about Demant Hatt and Johan Turi. Gratitude to Dan Lundberg, head archivist of the Musikverket in Stockholm, and Gunnar Ternhag, musicologist and author of a book about Karl Tirén, for reading a draft of the chapter on Tirén and Maria Persson and for answering multiple rounds of questions. Composer Frode Fjellheim also read the last version of that chapter, and I appreciate his comments. I was fortunate that Mattias Backström, author of an article on Hugo Samzelius, had some of his primary sources on hand and generously sent copies of nineteenth-century newspaper clippings. Tom G. Svensson, author of a study on Asa Kitok and her daughters, added details of his encounters with this remarkable family. For pointing me in fruitful directions, I also thank Gunlög Fur from Linköping University; Robert Pohjanen of Norrbottens Museum in Luleå; Jonas Monié Nordin from the Swedish Historical Museum; and Krister Stoor of Umeå University. I'm grateful to Ryös Antikvariat in Stockholm, which managed to get me difficult-to-find books in a timely way.

Praise to the scholars Ellen Alm in Trondheim and Rune Blix Hagen in Tromsø, both of whom study and write about *gand,* sorcery, and Sámi trials of the seventeenth century, and to Håkan Rydving, a scholar of religion, whose work on seventeenth-century drums in Sápmi has been crucial. In Tromsø I also thank Hanne Horsberg Hansen, an art historian, and Ivar Bjørklund, one of the editors of the recently published memoirs of Anders Bær and Lars Hætta. Thanks also to Pål Friis, who shared with me his work on Lars Hætta and J. A. Friis. Cathrine Baglo's impressive scholarship on living exhibitions of Sámi and their material possessions has been invaluable. I also benefited greatly from the research of Silje Opdahl Mathisen, both in her studies of Sámi museums in Norway and Sweden and in her work on the first ethnographic collections in Oslo. Trude Fonneland of the University of the Arctic in Tromsø, one of my reviewers, offered extensive and illuminating feedback on the initial proposal and a late draft. I also wish to acknowledge the important work being done in Finland by Eeva-Kristiina Harlin, Outi Pieski, and Rauna Kuokkanen. These three scholars and artists are at the forefront of exciting new developments in politics and art in Sápmi and Finland. I also benefited from correspondence at the National Museum of Finland with Eero Ehanti and Raila Kataja.

When it came to interviewing people for the last chapters on contemporary practices around exhibits and repatriation in Norway and Sweden, I am grateful to the staff at various museums in Norway: Eva Dagny Johansen in Alta, Ingvild Marie Bjørnå Pettersen in Varanger, Camilla Carlson in Kirkenes, Jenny Fjellheim in Røros, and Birgitte Skar and Randi Haugen at NTNU in Trondheim. I would particularly like to thank Johan Aslak Hætta, director of the Kautokeino Municipal Museum in Norway, for our Zoom conversation about Lars Hætta, and Mikael Jakobsson, curator of the Sámi collections at the Forest and Saami Museum in Lycksele, Sweden, for sharing personal reflections as well as information about the museum collections. Birger Nordin, a collector of Sámi *duodji,* kindly responded to all my questions. I am tremendously grateful to Káren Elle Gaup of the Norwegian Museum of Cultural History for meeting with me in 2016, answering important questions about the Bååstede project in Norway, and reading my chapter on that topic. I also thank Paula Rauhala at the Sámi Museum in

Karasjok, Erik Norberg at Saemien Sitje in Snåsa, and Christina Hætta, head of the Cultural Unit at the Saami Council, for research and language help.

I am responsible for my own interpretations and understandings of what has been shared with me and how I have read and responded to the scholarship of others. Sámi and Nordic museums are continually changing, adapting, and transforming their collections and displays. This is particularly true at the present moment as museums in Scandinavia have been hard at work digitizing their Sámi collections for greater public access and as Sámi museums in Norway have been upgrading their facilities in order to receive repatriated objects through the Bååstede project. This shifting museal landscape has been a challenge to capture at times but always fascinating and inspiring to write about.

For their assistance with illustrations, I thank Juhán Niila Stålka of Sami Duodji in Jokkmokk, Harrieth Aira of Árran Lule Sami Center, and Siv Eli Vuolab at the Sámi Parliament in Karasjok; Paula Rauhala at the Sámi Museum in Karasjok; Ellen Bals at the Kautokeino Municipal Museum; Anne Bryggman Tjikkom and Göran Sjöberg at Ájtte in Jokkmokk; Marie Tornehave at the Nordic Museum; and Staffan Lundmark, curator of the Tirén collection at the Umeå Municipal Museum. Thanks go to Jenni Laiti and Outi Pieski for the use of their artwork.

In the United Kingdom, I was assisted by my correspondence with Rachel Head of the Museum of Archaeology and Anthropology in Cambridge; Faye Belsey at the Pitt Rivers Museum in Oxford; and Judy Rudoe at the British Museum. For their help in my research of Hans Sloane's collections, I greatly thank Louisiane Ferlier of the Reconstructing Sloane project at the Royal Society and Alexandra Ortolja-Baird of Kings College, London.

Closer to home, I so appreciate the support of my good friend Katherine Hanson, who read my first draft and offered valuable comments on Norwegian history and much else. A second early reviewer, Holly Cusack-McVeigh, offered helpful, detailed comments on the original proposal. Librarian Mark D. Kelly at the University of Washington Libraries assisted me in getting material I needed. I also thank members of the Pacific Sámi Searvi in my own homeland, the Pacific Northwest, for their support.

Throughout the pandemic, Scandinavia House in New York and the National Nordic Museum in Seattle have offered multiple online programs, including a Sámi film festival and panels with Sámi writers, artists, and activists. The growing consciousness of Indigenous heritage within Nordic history and contemporary culture is encouraging to see. Through these programs I've continued to learn from Sámi activists, filmmakers, *duojárs,* and writers.

Once again, I've been fortunate to work with copy editor Anne Taylor and the fine staff at the University of Minnesota Press. My editor, Kristian Tvedten, contributed to the book from beginning to end and deserves the warmest thanks for seeing the project through.

Finally, love and gratitude to my friends and above all to my wife, Betsy, for companionship, laughter, and unflagging encouragement.

Notes

Introduction

1. Olaus Magnus, *A Description of the Northern Peoples, 1555,* vol. 1, ed. P. G. Foote (London: Hakluyt Society, 1996), 37.

2. For an overview of Sápmi's history, see Veli-Pekka Lehtola, *The Sámi People: Traditions in Transition* (Fairbanks: University of Alaska Press, 2002). For a contemporary grounding in Sámi political issues in Fennoscandia, see Rauna Kuokkanen, *Restructuring Relations: Indigenous Self-Determination, Governance, and Gender* (Oxford: Oxford University Press, 2019).

3. Nicholas Thomas, *The Return of Curiosity: What Are Museums For?* (London: Reaktion Books, 2016), 122.

Lapponia

1. Olaus Magnus, quoted in Ellen Alm, "So What Is 'Gand' Sorcery—Really?" *Norwegian SciTech News,* March 27, 2018, 4, https://www.norwegianscitechnews.com/2018/03/gand-sorcery-really/.

2. Johan Randulf, quoted in Alm, "So What Is 'Gand' Sorcery." See also Ellen Alm and Rune Blix Hagen, "Sámi Magic and Rituals from Historia Norwegie to Johannes Schefferus, c. 1150–1680," in *What Is North? Imagining the North from Ancient Times to the Present Day,* ed. Oisín Plumb, Alexandra Sanmark, and Donna Heddle (Turnhout, Belgium: Brepols, 2020), 153–73. *Gand* is also explored in Eldar Heide, "Gand, seid, og åndevind" (PhD diss., University of Bergen, Norway, 2006).

3. Johannes Schefferus, *The History of Lapland,* facsimile of the 1674 edition (Stockholm: Rediviva, 1971), 60.

4. Ibid.

5. For in-depth looks at Schefferus and *Lapponia,* see Jonas Nordin and Carl-Gösta Ojala, "Collecting, Connecting, Constructing: Early Modern Commodification and Globalization of Sámi Material Culture," *Journal of Material Culture* 23, no. 1 (2018): 58–82; and Mårten Snickare, "Kontroll, begär och kunskap: Den koloniala kampen om Goavddis," *Rig* 97, no. 2 (2014): 65–77.

6. See Eric Grundhauser, "The Man-Made Gut Stones Once Used to Thwart Assassination Attempts," *Slate,* August 12, 2016, https://slate.com/human-interest/2016/08/goa-stones-were-man-made-bezoars-that-were-said-to-cure-poison.html; Ivana Horacek, "Alchemy of the Gift: Things and Material Transformations at the Court of Rudolf II" (PhD diss., University of British Columbia, 2015).

7. See R. J. W. Evans, *Rudolf II and His World* (London: Thames and Hudson, 1997).

8. See Barbara Sjoholm, "Lapponia," *Harvard Review* 29 (2005): 6–19.

9. The word "shaman" is not found in Sámi languages. It originally came from the Tungus *samán* and entered Russian and European languages in the seventeenth century. Ideas about "Lappish shamans" were spread in Fennoscandia by ethnographers and linguists, such as J. A. Friis, and by the late nineteenth century the term was pervasive. In general, I refer only to *noaidis,* not shamans.

10. See Camilla Mordhorst, *Genstands Fortællinger: Fra Museum Wormianum til de moderne museer* (Copenhagen: Museum Tusculanums Forlag, 2009). This early drum, whose images are faded, is now identified as probably being from Ume Sápmi. With other objects from Ole Worm's collection, it was sold to the Royal Kunstkammer in Copenhagen. In 1849 it was moved to the newly constructed Ethnographic Museum and from there to the National Museum of Denmark. At some stage, its pointer and hammer were lost.

11. Quoted in Alm and Hagen, "Sámi Magic and Rituals," 155.

12. See Linda Andersson Burnett, "Translating Swedish Colonialism: Johannes Schefferus's *Lapponia* in Britain, c. 1674–1800," *Scandinavian Studies* 91, no. 1–2 (2019): 134–62.

13. Nicolas Lundius, quoted in Gunlög Fur, "'But in Itself, the Law Is Only White': Knowledge Claims and Universality in the History of Cultural Encounters," in *Fugitive Knowledge: The Loss and Preservation of Knowledge in Cultural Contact Zones,* ed. Andreas Beer and Gesa Mackenthun (Münster: Waxmann Verlag, 2015), 31.

14. Håkan Rydving, "The Saami Drums and the Religious Encounter in the Seventeenth and Eighteenth Centuries," in *The Saami Shaman Drum,* ed. Tore Ahlbäck and Jan Bergman, *Scripta Instituti Donneriani Aboensis* 14 (1991): 32.

15. Snickare, "Kontroll, begär och kunskap," 70.

16. Edith Seaton, *Literary Relations of England and Scandinavia in the Seventeenth Century* (Oxford: Clarendon Press, 1935), 193n.

17. Magalotti to Schefferus, September 1674, quoted in Juha Pentikäinen, "The Saami Shamanic Drum in Rome," in *Saami Religion,* ed. T. Ahlbäck, *Scripta Instituti Donneriani Aboensis* 12 (1987): 134.

18. Ernst Manker, *Die lappische Zaubertrommel* (Stockholm: Acta Lapponica, Part I, 1938), 750–55. Manker, in cataloging all the remaining drums he found in the 1930s, gave each a number. The drum presented to the Royal Society by Heysig-Ridderstjerna is no. 56. Like other scholars, Manker mentions that this drum could have come from the collections of either Olaf Rudbeck or Johannes Schefferus.

19. *Catalogue of the Royal Society Repository,* 1731, http://ttp.royalsociety.org/ttp/ttp.html?id=a462fb18-54c3-4173-8ce2-67509f3532b7&type=book.

Curiosity Cabinets

1. This account of the witchcraft trials in Finnmark, particularly the imprisonment and trial of Anders Poulsen (also Paulsen) in Vadsø, is shaped by Rune Blix Hagen, "Harmløs dissenter eller djevelsk trollmann? Trolldomsprosessen mot samen Anders Poulson i 1692," *Historisk tidsskrift* 81, no. 2–3 (2002): 319–46. Liv Helene Willumsen, *Witches of the North: Scotland and Finnmark* (Leiden: Brill, 2013), places the Poulsen case in the context of other witch trials in the seventeenth century. Willumsen also discusses how to read Poulsen's language filtered through the colonizing language of official Norwegian.

2. From the court trial, state archives, Tromsø, quoted in Willumsen, *Witches of the North,* 307, 302.

3. Quoted in Hagen, “Harmløs dissenter,” 324.

4. Ernst Manker, *Die lappische Zaubertrommel,* 813–17. Anders Poulsen’s drum (no. 71) was one of six in the National Museum of Denmark, until 2022.

5. Regarding the history of Sámi religion, Håkan Ryding’s monograph, *The End of Drum-Time: Religious Change among the Lule Saami, 1670s–1740s* (Stockholm: Almqvist & Wiksell, 1995), is a key source. Although Rydving writes specifically about Lule Sápmi, his observations about confrontations between Indigenous religion and Christianity apply to most regions in early modern Scandinavia. Gunlög Fur’s article, “Kolonisation och kulturmöten under 1600- och 1700-talen,” in *De historiska relationerna mellan svenska kyrkan och samerna,* ed. Daniel Lindmark and Olle Sundström (Skellefteå, Sweden: Artos & Norma bokförlag, 2016), 241–79, also discusses the cultural encounters between the missionaries and the Sámi.

6. See David King, *Finding Atlantis* (New York: Harmony Books, 2005), for a portrait of Olaf Rudbeck and his times in Uppsala.

7. Ole Worm, quoted in Mordhorst, *Genstands Fortællinger,* 37.

8. General background on Thomas von Westen comes from Rolf Grankvist, “Thomas von Westen,” in *Norsk biografisk leksikon,* online ed. (2009), https://nbl.snl.no/Thomas_Von_Westen; and from Dikka Storm, “A Network of Missionaries and the Establishment of Knowledge: Creating Space,” in *Networks, Interaction and Emerging Identities in Fennoscandia and Beyond,* ed. Charlotte Damm and Janne Saarikivi (Helsinki: Suomalais-Ugrilainen Seura, 2012), 263–83. From Rydving, *The End of Drum-Time,* comes a briefer and more critical assessment of von Westen. Birgitte Jørkov, “Den stærke tromme,” *Siden Saxo* 17, no. 1 (2000): 9–17, tells the story of how von Westen pursued Bendix Andersen and Jon Torchelsen for the drum in 1722–23. Jørkov also follows the fate of the drum through the next centuries.

9. Thomas von Westen, quoted in Fur, “Kolonisation och kulturmöten,” 264.

10. Quoted in Rydving, *The End of Drum-Time,* 36–37.

11. Jørkov, “Den stærke tromme,” 11.

12. Kristoffer Bayer, “University of Copenhagen History: The Fire of 1728,” *Uniavisen,* November 7, 2018, https://uniavisen.dk/en/university-of-copenhagen-history-the-fire-of-1728/.

13. See Mattias Ekman, “The Birth of the Museum in the Nordic Countries: Kunstkammer, Museology and Museography,” *Nordic Museology* 1 (2018): 5–26.

14. “Most of the exhibited Sámi and Siberian objects are from the early 1900s. At this time, the Sámi and Siberian peoples were exposed to the increasing colonization of their territories by the state forces as the industry demanded the region’s natural resources.” Text from exhibition, National Museum of Denmark, https://natmus.dk/historisk-viden/verden/arktis/samer-og-sibiriske-folk/.

15. Manker, *Die lappische Zaubertrommel,* 596–608 (no. 30).

The Magic Drum

1. Carl Linnæus, *The Lapland Journey; Iter Lapponicum 1732,* ed. and trans. Peter Graves (Edinburgh: Lockharton Press, 1995), 135–36.

2. J. P. Kohl, *Hamburgische Berichte von den neuesten Gelehrten Sachen* (1736), quoted in Edgar Reuterskiöld and K.B. Wiklund, “Linnés lappska trolltrumma,” *Fataburen* (1912): 159.

3. Carl Linnæus, *Lachesis Lapponica, or, A Tour in Lapland,* trans. James Smith (London: White and Cochran, 1811).

4. Nellejet Zorgdrager's "Linnæus as Ethnographer of Sámi Culture," *TijdSchrift voor Skandinavistiek* 29, no. 1–2 (2008): 45–76, provides a detailed review of Linnæus's journey through Lapland.

5. Linnæus, *Lapland Journey,* 50.

6. Ibid., 124–25.

7. Ibid., 125, 135.

8. Ibid., 152.

9. Sources on the church assemblies in Sweden in the 1720s when the Sámi drums were confiscated are Rydving, *The End of Drum-Time*; and Anna Westman and John E. Utsi, *Goabdesájgg: Sámij dålusj goabddáj jáhko birra/Drum-Time* (Jokkmokk, Sweden: Ájtte, svenskt fjäll- och samemuseum / Stockholm: Nordiska Museet, 1999), where a description of the assembly in Åsele is given. Information on Anders Nilsson Pont's trial and how the drum might have come into Linnæus's possession come from Bo Lundmark, "An Excursion on Linnæus's Drum from Sorsele," *Scripta Instituti Donneriani Aboensis* 14 (1991): 96–110; and Reuterskiöld and Wiklund, "Linnés lappska trolltrumma." Manker, *Die lappische Zaubertrommel,* 698–706, also gives an account of Pont's trial and the later journeys of the drum (no. 45).

10. Olle Hellström, "Nils Grubb," in *Svenskt biografiskt lexikon.* Riksarkivet, https://sok.riksarkivet.se/sbl/Presentation.aspx?id=13240.

11. Pehr Högström, quoted in Rydving, *The End of Drum-Time,* 86.

12. See Wilfred Blunt, *The Compleat Naturalist: A Life of Linneaus* (New York: Viking Press, 1971).

13. See James Delburgo, *Collecting the World: The Life and Curiosity of Hans Sloane* (London: Allen Lane, 2017).

14. See Adrian Tinniswood, *The Royal Society and the Invention of Modern Science* (New York: Basic Books, 2019).

15. Quoted in Andrea Wulf, *The Brother Gardeners* (New York: Random House, 2008), 58.

16. Delburgo, *Collecting the World,* 265.

17. Kaempfer's life and his collections acquired by Sloane are discussed in Delburgo, *Collecting the World,* 226–29. The drum bought from Kaempfer's estate is listed in Hans Sloane, *Catalogue of Miscellanea,* 111, object no. 1062, https://enlightenmentarchitectures.reconstructingsloane.org/cataloguemiscellanies.

18. The drum in the catalog from "Mr. Grubb, a Swede" is listed in Hans Sloane, *Catalogue of Miscellanea,* 152, object no. 1791, https://enlightenmentarchitectures.reconstructingsloane.org/cataloguemiscellanies.

19. A. Charlotta Adelkrantz, list of objects from Lapland: 7 July, 1736. Swed. and Engl., ff. 271, 272 A- Sloane MS 4054, British Library.

20. Hans Sloane, *Catalogue of Miscellanea,* 152, objects combined in no. 1787, https://enlightenmentarchitectures.reconstructingsloane.org/cataloguemiscellanies.

21. Jacob Serenius, *Dictionarium Suethico-Anglo-Latinum* (Stockholm, 1741).

22. See Pentikäinen, "The Saami Shamanic Drum in Rome," 126, for a mention of Göran

Törnqvist's role in facilitating the exchange between Charles X Gustav and the duke of Tuscany.

23. The British Museum has no record of these two drums in their registry, nor as being deaccessioned at any point.

24. British Museum, online accession note to drum "bequeathed by Sir Hans Sloane," https://www.britishmuseum.org/collection/object/H_Eu-SLMisc-1103.

25. British Museum, online accession note, https://www.britishmuseum.org/collection/object/H_Eu-5263.

26. Manker, *Die lappische Zaubertrommel,* 742–46 (no. 54). Also see MAA, Cambridge, online accession notes, https://collections.maa.cam.ac.uk/objects/457579.

Mr. Bullock's Exhibition of Laplanders

1. See Robert Altick on Bullock's Egyptian Hall and other collections and exhibitions in nineteenth-century England, *The Shows of London* (Cambridge, MA: Belknap Press of Harvard University Press, 1978).

2. William Bullock, *An Account of the Family of Laplanders, Which, with Their Summer and Winter Residences, Domestic Implements, Sledges, Herd of Living Reindeer, and a Panoramic View of the North Cape . . . Are Now Exhibiting at the Egyptian Hall, Piccadilly* (London: Printed for W. Bullock, 1822), 1.

3. Ibid., 2.

4. Arthur de Capell Brooke, *Travels through Sweden, Norway, and Finmark, to the North Cape, in the Summer of 1820* (London: Rodwell and Martin, 1823), 129.

5. See Stein R. Mathisen, "Mr. Bullock's Exhibition of Laplanders," *Ottar* 4 (2007): 11–18; and Cathrine Baglo, *På ville veger: Levende utstillinger av samer i Europa og Amerika* (Stamsund, Norway: Orkana Akademisk, 2017).

6. Carl Hagenbeck, *Beasts and Men, Being Carl Hagenbeck's Experiences for Half a Century among Wild Animals,* abridged trans. by Hugh S. R. Elliot and A. G. Thacker (London: Longmans, Green, 1909), 19.

7. For more on Sámi living exhibitions and reactions in the press, see Barbara Sjoholm, *Black Fox* (Madison: University of Wisconsin Press, 2017), 172–75.

8. Bullock, *An Account,* 35.

9. *Lapland Sketches, or Delineations of the Costume, Habits, and Peculiarities of Jens Holm and His Wife Karina Christian, with Accurate Representations of the Deer, Sledges, Huts, &c. As Exhibited at Bullock's Museum* (London: J. Harris and Son, 1822), 7.

10. Ibid., 6.

A Model Prisoner

1. For descriptions of the Kautokeino Uprising, see Lars Hætta and Anders Bær, *Erindringer: Samiske beretninger om Kautokeino-opprørets bakgrunn, etikk og moral,* ed. Nils Oksal, Johanna Johansen Ijäs, and Ivar Bjørklund (Stamsund, Norway: Orkana Akademisk, 2019); Jack Davy, "Lars Hætta's Miniature World: Sámi Prison Op-art Autoethnography," *Journal of Material Culture* 23, no. 3 (2017): 280–94; Sophus Tromholt, *Under the Rays of the Aurora Borealis,* vol. 2 (London: Low, Marston, Searle & Rivington, 1885).

2. Lars Hætta to J. A. Friis, undated (probably 1856–57), in Pål Friis, ed., *Brevene fra Lars Jakobsen Hætta til Jens Andreas Friis,* trans. Sara Marit Gaup (Guovdageaidnu, Norway: Pål Friis, 2019).

3. For biographical information on Hætta and Friis, see Bjørn Aarseth, "Lars Hætta," and Hans Lindkjølen, "J. A. Friis," in *Norsk biografisk leksikon.* See also Pål Friis, "Lars Jackobsen Hætta og Jens Andreas Friis: 30 års samararbeid for samisk skriftspråk," *Ottar* 5 (2020): 13–24.

4. J. A. Friis, *Lappisk Grammatik* (Christiania: J. W. Cappelen, 1856); *Lappiske sprogprøver. En samling af lappiske eventyr, ordsprog og gaader med ordbog* (Christiania: J. W. Cappelen, 1856).

5. Hætta and Bær, *Erindringer,* 101–2.

6. J. A. Friis, *Ordbog over det lappiske sprog; med latinsk og norsk forklaring samt en oversigt over sprogets grammatik* (Christiania: Dybwad, 1887).

7. See Silje Opdahl Mathisen, "A Record of Ethnographic Objects Procured for the Crystal Palace Exhibition in Sydenham," *Nordic Museology* 3 (2019): 8–24.

8. Robert Latham, *Norway and the Norwegians* (London: Richard Bentley, 1840), 264.

9. Yngvar Nielsen, *Universitetets ethnografiske samlinger 1857–1907: En historisk oversigt over deres tilblivelse, vaekst og udvikling* (Christiania: C. Fabritius & sønner, 1907), 45-46; and Cathrine Baglo, "The Disappearance of the Sea Sámi as a Cultural Display Category," *Nordic Museology* 27, no. 3 (2019): 25-44, https://doi.org/10.5617/nm.7725.

10. Nielsen, *Universitetets ethnografiske samlinger.* See also Magdalena Hillström, "Contested Boundaries: Nation, People and Cultural History Museums in Sweden and Norway, 1862–1909," *Culture Unbound: Journal of Current Cultural Research* 2 (2010): 583–607.

11. Hætta and Bær, *Erindringer,* 83.

12. Tromholt, *Under the Rays,* 85.

13. Ibid.

14. Ibid., 71.

15. See Mona Ringvej, "Tukthus og botsfengsel—fra asken til ilden," Norgeshistorie, University of Oslo, https://www.norgeshistorie.no/bygging-av-stat-og-nasjon/1418-tukthus-og-botsfengse-fra-asken-til-ilden.html.

16. Hætta and Bær, *Erindringer,* 67.

17. Ibid., 53.

18. J. A. Friis, *En sommer i Finmarken, Russisk Lapland og Nordkarelen* (Christiania, Norway: Cammermeyer, 1871).

19. Hætta and Bær, *Erindringer,* 50–51; Friis, *En sommer,* 87–88.

20. J. A. Friis, *Lappisk mytologi, eventyr og folkesagn* (Christiania, Norway: Cammermeyer, 1871).

21. J. A. Friis, *Fra Finmarken. Skildringer* (Christiania, Norway: Cammermeyer, 1881); J. A. Friis, *Lajla: A New Tale of Finmark,* trans. Ingerid Markhus (New York: G. P. Putnam's Sons, 1888).

22. J. A. Friis, *Lajla,* 202.

23. Quoted in Nils Oksal et al., "Introduction," in Hætta and Bær, *Erindringer,* 14n5, 6.

24. "Our History," Horniman Museum and Gardens, https://www.horniman.ac.uk/our-history/.

25. See Davy, "Lars Hætta's Miniature World," for specifics on the models at the Horniman.

26. Smithsonian Museum online catalog text of Hætta model reindeer and sled, https://collections.si.edu/search/detail/edanmdm:nmnhanthropology_8497908?q=Sami+%28Saami%29&record=3&hlterm=Sami%2B%28Saami%29.

27. Maria Doeke Boekraad and Knut Rio, "Kolonitidens lange røtter og den samiske samlingens aktualitet i dag," *Universitetsmuseets årbok* (Bergen: University of Bergen, 2019), 111. The miniatures made by Hætta and sent to the University of Bergen are now on loan to the Sámi Museum in Karasjok.

28. Nielsen, *Universitetets ethnografiske Samlinger,* 36–37.

29. Pitt Rivers Museum online catalog text of model reindeer in harness (1884.1.5), objects.prm.ox.ac.uk/pages/PRMUID124685.html.

Autumn Migration in Lule Lappmark

1. Sources on the von Dübens in Sápmi include Eva Dahlberg, *Lotten von Düben in Lapland* (Sweden: Alfabeta Bokforlag, 1991); and Gustaf von Düben, *Om Lappland och Lapparne, företrädesvis de Svenske* (Stockholm: P. A. Norstedt, 1873).

2. Anders Retzius, craniometry, and racial biology in Scandinavia are discussed in Maja Hagermann, *Käraste Herman* (Stockholm: Norstedts, 2015); and Jon Røyne Kyllingstad, *Measuring the Master Race: Physical Anthropology in Norway, 1890–1945* (Cambridge, UK: Open Book Publishers, 2014).

3. Quoted in Heidi Hansson, "An Arctic Eden: Alexander Hutchinson's *Try Lapland* and the Hospitable North," *Northern Review* 35 (Spring 2012): 147–65.

4. The term "salvage ethnography" is generally attributed to German–American anthropologist Franz Boas and his circle at Columbia University.

5. The stories of how Sámi crania were collected in Sápmi come from Carl-Gösta Ojala, "Sámi Prehistories: The Politics of Archaeology and Identity in Northernmost Europe" (PhD diss., Uppsala University, 2009).

6. Quoted in Ojala, "Sámi Prehistories," 245.

7. Von Düben, *Om Lappland,* iii.

8. See Mats Rehnberg, *The Nordiska Museet and Skansen* (Stockholm: Nordiska Museet, 1957). Eva Silvén explores how Sámi mannequins were displayed in Hazelius's early exhibits in "Staging the Sámi: Narrative and Display at the Nordiska Museet in Stockholm," in *Comparing: National Museums, Territories, Nation-Building and Change,* ed. Andreas Nyblom and Peter Aronsson (Linköping, Sweden: Linköping University Electronic Press, 2008), 311–19; and in "Scener och scenarier," in *För Sápmi i tiden,* ed. Christina Westergren and Eva Silvén (Stockholm: Nordiska Museets Förlag, 2008), 121–37. See also Cathrine Baglo, "Reconstruction as a Trope of Cultural Display," *Nordic Museology,* no. 2 (2015): 49–68; and Silje Opdahl Mathisen, "Still Standing: On the Use of Dioramas and Mannequins in Sámi Exhibitions," *Nordic Museology,* no. 1 (2017): 58–72.

9. Quoted in Ojala, "Sámi Prehistories," 244.

10. Gustaf Von Düben, *Crania Lapponica* (Stockholm: P. A. Norstedt, 1910).

11. Silje Opdahl Mathisen, "Still Standing," speaks of "equipage" to describe the frequent use of a mannequin driving a reindeer in images and models, a subject also explored by Leif Lindin and Ingvar Svanberg, "Ren dragande en ackja," *Västerbotten* 2 (1990): 110–19.

Razzias

1. Hazelius to Samzelius, April 27, 1891, quoted in Eva Silvén's text to the exhibit catalog *Sápmi–om att vara same i Sverige / Sápmi—makkár lea leahkit sápmelaš Ruotas / Sápmi—On Being Sami in Sweden* (Stockholm: Nordiska Museet, 2007), 47.

2. Hugo Samzelius, "Propaganda," *Malmberget* 94, November 27, 1890. Quoted in Mattias Bäckström, "Att skapa lappar: Om en debatt och två expeditioner till lappmarkerna," in *Regionernas bilder: Estetiska uttryck från och om periferin,* ed. Heidi Hansson, Maria Lindgren Leavenworth, and Lennart Pettersson (Umeå: Umeå University, Department of Language Studies, 2010), 84.

3. Quoted in Bäckström, "Att skapa lappar," 82.

4. Hazelius to Samzelius, February 22, 1891, quoted in Cecilia Hammarlund-Larsson, "Skärskådad samling: Samiskt kulturarv i Nordiska museet," in *För Sápmi,* ed. Westergren and Silvén, 91.

5. Ibid.

6. "Forskningsresorna i Lappland," *Vårt Land* 78, April 7, 1891.

7. Nordlund to Hazelius, May 5, 1891, quoted in Silvén, *Sápmi,* 56.

8. Hugo Samzelius, "I de arktiska lappmarkerna," *Stockholms Dagblad,* June 14, 1891.

9. Bäckström, "Att skapa lappar," 84.

10. See Heidi Hanson, "Henriette Kent and the Feminised North," *Nordlit* 22 (2007): 71–96, https://doi.org/10.7557/13.1572.

11. Emilie Demant Hatt, *With the Lapps in the High Mountains: A Woman among the Sámi 1907–1908,* ed. and trans. Barbara Sjoholm (Madison: University of Wisconsin Press, 2013), 148–49.

12. For comparison, see Ruth B. Phillips and Christopher B. Steiner, "Art, Authenticity, and the Baggage of Cultural Encounter," in *Unpacking Culture: Art and Commodity in Colonial and Postcolonial Worlds,* ed. Ruth B. Phillips and Christopher B. Steiner (Berkeley: University of California Press, 1999), 3–19.

13. "The History of Carl Wennberg," Carl Wennberg Kiruna-Sweden, http://www.wennberg.com/gb/content/6-history-of-wennberg.

14. Samzelius, *Stockholms Dagblad,* August 30, 1891.

15. Information on Christian Fandrem and trade in objects in Norway is described in Maria Doeke Boekraad and Knut Rio, "Kolonitidens lange røtter og den Sámiske samlingens aktualitet i dag," in *Universitetsmuseets årbok 2019* (Bergen: University of Bergen, 2019), 102–20, https://www.uib.no/universitetsmuseet/122993/%C3%A5rbokarkivet; and in "Handelsstedet Komagford," WikiStrinda, https://www.strindahistorielag.no/wiki/index.php/Handelsstedet_Komagfjord. The Tromsø Museum is now the Arctic University Museum of Norway.

16. Cedorph Ebeltoft, advertisement, 1894, quoted in Cathrine Baglo, "The Disappearance of the Sea Sámi as a Cultural Display Category," *Nordic Museology* 27, no. 3 (2019): 37, https://doi.org/10.5617/nm.7725.

17. Samzelius, *Stockholms Dagblad,* August 30, 1891.

18. Lilli Zickerman, quoted in Charlotte Hyltén-Cavallius, "Att göra en nation," in *Konsthantverk i Sverige, del 1,* ed. Christina Zetterlund, Charlotte Hyltén-Cavallius, and Johanna Rosenqvist (Botkyrka, Sweden: Mångkulturellt centrum, 2015), 28.

19. See Hillström, "Contested Boundaries."

20. Skansen's Lapp Camp, past and present, is described in Anna-Vera Nylund, "Sameliv på Skansen," in *För Sápmi,* ed. Westergren and Silvén; and Rehnberg, *Nordiska Museet.* The *sieidis* on Sacrifice Isle/Offerholmen are mentioned in "Lappland på Skansen och Djurgården," *Aftonbladet* 192, August 31, 1891. See also Hammarlund-Larsson, "Skärskådad samling," in *För Sápmi,* ed. Westergren and Silvén.

The Lappish Department

1. Ernst Manker, "Svart smike," in *På tredje botten* (Stockholm: LTs förlag, 1967), 163–69.

2. Along with Manker's own autobiographical and other writings, I've relied on biographical research, information, and analysis undertaken and presented by Eva Silvén, who writes from a museological perspective and particularly focuses on Manker's roles at the Nordic Museum. See, in particular, "Ernst Manker 1893–1972," in *Svenska etnologer och folklorister,* ed. Mats Hellspong and Fredrik Skott (Uppsala: Gustav Adolfs Akademien, 2010); "Constructing a Sami Cultural Heritage: Essentialism and Emancipation," *Ethnologia Scandinavica* 44 (2014): 59–74; "Sociomaterial Intertwinements in Sami Research: The Nordiska Museum in Stockholm and the Legacy of Ernst Manker," *Nordic Museology* 3 (2019): 96–117; *Friktion: Ernst Manker, Nordiska museet och det samiska kulturarvet* (Stockholm: Nordic Academic Press, 2021).

3. Ernst Manker, "Uppsala," in *På tredje botten,* 113–14.

4. Edgar Reuterskiöld, *De nordiska lapparnas religion* (Stockholm: Cederquists grafiska aktiebolag, 1912); Reuterskiöld and Wiklund, "Linnés lappska trolltrumma," 129–69.

5. Manker, "Uppsala," 115.

6. Manker's descriptions of the drums were part of every popular overview book on Sámi history and culture he published in his lifetime. Current scholars, such as Håkan Rydving, who have written extensively on the drums, generally dismiss many of Manker's explanations of the symbols.

7. Quoted in Hammarlund-Larsson, "Skärskådad samling," 89.

8. See Hammarlund-Larsson, "Skärskådad samling," and Silvén, *Friktion,* 36. The history of the Lappish Central Museum comes largely from Silvén, *Friktion,* 36–39.

9. Torsten Broberg, "Fint lappgods begärligt för uppköpare," 1934, quoted in Silvén, *Friktion,* 37.

10. Torkel Tomasson, Björn Collinder, and Ernst Manker, 1934, quoted in Silvén, *Friktion.* 37.

11. Elsa Laula, *Infor lif eller död? Sanningsord i de Lappska förhållandena* (Stockholm, 1904).

12. See Siri Broch Johansen, *Elsa Laula Renberg* (Karasjok, Norway: ČálliidLágádus, 2015). Information on Torkel Tomasson and the early decades of *SET* comes from Israel Ruong and Maja Ruong, *Index till samefolkets egen tidning-Samefolket 1918–1973* (Östersund, Sweden: Samefolket, 1985). A substantial account of the first fifty years of Sámi organizing in the twentieth century, including the establishment of *SET* and the media harassment of Elsa Laula, can be found in Patrik Lantto's important cultural history, *Tiden börjar på nytt: En analys av samernas etnopolitiska mobilisering i Sverige 1900–1950* (Umeå: Umeå University, 2000).

13. "Plan för ett lapskt centralmuseum," February 4, 1935, quoted in Silvén, *Friktion,* 37–38.

14. Torsten Broberg, *Social-Democrat,* 1935, quoted in Silvén, *Friktion,* 38.

15. The archivist at Norrbottens Museum in Luleå, Robert Pohjanen, provided me with information on a variety of Swedes in the North who donated to museums in Norrbotten and Västerbotten. Estimated numbers come from digital catalogs for Swedish museums or from curators, since not all objects are registered in the databases. For instance, Västerbottens Museum in Umeå has 1,062 Sámi cultural–historical objects per the museum's object antiquarian, Helena Forsberg (personal communication, March 19, 2021), far more than the registry lists online.

16. H. Hampusson Huldt, *Mönsterbok för lapsk hemslöjd i Västerbottens län* (Hälsingborg, Sweden: Schmidts Boktryckeri AB, 1920).

17. Ernst Manker, *De svenska fjällapparna* (Stockholm: Svenska turistföreningens förlag, 1947). The last chapter of this book was translated into English and formed the major part of Manker's *The Nomadism of the Swedish Mountain Lapps: The Siidas and Their Migratory Routes in 1945* (Stockholm: H. Geber, 1953).

18. Johan Turi, *Muitalus sámiid birra / En bog om lappernes liv,* ed. and trans. Emilie Demant (Stockholm: A.-B. Nordiska Bokhandeln, 1910); new English translation, Thomas A. DuBois, *An Account of the Sámi* (Chicago: Nordic Studies Press, 2011). Johan Turi and Per Turi, *Lappish Texts,* ed. Emilie Demant Hatt, trans. Gudmund Hatt (Copenhagen: Det Kongelige Danske Videnskabernes Selskab, 1918–19).

19. For accounts of the initial meeting and the long relationship between Johan Turi and Emilie Demant Hatt and of Manker's efforts to secure both their archives, see Sjoholm, *Black Fox.* Turi's book, *Muitalus sámiid birra,* is discussed at greater length in the next chapter.

20. Emilie Demant Hatt, *Med lapperne i højfjeldet* (Stockholm: A-B. Nordiska Bokhandeln, 1913); *With the Lapps in the High Mountains: A Woman among the Sami, 1907-1908,* ed. and trans. Barbara Sjoholm (Madison: University of Wisconsin Press, 2013); *Ved ilden: Eventyr og historier fra Lapland* (Copenhagen: J. H. Schultz Forlag, 1922); *By the Fire* (Minneapolis: University of Minnesota Press, 2019).

21. Ernst Manker, "I Johan Turis Marker," in *Viddernas Vandrare* (Stockholm: Folket i Bilds Förlag, 1959), 157.

22. Ibid., 159.

23. Ibid.

Making Histories

1. Ernst Manker, *Boken om Skum* (Stockholm: LTs Förlag, 1956). Additionally, Manker authored two books on Sámi art that tell parts of Skum's life story: *Näidkonst* (Stockholm. Stockholm LTs Förlag, 1965) and *Samefolkets konst* (Stockholm: Askild & Kärnekull, 1971).

2. Manker, *Boken om Skum,* 80.

3. Ibid., 26–29.

4. Ibid., 29.

5. Nils Nilsson Skum, *Same sita—lappbyn* (Stockholm: Bokförlags Aktiebolaget Thule, 1938), 12.

6. Ibid., 74–75.

7. Harald Gaski, "More Than Meets the Eye: The Indigeneity of Johan Turi's Writing and Artwork," *Scandinavian Studies* 83, no. 4 (2011): 593. Turi's artwork is also discussed in Svein Aarnold, "Johan Turi," in *Sámi Art and Aesthetics: Contemporary Perspectives,* ed. Svein Aarnold, Ulla Angkjær Jørgensen, and Elin Haugdal (Aarhus, Denmark: Aarhus Universitetsforlag, 2017), 69–97.

8. Manker, *Boken om Skum,* 52–53.

9. Ibid., 74.

10. E. Wretholm, "Einar Jolin och de primitiva," *Paletten,* no. 1 (1949), quoted in Skum's entry by Lars Thomasson in the *Svenskt biografiskt lexicon,* https://sok.riksarkivet.se/sbl/Presentation.aspx?id=6029.

11. Cecilia Widenheim, "Depth," Moderna Museet, https://www.modernamuseet.se/stockholm/en/exhibitions/10-stories/.

12. Manker, *Boken om Skum,* 79.

13. "Reindeer Man," *TIME* 48, no. 22, November 25, 1946.

14. *New York Times,* Dec. 28, 1951, 22.

15. Ernst Manker, Foreword, *Valla renar,* by Nils Nilsson Skum, with Ernst Manker, trans. Gunnar Pellijeff (Stockholm: Gerbers, 1955), 7–8.

16. Ernst Manker, "Lapparna som konstnärer," in *Primitive konst: Konst och konsthantverk hos primitiva folk,* ed. Sigvald Linné and Gösta Montell (Stockholm: Aktiebolaget Bokverk, 1947), 23–41.

17. Ørnulv Vorren and Ernst Manker, *Lapp Life and Customs* (Oslo: Oslo University Press, 1962).

18. Harry Fett, "Finnmarksviddens kunst. John Andreas Savio," *Kunst og kultur* 2 (1940): 246. For more on the early Sámi artists, including Savio, see Monica Grini, "Historiographical Reflections on Sámi Art and the Paradigm of the National in Norwegian Art History," in *Sámi Stories: Art and Identity of an Arctic People,* ed. Charis Gullickson and Sandra Lorentzen (Stamsund, Norway: Orkana Akademisk, 2014), 49–67; and Tuija Hautala-Hirvioja, "Early Sámi Visual Artists—Western Fine Art Meets Sámi Culture," *Barents Studies* 1, no. 1 (2014): 11–40.

19. Nils-Aslak Valkeapää, *Beaivi, áhčážan* (Kautokeino, Norway: DAT, 1988). *The Sun, My Father,* trans. Ralph Salisbury et al. (Kautokeino: DAT, 1997).

20. Hanna H. Hansen, "Sámi Artist Group 1978–1983: Otherness or Avant-Garde?," in *Decentering the Avant-Garde,* ed. Per Bäckström and Benedikt Hjartarson (Amsterdam: Rodopi, Avantgarde Critical Studies, 2014), 251–64.

21. The Sámi Museum in Karasjok is managed by the RiddoDuottarMuseat, a consortium of Sámi museums in northern Norway, and is discussed at greater length in the chapter "Returning: Norway."

22. For discussions about *dáidda* or art in contemporary Sámi culture, see Aarnold, *Sámi Art and Aesthetics.* The catalog for the 2016–17 exhibit at the Office for Contemporary Art Norway (OCA), *Let the River Flow,* with a focus on the Máze group, is available as a pdf through OCA, https://oca.no/publications/project-booklets/let-the-river-flow-the-sovereign-will-and-the-making-of-a-new-worldliness-english/. In conjunction with this exhibit, OCA also offers a series of film interviews with Sámi artists, including Synnøve

Persen. The series is titled "Thinking at the Edge of the World: Perspectives from the North," https://oca.no/audiovisual/.

23. Video interview with Synnøve Persen, "Thinking at the Edge of the World," October 2016.

24. A video that slowly scans the entire length of *Historjá* while a recording plays of Marakatt-Labba's father joiking is available at https://vimeo.com/201908843.

Roots and Spirals

1. See Silvén, *Friktion,* chap. 5, "Utställningar och uppvisningar," 130–63, for descriptions of the *Lapparna* exhibit of 1947. The full title of the exhibit was *Lapparna: Samerna,* but it was generally referred to only by the first word.

2. Ernst Manker, *The Lapps* (Stockholm: Nordiska Museet, 1962).

3. Lundius, quoted in Fur, "'But in Itself,'" 30.

4. Schefferus, *Lapponia,* from the Swedish translation, based on reports by his informants Samuel Rheen and Johannes Tornæus, quoted in Katarina Ågren, "Traditionsuppgifter om Västerbottnisk rotkorgslöjd," *Västerbotten* 4 (1983): 270.

5. Manker, *The Lapps,* 18.

6. Umeå's Handicraft Association (Umeå hemslöjdsförening), founded in 1909, was one of many handicraft associations set up in Sweden beginning in 1899. The national and regional handicraft associations are still very active in Sweden.

7. For biographical details on Emma Bergström-Andelius, see Kerstin Thörn, "Emma Andelius," in *Svenskt kvinnobiografisk lexicon,* https://skbl.se/en/article/EmmaAndelius0. See also H. Hampusson Huldt, *Mönsterbok för lapsk hemslöjd i Västerbottens län* (Hälsingborg, Sweden: Schmidts Boktryckeri AB, 1920).

8. Emma Bergström-Andelius, *Om lapska rotkorgar och deras bindning: För nomadskolor och arbetsstugor,* originally published February 7, 1932, reprinted in *Västerbotten* 4 (1983): 226–32.

9. See Israel Ruong and Maja Ruong, *Index till samefolkets egen tidning-Samefolket 1918–1973* (Östersund: Samefolket, 1985) for an overview of Sápmi mid-twentieth-century history in Sweden through the pages of *SET,* including material on Tomasson and Park.

10. K. B. Wiklund, *Nomadskolans läsebok, tredje boken* (Uppsala: Almqvist & Wiksell, 1929).

11. Bergström-Andelius, quoted in Ågren, "Traditionsuppgifter," 268.

12. For biographical information about Asa Kitok and her two daughters Margit and Ellen, I relied largely on Tom G. Svensson, *Asa Kitok och hennes döttrar: En studie om Sámisk rotslöjd* (Stockholm: Nordic Museet, Acta Lapponica 21, 1985), with supplementary correspondence with Svensson. Asa Kitok, Ellen Kitok Andersson, Margit Kitok Åström, and other Swedish *duojárs* are discussed in Kurt Kihlberg, *Giehta Dáidu / Den stora boken om samernas slöjd / The Great Book of Sámi Handicraft* (Rosvik, Sweden: Förlagshuset Nordkalotten, 1999). The website of the Sámi museum Ájtte also has information on root basketry, including examples by the three Kitoks, http://www.ajtte.com/att-leva-av-duodje-rot-och-silver/.

13. See Ruong and Ruong, *Index,* for information on Same Ätnam, Jokkmokk Folk High School, and Karin Stenberg. With Valdemar Lindholm, Stenberg coauthored the political

manifesto *Dat Läh Mijen Situd! Det är vår vilja: En vädjan till Svenska Nationen från Samefolket* (Stockholm: Svenska förlaget, 1920).

14. Same Ätnam's own collection is now at the Forest and Saami Museum in Lycksele, Sweden, https://skogsmuseet.se/Sámiska-samlingar.

15. Svensson, *Asa Kitok,* 155.

16. Ibid.

17. Ibid., 170.

18. Anna-Stina Svakko, quoted in Silvén, *Sápmi,* 32.

19. Contemporary discussions of *duodji* and *dáidda* can be found in *Duodji Reader,* ed. Harald Gaski and Gunvor Guttorm (Karasjok: Davvi Girji, 2022); Gunvor Guttorm, "The Power of Natural Materials and Environments in Contemporary *Duodji,*" in *Sámi Art and Aesthetics,* ed. Svein Aamold, Ulla Angkjær Jørgensen, and Elin Haugdal, 163–77. Background on Lars Levi Sunna comes from Thomas A. DuBois, *Sacred to the Touch: Nordic and Baltic Religious Wood Carving* (Seattle: University of Washington Press, 2018).

20. See Rose-Marie Huuva's "Object of Research—How Long?" at the Nordnorsk Kunstmuseum website, https://www.nnkm.no/.

21. Johan Sandberg McGuinne blog post, February 16, 2015; reprinted with permission. McGuinne also added this comment to me on April 17, 2021: "When it comes to duedtie/duöjjie/duodji as a gendered practice, a lot of it can be understood as an internalised form of colonialism; sewing was seen as a feminine practice by settlers, hence it's been coded as such by the majority society with regards to the Saami as well, and because of years of assimilation, we have come to accept this reading of our traditional handicrafts as somewhat set in stone, when the truth is that exceptions to the norms have existed for as long as we have been around."

Wax Cylinders, Sámi Voices

1. Karl-Erik Forsslund, *Som gäst hos fjällfolket* (Stockholm: A-B. Nordiska Bokhandeln, 1914), 94.

2. The verb "joik" (in North Sámi *juoigat*) is now regularly also used as a noun. I also employ "joiker" to refer to one who joiks. Joik, sometimes spelled "yoik," is not usually italicized in English.

3. Karl-Erik Forsslund, "Marknad och joikning i Arjeplog," *Dagens Nyheter,* March 2, 1913. A slightly revised account appears in Forsslund's travel book, *Som gäst hos fjällfolket,* 93–104, and is the source of all quotes about the 1913 winter market of Arjeplog. A further source on the winter market of 1913 and other expeditions is Gunnar Ternhag, *Song of the Sámi,* trans. Fred Lane (Stockholm: Svenskt visarkiv, 2019). I benefited from correspondence with Gunnar Ternhag and with Dan Lundberg, director of the Musikverket in Stockholm, which cares for the wax cylinders. The Musikverket site also has further details on Tirén and Persson and the collecting of joiks in Arjeplog and elsewhere, https://musikverket.se/svensktvisarkiv/karl-tiren/?lang=en. See also Richard Jones-Bamman, "'As Long as We Continue to Joik, We'll Remember Who We Are': Negotiating Identity and the Performance of Culture: The Saami Joik" (PhD diss., University of Washington, 1993).

4. Karl Tirén, *Die lappische Volksmusik* (Stockholm: Acta Lapponica, 1942), 18, quoted in Ternhag, *Song of the Sámi,* 17.

5. For Maria Persson's background, see Ternhag, *Song of the Sámi,* and Inger Stenman, "Maria Persson-Johansson frå Luokta-Mavas sameby: Karl Tiréns informant och 'nyckel' till jojkningens värld i 1910-talets Sápmi/Sameland," *Noterat* (1995): 87–106.

6. Tirén, quoted in Ternhag, *Song of the Sámi,* 17.

7. Quoted in Thomas Hilder, *Sámi Musical Performance and the Politics of Indigenity in Northern Europe* (Lanham, MD: Rowman and Littlefield, 2015), 74.

8. Von Düben, *Om Lappland,* 319.

9. K. B. Wiklund, *Lapparnes sång och music* (Uppsala: Småskrifter utgifna af Norrländska Studenters Folkbildningsförening, 1906), quoted in Ternhag, *Song of the Sámi,* 8.

10. Demant Hatt, *With the Lapps in the High Mountains,* 160.

11. Ibid., 120.

12. Staffan Lundmark, "Själens omedelbara spark," *Västerbotten* 2 (2014): 26–27.

13. Maria Himmelstrand, "På vandring i Lappland," *Svenska Turistföreningens Årskrift* (1913): 257–58.

14. Forsslund, *Som gäst,* 100–101.

15. See Mathias Boström, "Creating Audiences, Making Participants: The Cylinder Phonograph in Ethnographic Fieldwork," in *History of Participatory Media: Politics and Publics, 1750–2000,* ed. Anders Ekström (New York: Routledge, 2011), 49–62.

16. Forsslund, *Som gäst,* 98.

17. Stromboli is an island north of Sicily dominated by a volcano; Ternhag, *Song of the Sámi,* 31.

18. Torkel Tomasson, *Samefolkets egen tidning* (1926), quoted in Ternhag, *Song of the Sámi,* 96.

19. Matts Arnberg, Israel Ruong, and Håkan Unsgaard, *Jojk/Yoik* (Stockholm: Sveriges Radio, 1969).

20. For more on the renaissance of the joik in modern times, see Hilder, *Sámi Musical Performance*; Jones-Bamman, "'As Long'"; and Coppélie Cocq and Thomas A. DuBois, *Sámi Media and Indigenous Agency* (Seattle: University of Washington Press, 2020).

21. Ánde Somby, "Joik and the Theory of Knowledge," in *Dependency, Autonomy, Sustainability in the Arctic,* ed. Hanne Petersen and Birger Poppel, 275–76 (Aldershot: Ashgate, 1999).

22. Frode Fjellheim, personal communication, May 19, 2021.

23. Information on Frode Fjellheim's background and how he began to work with the Tirén collection comes from Jones-Bamman, "'As Long,'" 358–68, and from liner notes to Fjellheim's CD *Sangen vi glemte* (Idut, 1991), as well as from correspondence with Fjellheim.

24. Frode Fjellheim and Cantus, "Njoktje," after Kristina Johansson on *Spes* (2015).

25. Hilder, *Sámi Musical Performance,* 171.

Opening the Blue Chest

1. *Social Demokraten,* December 4, 1940.

2. For a register of all Emilie Demant Hatt's and Johan Turi's objects at the Nordic Museum in Stockholm, see https://digitaltmuseum.se.

3. Nils-Aslak Valkeapää, *Boares nauti: Johan Thuri* (Guovdageaidnu [Kautokeino], Norway: DAT, 1994).

4. Emilie Demant Hatt's paintings in the Nordic Museum can be viewed online at digitalmuseum.se.

5. Gilberg's list is found in Demant Hatt's papers in the Ethnographic Collection of the National Museum of Denmark (ESNM). The registers of her objects from Sápmi, with information on the accession dates and locations of objects collected by Demant Hatt, were only recently digitized, https://samlinger.natmus.dk/objectbrowse?media=image,rotation &keyword=samer,demant,hatt. I thank Inga Damm of the National Museum for providing me with printouts of the registers in 2016.

6. See Johan Turi, *An Account of the Sámi,* trans. Thomas A. DuBois (Chicago: Nordic Studies Press, 2011), 142–45.

7. Demant Hatt, *With the Lapps,* 24–25.

8. Emilie Demant to family, August 23, 1908, Emilie Demant Hatt Papers, Ethnographic Collection, National Museum of Denmark (ESNM) box K001.

9. Ibid.

10. Johan Turi to Emilie Demant Hatt, August 28, 1911, Emilie Demant Hatt Papers, E1b, Nordic Museum archives.

11. Gudmund Hatt, *Arktiske Skinddragter i Eurasien og Amerika: Et etnografisk studie* (Copenhagen: J. H. Schultz Forlag, 1914); "Arctic Skin Clothing in Eurasia and America: An Ethnographic Study," trans. Kirsten Taylor, *Arctic Anthropology,* vol. 5, no. 2 (1969): 3–132.

Recentering: Sweden

1. Marianne Nilsson and Inga-Maria Mulk, "Samerna och museerna i Sverige: En översiktlig inventering av Sámiska föremålssamlingar i Sverige" (Sweden, 1980).

2. Ibid., 9.

3. Ibid., 8.

4. Ibid., 29.

5. Ibid., 28.

6. Zoe-Hateehc Durrah Scheffy, "Sami Religion in Museums and Artistry," in *Creating Diversities: Folklore, Religion and the Politics of Heritage,* ed. Anna-Leena Siikala, Barbro Klein, and Stein R. Mathisen (Helsinki: Studia Finnica Folkloristica 14, 2004), 229. For more about the conflicts in the 1981 exhibit, see Silvén, "Sociomaterial Intertwinements in Sámi Research: The Nordiska Museum in Stockholm and the Legacy of Ernst Manker," *Nordic Museology* 3 (2019): 96–117; and Corine Ayélé Durand, *Anthropology in a Glass Case: Indigeneity, Collaboration, and Artistic Practice in Museums* (Riga, Latvia: VDM Verlag, 2010), 26–28.

7. Inga-Britt Blind, quoted in Durand, *Anthropology in a Glass Case,* 28.

8. Lars Thomasson, quoted in Silvén, "Sociomaterial Intertwinements," 108.

9. The museum's full name is Ájtte, the Swedish Mountain and Sami Museum.

10. James Clifford, "Museums as Contact Zones," in *Routes: Travel and Translation in the Late Twentieth Century* (Cambridge: Harvard University Press, 1997), 192.

11. See Scheffy, "Sámi Religion in Museums and Artistry," 225–64, and Silje Opdahl Mathisen, "Etnisitetens estetikk. Visuelle fortellinger og forhandlinger i Sámiske museumsutstillinger" (PhD dissertation, University of Oslo, 2014). Both studies analyze the Sámi exhibits at the Nordic and the exhibits at Åjtte in terms of styles of representation.

12. Silvén, *Sápmi,* 5.

13. Ibid., 15.

14. The reference group consisted of Sunna Kuoljok and Berit Inga, Ájtte; Ingwar Åhrén, Gaaltije; Sonia Larsson, Same Ätnam; Helge Sunna, Sameföreningen in Stockholm; Victoria Harnesk, Samernas Riksförbund; Annelie Päivo, Sámi Duodji; and Linda Mannela, Sáminuorra.

15. Silvén, *Sápmi,* 47–59.

16. The Nordic Museum has a website in Swedish dedicated to its Sámi collection and related exhibits and documents (https://www.nordiskamuseet.se/kunskapsomraden/Sámisk-historia-och-kultur) as well as links to the museum's Lotten von Düben website (http://webbplatser.nordiskamuseet.se/lvd/) and the website National Minorities in Sweden with videos in Swedish (http://nationellaminoriteter.nordiskamuseet.se/).

17. In January 2022, the Nordic Museum announced that the exhibit *Sápmi* would close in order to begin work on a new exhibition that would instead present a history of the Nordic region from the early 1500s to the present. In this exhibition, scheduled to open in 2023, stories of Sápmi past and present would be integrated into the larger narrative, according to comments by the Nordic's director, Sanne Houby-Nielsen. The intention is to involve Ájtte in creating the exhibition. Many in the Sámi community look forward to an updated exhibit, while others express some regret that there will be no specifically Sámi museum exhibit in Stockholm for visitors and schoolchildren. Since the time of Artur Hazelius's first *Autumn Migration in Lule Lappmark* display through the varied Nordic Museum exhibits of the twentieth and early twenty-first centuries, the question is still open whether inclusion or separation provides the better way of understanding Sámi culture and its place in Swedish and Nordic history.

18. Birger Nordin, personal communications, March 2021. See also information and a video on Nordin at the Forest and Saami Museum's website, https://skogsmuseet.se/samiska-samlingar.

19. Jon Henley, "Swedish Museum to Return Exhumed Skulls of 25 Sami People," *The Guardian,* August 7, 2019.

20. Mikael Jakobsson, personal communication, April 6, 2021.

Returning: Norway

1. Doug Mellgren, "Norway's King Apologizes for Treatment of Sámi People," Associated Press, October 7, 1997.

2. See Ivar Bjørklund, *Sápmi: Becoming a Nation* (Tromsø: Tromsø Museum, 2000), for a summary of Norwegianization's effects.

3. For detailed information on the three Sámi Parliaments and their differences and similarities, along with their relations with the three state governments, see Kuokkanen, *Restructuring Relations.*

4. See Oula-Antti Labba, "Norway: Saami Communities Contend with the Latest Form of Discrimination—'Green Colonialism,'" *Minority and Indigenous Trends 2020,* 167–70, https://minorityrights.org/trends2020/norway/. However, in a 2021 landmark case, the Norwegian Supreme Court held that the concession for a windfarm near Trondheim on

the Fosen Peninsula violated the Sámi people's rights in preventing them from herding reindeer in the area, thus setting an important precedent.

5. Leif Pareli, "Project Bååstede—Background and Process," in *Bååstede: The Return of Sámi Heritage,* ed. Káren Elle Gaup, Inger Jensen, and Leif Pareli (Oslo: Museumsforlaget, 2021), 32–41.

6. "Recalling Ancestral Voices," http://www.samimuseum.fi/heritage/english/index.html.

7. "Bååstede: Tilbakeføring av Sámisk kulturarv," Norsk Folkemusum et al., Oslo and Karasjok, March 1, 2012, https://dms-cf-05.dimu.org/file/032waVgq1L3z.

8. Summary of the agreements between Sámimuseum Siida and the National Museum of Finland provided by Raila Kataja, curator at the National Museum (personal communication, November 23, 2021).

9. They include Saemien Sitje in Snåsa; Årran Lule Sámi Center in Drag; Várdobáiki Museum in Evenskjer; and the Center of Northern Peoples in Manndalen. Two museum institutions consist of four consolidated museums in the same region: Tana-Varanger Museumsiida includes Varanger Samiske Museum, Tana museum, Ä'vv skoltesamisk museum, and the Savio Museum. RiddoDuottarMuseat (RDM) includes the Sámi Museum in Karasjok, Kautokeino Municipal Museum, Porsanger Museum, and Kokelv Coastal Sámi Museum. RDM also administers the Sámi Art Collections in Karasjok.

10. Norwegian Museum of Cultural History / Norsk Folkemuseum, https://norskfolkemuseum.no/en/the-history-of-the-museum.

11. In 1993 the Ethnographic Museum in Oslo, now the Museum of Cultural History (KHM), borrowed back various Sámi objects from the NFM for a permanent exhibit on the Arctic, where Sámi material culture was displayed with that of other peoples of the circumpolar north. For a critical look at this exhibit, see Monica Grini, *Samisk kunst og norsk kunsthistorie* (Stockholm: Stockholm University Press, 2021), 100–107. The KHM has since updated its permanent Arctic exhibit with *Ten Sami Time Frames,* a contemporary documentation of Sámi life with photographs and texts, https://www.khm.uio.no/english/visit-us/historical-museum/exhibitions/arctic/ten-sami-time-frames/index.html.

12. For an overview and background of the NFM's Sámi collections, see S. O. Mathisen, *Etnisitetens estetikk.*

13. Káren Elle Gaup, "Introduction," in *Bååstede,* 25.

14. Lars Magne Andreassen, "Forvaltning av egen kulturhistorie eller forvaltning av kulturell uverdignet?" *Museumnytt,* January 2015, 31.

15. Aili Keskitalo, "The Repatriation of Culture: Opening Remarks," in *Bååstede,* 30.

16. Amanda Lind, *Barents Observer,* June 17, 2020.

17. The Commission to Investigate the Norwegianisation Policy and Injustice against the Sámi and Kvens/Norwegian Finns, University of Tromsø, https://uit.no/kommisjonen/mandat.en.

18. Tore Johnsen, "Acknowledged History and Renewed Relationships," in *The Sámi and the Church of Sweden: Results from a White Paper Project,* ed. Daniel Lindmark and Olle Sundström (Östersund, Sweden: Gidlunds Förlag, 2018), 104.

19. John Last, "Canadian-Style Reconciliation Commissions Draw Mixed Reaction

across Arctic Europe," CBC News, July 20, 2020, www.cbc.ca/canada/north/Sámi-truth-commissions.

20. Rauna Kauokkanen, quoted in Last, "Canadian-Style Reconciliation."

21. Rauna Kauokkanen, "Reconciliation as a Threat or Structural Change? The Truth and Reconciliation Process and Settler Colonial Policy Making in Finland," *Human Rights Review* 21, no. 4 (2020): 303.

22. Sylvia Sparrock, "Ways Forward," in *The Sámi and the Church of Sweden,* ed. Lindmark and Sundström, 171.

23. Várjjat Sámi Musea—Varanger Sámi Museum, https://dvmv.no/varanger-samiske-mus/hjem/.

24. See S. O. Mathisen, *Etnisitetens estetikk,* for detailed descriptions of the VSM's displays.

25. Ingvild Marie Bjørnå Pettersen, personal communication, November 26, 2020.

26. Várdobáiki, http://www.vardobaiki.no.

27. Árran Julevsáme guovdásj / Lule Sámi Center, https://arran.no/?id=1018051654.

28. Ä'vv Saa'mi mu'zei, the Skolt Sámi Museum, is a good guide to the region and history, https://dvmv.no/vv-skoltesamisk-muse/hjem/

29. Camilla Carlson, personal communication, November 20, 2020.

30. Johan Aslak Hætta, personal communication (Zoom), November 16, 2020.

31. English text from *Who Owns the Story?* 2017, NTNU Museum, supplied by Randi Haugen.

32. Jenny Fjellheim, personal communication, December 4, 2020.

Recollecting: Sápmi

1. Sophie Page and Marina Wallace, *Spellbound: Magic, Ritual and Witchcraft* (Oxford: Ashmolean Museum, 2018), 123. "Fig 108. Finnish Shaman's Drum, seventeenth-eighteenth centuries © Trustees of the British Museum."

2. British Museum, exhibition page of Sámi "Magic Drum": https://www.britishmuseum.org/the_museum/museum_in_london/london_exhibition_archive/archive_Sámi_drum.aspx. Collection notes on drum: https://www.britishmuseum.org/research/collection_online/collection_object_details.aspx?objectId=671371&partId=1.

3. Jonathan Jones, "Shamanism Casts a Spell at the British Museum," *The Guardian,* January 8, 2009, https://www.theguardian.com.

4. Eeva-Kristiina Harlin, "Sámi Objects in Museum Collections and the Change of Paradigm," in *Bååstede: The Return of Sámi Heritage,* ed. Káren Elle Gaup, Inger Jensen, and Leif Pareli (Oslo: Museumsforlaget, 2021), 122–23.

5. United Nations, "Norway's Report on Repatriation of Ceremonial Objects and Human Remains under the UN Declaration of the Rights of Indigenous Peoples," Office of the High Commissioner for Human Rights, 2019, 2.

6. "Kulturministeren giver tilladelse til udskillelse af samisk tromme," press release, Danish Cultural Ministry, January 24, 2022, https://kum.dk/aktuelt/nyheder/kulturministeren-giver-tilladelse-til-udskillelse-af-samisk-tromme.

7. Anne May Olli, quoted in "Danmark gir fra seg sjamantromme—Udendelig glad,"

Martin Lægland, *VG,* January 24, 2022, https://www.vg.no/nyheter/innenriks/i/JxG2K8/danmark-gir-fra-seg-samisk-sjamantromme-uendelig-glad.

8. For more on Ethel John Lindgren-Utsi and Mikel Utsi, see Sjoholm, *Black Fox,* 315–16.

9. Scott Research Institute, Mikel Utsi collection, https://www.spri.cam.ac.uk/museum/catalogue/armc/search/?q=Utsi.

10. Anna Westman and John E. Utsi, *Goabdesájgge: Sámij dålusj goabddáj jáhko birra / Drum-Time: The Drums and Religion of the Sámi* (Jokkmokk, Sweden: Ájtte, svenskt fjäll- och samemuseum / Stockholm: Nordiska museet, 1999).

11. Durand describes the process of observing Helge Sunna at work on the drum in *Anthropology in a Glass Case,* 129–35.

12. Helge Sunna, featured on the website of Arctic Indigenous Design Archives (AIDA), which conserves the archives of Sámi *duojárs,* https://arkisto.fi/aida/en/duojar-archives/surname-s/sunna-helge-archive.

13. Gunvor Guttorm, "Duodji: A New Step for Art Education," *International Journal of Art & Design Education* 31, no. 2 (2012): 180–90, https://doi.org/10.1111/j.1476-8070.2012.01712.x. See also the recent *Duodji Reader,* edited by Gunvor Guttorm and Harald Gaski (Karasjok, Norway: Davvi Girji, 2022).

14. Jelena Porsanger, Paula Rauhala, Maaike Halbertsma, "Keeping Sámi Weaving Tradition Alive," Safeguarding Practices, 2016–17, https://safeguardingpractices.com/good-practice/keeping-sami-weaving-tradition-alive/.

15. Heidi Person, "I formødrenes fotspor—Mahttaráhkkuid bálggái: En studie av hornluen som en sjøsamisk tradisjon," master's thesis, Universitetet i Sørøst-Norge, 2019, https://openarchive.usn.no/usn-xmlui/handle/11250/2672727.

16. Eva Dagny Johansen, personal communication, November 3, 2020.

17. Eeva-Kristiina Harlin, "The Ládjogahpir," Societal Dimensions of Sámi Research, https://sodisami.net/portfolio-item/the-ladjogahpir/.

18. Eeva-Kristiina Harlin and Outi Pieski, *Ládjogahpir: The Foremothers' Hat of Pride* (Karasjok: Davvi Girji, 2020), 116.

19. Henrik Ole Magga, quoted in Hanna Horsberg Hansen, "The Sámi Art Museum: There Is No—or Is There?" *Nordlit* 46 (2020): 226.

20. Sapmi Park in Karasjok, https://www.scandichotels.com/hotels/norway/karasjok/sapmi-park. The text I quote has since been removed from the website, but the Magic Theatre is still showing the film.

21. Trude Fonneland, *Contemporary Shamanisms in Norway: Religion, Entrepreneurship, and Politics* (Oxford: Oxford University Press, 2017).

22. Website text from the Office for Contemporary Art Norway for a screening of Sissel Bergh's film, *Dalvedh,* February 2, 2019, https://www.oca.no/programme/mezzanine-series/screening-dalvedh-a-film-by-sisselm-bergh-20190202-1230 (https://www.youtube.com/watch?v=UoENKsowKrg).

23. Anders Sunna interview in Gabriel Kuhn, *Liberating Sápmi: Indigenous Resistance in Europe's Far North* (Oakland, CA: PM Press, 2021), 153.

24. The OCA was founded in Norway in 2001 by the Norwegian Ministries of Culture and Foreign Affairs. These days on their website it reads: "OCA acknowledges the Sámi as one people, and as the Indigenous people of the Fennoscandian region. On the land of

this region, Sápmi, the Sámi people have lived since time immemorial, respectfully harvesting from nature by fishing, farming, hunting and following reindeer, amongst other activities. We pay respect to the deep knowledge of land and water, as well as to the spiritual principles and world perspectives that have and continue to inspire Sápmi across all of its communities."

25. "Jenni Laiti: Forewalkers," Art Ii Biennial, https://artii.fi/artists/jenni-laiti-2/.

26. Interviews with Pieski and Laiti on YouTube, https://artii.fi/artists/jenni-laiti-2/.

Selected Bibliography

Aamold, Svein, Ulla Angkjær Jørgensen, and Elin Haugdal, eds. *Sámi Art and Aesthetics: Contemporary Perspectives*. Aarhus, Denmark: Aarhus Universitetsforlag, 2017.

Aarseth, Bjørn, "Lars Hætta." In *Norsk biografisk leksikon*, online ed., 2009. https://nbl.snl.no/Lars_Hætta.

Ågren Katarina. "Traditionsuppgifter om Västerbottnisk rotkorgslöjd." *Västerbotten* 4 (1983): 255–72.

Alm, Ellen. "So What Is 'Gand' Sorcery—Really?" *Norwegian SciTech News*, March 27, 2018. https://www.norwegianscitechnews.com/2018/03/gand-sorcery-really/.

Alm, Ellen, and Rune Blix Hagen. "Sámi Magic and Rituals from Historia Norwegie to Johannes Schefferus, c. 1150-1680." In *What Is North? Imagining the North from Ancient Times to the Present Day*, edited by Oisín Plumb, Alexandra Sanmark, and Donna Heddle, 153–73. Turnhout, Belgium: Brepols, 2020.

Altick, Robert D. *The Shows of London*. Cambridge, MA: Belknap Press of Harvard University Press, 1978.

Andreassen, Lars Magne. "Forvaltning av egen kulturhistorie eller forvaltning av kulturell uverdignet?" *Museumnytt*, January 2015, 31.

Arnberg, Matts, Israel Ruong, and Håkan Unsgaard. *Jojk /Yoik*. Stockholm: Sveriges Radio, 1969.

"Bååstede: Tilbakeføring av samisk kulturarv." Norsk Folkemuseum et al. Karasjok and Oslo, March 2012. https://dms-cf-05.dimu.org/file/032waVgq1L3z.

Bäckström, Mattias. "Att skapa lappar: Om en debatt och två expeditioner till lappmarkerna." In *Regionernas bilder: Estetiska uttryck från och om periferin*, edited by Heidi Hansson, Maria Lindgren Leavenworth, and Lennart Pettersson, 74–87. Umeå: Umeå University, Department of Language Studies, 2010.

Baglo, Cathrine. "The Disappearance of the Sea Sami as a Cultural Display Category." *Nordic Museology*, no. 3 (2019): 25–44.

Baglo, Cathrine. *På ville veger: Levende utstillinger av samer i Europa og Amerika*. Stamsund, Norway: Orkana Akademisk, 2017.

Baglo, Cathrine. "Reconstruction as a Trope of Cultural Display." *Nordic Museology*, no. 2 (2015): 49–68.

Bayer, Kristoffer. "University of Copenhagen History: The Fire of 1728." *Uniavisen*, November 7, 2018. https://www.uniavisen.dk/en/university-of-copenhagen-history-the-fire-of-1728/.

Bergström-Andelius, Emma. *Om lapska rotkorgar och deras bindning: För nomadskolor och arbetsstugor*. Stockholm: Norstedt, 1932; reprinted in *Västerbotten* 4 (1983): 226–31.

Bjørklund, Ivar. *Sápmi: Becoming a Nation*. Tromsø: Tromsø Museum, 2000.

Blunt, Wilfred. *The Compleat Naturalist: A Life of Linneaus.* New York: Viking Press, 1971.

Boekraad, Maria Doeke, and Knut Rio. "Kolonitidens lange røtter og den samiske samlingens aktualitet i dag." In *Universitetsmuseets årbok 2019,* 102–20. Bergen: University of Bergen, 2019. https://www.uib.no/universitetsmuseet/122993/%C3%A5rbokarkivet.

Boström, Mathias. "Creating Audiences, Making Participants: The Cylinder Phonograph in Ethnographic Fieldwork." In *History of Participatory Media: Politics and Publics, 1750–2000,* edited by Anders Ekström, 49–62. New York: Routledge, 2011.

Brooke, Arthur de Capell. *Travels through Sweden, Norway, and Finmark: To the North Cape, in the Summer of 1820.* London: Rodwell and Martin, 1823.

Bullock, William. *An Account of the Family of Laplanders, Which, with Their Summer and Winter Residences, Domestic Implements, Sledges, Herd of Living Reindeer, and a Panoramic View of the North Cape . . . Are Now Exhibiting at the Egyptian Hall, Piccadilly.* London: Printed for W. Bullock, 1822.

Burnett, Linda Andersson. "Translating Swedish Colonialism: Johannes Schefferus's *Lapponia* in Britain, c. 1674–1800." *Scandinavian Studies* 91, no. 1–2 (2019): 134–62.

Clifford, James. *Routes: Travel and Translation in the Late Twentieth Century.* Cambridge, MA: Harvard University Press, 1997.

Cocq, Coppélie, and Thomas A. DuBois. *Sámi Media and Indigenous Agency in the Arctic North.* Seattle: University of Washington Press, 2020.

Dahlberg, Eva. *Lotten von Düben in Lapland.* Sweden: Alfabeta Bokforlag, 1991.

Davy, Jack. "Lars Hætta's Miniature World: Sámi Prison Op-art Autoethnography." *Journal of Material Culture* 23, no. 3 (2017): 280–94. https://doi.org/10.1177/1359183517745716.

Delburgo, James. *Collecting the World: The Life and Curiosity of Hans Sloane.* London: Allen Lane, 2017.

Demant Hatt, Emilie. *With the Lapps in the High Mountains: A Woman among the Sami, 1907–1908.* Edited and translated by Barbara Sjoholm. Madison: University of Wisconsin Press, 2013.

DuBois, Thomas A. *Sacred to the Touch: Nordic and Baltic Religious Wood Carving.* Seattle: University of Washington Press, 2018.

Durand, Corine Ayélé. *Anthropology in a Glass Case: Indigeneity, Collaboration, and Artistic Practice in Museums.* Riga, Latvia: VDM Verlag, 2010.

Edbom, Gunilla. "Samiskt kulturarv i samlingar: Rapport från ett projekt om återföringsfrågor gällande samiska föremål." Jokkmokk, Sweden: Ájtte, 2005.

Ekman, Mattias. "The Birth of the Museum in the Nordic Countries: Kunstkammer, Museology and Museography." *Nordic Museology* 1 (2018): 5–26.

Evans, R. J. W. *Rudolf II and His World.* London: Thames and Hudson, 1997.

Fett, Harry. "Finnmarksviddens kunst. John Andreas Saivo." *Kunst og kultur* 26 (1940): 221–46.

Fonneland, Trude. *Contemporary Shamanisms in Norway: Religion, Entrepreneurship, and Politics.* Oxford: Oxford University Press, 2017.

Forsslund, Karl-Erik. *Som gäst hos fjällfolket.* Stockholm: A-B. Nordiska Bokhandeln, 1914.

Friis, J. A. *En sommer i Finmarken, Russisk Lapland og Nordkarelen.* Christiania, Norway: Cammermeyer, 1871.

Friis, J. A. *Fra Finmarken. Skildringer.* Christiania, Norway: Cammermeyer, 1881.

Friis, J. A. *Lajla: A New Tale of Finmark.* Translated by Ingerid Markhus. New York: G. P. Putnam's Sons, 1888.

Friis, J. A. *Lappisk mytologi, eventyr, og folkesagn.* Christiania, Norway: Cammermeyer, 1871.

Friis, Pål. "Lars Jakobsen Hætta og Jens Andreas Friis: 30 års samarbeid for samisk skriftspråk." *Ottar* 5 (2020): 13–24.

Friis, Pål, ed. *Brevene fra Lars Jakobsen Hætta til Jens Andreas Friis.* Translated by Sara Marit Gaup. Guovdageaidnu, Norway: Pål Friis, 2019.

Fur, Gunlög. "'But in Itself, the Law Is Only White': Knowledge Claims and Universality in the History of Cultural Encounters." In *Fugitive Knowledge: The Loss and Preservation of Knowledge in Cultural Contact Zones,* edited by Andreas Beer and Gesa Mackenthun, 29–49. New York: Waxmann Verlag, 2015.

Fur, Gunlög. "Kolonisation och kulturmöten under 1600-och 1700-talen." In *De historiska relationerna mellan svenska kyrkan och samerna,* edited by Daniel Lindmark and Olle Sundström, 241–79. Skellefteå, Sweden: Artos & Norma bokförlag, 2016.

Gaski, Harald. "More Than Meets the Eye: The Indigeneity of Johan Turi's Writing and Artwork." *Scandinavian Studies* 83, no. 4 (2011): 591–608.

Gaski, Harald. "When the Thieves Became Masters in the Land of the Shamans." *Nordlit* 15 (2004): 35–45.

Gaup, Káren Elle, Inger Jensen, and Leif Pareli, eds. *Bååstede: The Return of Sámi Heritage.* Oslo: Museumsforlaget, 2021.

Grankvist, Rolf. "Thomas von Westen." In *Norsk biografisk leksikon,* online ed., 2009. https://nbl.snl.no/Thomas_Von_Westen.

Grini, Monica. "Historiographical Reflections on Sámi Art and the Paradigm of the National in Norwegian Art History." In *Sámi Stories: Art and Identity of an Arctic People,* edited by Charis Gullickson and Sandra Lorentzen, 49–67. Stamsund, Norway: Orkana Akademisk, 2014.

Grini, Monica. *Samisk kunst og norsk kunsthistorie.* Stockholm: Stockholm University Press, 2021.

Grundhauser, Eric. "The Man-Made Gut Stones Once Used to Thwart Assassination Attempts." *Slate,* August 12, 2016. https://slate.com/human-interest/2016/08/goa-stones-were-man-made-bezoars-that-were-said-to-cure-poison.html.

Gunvor Guttorm. "The Power of Natural Materials and Environments in Contemporary *Duodji.*" In *Sámi Art and Aesthetics,* ed. Svein Aamold, Ulla Angkjær Jørgensen, and Elin Haugdal, 163–77. Aarhus, Denmark: Aarhus Universitetsforlag, 2017.

Guttorm, Gunvor, and Harald Gaski, eds. *Duodji Reader: Guoktenuppelot čállosa duoji birra sámi duojáriid ja dutkiid bokte maŋimus 60 jagis.* Karasjok, Norway: Davvi Girji, 2022.

Hætta, Lars, and Anders Bær. *Erindringer: Samiske beretninger om Kautokeino-opprørets bakgrunn, etikk og moral,* edited by Nils Oskal, Johanna Johansen Ijäs, and Ivar Bjørklund. Stamsund, Norway: Orkana Akademisk, 2019.

Hagen, Rune Blix. "Harmløs dissenter eller djevelsk trollmann? Trolldomsprosessen mot samen Anders Poulson i 1692." *Historisk tidsskrift* 81, no. 2–3 (2002): 319–46.

Hagenbeck, Carl. *Beasts and Men, Being Carl Hagenbeck's Experiences for Half a Century among Wild Animals*. Abridged translation by Hugh S. R. Elliot and A. G. Thacker. London: Longmans, Green, 1909.

Hagermann, Maja. *Käraste Herman: Rasbiologen Herman Lundborgs gåta*. Stockholm: Norstedts, 2015.

Hammarlund-Larsson, Cecilia. "Skärskådad samling: Samiskt kulturarv i Nordiska museet." In *För Sápmi i tiden*, edited by Christina Westergren and Eva Silvén, 85–120. Stockholm: Nordiska Museets Förlag, 2008.

Hansen, Hanna Horsberg. "The Sámi Art Museum: There Is No—or Is There?" *Nordit* 46 (2020): 222–41.

Hansen, Hanna Horsberg. "Sami Artist Group 1978–1983: Otherness or Avant-Garde?" In *Decentering the Avant-Garde*, edited by Per Bäckström and Benedikt Hjartarson, 251–64. Amsterdam: Rodopi, Avantgarde Critical Studies, 2014.

Hanson, Heidi. "An Arctic Eden: Alexander Hutchinson's *Try Lapland* and the Hospitable North." *Northern Review* 35 (Spring 2012): 147–65.

Hanson, Heidi. "Henrietta Kent and the Feminized North." *Nordlit* 22 (2007): 71–96.

Harlin, Eeva-Kristiina. "Recording Sámi Heritage in European Museums: Creating a Database for the People." In *Provenienzforschung in ethnologischen Sammlungen der Kolonialzeit*, edited by Larissa Förster, Iris Edenheiser, Sarah Fründt, and Heike Hartmann, 69–84. München, Germany: Museum Fünf Kontinente, 2017.

Harlin, Eeva-Kristiina, and Outi Pieski. *Ládjogahpir: The Foremothers' Hat of Pride*. Karasjok: Davvi Girji, 2020.

Hautala-Hirvioja, Tuija. "Early Sámi Visual Artists: Western Fine Art Meets Sámi Culture." *Barents Studies* 1, no. 1 (2014): 11–40.

Heide, Eldar. "Gand, seid, og åndevind." PhD diss., University of Bergen, Norway, 2006. http://hdl.handle.net/1956/4441.

Hellström, Olle. "Nils Grubb." In *Svenskt biografiskt lexikon*. Riksarkivet. https://sok.riksarkivet.se/sbl/Presentation.aspx?id=13240.

Hilder, Thomas B. *Sámi Musical Performance and the Politics of Indigeneity in Northern Europe*. Lanham, MD: Rowman and Littlefield, 2015.

Hillström, Magdalena. "Contested Boundaries: Nation, People and Cultural History Museums in Sweden and Norway, 1862–1909." *Culture Unbound: Journal of Current Cultural Research* 2 (2010): 583–607.

Himmelstrand, Maria. "På vandring i Lappland." *Svenska Turistföreningens Årskrift 1913*, 252–89.

Hjorth, Ingeborg. "Tråante 2017—To nye utstillinger åpner øyene for samsisk kulturv." *Heimen* 54, no. 1 (2017): 105–8. www.idunn.no/heimen.

Horacek, Ivana. "Alchemy of the Gift: Things and Material Transformations at the Court of Rudolf II." PhD diss., University of British Columbia, 2015.

Hyltén-Cavallius, Charlotte. "At göra en nation." In *Konsthantverk i Sverige, del 1*, edited by Christina Zetterlund, Charlotte Hyltén-Cavallius, and Johanna Rosenqvist, 23–31. Botkyrka, Sweden: Mångkulturellt centrum, 2015.

Johansen, Siri Broch. *Elsa Laula Renberg*. Karasjok, Norway: ČálliidLágádus, 2015.

Jones-Bamman, Richard. "'As Long as We Continue to Joik, We'll Remember Who We

Are': Negotiating Identity and the Performance of Culture: The Saami Joik." PhD diss., University of Washington, 1993.
Jørkov, Birgitte. "Den Stærke Tromme." *Siden Saxo* 17, no. 1 (2000): 9–17.
Kihlberg, Kurt. *Giehta Dáidu / Den stora boken om samernas slöjd / The Great Book of Sami Handicraft.* Rosvik, Sweden: Förlagshuset Nordkalotten, 1999.
King, David. *Finding Atlantis.* New York: Harmony Books, 2005.
Kuhn, Gabriel. *Liberating Sápmi: Indigenous Resistance in Europe's Far North.* Oakland, CA: PM Press, 2021.
Kuokkanen, Rauna. "Reconciliation as a Threat or Structural Change? The Truth and Reconciliation Process and Settler Colonial Policy Making in Finland." In *Human Rights Review* 21, no. 4 (2020): 293–312. https://doi.org/10.1007/s12142-020-00594-x.
Kuokkanen, Rauna. *Restructuring Relations: Indigenous Self-Determination, Governance, and Gender.* Oxford: Oxford University Press, 2019.
Kyllingstad, Jon Røyne. *Measuring the Master Race: Physical Anthropology in Norway, 1890–1945.* Cambridge, UK: Open Book Publishers, 2014.
Lantto, Patrik. *Tiden börjar på nytt: En analys av samernas etnopolitiska mobilisering i Sverige 1900–1950.* Umeå: Umeå University, 2000.
Lapland Sketches, or Delineations of the Costume, Habits, and Peculiarities of Jens Holm and His Wife Karina Christian, with Accurate Representations of the Deer, Sledges, Huts, &c. as Exhibited at Bullock's Museum. London: J. Harris and Son, 1822.
Latham, Robert Gordon. *Norway and the Norwegians.* London: Richard Bentley, 1840.
Lehtola, Veli-Pekka. *The Sámi People: Traditions in Transition.* Fairbanks: University of Alaska Press, 2002.
Lindin, Leif, and Ingvar Svanberg. "Ren dragande en ackja." *Västerbotten* 2 (1990): 110–19.
Lindkjølen, Hans. "J. A. Friis." *Norsk biografisk leksikon,* online ed., 2009. https://nbl.snl.no/J_A_Friis.
Lindmark, Daniel, and Olle Sundström, eds. *The Sami and the Church of Sweden: Results from a White Paper Project.* Östersund, Sweden: Gidlunds Förlag, 2018.
Linnaeus, Carl. *Lachesis Lapponica, or, A Tour in Lapland.* Translated by James Smith. London: White and Cochran, 1811.
Linnaeus, Carl. *The Lapland Journey; Iter Lapponicum 1732.* Edited and translated by Peter Graves. Edinburgh: Lockharton Press, 1995.
Lundmark, Bo. "An Excursion on Linnæus's Drum from Sorsele." *Scripta Instituti Donneriani Aboensis* 14 (1991): 96–110.
Lundmark, Staffan. "Själens omedelbara spark." *Västerbotten* 2 (2014): 19–27.
Magnus, Olaus. *A Description of the Northern Peoples, 1555.* Vol. 1. Edited by P. G. Foote. London: Hakluyt Society, 1996.
Manker, Ernst. *Boken om Skum.* Stockholm: LTs Förlag, 1956.
Manker, Ernst. *De svenska fjällapparna.* Stockholm: Svenska turistföreningens förlag, 1947.
Manker, Ernst. *Die lappische Zaubertrommel.* Stockholm, Acta Lapponica, part I, 1938; part II, 1950.
Manker, Ernst. "Lapparna som konstnärer." In *Primitive konst: Konst och konsthantverk*

hos primitiva folk, edited by Sigvald Linné and Gösta Montell, 23–41. Stockholm: Aktiebolaget Bokverk, 1947.

Manker, Ernst. *The Lapps: Guide to the Exhibits.* Stockholm: Nordiska Museet, 1962.

Manker, Ernst. "Lapska Kulturrester." *Fataburen* (1945): 77–100.

Manker, Ernst. *Näidkonst.* Stockholm: LTs Förlag, 1965.

Manker, Ernst. *Nomadism of the Swedish Mountain Lapps: The Siidas and Their Migratory Routes in 1945.* Stockholm: H. Geber, 1953.

Manker, Ernst. *På tredje botten.* Stockholm: LTs Förlag, 1967.

Manker, Ernst. *Samefolkets konst.* Stockholm: Askild & Kärnekull, 1971.

Manker, Ernst. *Viddernas vandrare.* Stockholm: Folket i Bild Förlag, 1959.

Mathisen, Silje Opdahl. "Etnisitetens estetikk: Visuelle fortellinger og forhandlinger i samiske museumsutstillinger." PhD diss., University of Oslo, 2014.

Mathisen, Silje Opdahl. "A Record of Ethnographic Objects Procured for the Crystal Palace Exhibition in Sydenham." *Nordic Museology* 3 (2019): 8–24.

Mathisen, Silje Opdahl. "Still Standing: On the Use of Dioramas and Mannequins in Sámi Exhibitions." *Nordic Museology* 1 (2017): 58–72.

Mathisen, Stein R. "Mr. Bullock's Exhibition of Laplanders." *Ottar* 4 (2007): 11–18.

Mordhorst, Camilla. *Genstands Fortællinger: Fra Museum Wormianum til de moderne museer.* Copenhagen: Museum Tusculanums Forlag, 2009.

Nielsen, Yngvar. *Universitetets ethnografiske Samlinger 1857–1907: En historisk oversigt over deres tilblivelse, vaekst og udvikling.* Christiania, Norway: C. Fabritius & sønner, 1907.

"Nils Skum Is Dead; Swedish Artist, 79." *New York Times,* December 28, 1951, 22.

Nilsson, Marianne, and Inga-Maria Mulk. "Samerna och museerna i Sverige: En översiktlig inventering av samiska föremålssamlingar i Sverige." Sweden, 1980.

Nordin, Jonas, and Carl-Gösta Ojala. "Collecting, Connecting, Constructing: Early Modern Commodification and Globalization of Sámi Material Culture." *Journal of Material Culture* 23, no 1 (2018): 58–82.

Nylund, Anna-Vera. "Sameliv på Skansen." In *För Sápmi i tiden,* edited by Christina Westergren and Eva Silvén, 138–57. Stockholm: Nordiska Museets Förlag, 2008.

Ojala, Carl-Gösta. "Sámi Prehistories: The Politics of Archaeology and Identity in Northernmost Europe." PhD diss., Uppsala University, 2009.

Page, Sophie, and Marina Wallace. *Spellbound: Magic, Ritual and Witchcraft.* Oxford: Ashmolean Museum, 2018.

Pentikäinan, Juha. "The Saami Shamanic Drum in Rome." In *Saami Religion,* edited by Tore Ahlbäck. *Scripta Instituti Donneriani Aboensis* 12 (1987): 124–49.

Person, Heidi. "I formødrenes fotspor—Mahttaráhkkuid bálggái: En studie av hornluen som en sjøsamisk tradisjon." Master's thesis, Universitetet i Sørøst-Norge, 2019. https://openarchive.usn.no/usn-xmlui/handle/11250/2672727.

Phillips, Ruth B., and Christopher B. Steiner. "Art, Authenticity, and the Baggage of Cultural Encounter." In *Unpacking Culture: Art and Commodity in Colonial and Postcolonial Worlds,* edited by Ruth B. Phillips, and Christopher B. Steiner, 3–19. Berkeley: University of California Press, 1999.

Rehnberg, Mats. *The Nordiska Museet and Skansen.* Stockholm: Nordiska Museet, 1957.

"Reindeer Man." *TIME* 48, no. 22, November 25, 1946.

Reuterskiöld, Edgar. *De nordiska lapparnas religion.* Stockholm: Cederquists grafiska aktiebolag, 1912.
Reuterskiöld, Edgar, and K. B. Wiklund. "Linnés lappska trolltrumma." *Fataburen* (1912): 129–69.
Ringvej, Mona. "Tukthus og botsfengsel—fra asken til ilden." Norgeshistorie, University of Oslo. https://www.norgeshistorie.no/bygging-av-stat-og-nasjon/1418-tukthus-og-botsfengse-fra-asken-til-ilden.html/.
Ruong, Israel, and Maja Ruong. *Index till Samefolkets egen tidning-Samefolket, 1918–1973.* Östersund, Sweden: Samefolket, 1985.
Rydving, Håkan. *The End of Drum-Time: Religious Change among the Lule Saami, 1670s–1740s.* 2nd ed. Stockholm: Almqvist & Wiksell, 1995.
Rydving, Håkan. "The Saami Drums and the Religious Encounter in the 17th and 18th Centuries." In *The Saami Shaman Drum,* edited by Tore Ahlbäck and Jan Bergman. *Scripta Instituti Donneriani Aboensis* 14 (1991): 28–51.
Samzelius, Hugo. "I de arktiska lappmarkerna." *Stockholms dagblad.* Diary during research trips for the Nordiska Museet. Published in four installments, April 19, 1891; June 14, 1891; August 30, 1891; September 13, 1891.
Schefferus, Johannes. *The History of Lapland.* Facsimile of the 1674 edition. Stockholm: Rediviva, 1971.
Scheffy, Zoe-Hateehc Durrah. "Sami Religion in Museums and Artistry." In *Creating Diversities: Folklore, Religion and the Politics of Heritage,* edited by Anna-Leena Siikala, Barbro Klein, and Stein R. Mathisen, 225–64. Helsinki: Studia Finnica Folkloristica 14, 2004.
Silvén, Eva. "Ernst Manker 1893–1972." In *Svenska etnologer och folklorister,* edited by Mats Hellspong and Fredrik Skott, 135–41. Uppsala: Kungl. Gustav Adolfs akademien för svensk folkkultur, 2010.
Silvén, Eva. *Friktion: Ernst Manker, Nordiska Museet och Konstruktionen av Samiskt Kulturarv.* Stockholm: Nordic Academic Press, 2021.
Silvén, Eva. *Sápmi–om att vara same i Sverige / Sápmi–makkár lea leahkit sápmelaš Ruotas / Sápmi–On Being Sami in Sweden.* Stockholm: Nordiska Museet, 2007.
Silvén, Eva. "Scener och scenarier." In *För Sápmi i tiden,* edited by Christina Westergren and Eva Silvén, 121–37. Stockholm: Nordiska Museets Förlag, 2008.
Silvén, Eva. "Sociomaterial Intertwinements in Sami Research: The Nordic Museum in Stockholm and the Legacy of Ernst Manker." *Nordic Museology,* no. 3 (2019): 96–117.
Silvén, Eva. "Staging the Sámi: Narrative and Display at the Nordiska Museet in Stockholm." In *Comparing: National Museums, Territories, Nation-Building and Change,* edited by Andreas Nyblom and Peter Aronsson, 311–19. Linköping, Sweden: Linköping University Electronic Press, 2008.
Sjoholm, Barbara. *Black Fox: A Life of Emilie Demant Hatt, Artist and Ethnographer.* Madison: University of Wisconsin Press, 2017.
Sjoholm, Barbara. "Lapponia." *Harvard Review* 29 (2005): 6–19.
Sjoholm, Barbara. "Things to Be Marveled at Rather Than Examined: Olaus Magnus and 'A Description of the Northern Peoples.'" *Antioch Review* 62, no. 2 (2004): 245–54.
Skum, Nils Nilsson. *Same Sita—Lappbyan,* edited by Ernst Manker. North Sami and

Swedish text translated by Israel Ruong. Stockholm: Bokförlags Aktiebolag Thule (Acta Lapponica 2), 1938.

Skum, Nils Nilsson. *Valla renar.* With Ernst Manker. Translated from Finnish by Gunnar Pellijeff. Stockholm: Gerbers, 1955.

Snickare, Mårten. "Kontroll, begär och kunskap: Den koloniala kampen om Goavddis." *Rig* 97, no. 2 (2014): 65–76.

Somby, Ánde. "Joik and the Theory of Knowledge." In *Dependency, Autonomy, Sustainability in the Arctic,* edited by Hanne Petersen and Birger Poppel, 275–76. Aldershot: Ashgate, 1999.

Stenman, Inger. "Maria Persson-Johansson frå Luokta-Mavas sameby: Karl Tiréns informant och 'nyckel' till jojkningens värld i 1910-talets Sápmi/Sameland." *Noterat* (1995): 87–106.

Stoor, Krister. "Juoiganmuitalusat-Jojkberlittelser: En studie av jojkens narrativa egenskaper." PhD diss., Umeå University, 2007.

Storm, Dikka. "A Network of Missionaries and the Establishment of Knowledge: Creating Space." In *Networks, Interaction and Emerging Identities in Fennoscandia and Beyond,* edited by Charlotte Damm and Janne Saarikivi, 263–83. Helsinki: Suonalais-Ugrilainen Seura, 2012.

Svensson, Tom G. *Asa Kitok och hennes döttrar: En studie om samisk rotslöjd.* Stockholm: Nordiska Museet (Acta Lapponica 21), 1985.

Ternhag, Gunnar. *Jojksamlaren Karl Tirén.* Umeå, Sweden: DAUM, 2000. English edition, *Song of the Sámi.* Translated by Fred Lane. Stockholm: Svensk visarkiv, 2019.

Thomas, Nicholas. *The Return of Curiosity: What Are Museums For?* London: Reaktion Books, 2016.

Thomasson, Lars. "Nils Nilsson Skum." In *Svenskt biografiskt lexikon.* Riksarkivet. https://sok.riksarkivet.se/sbl/Presentation.aspx?id=6029.

Thörn, Kirsten. "Emma Andelius." In *Svenskt kvinnobiografisk lexikon.* https://skbl.se/en/article/EmmaAndelius0.

Tinniswood, Adrian. *The Royal Society and the Invention of Modern Science.* New York: Basic Books, 2019.

Tirén, Karl. *Die lappische Volksmusik.* Stockholm: Acta Lapponica, 1942.

Tromholt, Sophus. *Under the Rays of the Aurora Borealis,* vol. 2. London: Low, Marston, Searle & Rivington, 1885.

Turi, Johan. *Muitalus sámiid birra / En bog om lappernes liv.* Translated, edited, and with an introduction by Emilie Demant. Stockholm: A.-B. Nordiska Bokhandeln, 1910. New English translation by Thomas A. DuBois, *An Account of the Sámi.* Chicago: Nordic Studies Press, 2011.

Turi, Johan, and Per Turi. *Lappish Texts.* With the cooperation of K. B. Wiklund. Translated by Gudmund Hatt. Edited, with preface and notes, by Emilie Demant Hatt. Copenhagen: Det Kongelige Danske Videnskabernes Selskab, 1918–19.

Valkeapää, Nils-Aslak. *Boares nauti: Johan Thuri.* Guovdageaidnu (Kautokeino), Norway: DAT, 1994.

Von Düben, Gustaf. *Crania Lapponica.* Edited by C. G. Santesson. With a preface by Gustaf Retzius. Stockholm: P. A. Norstedt, 1910.

Von Düben, Gustaf. *Om Lappland och Lapparne. Företrädesvis de Svenske.* P. A. Norstedt, 1873.

Vorren, Ørnulv, and Ernst Manker. *Lapp Life and Customs.* Translated by Kathleen McFarlane. London: Oxford University Press, 1962.

Westman, Anna, and John E. Utsi. *Goabdesájgge: Sámij dålusj goabddáj jáhko birra / Drum-Time: The Drums and Religion of the Sámi.* Jokkmokk: Ájtte, svenskt fjäll -och samemuseum / Stockholm: Nordiska museet, 1999.

Wiklund, Karl Bernhard. *Lapparnas sång och poesi.* Uppsala: W. Schultz, 1906.

Willumsen, Liv Helene. *Witches of the North: Scotland and Finnmark.* Netherlands: Brill, 2013.

Wulf, Andrea. *The Brother Gardeners.* New York: Random House, 2008.

Zorgdrager, Nellejet. "Linnæus as Ethnographer of Sami Culture." *TijdSchrift voor Skandinavistiek* 29, no. 1–2 (2008): 45–76.

Index

Page numbers in italic refer to illustrations.

Barbara Sjoholm is the author of *The Palace of the Snow Queen: Winter Travels in Lapland* and *Black Fox: A Life of Emilie Demant Hatt, Artist and Ethnographer,* as well as the editor and translator of Demant Hatt's collection of Sami folktales, *By the Fire* (Minnesota, 2019), and travel ethnography, *With the Lapps in the High Mountains.* Her translations from Norwegian and Danish have received awards and fellowships from the American-Scandinavian Foundation and the National Endowment for the Arts.